INDIGENOUS PEOPLES AND THE FUTURE OF FEDERALISM

Edited by Amy Swiffen and Joshua Nichols

As a settler state, Canada's claims to sovereign control over territory are contested by Indigenous claims to land and to self-determination. *Indigenous Peoples and the Future of Federalism* presents legal analyses that explore forms of federalism and their potential to include multiple and divided sovereignties.

This collection aims to advance reconciliation with Indigenous peoples in Canada and elsewhere by developing jurisprudence on the possibilities for a nation-to-nation relationship between Indigenous nations and Crown sovereignty. Contributors use legal creativity to explore how federalism can be structured to include the constitutional jurisdiction of Indigenous nations. Several chapters are grounded in the Canadian context while others connect the issues to international law and other settler colonial jurisdictions, recognizing how Indigenous resistance to settler laws and government decisions can at the same time be the enactment of Indigenous legalities and constitutional cultures. Ultimately, *Indigenous Peoples and the Future of Federalism* offers innovative ways for Canada to move forward from this challenge using existing constitutional mechanisms to give life to a plurinational Canadian federalism inclusive of the jurisdiction of Indigenous peoples.

AMY SWIFFEN is an associate professor in the Department of Sociology and Anthropology at Concordia University.

JOSHUA NICHOLS is an assistant professor in the Faculty of Law at McGill University.

Indigenous Peoples and the Future of Federalism

EDITED BY AMY SWIFFEN
AND JOSHUA NICHOLS

UNIVERSITY OF TORONTO PRESS
Toronto Buffalo London

© University of Toronto Press 2024
Toronto Buffalo London
utorontopress.com

ISBN 978-1-4875-5209-1 (cloth)   ISBN 978-1-4875-6098-0 (EPUB)
ISBN 978-1-4875-5571-9 (paper)   ISBN 978-1-4875-5901-4 (PDF)

Library and Archives Canada Cataloguing in Publication

Title: Indigenous peoples and the future of federalism / edited by Amy
   Swiffen and Joshua Nichols.
Names: Swiffen, Amy, editor. | Nichols, Joshua, 1978– editor.
Description: Includes bibliographical references and index.
Identifiers: Canadiana (print) 20230581501 | Canadiana (ebook)
   20230581625 | ISBN 9781487552091 (hardcover) | ISBN 9781487555719
   (softcover) | ISBN 9781487560980 (EPUB) | ISBN 9781487559014 (PDF)
Subjects: LCSH: Indigenous peoples – Canada – Government relations. |
   LCSH: Indigenous peoples – Civil rights – Canada. | LCSH: Self-
   determination, National – Canada. | LCSH: Canada – Politics and
   government.
Classification: LCC E92.I54 2024 | DDC 323.1197/071 – dc23

Cover design: John Beadle

We wish to acknowledge the land on which the University of Toronto Press
operates. This land is the traditional territory of the Wendat, the Anishnaabeg,
the Haudenosaunee, the Métis, and the Mississaugas of the Credit First Nation.

This book has been published with the help of a grant from the Federation
for the Humanities and Social Sciences, through the Awards to Scholarly
Publications Program, using funds provided by the Social Sciences and
Humanities Research Council of Canada.

University of Toronto Press acknowledges the financial support of the
Government of Canada, the Canada Council for the Arts, and the Ontario Arts
Council, an agency of the Government of Ontario, for its publishing activities.

Contents

Foreword vii
JAMES (SA'KE'J) YOUNGBLOOD HENDERSON

Introduction: Indigenous Peoples in Federal Contexts 3
AMY SWIFFEN WITH SHOSHANA PAGET

Part One: Futures of Canadian Federalism

1 Creating Inclusive Canadian Federalism 13
JAMES (SA'KE'J) YOUNGBLOOD HENDERSON

2 Consent and the Resolution of Political Relations between Indigenous Peoples and the Canadian State 42
MICHAEL ASCH

3 Struggles against Domestication: The United Nations Declaration on the Rights of Indigenous Peoples and Constitutional Pluralism 61
GORDON CHRISTIE

Part Two: Decolonizing Constitutionalism

4 Politicizing Indigenous Self-Determination: The UNDRIP and Legal and Political Constitutionalism 91
YANN ALLARD-TREMBLAY

5 A Theory of Decolonial Constitutionalism: Insights from Latin America 117
ROGER MERINO

6 The UNDRIP, the Treaty of Waitangi, and the
 Developing Constitution of Aotearoa New Zealand   142
 CARWYN JONES

Part Three: Plurinational Federalism

7 Treaty Federalism, the *Canadian Charter of Rights and Freedoms*, and Section 25 as a Bridge across Legal Cultures   169
 AMY SWIFFEN

8 Positivism and Pluralism: The Legal Imagination of Sovereignty in Indigenous–State Relations   200
 RYAN BEATON

9 "To Invite New Worlds": Indigenous Constitutionalism and the Search for a Jurisgenerative Federalism in Canada   249
 ROBERT HAMILTON

Conclusion: The Futures of Federalism   283
JOSHUA NICHOLS

Foreword

In 2015, Prime Minister of Canada Justin Trudeau stated: "It is time for a renewed, nation-to-nation relationship with Indigenous peoples, based on recognition of rights, respect, co-operation, and partnership." As part of this renewed relationship, Canada "will do more to make sure that the voices of Indigenous peoples are heard in Ottawa." Since self-rule was granted to the colonial immigrant-settlers in the various constitutional acts of imperial Parliament, generating a shared Aboriginal voice in the national government has remained a quandary. The renewed nation-to-nation relationship generates alternative and preferable futures for the national institutions to develop honourable government. It builds on the vibrant tradition of a complex of time, place, lived experiences, and compromises at the heart of constitutional history and law. This future will be more complicated and should be more inclusive than in the past.

The chapters in this book about the future of federalism represent some approaches to how the nation-to-nation relationship could generate a constitutional form of federalism for the patriated or decolonized nation. These writings find Canadian federalism as contested – it needs analysis, deliberation, and changes. They present a synthesis of the transformation of United Nations (UN) law to decolonization by self-determination and human rights, both formally and informally, which could guide Canadian federalism.[1] In addition, the authors focus on the concept of constitutional supremacy in Canada rather than the parliamentary supremacy of the past. They urge that prospective thinking about law and politics is not only desirable but required for generating systemic justice. Their innovative works focus on institutional changes, analysis, applications, and opportunities. They reopen the political and legal imagination of alternative futures and rescue us from the colonial past and the powerful present that is neither fair nor sustainable.

The federalism of the future can build on the incomplete federalism of the past. The nation-to-nation relationship has existed on this continent for a long time, with the dominate model being that of various nations uniting in the form of confederacies of Indigenous nations. In contrast with European thought, where federations were often thought of as deviations from the ideal unitary sovereign state familiar from the Westphalian world order, the Indigenous nations in the Americas generated the oldest and continuous forms of federalism.

In part of this book, the authors attempt to reconcile the intractable problems of the exclusion of treaty and Aboriginal nations from federal and provincial institutions to generate an authentic national Parliament. While the Elders and knowledge keepers of the treaty nations have always acknowledged and argued for the central importance of the federation with the British sovereign and the United States,[2] Indigenous federalism and its reliance on laws has been ignored and understudied by the colonists/settlers.[3] The Indigenous federations are comprised of the Mi'kmaw Nation and its seven districts, the Wabanaki Confederacy of more than fourteen nations, the Huron (Wendat) Confederacy, the Haudenosaunee Confederacy of six nations, the Seven Fires Confederacy, the Three Fires Confederacy, the Cree (or Néhinaw) Confederacy, the Blackfoot Confederacy, and so on. The Indigenous confederacy was conceptualized as many families living in one lodge and represented by a circle of Wampum, with an outside circle of two strands representing knowledge and protection, and the internal strands representing the united nations joined together in peace and unity. It is also represented by various Wampum Belts that represent the complex "chain" of the federated nations or the "linking of arms together."

The Indigenous concept of federation was extended by sovereign treaties to the sovereign of Great Britain and its unitary state to generate a transatlantic treaty federalism or commonwealth. This is the foundational federalism in British North America and the United States. These imperial treaties created the federal principle or federacy covenant among the confederacies and nations in North America. They were crafted in the language of sovereignty and power. They created a shared rule and cooperative governance founded on the ancient teaching of peace, friendship, protection, and respect. From the perspective of the treaty nations, all inherent powers were retained that were not delegated to the British sovereign.

In the last four centuries, Indigenous nations have extended treaty federalism across the continent as they sought to reconcile with the sovereigns of Great Britain and the United States. The early federations were represented by new Wampum Belts reflected in the new strands of the covenant chains. Similar treaties were made with Aboriginal nations in other continents. The modern-day treaties in Canada are represented by lengthy land claims documents. These treaties generated a confederation of nations with the British sovereign.

Canadian parliamentary federation looks different from the perspective of the uniting provinces than from the perspective of the excluded treaty nations. It has remained more a constitutional convention rather than theoretical or legal.[4] It is a concept in progress, moving from its colonial role of enabling collective action to its postcolonial role of limiting collective action. As Northrop Frye insightfully noted, Canada "has passed from a pre-national to a post-national phase without ever having become a nation."[5] While the imperial treaties were the existing foundation and generative force behind the constitutional order in North America, the colonists' self-rule ignored or left the treaties and the treaty obligations in the background.

The exclusions of treaty and Aboriginal nations from the provincial union has never been generated by the treaty nations – it has been in the colonial settler's odyssey of self-rule that was established through the *Constitution Act, 1867*. It was not generated by autonomous sovereigns but rather by British colonialism. The partnership of the English and French colonists established the union of the provinces by imperial Parliament. Colonial racism, eugenics, and self-interests provide the blinders to imperial obligations to the treaty nations. In the treaties, the treaty nations did not consent to nor surrender any authority to the imperial Parliament to generate the self-rule of the colonists. The imperial acts established the fundamental contradiction of the rule of law and representative democracy in Canada.

The development of the Dominion of Canada with enumerated authority over Indians without their consent or participation generated a coercive federalism that oppressed them.[6] The federal Parliament displaced treaty rights with oppressive federal laws that were injudicious, dominating, and assimilating. They dictated to the treaty nations what they must do and not do. Political ideology replaced law. The treaty and Aboriginal nations rejected their exclusion from a coercive federation that enacted laws that were not only unjust and inefficient, but which generated distrust.

Notwithstanding colonial self-rule, the imperial treaties with Aboriginal nations remained integral to the constitutional foundation and justification for the existence of the provinces and their union, rather than colonial sovereigns. With the patriation of Canada from the control of the Parliament of the United Kingdom in the *Canada Act, 1982*, the treaties were made part of the supreme law of Canada. By this imperial act, treaty rights were transferred from the United Kingdom to Canada.[7] This constitutional right represents the rejection of colonial law and a decolonization moment towards nationhood. It is the emergence of a new conscience speaking through various decision-makers and empowered by the Constitution, which affirmed the treaty nations' reliance on law to protect their inherent sovereignty. It generates an emergent national consciousness towards nation building – a nation arguing with its colonial and racial conscience.

Most treaty nations are considering innovative electoral reforms for their constitutional rights. They argue that the present electoral system, derived from British traditions, is not inclusive. They argue that Canadian federalism has responded to key events by compromising the Constitution, and that it should resolve these issues that arise to transform into a just society. Treaty nations' solution to historical injustice and constitutional reconciliation is not in the courts; it is in redesigning the national and provincial institutions of good government to honourable government by a trans-systemic approach, which includes their delegates in the political institutions.[8] Aboriginal nations without treaties will have to make their own decisions about how they should be included in political institutions.

These constitutional tensions and cleavages in a trans-systemic reconciliation cannot be eased by denial, formulaic responses, or policy prescriptions.[9] Reconciliation has to be based on a merging of Aboriginal law and Canadian law.[10] The national government of Canada should reflect its constitutional order with interdependence, multiple communities, and overlapping jurisdictions. Its national institutions need to accept (and perhaps even celebrate) the potentially jurisgenerative and creative role constitutional rights might play in a parliamentary system.

In this book, the authors begin to conceptualize constitutional federalism from an innovative architectural view of federalism that includes Aboriginal nations, treaty nations, provinces, and territories.[11] Many voices say that the existing federation is broken and needs repair. The historical and existing provincial federalism represents a small part of a much larger range of possibilities. It is exclusive; it represents the interests of the provinces and its peoples, ignoring the interests of the treaty nations and other Aboriginal peoples under their constitutional rights.

The treaty nations view the people of the provinces as having double representation – one at the provincial level and another at the federal level – that is detrimental to democratic representation. They have captured governmental power by arbitrarily excluding and oppressing the treaty nations. When treaty nations question the legitimacy of this double representation of non-Aboriginal peoples and their exclusions of Aboriginal peoples, it exposes the historical and current discriminatory and hidden fault lines of provincial federalism that have been tacitly accepted by Canadians.

So, the task of these assembled scholars (and Canadians as a whole) is not to fetishize the existing federalism of the colonial era, but to study its dynamics and explore how a constitutional federalism can serve better the future of the living constitution that demands more flexibility and sensitivity from an honourable government.

For the national confederation to be a sustainable and living constitution in the future, Canada must commit to permanent nation building and structural changes within its institutions of power, not through smoke and sound bites about British conventions. Canadians will not be able to define, let alone resolve, our fundamental constitutional problems until we confront the necessary transformations to represent the postcolonial nation and its complex composition. The existing national institutions cannot continue to compartmentalize these interests and challenges; constitutional fidelity requires that they establish an interconnected approach to power and decision-making. An approach has to respect the fundamental compacts that establish legitimate powers and the fundamental and inherent dignity and human rights of all peoples to establish responsible and effective laws and policies.

From a triadic perspective of the nation-to-nation relationship, the existing theory and practice of Canadian federalism deserves this reconceptualization and reform. The Supreme Court in *Reference re Secession of Quebec* noted that a constitution should "ensure that vulnerable minority groups are endowed with the institutions and rights necessary to maintain and promote their identities against the assimilative pressures of the majority."[12]

An architectural approach of uniting the treaty nations' relationship and role to the federal and provincial powers needs to reflect the critical roles of design, culture, harmony, and creativity required by the multidimensional nature of Canadian democracy and constitutionalism. This approach should aspire to be open to the art of the possible, the transformation of institutions, the dynamics of cooperation, and the spirit of constitutional accommodation and reconciliation of constitutional powers and rights. A patriated constitutional federalism needs to be premised on the ideal of the symbiotic relationship between constitutional powers and rights being reflected in our institutions and practices. It needs to reflect the triadic structure of a patriated constitution.[13] A generative federalism must be designed not to eliminate competing views in an attempt to generate a singular vision but rather accept and mediate such diversity. In so doing, it should seek to provide systems and practices whereby these conflicts can be negotiated and reconciled rather than developing into open antagonism or partisanship. A central feature of a generative federalism will invariably agree on one point: there is only one Constitution in Canada that controls the interconnected uses of legitimate power.

Guided by the global consensus of UN law ratified by Canada and constitutional supremacy, the promise of constitutional federalism in Canada has many institutional possibilities. By establishing an honourable national federalism, Canadians will repair what must be repaired and reform what must be reformed. These political reforms should be derived from the optimism of conciliatory nation building and the necessity of constitutional reconciliation of multifarious interests. The new judicial recognition of cooperative federalism has breached the previously impermeable boundaries of the constitutional distribution of the powers of the colony and provided a pathway for the treaty nations and governments to now be able to take seriously an innovative design of constitutional federalism. Of course, an honourable federalism will require constitutional wisdom and trans-systemic commitment to flourish.

James (Sa'ke'j) Youngblood Henderson[*]

NOTES

[*] Research Fellow, Wiyasiwewin Mikiwahp Native Law Centre of Canada, College of Law, University of Saskatchewan. *Ababinilli, maheoo, niskam*, and others provided guidance; however, I assume full responsibility for interpretation.

1 The formal international law is the treaty-based international organization of the United Nations that generates formal treaties, conventions, declarations, and other traditional sources of international law. The informal international law is generated by loosely organized networks or forums that generate guidelines, standards, declarations, and policy coordination or exchange that are part of the international law or rulemaking process. Joost Pauwelyn, Ramses A. Wessel, and Jan Wouters, eds., *Informal International Lawmaking* (Oxford: Oxford University Press, 2012).

2 In United States law, see Felix S. Cohen, *Handbook of Federal Indian Law* (Washington, DC: US Government Printing Office, 1942), 33–4, 39–40, 122; Russell Lawrence Barsh and James (Sa'ke'j) Youngblood Henderson, *The*

Road: Indian Tribes and Political Liberty (Berkeley: University of California Press, 1980), 270; "Indian Canon Originalism," *Harvard Law Review* 126, no. 4 (February 2013): 1100; Maggie Blackhawk, "Federal Indian Law as Paradigm within Public Law," *Harvard Law Review* 132, no. 7 (2019): 1787. In Canada, see Andrew Bear Robe, "Treaty Federalism," *Constitutional Forum* 4, no. 1 (Fall 1992): 6, 8; James (Sa'ke'j) Youngblood Henderson, "Empowering Treaty Federalism," *Saskatchewan Law Review* 58, no. 2 (1994): 258–65; Thomas O. Hugelin, "Exploring Concepts of Treaty Federalism: A Comparative Perspective" (paper prepared for the Royal Commission on Aboriginal Peoples, 1994); Kiera L. Ladner, "Treaty Federalism: An Indigenous Vision of Canadian Federalisms," in *New Trends in Canadian Federalism*, ed. François Rocher and Miriam Smith, 2nd ed. (Peterborough, ON: Broadview Press, 2003), 167.

3 Graham White, "Treaty Federalism in Northern Canada: Aboriginal-Government Land Claims Boards," *Publius* 32, no. 3 (Summer 2002): 89–114.

4 *Reference re Amendment of Constitution of Canada*, [1981] 1 SCR 753 articulating a constitutional convention requiring substantial provincial consent for amendments affecting provincial powers.

5 Northrop Frye, quoted in Seymour Martin Lipset, *Continental Divide: The Values and Institutions of the United States and Canada* (London: Routledge, 1990), 6.

6 For a history and analysis, see Royal Commission on Aboriginal Peoples (RCAP), *Report of the Royal Commission on Aboriginal Peoples*, vol. 1, *Looking Forward, Looking Back* (Ottawa: Supply and Services Canada, 1996); *Report of the Royal Commission on Aboriginal Peoples*, vol. 2, *Restructuring the Relationship* (Ottawa: Supply and Services Canada, 1996). See also Truth and Reconciliation Commission of Canada, *Final Report of the Truth and Reconciliation Commission of Canada*, 6 vols. (Montreal: McGill-Queen's University Press, 2015).

7 Lord Denning, *R. v. Secretary of State for Foreign and Commonwealth Affairs*, [1982] 2 All E.R. 118, at 129–30; James (Sa'ke'j) Youngblood Henderson, *First Nations Jurisprudence and Aboriginal Rights: Defining the Just Society* (Saskatoon: Native Law Centre, University of Saskatchewan, 2006), chap. 1.

8 The Supreme Court agrees; see *Reference re Secession of Quebec*, [1998] 2 SCR 217 [hereafter *Quebec Secession Reference*], at para 101: "The reconciliation of the various legitimate constitutional interests outlined above is necessarily committed to the political rather than the judicial realm."

9 See Peter W. Hogg and Mary Ellen Turpel, "Implementing Aboriginal Self-Government: Constitutional and Jurisdictional Issues," *Canadian Bar Review* 74, no. 2 (1995): 187–224.

10 The best example of a trans-systemic negotiation is the Indian Residential Schools Agreement of 2006; see Kathleen Mahoney, "The Untold Story: How Indigenous Legal Principles Informed the Largest Settlement in Canadian Legal History," *University of New Brunswick Law Journal* 69 (2018): 198. See also Sari Graben, "The Nisga'a Final Agreement: Negotiating Federalism," *Indigenous Law Journal* 6, no. 2 (2007): 63; Sari Graben and Matthew Mehaffey, "Negotiating Self-Government Over and Over and Over Again: Interpreting Contemporary Treaties," in *The Right Relationship: Reimagining the Implementation of Historical Treaties*, ed. John Borrows and Michael Coyle (Toronto: University of Toronto Press, 2017), 164–84.
11 James Tully, *Strange Multiplicity: Constitutionalism in an Age of Diversity* (Cambridge: Cambridge University Press, 1995); Jean Leclair, "Socrates, Odysseus, and Federalism," *Review of Constitutional Studies* 18, no. 1 (2013): 1–18; Social Sciences and Humanities Research Council, *Toward a Successful Shared Future for Canada: Research Insights from the Knowledge Systems, Experiences and Aspirations of First Nations, Inuit and Métis Peoples* (August 2018), https://www.sshrc-crsh.gc.ca/society-societe/community-communite/ifca-iac/03-aboriginal_peoples_in_Canada_report-les_peuples_autochtones_en_Canada_rapport-eng.aspx.
12 *Quebec Secession Reference*, at para 74.
13 *Tsilhqot'in Nation v. British Columbia*, [2014] 2 SCR 257, at paras 117–52. See also ibid., at para 152: "The s. 35 framework applies to exercises of both provincial and federal power."

INDIGENOUS PEOPLES AND THE FUTURE OF FEDERALISM

Introduction:
Indigenous Peoples in Federal Contexts

AMY SWIFFEN WITH SHOSHANA PAGET

As a settler state, Canada's claims to sovereign control over territory are contested by Indigenous claims to land and to self-determination. Currently, while Canadian courts have recognized the sovereignty of Indigenous peoples prior to colonization, they have not articulated a plausible account of how that sovereignty was lost. The legal doctrines they draw on require sovereignty to have been transferred or acquired by cession or conquest, yet neither has been accepted as the basis for state sovereignty in Canada, which remains attached to the idea of settlement, effectively, *terra nullius* (unoccupied land). Australia and New Zealand grapple with the same constitutive flaw. The chapters in this book offer innovative ways for Canada to move forward from this challenge using existing constitutional mechanisms to give life to a plurinational Canadian federalism inclusive of the jurisdiction of Indigenous peoples. There has not been much sustained analysis of this possibility in mainstream legal scholarship. One reason is because the focus of legal reform efforts has been diverted by the appellate courts, which have insisted that the issue of the foundation of state sovereignty is non-justiciable. In other words, the courts have decided they are unable to review the legitimacy of state sovereignty, as their own authority to decide legal matters is dependent on state sovereignty. Through this form of reasoning, questions about Indigenous sovereignty are displaced beyond the scope of settler government institutions.

The chapters in this book are unique in that they address this challenge in ways that assume Indigenous viewpoints. Indigenous nations' long experience with federalism in their dealings with one another and with settler governments are critical contributions to these debates. Consequently, many of the chapters do not begin at the usual place – with the reasoning of government officials and state institutions – but with Indigenous legal and political theories, and from the standpoint of Indigenous nations. As a result, the chapters mainly address the legal fictions that sustain state sovereignty in opposition to Indigenous legalities in Canada. This may not seem at first to be a methodological innovation, but it is, because the chapters take seriously the fact that Indigenous peoples have not been included with the Canadian nation or theory of the state as polities. Crucially, they have not been asked for their consent to current arrangements of power and law, nor have they actively engaged in the design of these arrangements. While there are glimmers of a better approach in, for example, historic treaty-making and the promise of "treaty federalism" developed in some of the chapters in this book, these Indigenous insights and practices have not yet been taken up in a productive and just way by settler officials. As James (Sa'ke'j) Youngblood Henderson notes in the foreword to this volume:

> While the Elders and knowledge keepers of the treaty nations have always acknowledged and argued for the central importance of the federation with the British sovereign and the United States, Indigenous federalism and its reliance on laws has been ignored and understudied by the colonists/settlers.

This tension lies at the heart of this book. The authors propose, in different idioms and from different standpoints, a range of ways forward that address the incompleteness of Canada's constitutional framework. Some begin by positioning Indigenous nations as outside the constitutional frame and therefore not bound or limited by it, and others point to the ways that the Constitution and the *Canadian Charter of Rights and Freedoms* can be better implemented and interpreted in ways that support the interests of Indigenous nations. The two approaches are not incompatible, as both bring pressure to bear on mainstream settler thinking on these issues.

The book is organized into three parts. The first focuses on Canadian federalism, considering the opportunities offered by the ideas of treaty federalism and "voluntary consent, mutually given" to create space for plural legal orders. The second part of the book looks at Indigenous jurisdiction from the perspective of constitutionalism through an examination of multicultural constitutionalism in Latin America, a critique of legal constitutionalism, and an exploration of the relationship between Indigenous peoples and the state of New Zealand. The final part of the book explores plurinational federalism as a model for constitutional reconciliation, the relationship between Indigenous governments and the *Charter*, and how the United Nations Declaration on the Rights of

Indigenous Peoples (UNDRIP) might move Canada towards plurinational federalism.

The chapters in part one each address challenges to reconciliation within the current framework of Canadian constitutionalism. Chapter 1, by James (Sa'ke'j) Youngblood Henderson, argues that much of Canada's written and unwritten constitution is not based on British political practices but on the confederacies of Indigenous nations and treaties made between those nations and the British Crown. Henderson argues that foundational principles of federalism embodied in those treaties should be integrated with Canada's existing institutional and governmental structures. The problem Henderson addresses is the need to reconcile Indigenous and settler jurisdictions, when the source of each differs. His answer is to draw on Indigenous traditions of federalism, partially realized and extended through the treaties with imperial and colonial governments. This concept of treaty federalism envisions a symbiotic and balanced relationship among diverse peoples, and a recognition of the inherent powers of Indigenous peoples. As Henderson explains, it includes a "multi-tiered government, combining elements of shared-rule and regional self-rule" consistent with Canada's principles of federalism. Henderson offers several concrete proposals of such mutually constitutive forms of representation, including treaty delegates and mutually agreed dispute resolution mechanisms.

In chapter 2, Michael Asch explores how the relationship between Indigenous peoples and the Canadian state might evolve using social contract theory and the idea of "voluntary consent, mutually given." Asch emphasizes that while Canada now acknowledges that Indigenous peoples were living in sovereign nations when settlers arrived, it still relies on *terra nullius* to legitimate the establishment of the state. Asch's proposal addresses the need to overcome reliance on this doctrine to justify the occupation of Canada. Instead, he suggests a constitutional agreement that enables Indigenous peoples and settlers to live together relationally in a federation based on an understanding of consent, not as a single act but as an ongoing process that moves parties closer to a common objective. Asch applies the concept to treaty-making, which he argues is a process whereby Canada could develop a political relationship with Indigenous peoples that is arrived at through step-by-step consensus.

Chapter 3, by Gordon Christie, takes on the idea that a basis for constitutional pluralism can be found in section 35 of the Constitution. Christie tackles the tension between external and internal approaches to constitutionalism and considers the impact of the UNDRIP on domestic debates. Using *R. v. Sparrow* as an example, he examines arguments made by Michael Asch and Patrick Macklem that read the *Sparrow* decision using an "inherent rights" approach to section 35, and that are therefore compatible with constitutional pluralism. However, subsequent case law shows that the Supreme Court has avoided the constitutional implications of recognizing that Indigenous peoples have always had "politically structured societies." In doing so, the Court avoided the possibility of finding an inherent right to Indigenous self-government and constitutional pluralism. There have been no indications since *Sparrow* that the Court thinks section 35 requires an understanding that constitutional pluralism is embedded in the Constitution. Instead, jurisprudence grounded in the assumption of Crown sovereignty continues to grow. Exploring why this is, Christie turns to the question of how arguments are supposed to function and how they actually do function in the workings of the courts. In examining section 35, he suggests the Court understands the problems and develops solutions that are already framed by a liberal discourse in which constitutional pluralism has no place.

Part two of the book contains three chapters that turn away from the Canadian legal order and look at Indigenous jurisdiction from the perspective of theories of constitutionalism and a critique of legal constitutionalism. In chapter 4, Yann Allard-Tremblay suggests that political constitutionalism may offer a way to enable Indigenous self-determination. He contrasts political constitutionalism with legal constitutionalism and identifies the danger in the latter that legal forms can come to be understood as exhaustive of the content of political rights and the political practices they represent. Self-determination, he argues, is especially susceptible to this misunderstanding. Allard-Tremblay's chapter draws attention to the politics of recognition and refusal in a way that provides a lens for the book as a whole. He points out that the United Nations Declaration on the Rights of Indigenous Peoples assumes full sovereignty is not possible for Indigenous peoples. The UNDRIP exemplifies this logic even as it seeks to formulate universal norms that protect Indigenous self-determination. Allard-Tremblay critiques the UNDRIP for how it fits with the goal of settler colonialism as it has shifted from the domination of Indigenous peoples to their incorporation as minorities. He also objects to making rights claims the focal point of political action. Against this, he argues that Indigenous self-determination must be politicized and politics become the way to realize self-determination. In this theorization, the rights recognized in the UNDRIP are acknowledged through a nation-to-nation relationship within which different political entities engage over terms of governance.

In chapter 5, Roger Merino explores constitutionalism through an examination of multicultural and plurinational constitutions in Latin America and suggests an approach to decolonial constitutionalism that recognizes Indigenous political objectives expressed through social struggle. In Peru, the autonomy of Indigenous communities – embodied in rights to land and power to solve internal disputes – is recognized. However, these rights do not extend to natural resources, which are instead subjected to the national interest. In Columbia, the Constitution recognizes the rights of ethnic groups to land, self-government, and resource management, but natural resources remain controlled by the state. Bolivia and Ecuador also employ plurinational constitutionalism in an effort to address the colonial foundations of their respective states. In Ecuador, however, certain strategic and natural resources remain controlled by the state, even in Indigenous territories. In Bolivia, similarly, rights over natural resources that pertain to the Bolivian people (i.e., the national interest) remain controlled by the state. Thus, while the constitutions of these countries promise decolonization, Merino points out that the political economy of resource extraction still structures the hegemony of states in their dealings with Indigenous peoples. Therefore, these constitutional arrangements are ineffective because political power depends on the control of resources. The takeaway of Merino's chapter is that decolonial constitutionalism must involve concrete measures to provide for Indigenous jurisdiction over natural resources.

The final chapter in part two, by Carwyn Jones, considers how the United Nations Declaration on the Rights of Indigenous Peoples presents new opportunities to transform the unwritten constitution of Aotearoa New Zealand to give effect to the relationship established in the Treaty of Waitangi between the Māori and the New Zealand state. He suggests that the UNDRIP can support this relationship if it is interpreted in light of "Treaty principles" of Māori constitutionalism. The Treaty of Waitangi is a founding document in the constitutional framework of Aotearoa New Zealand, and legal institutions recognize its principles as providing constraints on the exercise of public power. Jones argues that applying these principles in other contexts would be a way to give effect to the relationship established in the Treaty. The chapter contains useful elaborations of the principles within Māori law and legal theory that could be drawn on to make the most of the Treaty's transformative potential. Jones takes the Te Awa Tupua settlement as an example of how the Treaty of Waitangi can be used as a framework to restructure the relationship between the Crown and the Māori. For Jones, changes to social policy structured by Māori legal principles reflect the beginnings of a kind of Indigenous constitutionalism based on mutual recognition.

The essays in the third and final part of the book use legal creativity to explore the idea of plurinational federalism as a possible model for reconciliation. In chapter 7, Amy Swiffen addresses an undertheorized aspect of the Canadian Constitution, specifically the application of the *Canadian Charter of Rights and Freedoms* as it relates to section 25, which states that the *Charter* must not abrogate or derogate from Aboriginal rights. Swiffen argues that section 25 could be central to Indigenous jurisdiction in Canadian federalism, suggesting it generates a "reverse duty of cognizability." Swiffen shows how the Canadian courts have come to see section 25 as a shield for Aboriginal rights, sometimes giving precedence to *Charter* rights, and sometimes to Aboriginal rights in cases where these rights cannot be reconciled. In general, however, the juridical consensus seems to be that section 25 shields actions of an Aboriginal government from internal *Charter* challenges. However, the existing case law only pertains to external restrictions aimed at protecting Aboriginal rights from non-Aboriginal individuals. It is unclear how it would apply if an Indigenous government faced a *Charter* challenge. For Swiffen, this gap is an opportunity to think creatively about the relationship between the *Charter* and Indigenous legalities. She suggests that instead of a shield, which pits different forms of rights against each other, section 25 can be seen as a way to bridge legal cultures and engage Indigenous legalities in *Charter* interpretation.

In chapter 8, Ryan Beaton provides a novel take on the Marshall trilogy, something not easy to do given the venerableness of those judgments. *Johnson v. M'Intosh*, decided in 1823 by the US Supreme Court, has become the foundation for the legal doctrine on Indigenous land rights in the US and Canada. Beaton notes how the Court rejects the power to make judgments on the legal validity of assertions of state sovereignty. The "*M'Intosh* exclusion" is perhaps the biggest jurisprudential hurdle facing Indigenous peoples' claims to sovereignty in Australia, New Zealand, Canada, and the US and is worth interrogating in the way he does. However, Beaton also illustrates how despite this exclusion, courts *do* discuss and reinterpret the legal significance of these assertions based on the changing social and political contexts of Indigenous–state relations. For example, Beaton finds that Chief Justice Marshall used the term "conquest" in a way that did not fit its everyday usage but rather fit with established bodies of law. He also examines the Caron case (*Caron v. Alberta*) as a contemporary example, noting how the difference between the majority and the dissent centred on the way in which the agreement between Canada and the provisional Indigenous government was interpreted. As Beaton suggests, the fact that the majority and dissent made contrasting interpretive manoeuvres reflects the existence of contrasting juridical understandings of constitutional Indigenous–state agreements. Thus, he argues while the courts do not appear likely to depart from the *M'Intosh* exclusion, they should acknowledge space for the legal creativity to which the exclusion itself points.

The last chapter in the collection, by Robert Hamilton, suggests that to include Indigenous jurisdiction, Canadian federalism must be reformed so multiple legal orders can coexist. He argues that this requires the courts to adopt a "jurisgenerative" approach to legal interpretation. He draws from the work of Robert Cover to distinguish this from a jurispathic form of legal interpretation. Whereas *jurisgenerative* refers to the shared production of legal meaning by a community, *jurispathic* legal interpretation seeks to snuff out alternative legal meanings. As Hamilton argues, jurispathic approaches can be seen in decisions made by colonial courts that eliminate an Indigenous legality in favour of its own. Historically, courts have used jurispathic methods to ignore the existence of Indigenous law. Hamilton asks, therefore, how the jurispathic practices of the courts can be changed to create space for the development of jurisgenerative law. If the courts recognize their jurispathic role, Hamilton suggests, they may choose to adopt a more flexible approach to the construction of legal meaning. For instance, what he terms "dialogical federalism" depends on ongoing dialogue among multiple interpretative communities to give laws meaning. To do this, courts must create spaces for negotiations over contested norms with equal negotiating power between parties.

Taken together, the chapters in this book argue that there is a need to acknowledge the plural legal jurisdictions that exist in Canada today. They suggest that to adequately respect Indigenous jurisdiction, the federal government and judiciary must adapt to the existence of Indigenous legalities. They also remind readers that constitutions are not limited to formal written texts but remain in part unwritten, existing outside of the formal government and embodied in diverse communities that develop and practice constitutional law. Importantly, the chapters also recognize how Indigenous resistance to settler laws and government decisions can at the same time be the enactment of Indigenous legalities and constitutional cultures. They attempt to show that there are ways for the court system to accept, work with, and support

Indigenous legalities and jurisdiction. They ask the Canadian courts to consider what they can do, not only what they cannot, and how they can think about and work creatively to build a plurinational federalism. While each chapter offers a different approach, they all highlight the urgency of reimagining federalism so that Canada can truly become a democratic federation with Indigenous peoples.

PART ONE

Futures of Canadian Federalism

1 Creating Inclusive Canadian Federalism

JAMES (SA'KE'J) YOUNGBLOOD HENDERSON*

Introduction

Much of what we mean by the Constitution of Canada cannot be found in the visible text of its documents. The foundation of the Constitution began with the various Indigenous nations entering into a transatlantic federation with the British sovereign in foreign affairs by royal prerogatives and imperial laws that permitted British settlement in Indigenous territories.[1] Based on the treaty delegations, the Parliament of the United Kingdom created the second part of the Constitution through constitutional acts that created colonial governance by an implied social contract.[2] The animating spirit of the constitutional documents was the colonists seeking self-rule[3] in domestic affairs and the limiting of the imposed colonial script of domination and dependence on the Parliament of the United Kingdom. The colonial visions of the confederation of the provinces were not based on the existing British political theory of a unicameral Parliament. Instead, the innovative confederacies of Aboriginal nations and tribes in North America informed part of the provinces' visions of self-rule. To this remarkable tradition, the colonists added a narrative of an irresistible desire for self-rule by two settler communities with similar knowledge systems but with different languages, cultures, and legal systems. The contingencies of self-rule within the British Empire were a resolution of continuing tensions over the exercise of authority and the generating of the institutional structures of a new political life. It was a rejection of the political world of colonialism they inhabited that guided their proposed political compromise.

At least two competing visions by the colonial elite generated their concept of provincial union. One vision, based on the unitary institutions of Great Britain, requested the establishment of delegated powers to a central or federal government with overarching authority over the provinces that joined the union. The other vision pursued provincial autonomy to maintain the political, legal, and cultural integrity of the French settlers in Quebec against the British provinces. The Parliament of the United Kingdom enacted self-rule in the *Constitution (British North America) Act, 1867* that reflected both visions and their tensions.[4] This political deal established an overarching and residual authority in the new national dominion to make laws for the peace, order, and good government of Canada, the power to disallow provincial legislation, and a list of specific powers in subject matter not delegated to the confederating provinces. In particular, the Dominion was transferred the power over Indians and land reserved for Indians[5] and the necessary and proper power to implement imperial treaties.[6] Under the explicit promises of the confederation and a competing list of delegated powers, the existing social and cultural integrity of the provinces was protected from federal powers through a division of power or competences.[7]

As imperial law, the *Constitution Act, 1867* was an unfinished union. Since 1867, five constitutional amendments have incrementally adjusted the colonial constitution to new situations.[8] More than these constitutional amendments, the courts have established the guiding principles that mediate the division of powers. The judicial interpretative trajectory has been to accommodate a decentralized division of power within the frame of the imperial constitution.[9] The courts adopted the underlying principle of Canadian federalism to explain the imperial union or confederacy of colonies, deriving *federalism* from the wording of the "federally united" that they held was implicit in the preamble of the imperial constitution.[10] As defined by the *Oxford English Dictionary*, the root of *federalism* is the term "federal" (*foedus*), which initially meant "of or pertaining to a league covenant, compact or treaty" and was expanded to include a form of government in which two or more states, provinces, or colonies constitute a political union. However, even the judicial interpretation of the imperial constitution did not promote or manage successfully its deeply entwined intergovernmentalism and its fiscal relationship. The judicial articulation of the principles of settler federalism promotes national unity through provincial diversity. The judicial construction of the purpose of settler federalism was to maintain and protect distinct cultural and regional communities within an overall political, economic, and social union. The courts interpreted the division of constitutional powers to protect the autonomy of the component units and provide for their participation in common institutions.

At least three other constitutional amendments have occurred that have changed constitutional intergovernmentalism and the division of powers. The years following the Second World War saw the rise of an activist federal government that enacted social welfare legislation to resolve various hardships and recognized bilingualism, multiculturalism, and nationalism.[11] Over the past four decades, Canadians have been working towards reforms of their setter constitution. The *Canada Act, 1982* was an incremental adjustment of the colonial constitution that established constitutional rights in the peoples of Canada.[12] The normative vision of this imperial act was derived from international decolonization efforts. Without the participation of Quebec, it established a new amending formula to heighten the principle of the "equality" of the provinces. The constitutional renewal accommodated the existing Aboriginal and treaty rights of the Aboriginal peoples,[13] and the *Canadian Charter of Rights and Freedoms* generated rights for all Canadians against governmental authority.[14] The perceived need for more constitutional reform is illustrated by the failure of the Meech Lake and Charlottetown Accords, where the agreements between Canada and the provincial governments attempted to change Canadian governance, including Indigenous representation in Parliament. The failure of these Accords emphasizes the need to resolve the colonial structural weaknesses in the electoral systems and federal institutions by creating an inclusive constitution.[15]

Treaty nations feel the current federal system is unfair to them and needs to include them. Their key objectives are institutional. They have seen that the present parliamentary and federal institutions favour the settlers. Indeed, much of the structure and text of the written Constitution is silent on its Indigenous foundations. In the constitutional reforms of the *Canada Act, 1982*, the structural provisions of the colonial constitution, which create the institutional framework for federalism and representative governments, were limited by the new rights that placed limitations on governmental powers. The affirmation of treaty rights challenges the existing identification of the federal institutions as the institutional arrangements for the exclusive benefit of the settler communities based on various prejudices and bias, both conscious and unconscious. The institutional arrangement of the settlers with the Parliament of the United Kingdom as the contingent outcome of political struggles is represented as a mythical narrative of constitutionalism, democracy, and private rights. These mythical narratives make these institutions look natural in retrospect. Yet the existing institutions are a subset of broader treaty federalism that is unrealized and ignored.

In 1998, the Supreme Court of Canada (hereafter the Court), in the *Reference re Secession of Quebec*, articulated the new principles of constitutional interpretation in the postcolonial reforms. The unanimous

Court comprehended that the postcolonial Constitution of Canada is more than a written text. In its analysis of the Constitution, the Canadian courts have considered its underlying legacies and principles. A superficial or fragmented reading of provisions of the written imperial acts enacted by the Crown-in-Parliament in the United Kingdom, known as constitutional acts, may be incomplete, if not misleading, about the sources and nature of constitutional authority. A more comprehensive reading is necessary to grasp the implicit and underlying principles animating the constitutional structure identified by the Court: "federalism, democracy, constitutionalism and the rule of law, and respect for minorities."[16] These implicit principles are founded more on Aboriginal thought than on British or French thought.[17]

The various written imperial acts were a veneer that concealed an even longer historical legacy about the source and nature of governmental authority and legitimacy. This legacy embraces the unwritten traditions and principles of centuries of confrontation between the king and Parliament that forged the unwritten British constitution, as well as the global framework of consensual rules and principles governing the exercise of constitutional authority in Canada.[18] In North America, these legacies rest on the ignored legacies of the inherent sovereignty of the Aboriginal nations and their treaty reconciliations with the British sovereign in the law of nations. These imperial treaties from many Aboriginal nations established the fundamental delegation of authority that informs the source and nature of British authority in North America.[19] Under the residual jurisdictional rule in treaties, namely that in the absence of any special provision in a treaty that delegates authority to the British sovereign, the Aboriginal confederations and nations retain jurisdiction over these subject matters. Thus, in the absence of treaty direction, it is assumed that the subject matter is retained by the Aboriginal nations. This rule prevents the British sovereign from arrogating jurisdiction over a subject matter retained by the Aboriginal nations.

The various constitution acts enacted by the Parliament of the United Kingdom, for example, are supported by a deep and invisible foundation of Aboriginal sovereignty and treaty reconciliations with the imperial Crown of Great Britain, which provides the architecture for imperial acts and gives the text its meaning. Following the constitutional patriation of Canada, the United Kingdom expressly affirmed these resilient and foundational powers. It renewed the oldest legal foundation of the Canadian nation and affirmed these foundational powers as constitutional rights protected by constitutional supremacy. These legacies have much to contribute in reformulating and reimagining the patriated Constitution.

Little in the text of the Constitution informs us on how to give meaning to the context or text of the constitutional acts, much less to Aboriginal and treaty rights. More importantly, nothing in the text of the Constitution reveals how to read the treaties and acts together. Justice McLachlin for the Court has articulated the controlling doctrine of constitutional convergence among its parts: "It is a basic rule ... that one part of the Constitution cannot be abrogated or diminished by another part of the Constitution."[20] This doctrine of horizontal constitutionalism requires the courts to generate a "symbiosis" of the different parts of the Constitution that compose the supreme law of patriated Canada, but none is absolute over the other.[21]

The goal of this chapter is to make the foundational principles of treaty federalism as part of the unwritten and written text of the treaties more visible, and to reveal how to reconcile and integrate these principles with the institutional and governmental future. The acknowledgment of treaty federalism should be an integral part of implementing constitutional reform and institution building in postcolonial Canada. I argue that treaty federalism should be in a symbiotic and balanced relationship that reflects the underlying complexity of our constitutional unity among a diverse network of peoples for today and tomorrow. This chapter also expands the institutional concept of federalism as one that pursues the protection of constitutional rights and promotes balanced participation by all in federal government.

Renewing Transatlantic Treaty Federalism

In 2015, Canada embarked on another moment of national reconstitution and constitutional adjustments. It addressed as an essential part of constitutional reconciliation how treaty nations can make self-determining decisions for themselves to rebuild their nations.[22] Constitutional reconciliation involves regenerating a constitutional convergence among treaty rights and the other constitutional powers. The nation-to-nation reconstruction of the treaty nations is an affirmation of constitutional supremacy and the rule of law. It is an attempt to symbiotically connect the imperial treaties, instructions, proclamations, and acts to reconfigure patriated Canada as a nation in the enduring future.

In the nation rebuilding process, Canada will transition from its historical role of enslaving the treaty nations as "wards" of the federal government, and its current role of designing and administering law programs over the lives of treaty people as well as providing services under the federal *Indian Act*,[23] to a role that supports the self-determination of treaty nations and their constitutional relationship with Canada and the provinces. The pernicious *Indian Act* has always been the antithesis of self-determination. The nation rebuilding seeks to reweave the past treaties into the future.

When adequately understood by the interpretative principles developed and revealed by the Court, the imperial treaties with distinct nations are one of the grand inventions of modern legal consciousness. The treaty authority of each nation was based on their inherent powers, *ex proprio vigore* (of its own force). The treaties reveal the existence of these inherent powers of the Aboriginal nations that establish the foundational nation-to-nation relationship that supports the imperial acts that determine the Constitution of Canada but lie outside of them.

Against the background of the European law of nations, the treaty negotiations, the oral promises in the negotiations, and the written terms of the treaties illuminate a coherent and conceptual legal order and the relationship between the sovereigns.[24] The treaties posit a consensual relationship that preserved the cohesive families of the treaty nations, their control over a particular territory, and their identities. The sovereigns' treaties created and sustained an innovative way of structuring British North America and its expansion across the continent on mutual promises. These treaties generated a commonwealth with the British sovereign, which accords with the initial concept of federal as a covenant, compact, or treaty, solemnly enacted, which established friendship and the peace of alliance. Through distinct world views, languages, and legal systems, the treaty reconciliations merge desire and power with the capabilities of compromise and trust. The promises invoke optimism of shared beliefs that speaks consensually, rationally, and authoritatively about future relations and jurisdictions.

The shared intent, purpose, and principles of the sovereigns in the imperial treaties resolve the challenge of facing a conquest, war, or subordination to existing orders of either party. The sovereigns committed to a vision of the transatlantic rule of law and a feasible, necessary structure of a consensual and desirable treaty commonwealth or federation. The sovereigns created treaties based on mutual consent[25] and which required the strict construction of rights guided by the understanding of the treaty nations that is founded on a trans-systemic synthesis founded in Aboriginal law and imperial constitutional law. The imperial treaties were not one-time historical events that extinguished the treaty nations, their jurisdictions, treaty tenure, or their rights; instead, they create a continuous, forward-looking relationship and structured process for building an imperial constitutional order in North America.

In the treaties, the sovereigns made intelligible the framework of treaty federation in imperial constitutional law.[26] The various terms of the imperial treaties over time reveal structural similarities within the treaty relationship, with the treaty nations delegating specific jurisdictions and obligations to the British sovereign. These similarities are drawn from the inherent powers of each nation, not from rights. The British sovereign recognizes, affirms, and respects the treaty nations' inherent sovereignty, which existed prior to, and apart from, the treaties. The treaty nations granted to the British sovereign delegated rights in the imperial treaties. In these treaties, the British sovereign did not grant many new rights to the treaty nations.[27] The imperial treaties stabilize and protect these inherent powers in the imperial reconciliation with the pre-existing Aboriginal nations' order, law, and territories.

The imperial treaties inaugurate the basic transatlantic treaty commonwealth or federation with the United Kingdom as the foundation of the Constitution of Canada.[28] The treaty federation, however incomplete, generated the invariant foundation for the liminal imperial proclamation, instructions, and acts directed towards responsible and good governance and the division of powers in the Constitution of Canada.

In the imperial treaties, the various treaty nations chose to retain inherent powers, independence, and liberties under the protection of Great Britain. The continuity of treaty sovereignty and governance was affirmed implicitly or expressly in most treaties. The treaty nations did not agree to foreign rule in the treaties. The treaty nations' delegation to the imperial Crown authorized settlements and immigration, but it never authorized imperial authority or colonization over them.[29] Treaty nations and tribes, in the spirit and intent of peace and friendship in the Georgian treaties, retained their inherent power to governance. In the Victorian treaties, Aboriginal self-rule was vested in the treaty chiefs to maintain "peace and good order" in the transferred territory over all inhabitants.[30] The treaties reveal the inescapable reliance among the treaty nations in governing themselves and offer no evidence of toleration for federal or provincial governance over them. Their express and incidental rights established their self-rule based on an innovative and inspired vision of foundational and complementary legal systems operating on consent and trust.

The oral promises and written terms of the imperial treaties delegate and determine the shape and limits of an innovative and normative treaty confederation.[31] They resolved issues consensually, which would otherwise be indeterminate among the nations, by leaving flexible and residual authority in treaty nations to apply their laws over specific peoples and territories. They seek to ensure that even the unknown and the unforeseeable can be subject to consensual negotiations and dialogical and honourable reconciliation. Their express terms and incidental rights establish an innovative and inspired vision of honourable governance.

Reconciling Provincial Federalism with Treaty Federalism

The treaty nations' recrimination against the federal government is long standing.[32] The transfer of jurisdiction over the treaty nations from the provinces to the federal government was designed to protect the treaty nations from the provinces and ensure a separate existence in federal institutions.[33] The federal government ignored and failed to implement the treaties and the lands reserved for them, but instead sought to assimilate them under constitutional tutelage as individuals rather than partners in confederation. In the last three decades, the federal government has sought to reconcile the treaties and grant delegated self-government rights to all Indigenous peoples. The treaty nations have rejected self-government for the affirmation of treaty federalism as the foundational order of Canada. Section 35 of the *Constitution Act, 1982*, part of the *Canada Act, 1982*, belatedly affirms and preserves, from within the Constitution itself, this foundational nation-to-nation order of the treaty nations.[34] Constitutional affirmation of treaty rights amalgamated the treaty nations into the patriated nation. They reveal the foundational benchmark of constitutional law and analysis. The purpose of the belated confirmation of these treaty rights was to create a constitutional shield against parliamentary supremacy; the existence of treaty nations could no longer be denied, displaced, or denigrated simply because they were not explicitly mentioned in the constitutional text.

The *Constitution Act, 1982* renewed and revived the underlying principle of the treaty promises, rights, and partnership as part of constitutional supremacy of the postcolonial nation. It unsettled the prevailing narrative of national federalism and its distribution and limitation of power. This decolonizing imperial act was intended to eliminate the dark era of colonialism and racism of Canadian nationalism that obstructed the achievement of treaty federalism as part of the shared rule in Canada. Nonetheless, the existing treaty order that generated British North America and now Canada has remained ignored and excluded in provincial federalism. This exclusion illustrates the incompleteness of constitutional governance, both descriptively and normatively.

Many reasons for the exclusion exist. The imperial Crown did not effectively translate or transmit the meaning of the treaties to the colonialists or their governmental entity. This miscommunication caused the treaties to remain a nation-to-nation agreement in the international or foreign affairs and imperial constitutional law. While the federal Parliament was authorized to implement these treaties,[35] they did not. Colonial provinces and federal Parliament avoided and ignored the interests and rights of the treaty nations.[36] The local authorities created and propagated negative images of the treaty nations as uncivilized to justify the assimilation of members of treaty nations to British colonial society.[37] Parliament's endless array of creative and argumentative strategies and abeyances around treaty implementation and judicial interpretation reveals a dark and destructive legacy.

Colonialism[38] and the artefacts of colonial law have been rigidly woven into constitutional abeyances. They narrowly focused on the relations between Great Britain and its subjects in foreign lands or colonies.[39] This system of rules that established constitutional law was based on the treaty federation with the treaty nations. Since the colonialists were forced to live by prerogatives of the imperial Crown and then the imperial Parliament, the very concept of imperial treaty rights acquired a nuance of domination. The imperial authorities were distant, negligent, and rarely legislated or provided oversight for the colonies. British colonists became comfortable in believing that Canadian federalism grew out of the mystical traditions of Great Britain as they moved from the Blackstonian or Whig sovereignty of an unwritten constitution to legal pluralism and a written constitution. These beliefs are as much a matter of prejudice as they are of convenience.[40] These imperial acts need fundamental rethinking with respect to how to protect treaty nations with constitutional rights.[41]

Under constitutional reforms in the *Constitution Act, 1982*, inviolable treaties and treaty nations are revealed as the source of the ancient constitution that justifies the limited sovereign authority of Great Britain in North America. The Aboriginal nations' delegated authority to the British sovereign in the treaties was the source and foundation for most of the provinces and the federal government. Thus, much of constitutional law is based on treaty federalism and is integral to constitutional interpretation.

Regardless of the legacy of denial, unfulfilled promises, and avoidance of treaty rights and responsibilities as constitutional rights and responsibilities, the affirmative rights and obligations of the treaties require Canada to constitutionally reconcile the imperial acts with the imperial treaties. The spirit and wording of section 35 of the *Constitution Act, 1982*, the 1996 final report of the Royal Commission on Aboriginal Peoples (RCAP), and the Court's decisions have rejected the malevolent assumptions of British colonialism, racism, and the legal interpretations of the meaning of the treaties. Section 35 denies organizing the future of Canada on the colonial quest for self-rule that camouflaged treaty rights and responsibilities.

The final report of the RCAP concluded that, because of false colonial premises, it is "indisputable that ... existing treaties have been honoured by governments more in the breach than in the observance."[42] It stated that the treaty relationship between treaty nations and the Canadian government was "mired in ignorance, mistrust and prejudice. Indeed, this has been the case for generations."[43] The RCAP's findings characterized the dishonoured treaties as part of the harmful "ghosts" of Canadian history.[44] Moreover, it stated that "[a] country cannot be built on a living lie."[45]

The report also referred to the constitutional recognition and affirmation of treaty rights in section 35(1) of the *Constitution Act, 1982*[46] as the "bedrock" of Canadian law[47] that have paved the way for Canada's federalistic and pluralistic society.[48] It affirmed the existing imperial treaties are "sacred," and that they create "sacred compacts."[49] It said the treaty nations are the "bearers of ancient and enduring powers"[50] that created "treaty federalism" in Canada, which "is an integral part of the Canadian constitution."[51] The report noted that the existing treaties are comparable to the "terms of union where former British colonies entered Confederation as provinces."[52] It interpreted section 35 as confirming the status of treaty nations as equal partners in the complex arrangements that make up patriated Canada.[53]

In *People to People, Nation to Nation*, a volume of highlights, the RCAP stated that "[a]n agreed treaty process can be the mechanism for implementing virtually all the recommendations in our report – indeed, it may be the only legitimate way to do so."[54] Recommendation 2.2.1 of the report restated the fundamental principle of treaty federalism or confederalism: authority is derived from the agreements of treaty nations with the British sovereign rather than from parliamentary sovereignty.[55] It recommended that the Canadian governments enter into new treaty negotiations with Aboriginal peoples who do not have a treaty relationship with Canada. It said that a secure constitutional foundation must replace false colonial premises.[56]

The Court has spoken about the implicit and underlying principles of Canadian federalism[57] and the inclusive, dynamic, and cooperative nature of these principles.[58] These decisions underscore the flexible nature of our constitutionalized federalism to meet the changing realities of Canadians. They reflect one of the enduring strengths of the Canadian federation – its ability to allow diverse nationalities and peoples to cohabit and prosper within postcolonial institutions of governance in a democratic nation.

The Court has established that section 35(1) affirms the fair and just reconciliation between treaty nations and the shared Crown.[59] The honour of the Crown is a controlling principle that arises from the "Crown's assertion of sovereignty over an Aboriginal peoples."[60] Since reconciliation is conceived as an ongoing process, the acknowledgment of treaty reconciliation presents an existing, consensual, and vested reconciliation, which requires the federal duty to respect the treaty nations' constitutionally protected agreements, to maintain the honour of the Crown, and to make the constitutional power of the federal government to legislate for treaty nations to be consistent with the spirit, intent, and text of the treaties.[61] Harmonizing treaty reconciliation with federal and provincial powers and laws does not involve the balancing of distinct rights but rather the convergence and implementation of treaty rights with the existing constitutional powers and their institutional and governance structures.[62] Writing on behalf of a unanimous Court, Chief Justice McLachlin observed that "[t]reaties serve to reconcile pre-existing Aboriginal sovereignty with assumed Crown sovereignty."[63] Treaty reconciliations cannot undermine the existing treaty rights or inherent powers retained by the treaty nations. Neither the treaty nations nor the framers of section 35(1) deliberately chose to subordinate the exercise of treaty rights to the good of British or Canadian society.[64]

The imperial treaties reveal the underlying principles of treaty federalism. The proposed treaty federalism is consistent with the most fundamental federal principle in Canada, which recognizes a "multi-tiered government combining elements of shared-rule and regional self-rule."[65] Treaty federalism is the foundation and operates similarly to the imperial acts that united the federation of the colonies into a Canadian federation as a response to the aspirations of diverse political colonialists, particularly the British and French. Treaty federalism under the Constitution of Canada is similar to the spirit and intent of the Balfour Declaration's reference to "autonomous Communities ... equal in status, in no way subordinate to one another in any aspect of their domestic or external affairs, though united by a common allegiance to the Crown."[66] Chief Justice Thibaudeau Rinfret reminded Canada and the provinces in the Nova Scotia Interdelegation case of 1951: "The constitution of Canada does not belong either to Parliament, or to the Legislatures; it belongs to the country and it is there that the citizens of the country will find the protection of the rights to which they are entitled."[67]

The Court has affirmed that a constitutional purpose of section 35 is to protect, recognize, and enhance the survival of Aboriginal peoples' distinctive communities.[68] It has established that one of the purposes of the federal structure of Canada was for the protection of cultural and linguistic diversity and local autonomy of Aboriginal peoples.[69] Given that "a review of the written provisions of the Constitution does not provide the entire picture"[70] of Canadian federalism, reconceptualizing and establishing a unified federation that includes treaty nations is required to "fill out gaps in the express terms of the constitutional scheme."[71] Legal and academic commentators have noted the value of this approach.[72] Canada and the provinces are constitutionally required to pursue the reconciliation process as laid out by the Court, which distances Canada from past efforts at colonialism, racism, and assimilation, by restoring treaty nations to a place within the Canadian constitutional order and forging a new relationship marked by collaboration and partnership.

In the way forward, no one way of thinking, talking, writing, or symbolizing enjoys the privilege of best representing reconciliation of the concept of treaty federalism in a nation-to-nation relationship or the expression of treaty self-determination or governance. The Government of Canada has affirmed the United Nations Declaration on the Rights of Indigenous Peoples (UNDRIP) and has statutorily implemented it.[73] It is integral to Canada's declaration of principles respecting Canada's relationship with Indigenous peoples[74] that Indigenous self-government is part of Canada's evolving system of cooperative federalism and distinct orders of government.

Consolidation of Treaty Federalism with Provincial Federalism

The constitutional federation remains unfinished. The *Constitution Act, 1982* sought to resolve these incoherencies about legitimate authority in Canada. The final report of the Royal Commission on Aboriginal Peoples and the decision of the Court provided a supporting set of ideas to guide the reconciliation and reconstruction of the governing institutions of Canada. It reaffirmed that Canadian federalism arose out of treaty federalism.[75] The source of Canadian federalism arose from the authority of these imperial treaties and acts that were initially derived from the treaty nations' consensual delegation to the imperial Crown, rather than from the inherent sovereignty of the imperial Crown. Out of the derivative rights arising from the sovereign or imperial treaties with Aboriginal nations, the imperial Crown established the provinces in British North America and the subsequent provincial federalism by imperial acts.

However, the imperial Crown-in-Parliament unilaterally used its political conventions and rules to establish these provinces and responsible government without the consent of the treaty nations in the treaties. These imperial acts failed to define the processes of selecting a government. Instead, the preamble of the *Constitution Act, 1867* provides for a federal union with "a constitution similar in principle" to that of the United Kingdom.[76] The royal prerogative, treaties, and law of nations are integral parts of the imperial transatlantic constitutional law of the United Kingdom.[77] Thus, they are part of the global law. No prohibition exists with these principles against treaty nations being part of the union.

Because of section 35(1), the final report of the RCAP concluded that a profound need exists for new processes that will allow Aboriginal peoples the opportunity to restructure existing governmental institutions and to participate as partners in the Canadian federation on terms they freely accept. It recommended that all governments in Canada recognize that section 35 provides the basis for an Aboriginal order of government that coexists within the framework of Canada along with the federal and provincial orders of government. Each order of government operates within its distinct sovereign sphere, as defined by the Constitution, and exercises authority within spheres of jurisdiction that have both overlapping and exclusive components.[78]

The RCAP report also argued for the unification of treaty federalism with provincial federalism as an integral part of displacing the colonial legacy in Canada with a constitutional legacy.[79] This unification needs institutional reform to implement the constitutional transformation of treaty rights that could lead to actualizing a shared future by creating an authentic Canadian federation, creating authentic democracy, consolidating treaty federalism, and implementing good faith into treaty rights and obligations.

Concerning the existing historical treaties, the RCAP recommended that the parties implement them from the perspectives of both justice and reconciliation. Since treaty promises were part of the foundation of Canada (and keeping those promises is a challenge to the honour and legitimacy of Canada), the implementation of legally recognized rights under the treaties will demonstrate that the Crown's honour is reflected in the Crown's actions. Justice requires the fulfilment of the agreed-upon terms of the treaties as recorded in the treaty text and supplemented by oral evidence. Reconciliation involves the establishment of proper principles to govern the continuing treaty relationship and to complete treaties that are incomplete because of the absence of consensus.[80]

Since the affirmation of treaty rights as part of the supreme law of Canada, the constitutional rights of treaty nations must be reflected in

Canadian federalism and their cultural realities protected in the constitutional order. The affirmation provides the constitutional authority for the protection of these inherent powers and rights against majority tyranny and for institutional transformation. The underlying constitutional architecture for the change exists; what is required is a fresh examination of provincial federalism from the constitutionally required lens of the treaties, the honour of the Crown, reconciliation, and dialogical governance.[81] The courts have established constitutional principles that should guide these political processes and principled negotiations.[82] These constitutional principles extend back to remedy the past avoidance of Aboriginal and treaty rights by courts and politicians. They also continue forward to embrace a political commitment to negotiate a more positive and durable relationship based on constitutional supremacy. In short, these principles create a shared future and sovereignty.

Section 35 of the *Constitution Act, 1982* affirms the residual right of self-determination of the treaty nations through the exercise of their existing treaty rights and its territorial boundaries as treaty governance. Treaty governance is an affirmative treaty right. It is the territorial jurisdiction created by the treaties for the exercise of inherent powers, federal implementation of affirmative promissory obligations in the treaties, and other rights and freedoms.[83]

Section 35 also limits the authority of the federal Parliament and the provinces over treaty rights.[84] Constitutional supremacy and the honour of the Crown requires institutional reforms involving treaty rights in the nation-to-nation relationship that will create an inclusive Canada, distinct from colonial Canada.[85] These reforms require merging treaty federalism with provincial federalism to improve and generate an inclusive Canadian federalism, democracy, and government. The "core," "centrepiece," or "heart" of Canadian federalism and governance is a legitimate governmental authority.

Additionally, the *Charter* sought to impose the rule of law and placed limits on federal and provincial governmental power over Canadians. Under the global vision of self-determination and human rights of the UNDRIP, the patriated constitutional order should link provincial federalism and treaty federalism into an authentic Canadian federation. All of these constitutional changes affirm the right to belated nation building and the need for reconciliation based on the right of self-determination.

The constitutional reforms, the decisions of the Court, the final report of the Royal Commission of Aboriginal Peoples, and the UNDRIP have established the foundation to reconcile treaty nations into a shared constitutional future and build a society that is uncontaminated by colonial thinking and laws.[86] Canada has started to comprehend that a dynamic nation-to-nation relationship is a necessary reform to the existing institutional systems and to imagine a creative pluralistic future of new chances and unlimited possibilities; we shall begin to share our future.

A coherent and authentic patriated Canada can only be created by understanding the necessity of acknowledging treaties established by the territorial jurisdiction of treaty governance.[87] This territorial jurisdiction of treaties has to be respected equally with provincial jurisdiction. The treaty boundaries and provincial boundaries generate ecological, political, and social identities. These territorial jurisdictions of the treaties are simultaneously cartographical, normative, and discursive service delivery areas. These jurisdictions have the inherent authority to define their laws and their systems of governance and implement their treaty rights. These elements cannot be neatly severed. They are an inherent part of the Constitution.

Further, Canada has to reconcile treaty and provincial federalism into a national federation based on the rights of free association and self-determination. To combine treaty federalism with provincial federalism is a transformation from colonialism to inclusive constitutionalism. The goal of the consolidation is to create institutional reforms rather than replace existing institutions with others. It must change the character as well as the content of the institutions. Such reforms should reimagine and remake parts of the constitutional governance framework to include treaty nations. Reconciling treaty federalism with provincial federalism would be a necessarily belated nation building process that would create a significant patriated nation, federation, and democratic society. Without such a convergence, Canada does not have a coherent vision of federalism or democracy that is consistent with its Constitution. Canada's political conventions imported from Great Britain have established structural inequalities that are not only inconsistent with its Constitution but have also blocked effective free association of the treaty nations and participation and representation in both treaty governance and Canadian governance.[88]

Constitutional reform requires Canada to provide national leadership on uniting provincial federalism with treaty federalism. Both territorial jurisdictions need to be unified in Parliament. Treaty jurisdictions are foundational; provincial jurisdiction is synthetic and derivative; federal jurisdiction is epiphenomenal. Each jurisdiction is equally essential to patriated Canada.

Many structural or institutional reforms are necessary for consolidation. The existing treaty relationship and constitutional rights need the establishment of both an attorney general for treaty nations[89] and a

Queen's Treaty Council similar to the current Privy Council. Both these institutional reforms are needed to develop and ensure a treaty strategy on the implementation of rights or settling disputes. They should study and implement law reform initiatives, process mapping, reversals of administrative boards and agencies, and be a central clearing house for discussions and disputes about the interpretation, application, and management of the various treaty relationships that have created Canada. They could develop mechanisms and processes to identify and potentially resolve treaty gaps, disputes, or accommodations. They could generate a wide variety of options for managing and strengthening the treaty relationships, and supplemental agreements on disputed issues based on baseline studies, transitional planning, and cumulative effects synthesis.

Generating Canadian Democracy

In addition to consolidating treaty federalism with provincial federalism to establish honourable federal governance, Canadian governments should revise their electoral systems to create authentic boundaries of representative democratic governance. Equally as important, provincial governments should be fundamentally reformed to include representation from treaty nations. The unique constitutional rights of treaty nations must be recognized as politically equal with provincial powers. This recognition can be an effective bridge between communities that respects, rather than subverts, the equitable distribution of political power. Canadian institutions need to include treaty delegates from the treaty nations to have a coherent and democratic constitution. I would suggest that one male and one female delegate be elected or appointed to represent the constitutional rights of each treaty on a nation basis, which is about forty delegates.

At the centre of existing federalism rests the question of how power ought to be distributed to optimize representation, avoid corruption, and prevent majority abuse. The existing electoral system was copied from British political conventions, mostly unwritten, that have established structural inequalities for treaty nations. The inequalities have blocked effective participation and representation by treaty nations.[90] It is challenging for the treaty nations to view the existing forms of governance as anything but segregation. Moreover, the courts have acknowledged that these non-representative governments have the implied power to infringe on the constitutional rights protecting Aboriginal peoples if justified. No legitimate reason exists for Canadian democracy to exclude the treaty nations from political institutions.

Canada has a history of uneven steps towards the political franchise as it developed a responsible government based on compromises and deals that protect diversity and minorities against the tyranny of the majority.[91] The facts reveal that the colonialists have never allowed participation of treaty nations in the political process. These constitutional voices have been excluded from the debate on public policy and the law-making process. As a consequence of their exclusion from Parliament, the treaty nations have engaged with law-making through non-electoral mechanisms and protests.

I do not think it is provocative to say that a representative democracy lacks legitimacy if ruled solely by an elite minority or certain majority. All democratic ideals follow the principle that governments "must not fall permanently hostage to a faction, however broadly the term faction may be defined."[92] Canadian democracy was created by the colonists to serve their purposes. At every level, democracy in Canada and the provinces has been controlled by the colonialist-immigrant faction; this dynamic has generated systemic inequality and political segregation for treaty nations. While treaty nations governance of its peoples is a practical necessity for self-determination within the treaty's territorial boundaries, without representation in Parliament and legislative assemblies, this systemic inequality cannot be resolved. Without a restructuring of Canadian democracy to include representation of the treaty nations, Canadian democracy will remain more a fiction than a reality, more hypocritical than humanistic, and more tyrannical than national.

A true patriated federalism and democracy can be created by understanding the necessity of the equality of treaty federalism in Canadian legislatures as a constitutional right of self-determination. Rather than a minority interest limiting majority power, treaty federalism can empower treaty nations based on the idea of treaty allies and constitutional equality. Constitutional equality is an antidote to the individual franchise of the modern electoral system. It embraces treaty jurisdiction as a means of protecting treaty nations and rights from hegemonic oppression and compulsory assimilation of a unitary and repressive colonialist culture of the past. The oppressive project of political apartheid must yield to respect the uniqueness of treaty difference.

The constitutional doctrine of the honour of the Crown and duty to consult and accommodate with treaty nations[93] as well as the right to free, prior, and informed consent are proxies for the non-representative nature of Canadian Parliament and provincial legislative assemblies. If the treaty nations were directly represented in these representative institutions of Canadian governance, the reliance on consent, consultation, and accommodation would be lessened.

The recent decision of the Court that the constitutional treaty right to consultation does not apply to Parliament demonstrates and enforces the need for treaty delegates to be an active participant in Parliament and in provincial legislative assemblies.[94] Under the inherent authority of the treaties, the treaty nations should send treaty delegates to Parliament and to the provincial legislative assemblies to represent their constitutional rights in law-making. Treaty delegates will generate a new partnership in revitalized federalism and an extraordinary democracy and resolve their subordination.

Recently, some First Nations, Métis, and Inuit peoples have represented an existing riding as individuals, but none have been delegated as authorized to speak for treaty rights. While the federal *Electoral Boundaries Readjustment Act* of 1985[95] allows for communities of interests and identities to be taken into account in drawing electoral boundaries, federal legislation has not been responsive to the constitutional interests of treaty nations. Current electoral laws fail to recognize treaty rights as defining new constitutional communities of interest distinct from other "group interests." Especially important is their right to cultural association.[96]

The tremendous effort made through dialogues with the United Nations and the Organization of American States (OAS) to empower powerless Indigenous peoples has proven the validity of Indigenous peoples as change agents in overcoming the hardened resistance of Eurocentric colonial thought. Independent Indigenous senators in Canada have demonstrated the same dialogical abilities could prevail in Parliament and provincial governments.

While creating authentic self-determination and democratic government in Canada, a constitutional reconciliation of treaty federalism and provincial federalism can be accomplished without undermining the constitutional foundations of Canada.[97] Article 19 of the UNDRIP reads: "States shall consult and cooperate in good faith with the indigenous peoples concerned through their own representative institutions in order to obtain their free, prior and informed consent before adopting and implementing legislative or administrative measures that may affect them."[98] Moreover, the 2016 American Declaration on the Rights of Indigenous Peoples of the OAS has expressly declared that Indigenous peoples have the right to equal opportunities to access and participate fully and effectively as peoples in all national institutions and forums, including deliberative bodies.[99] Both of these international documents are consistent with the idea of Treaty delegates.

The establishment of treaty delegates will not require constitutional amendments; this reconciliation can proceed under electoral reforms or federal legislation applying section 35 of the *Constitution Act, 1982* to federal election laws. The treaty delegates can be elected from the existing treaty boundaries similarly to the provincial and territorial boundaries.[100] They should be elected following treaty nations' laws. Each federal, territorial, and provincial government has the constitutional obligation to fulfil the treaty promises within the division of powers under the Constitution.[101] The treaty voice must be included in the election laws of federal, territorial, and provincial governments.

How long should treaty nations wait for Canadian governments to reconcile the democratic principle they uphold with the existing structural inequality and extravagant powers Canadian institutions unjustly maintain over them? Most treaty nations realize Canadian political elites have perverted treaty and human rights through systemic racism, greed, and preferential rights. Thus, treaty nations have been prevented from becoming equal partners in Canada, and Canada has been prevented from becoming a constitutional democracy. This situation must be resolved.

Conclusion

In interpreting the Constitution, the courts have developed a more holistic concern for cooperative federalism with overlapping powers and the just distribution of power.[102] The silence of the watertight structure and text of the Constitution should not be construed as denying institutional change that urges reconciliation with the existing treaty nations. It must be remembered that the entire text of the Constitution is silent concerning watertight or cooperative federalism[103] and democracy.[104] The judiciary discovered these implicit concepts in the structure and text of the Constitution, and they defined and normalized them. It is indefensible to treat these implied concepts as though they reflect strategic choices to exclude the treaty nations forever. The inherent powers of the Aboriginal nations are the oldest foundation of the Constitution.[105]

Cooperative federalism requires a new, connected, patriated structure for Canadian federalism and democracy in Canada consistent with constitutional reforms and the pre-emptive norms of self-determination found in the UNDRIP.[106] As the Court has stated:

> The Constitution, though a legal document, serves as a framework for life and for political action within a federal state, in which the courts have rightly observed the importance of cooperation among government actors to ensure that federalism operates flexibly.[107]

As a constitutional standard of Canada, treaty federalism is not a racial, ethnic, religious, linguistic, or minority standard. Instead, the concept focuses on constitutional rights that are interlinked to create a patriated Canada rather than on the fate of being born into a particular racialized group or culture. It is a concept and mechanism that is essential for the elimination of the adverse effects of colonialism and systemic racism in the modern constitutional debate between colonial and treaty nations about the meaning of Canada.

Merging treaty federalism with provincial federalism into cooperative federalism by federal laws must explicitly require the governments to obtain the legitimate consent of each treaty nation. Each treaty nation must determine its relation with Canada and the provinces. Only a fair and honourable constitutional reconciliation process will allow treaty nations to take over their affairs and destiny. Treaty nations and Canadians continue to value their collective knowledge systems, heritages, and identities, but they are no long the prisoners of any one identity that dictates every dream, thought, or action.

Treaty federalism in a renewed nation-to-nation relationship is not about merely moving boxes around in organizational charts. It requires structural and institutional changes in the idea of federalism and representative governments. It has at least eight vectors: (1) recognizing the legal personality of treaty nations already acknowledged by imperial treaties; (2) consolidating and implementing the existing treaties; (3) the immediate vesting of the specific power of self-determination of treaty nations; (4) including treaty nations in the national equalization formula; (5) limiting the powers of federal and provincial governments over treaty nations to those that were formally delegated to the Crown in the treaties; (6) broadly acknowledging the right of Aboriginal nations to enter into new treaties where there are no existing treaties; (7) including the treaty nations in the electoral apportionment of federal and provincial governments; and (8) filling gaps in the old treaties in accordance with UN human rights covenants. These reforms can be achieved by federal law without constitutional amendment.

These eight goals are essential to a renewed Canadian federalism and completing Canadian democracy. They are necessary for an institutional and symbolic renewal of the principles of federation. They are necessary to heal the deep intergenerational recrimination and wounds of the treaty nations generated by being "wards" of the federal government, a Canadian form of slavery. These goals are based on the principles of cultural integrity, political liberty, equality of economic opportunity, and human dignity. Canadians are not being asked to accept or advance unfamiliar values, but only to apply existing constitutional values to the treaty nations. The union of treaty federalism and provincial federalism is based on the idea that humans can come to honourable agreements on the terms of life and relationships. It is a belief in the unlimited potential of mutual problem-solving that enhances collective and individual life choices. This capacity can overcome the power of hierarchies of nationality, class, race, and gender. It is an enduring, covenantal relationship – not just an idea or an empty promise. The greatness of Canada lies in future relationships and new ways of living together as well as healing past wrongs.

NOTES

* Research Fellow, Wiyasiwewin Mikiwahp Native Law Centre of Canada, College of Law, University of Saskatchewan. *Ababinilli, maheoo, niskam,* and others provided guidance; however, I assume full responsibility for interpretation.
1 See James (Sa'ke'j) Youngblood Henderson, *Treaty Rights in the Constitution of Canada* (Toronto: Carswell, 2007); "Empowering Treaty Federalism," *Saskatchewan Law Review* 58, no. 2 (1994): 258–65.
2 The metaphor of an implied social contract as the hidden cornerstone of the rule of law is embedded in the various constitution acts in section 52(2) of the *Canada Act, 1982* (UK), 1982, c 11 [hereafter *Canada Act, 1982*] that comprise the Constitution of Canada, *Reference re Secession of Quebec*, [1998] 2 SCR 217 [hereafter *Quebec Secession Reference*], at para 32. The source of the implied social contract is the political philosophy of Thomas Hobbes, *Hobbes's Leviathan* (first published 1651, this edition, Oxford: Oxford University Press, 1909); John Locke, *Two Treatises of Government and A Letter Concerning Toleration*, ed. Ian Shapiro (first published 1690, this edition, New Haven, CT: Yale University Press, 2003); Jean-Jacques Rousseau, *The Social Contract and The First and Second Discourses*, ed. Susan Dunn (first published 1762, this edition, New Haven, CT: Yale University Press, 2002). The theory of the social contract in the constitution acts has to be contrasted with the trans-systemic treaties between the Indigenous nations and the British sovereign.
3 Peter Burroughs, "Colonial Self-Government," in *British Imperialism in the Nineteenth Century*, ed. C.C. Eldridge (London: Palgrave, 1984), 39–64.
4 *Constitution Act, 1867* (UK), 30–31 Vict, c 3, s 91, reprinted in RSC 1985, Appendix II, No 5.
5 Ibid., at s 91(24).
6 Ibid., at s 132.
7 Ibid., at ss 92, 93, 109.

8 See list in *Constitution Act, 1982*, s 52(2) of *Canada Act, 1982*.
9 *Quebec Secession Reference*, at paras 43–4, 55–60; A. Wayne MacKay, "The Supreme Court of Canada and Federalism: Does/Should Anyone Care Anymore?," *Canadian Bar Review* 80, no. 1 (2001): 241–80; Gerald Baier, *Courts and Federalism: Judicial Doctrine in the United States, Australia, and Canada* (Vancouver: UBC Press, 2006), chaps 2, 5.
10 *Quebec Secession Reference*, at paras 56–7.
11 John D. Whyte, "Federalism Dreams," *Queen's Law Journal* 34, no. 1 (2008–9): 1–28; James Bickerton, "Deconstructing the New Federalism," *Canadian Political Science Review* 4, no. 2–3 (2010): 56–72.
12 *Canada Act, 1982*.
13 *Constitution Act, 1982*, being Schedule B to the *Canada Act, 1982*, s 35 [hereafter *Constitution Act, 1982*].
14 *Canadian Charter of Rights and Freedoms*, Part 1 of the *Constitution Act, 1982*, being Schedule B to the *Canada Act, 1982* [hereafter *Charter*].
15 Andrew Cohen, *A Deal Undone: The Making and Breaking of the Meech Lake Accord* (Vancouver: Douglas & McIntyre, 1990); Kenneth McRoberts and Patrick J. Monahan, *The Charlottetown Accord, the Referendum, and the Future of Canada* (Toronto: University of Toronto Press, 1993).
16 *Quebec Secession Reference*, at para 49. See also paras 44, 50–4.
17 See political philosopher John Ralston Saul's insights in *A Fair Country: Telling Truths about Canada* (Toronto: Viking Canada, 2008). In the first part of the book, Saul argues that Canadian political thought is heavily influenced and shaped by Aboriginal ideas.
18 *Quebec Secession Reference*, at paras 32, 49.
19 Ibid., at para 82.
20 See *New Brunswick Broadcasting Co. v. Nova Scotia (Speaker of the House of Assembly)*, [1993] 1 SCR 319 [hereafter *New Brunswick*], at 373. See also *Quebec Secession Reference*, at para 49.
21 See *Quebec Secession Reference*, at paras 49–50. See also *R. v. Sparrow*, [1990] 1 SCR 1075 [hereafter *Sparrow*], at 1109; *R. v. Van der Peet*, [1996] 2 SCR 507 [hereafter *Van der Peet*], at paras 42, 49–50; *Delgamuukw v. British Columbia*, [1997] 3 SCR 1010 [hereafter *Delgamuukw*], at paras 82, 148. See the partial attempts in *R. v. Badger*, [1996] 1 SCR 771 [hereafter *Badger*].
22 See the Honourable Jody Wilson-Raybould, "Assembly of First Nations, Annual General Assembly" (speech, Niagara Falls, ON, 12 July 2016), Government of Canada, http://www.canada.ca/en/department-justice/news/2016/07/assembly-of-first-nations-annual-general-assembly.html. The concept of nation to nation was inherent in the various treaty federations with the British sovereign; see Henderson, *Treaty Rights*, 1003–53.
23 *Indian Act*, RSC 1985, c I-5, originally enacted in 1867.

24 These treaties are discussed in Henderson, *Treaty Rights*, 143–282.
25 This is usually represented by the phrase "said chiefs and principal men do freely, fully and voluntarily" surrender a tract of land for money. See "Copy of the Robinson Treaty Made in the Year 1850 with the Ojibewa Indians of Lake Huron Conveying Certain Lands to the Crown," Government of Canada, accessed 25 April 2023, https://www.rcaanc-cirnac.gc.ca/eng/1100100028984/1581293724401; "Copy of the Robinson Treaty Made in the Year 1850 with the Ojibewa Indians of Lake Superior Conveying Certain Lands to the Crown," Government of Canada, accessed 25 April 2023, https://www.rcaanc-cirnac.gc.ca/eng/1100100028984/1581293724401.
26 For discussion of imperial law and treaties, see Mark Walters, "Mohegan Indians v. Connecticut (1705–1773) and the Legal Status of Aboriginal Customary Laws and Government in British North America," *Osgoode Hall Law Journal* 33, no. 4 (1995): 785–829.
27 *United States v. Winans*, [1905] 198 US 371, at 381 (A treaty is "not a grant of rights to the Indians, but a grant of right from them – a reservation of those not granted"); Felix S. Cohen, *Cohen's Handbook of Federal Indian Law*, ed. Nell Jessup Newton et al. (Newark, NJ: LexisNexis, 2005), 26 ("Treaties must be understood as grants of rights from Indian people who reserved all rights not granted"); "Indian Canon Originalism," *Harvard Law Review* 126, no. 4 (February 2013): 1100.
28 See James (Sa'ke'j) Youngblood Henderson, *Wabanaki Compact: The Foundations of Treaty Federalism in North America, 1621–1728* (Saskatoon: Indigenous Law Centre, 2020); *Elikewake Compact: The Mi'kmaw, Wolastoqey, and Passamaquoddy Nations' Confederation with Great Britain, 1725–1779* (Saskatoon: Indigenous Law Centre, 2021).
29 See Royal Commission on Aboriginal Peoples (RCAP), *Partners in Confederation: Aboriginal Peoples, Self-Government, and the Constitution* (Ottawa: Supply and Services Canada, 1993), 25–6. See also Michael Asch and Patrick Macklem, "Aboriginal Rights and Canadian Sovereignty: An Essay on *R. v. Sparrow*," *Alberta Law Review* 29, no. 2 (1991): 498.
30 See Henderson, "Empowering Treaty Federalism," 258–65.
31 See *Badger*.
32 RCAP, *Partners in Confederation*; *Report of the Royal Commission on Aboriginal Peoples*, vol. 1, *Looking Forward, Looking Back* (Ottawa: Supply and Services Canada, 1996).
33 See Great Britain, Select Committee on Aborigines, *Report of the Select Committee on Aborigines* (London, 1837), 77–8, https://babel.hathitrust.org/cgi/pt?id=nyp.33433000271902&view=1up&seq=83.
34 *Constitution Act, 1982*, s 35. Justice Marie Deschamps in a minority decision in *Beckman v. Little Salmon/Carmacks First Nation*, [2010] 3 SCR 103, at

para 97 stated that the treaties with Aboriginal are one of the three basic compacts that are interwoven into constitutionalism.
35 In this regard, sections 91(24) and 132 of the *Constitution Act, 1867* must not only be read with one another but also with section 35 of the *Constitution Act, 1982* and section 25 of the *Charter*.
36 Select Committee on Aborigines, *Report*, 77–8.
37 RCAP, *Looking Forward, Looking Back*; *Report of the Royal Commission on Aboriginal Peoples*, vol. 2, *Restructuring the Relationship* (Ottawa: Supply and Services Canada, 1996); *Report of the Royal Commission on Aboriginal Peoples*, vol. 3, *Gathering Strength* (Ottawa: Supply and Services Canada, 1996); *Report of the Royal Commission on Aboriginal Peoples*, vol. 4, *Perspectives and Realities* (Ottawa: Supply and Services Canada, 1996); *Report of the Royal Commission on Aboriginal Peoples*, vol. 5, *Renewal: A Twenty-Year Commitment* (Ottawa: Supply and Services Canada, 1996); see especially vols. 1 and 2. See generally the Honourable Jane Stewart, "On the Occasion of the Unveiling of *Gathering Strength – Canada's Aboriginal Plan*" (speech, Ottawa, ON, 7 January 1998), Government of Canada, https://www.rcaanc-cirnac.gc.ca/eng/1100100015725/1571590271585.
38 James (Sa'ke'j) Youngblood Henderson, "Postcolonial Ghost Dancing: Diagnosing European Colonialism," in *Reclaiming Indigenous Voice and Vision*, ed. Marie Battiste (Vancouver: UBC Press, 2000), 161.
39 See Antony Anghie, "Finding the Peripheries: Sovereignty and Colonialism in Nineteenth-Century International Law," *Harvard International Law Journal* 40, no. 1 (Winter 1999): 1; Kenneth Roberts-Wray, *Commonwealth and Colonial Law* (New York: F.A. Prager, 1966); Charles Clark, *A Summary of Colonial Law: The Practice of the Court of Appeals from the Plantations, and of the Laws and Their Administration in All the Colonies* (London: S. Sweet, 1834).
40 See generally Andrew W. Fraser, *The Spirit of the Laws: Republicanism and the Unfinished Project of Modernity* (Toronto: University of Toronto Press, 1990).
41 See, in particular, *Constitution Act, 1930* (UK), 20–21 Geo 5, c 26, reprinted in RSC 1970, Appendix II, No 25; see *Badger*, at paras 41–8, 83–5.
42 RCAP, *Restructuring the Relationship*, 3.
43 Ibid., 35.
44 RCAP, *People to People, Nation to Nation: Highlights from the Report of the Royal Commission on Aboriginal Peoples* (Ottawa: Supply and Services Canada, 1996), 4–5. In *Sparrow*, at 1103–4, the Court alluded to a similar vision of history marked by denial and domination, where governments and legal institutions ignored Aboriginals' legal rights, claims, and perspectives and primarily served non-Aboriginal interests.
45 RCAP, *Restructuring the Relationship*, 1.
46 Ibid., 20–1.

47 Ibid., 33. This is comparable to A.V. Dicey's assertion that the doctrine of parliamentary sovereignty is "the very keystone of the law of the [United Kingdom] constitution." A.V. Dicey, *Introduction to the Study of the Law of the Constitution*, 9th ed. (London: Macmillan and Co, 1939), 70. See also ibid., 39.
48 RCAP, *Restructuring the Relationship*, 14 (pluralism), 356 (federalism).
49 Ibid., 17–18 (sacred), 19 (social contract), 17, 48 (sacred compact).
50 RCAP, *Partners in Confederation*, 36.
51 RCAP, *Restructuring the Relationship*, 184.
52 Ibid., 16, 19, 20.
53 Ibid., 231.
54 RCAP, *People to People*, 51.
55 RCAP, *Restructuring the Relationship*, 20; and see 18–22 for commentary, and 195–6 for discussion on parliamentary sovereignty and inherent rights.
56 RCAP, *Looking Forward, Looking Back*, 685.
57 See *Quebec Secession Reference*, at para 43.
58 *Reference re Same-Sex Marriage*, [2004] 3 SCR 698, at paras 22–4.
59 See *Sparrow*, at 1109; *Van der Peet*, at paras 43 (Chief Justice Lamer), 230 (Justice McLachlin, dissenting); *Delgamuukw*, at para 186; *Haida Nation v. British Columbia (Minister of Forests)*, [2004] 3 SCR 511 [hereafter *Haida Nation*], at para 20; *Taku River Tlingit First Nation v. British Columbia (Project Assessment Director)*, [2004] 3 SCR 550, at para 24.
60 See *Haida Nation*, at para 32. See also ibid., at para 38. This unanimous decision embodies the dissent of Justice McLachlin (as she then was) in *Van der Peet*, at para 310, questioning how the majority's version of reconciliation of the different legal cultures could be accomplished: "More particularly, does the goal of reconciliation of aboriginal and non-aboriginal interests require that we permit the Crown to require a judicially authorized transfer of the aboriginal right to non-aboriginals without the consent of the aboriginal people, without treaty, and without compensation? I cannot think it does."
61 See *Sparrow*, at 1106–7; *Mikisew Cree First Nation v. Canada (Minister of Canadian Heritage)*, [2005] 3 SCR 388 [hereafter *Mikisew Cree*], at paras 51, 54, 57.
62 See *Grassy Narrows First Nation v. Ontario (Natural Resources)*, [2014] 2 SCR 447 [hereafter *Grassy Narrows*], at para 35.
63 See *Haida Nation*, at para 20.
64 See *R. v. Marshall*, [1999] 3 SCR 533 [hereafter *Marshall*], at para 45, 179 DLR (4th) 193; *Van der Peet*, at paras 308, 315 (Justice McLachlin, dissenting).
65 See Ronald L. Watts, *Comparing Federal Systems*, 3rd ed. (Montreal: McGill-Queen's University Press, 2008), 8.

38 James (Sa'ke'j) Youngblood Henderson

66 "Report of the Inter-Imperial Relations Committee," in *The Colonial and Imperial Conferences from 1887 to 1937*, vol. 3, *Imperial Conferences*, ed. Maurice Ollivier (Ottawa: Edmond Cloutier, 1954), 146.
67 *Attorney General of Nova Scotia v. Attorney General of Canada*, [1951] SCR 31, at 34. See also *Quebec Secession Reference*, at para 85: "The Constitution is the expression of the sovereignty of the people of Canada."
68 See *R. v. Powley*, [2003] 2 SCR 207, at paras 13, 17.
69 See *Quebec Secession Reference*, at paras 43, 59–60.
70 Ibid., at para 55.
71 See *Reference Re Remuneration of Judges of the Provincial Court of Prince Edward Island*, [1997] 3 SCR 3, at 95. See also *Mitchell v. M.N.R.*, [2001] SCR 911, at paras 129, 135; *Campbell v. British Columbia (Attorney General)*, [2000] BCSC 1123, at paras 68, 80–81.
72 See Henderson, "Empowering Treaty Federalism"; Brian Slattery, "The Organic Constitution: Aboriginal Peoples and the Evolution of Canada," *Osgoode Hall Law Journal* 34, no. 1 (1996): 101; Patrick Macklem, *Indigenous Difference and the Constitution of Canada* (Toronto: University of Toronto Press, 2001). See also the work of political scientists such as Kiera L. Ladner, "Treaty Federalism: An Indigenous Vision of Canadian Federalisms," in *New Trends in Canadian Federalism*, ed. François Rocher and Miriam Smith, 2nd ed. (Peterborough, ON: Broadview Press, 2003), 167.
73 UN General Assembly, United Nations Declaration on the Rights of Indigenous Peoples (UNDRIP), 2 October 2007, A/RES/61/295, Article 37(1). In 2015, Canada announced that it was a full supporter, without qualification, of the UNDRIP under the Canadian Constitution. See Tim Fontaine, "Canada Officially Adopts UN Declaration on Rights of Indigenous Peoples," *CBC News*, 10 May 2016, https://www.cbc.ca/news/indigenous/canada-adopting-implementing-un-rights-declaration-1.3575272. See also John Borrows, Larry Chartrand, Oonagh E. Fitzgerald, and Risa Schwartz, eds., *Braiding Legal Orders: Implementing the United Nations Declaration on the Rights of Indigenous Peoples* (Waterloo, ON: Centre for International Governance Innovation, 2019).
74 *United Nations Declaration on the Rights of Indigenous Peoples Act*, SC 2021, c 14. See Department of Justice Canada, "Principles Respecting the Government of Canada's Relationship with Indigenous Peoples," Government of Canada, last modified 14 February 2018, https://justice.gc.ca/eng/csj-sjc/principles-principes.html.
75 RCAP, *Restructuring the Relationship*, 15: "Canadians are not taught that Canada was built on the formal treaty alliances that European explorers, military commanders and later civil authorities were able to forge with the nations they encountered on this continent."
76 *Constitution Act, 1867*, preamble. The *Constitution Act, 1867* provides for the confederating provinces to "be federally united into One Dominion

under the Crown of the United Kingdom of Great Britain and Ireland, with a Constitution similar in Principle to that of the United Kingdom." See generally *New Brunswick*, where the court found that the doctrine of parliamentary privilege is included in the Constitution of Canada, although it is not mentioned in section 52(2) of the *Constitution Act, 1982*.

77 The boundaries of the constitutional law of the United Kingdom have never been satisfactorily defined. See Hardinge Stanley Giffard Halsbury and Gerald D. Sanagan, *Halsbury's Laws of England*, 3rd ed., vol. 8 (London: Butterworths, 1954), at paras 801, 889–1082. But as part of the constitutional law, treaties are included in the royal prerogatives (ibid., at paras 985–6) and the United Nations (ibid., at para 988).

78 See Recommendation 2.3.12 in RCAP, *Restructuring the Relationship*, 244.

79 RCAP, *Restructuring the Relationship*, 188–201. See also *Simon v. The Queen*, [1985] 2 SCR 387, at 404 and its effect on *R. v. Syliboy*, [1929] 1 DLR 307; *R. v. Côté*, [1996] 3 SCR 139, at paras 52–3; *Marshall*, at para 45 (describing the purpose of section 35(1) by rejecting the idea that non-treaty nations' licenses or privileges can displace the constitutional rights of Aboriginal peoples).

80 Recommendation 2.2.2 in RCAP, *Restructuring the Relationship*, 46.

81 The idea of governance by a continuous dialogue among competing constitutional interests rather than legislation is emerging in many contemporary sites. See the constitutional discussion of negotiations in *Quebec Secession Reference*, at para 63. See also James (Sa'ke'j) Youngblood Henderson, "Dialogical Governance: A Mechanism of Constitutional Governance," *Saskatchewan Law Review* 72, no. 1 (2009): 29; A. Wayne MacKay, "The Legislature, the Executive and the Courts: The Delicate Balance of Power or Who Is Running This Country Anyway?," *Dalhousie Law Journal* 24, no. 2 (2001): 37.

82 See *Delgamuukw*, at para 207; *Quebec Secession Reference*, at paras 94–104.

83 See *Charter*, ss 25 6. Section 26 provides the following: "The guarantee in this Charter of certain rights and freedoms shall not be construed as denying the existence of any other rights or freedoms that exist in Canada." This rule of construction defines the other unenumerated "rights and freedoms" clause in section 25, which together can be interpreted as applying the UNDRIP to Aboriginal peoples of Canada. Article 1 of the UNDRIP provides that "Indigenous peoples have the right to the full enjoyment, as a collective or as individuals, of all human rights and fundamental freedoms as recognized in the Charter of the United Nations, the Universal Declaration on Human Rights, and international human rights law." Canada has affirmed the UNDRIP in the *United Nations Declaration on the Rights of Indigenous Peoples Act*, SC 2021, c 14. In consultation and cooperation with Indigenous peoples, the Government of Canada must take all measures necessary to ensure that the laws of Canada are consistent with the UNDRIP.

84 See, for example, *Mitchell v. Peguis Indian Band*, [1990] 2 SCR 85.
85 See *Quebec Secession Reference*, at paras 70–8.
86 "Treaty Federalism," special issue, *Review of Constitutional Studies* 24, no. 1 (June 2019).
87 See Henderson, "Empowering Treaty Federalism," 250–69.
88 See Committee for Aboriginal Electoral Reform (CAEF), "The Path to Electoral Equality," in *Reforming Electoral Democracy*, vol. 4 (Ottawa: Communication Group, 1991), 241–5.
89 See James (Sa'ke'j) Youngblood Henderson, "Aboriginal Attorney General," *Windsor Yearbook of Access to Justice* 22 (2003): 265.
90 See CAEF, "Path to Electoral Equality," 241–5.
91 See *Quebec Secession Reference*, at paras 63–9.
92 See Roberto Mangabeira Unger, *The Critical Legal Studies Movement* (Cambridge, MA: Harvard University Press, 1986), 27. See also ibid., 28–31.
93 See *Mikisew Cree*, at paras 51–8 for greater discussion of the honour of the Crown and duty to consult.
94 See *Mikisew Cree First Nation v. Canada (Governor General in Council)*, [2018] 2 SCR 765, at paras 32–3, 38–40.
95 *Electoral Boundaries Readjustment Act*, RSC 1985, c E-3.
96 See United Nations Human Rights Committee, *Selected Decisions under the Optional Protocol (Second to Sixteenth Sessions)* (New York: United Nations, 1985), 83.
97 See *Delgamuukw*, at para 82, citing *Van der Peet*, at para 49: "accommodation of [Aboriginal rights] must be done in a manner which does not strain 'the Canadian legal and constitutional structure.'" Treaties are the foundational architecture of the legal and constitutional structure of British North America (or Canada).
98 UNDRIP, Article 19.
99 Organization of American States (OAS), General Assembly, 46th Sess, American Declaration on the Rights of Indigenous Peoples, OR OEA/Ser.P/AG/RES.2888 (XLVI-O/16) (2016) Article 21, at para 2.
100 See CAEF, "Path to Electoral Equality," 259–60, 273–7.
101 See *Grassy Narrows*, at para 35.
102 See *Canadian Western Bank v. Alberta*, [2007] 2 SCR 3 [hereafter *Canadian Western Bank*], at paras 24, 37, 42; *Reference re Pan-Canadian Securities Regulation*, [2018] 3 SCR 189, at paras 17–19; *Tsilhqot'in Nation v. British Columbia*, [2014] SCR 256, at paras 148–50.
103 See *Quebec Secession Reference*, at paras 55–6.
104 Ibid., at para 62.
105 See *Charter*, ss 25–6.

106 *Quebec Secession Reference*, at para 74: "a constitution may provide an added safeguard for fundamental human rights and individual freedoms which might otherwise be susceptible to government interference."
107 *Canadian Western Bank*, at para 42.

2 Consent and the Resolution of Political Relations between Indigenous Peoples and the Canadian State

MICHAEL ASCH[*]

Introduction

We are at a particularly difficult moment in the history of the relationship between Indigenous peoples and the settler state of Canada. Right now, it is hard to imagine how we can move from what has been revealed to be a deadlock caused largely by Canada's refusal to even begin in the wholehearted investment of building a just and equitable political and economic relationship with those on whose lands the state was built. Nonetheless, I feel it is useful, if optimistic, to begin to think through how the establishment of such a relationship might evolve. What follows, then, is a discussion of one possible path forward. It is based on social contract theory and is imagined through the lens of consent theory – particularly, what is meant in this context by the phrase "voluntary consent, mutually given."

To that end, let me go out even further on a limb and lay out the rough shape of what I imagine would be the outcome of a process based on voluntary consent as understood in social contract theory. It is, of course, completely hypothetical in that, as will become clear, at the end of the day the approach I describe will not be to a predefined end point but will result from the consequences of steps taken along the way. Nonetheless, here is what I imagine.

In my belief, this process will reach an agreement based on voluntary consent that enables us all to live within the geographic region of Canada (or, if you are of the view, within Quebec).[1] The ultimate objective, then, expressed as an initial condition, is to establish such a relationship without it causing the dissolution of Canada. That is, I believe that what we seek is an agreement that not only enables us to inhabit the same territory but actually to live together relationally. Given this, I also assume that the state would most likely be configured as a confederation with a consociational orientation.[2] I anticipate that this is the form of governance that would result were we to negotiate through a process based on mutual consent, voluntarily given.[3]

This chapter, then, is aimed at describing, in a preliminary way, what would constitute "voluntary consent, mutually given" in the context of building any relationship between Indigenous peoples and Canada, and which is in my view most likely to move in the direction of the outcome I describe above. In this regard, I will argue that rather than being a single act, as is imagined in classical social contract theory, voluntary consent is a process intended to move the parties closer to an objective that becomes more defined as it progresses. It is one that proceeds as much through consensus as by formalized events, although the latter will likely play a crucial role by marking key moments along the way.

At the same time, while a depiction of this process is my ultimate goal, to get there I will first lay out how I understand the concept of consent in social contract theory through a lens offered by Jeremy Webber as well as the standing of Canada's current relationship with Indigenous polities as expressed within that frame. This will involve first discussing three concepts on which I rely: (1) "consent," as that term is used with regard to political relations between Indigenous peoples and settler states; (2) what would constitute "voluntary consent, mutually given" in that context; and (3) the relationship between the doctrine of *terra nullius*, social contract theory, and the manner in which Canada justifies the legitimacy of its assertion of sovereignty. Then, before closing, I will quickly address impediments to even beginning the process, resulting from the historic wrongs consequent to Canada's justification.

On Consent

Based on my reading of relevant official contemporary documents of the United Nations, "consent" of an Indigenous party in the context of Indigenous–State relations takes one of two forms.[4] The first is what I will call "reactive consent." It arises from the way the word is used in the 2007 United Nations Declaration on the Rights of Indigenous Peoples (UNDRIP).[5] Here, the right of Indigenous peoples in states like Canada to "free, prior and informed consent" only arises as a response to initiatives of the state and is applied only with regard to specified matters. These are: relocation from their lands (Article 10); compensation for cultural and other "non-tangible" property taken without permission (Article 11.2); the state's adoption or implementation of "legislative or administrative measures that may affect them" (Article 19); redress for lands and resources they have traditionally owned or occupied and have been "confiscated, taken, occupied, used or damaged" without it (Article 28.1); the storage or disposal of hazardous materials on their lands or territories (Article 29.2); and with respect to developments on their lands (Article 32.2). Furthermore, according to UNDIP's Article 28.1, when Indigenous parties do not give consent, redress is limited to the right to seek "just, fair and equitable compensation."

Thus, it would follow that in the situation discussed here, it would be perfectly acceptable for Canada to present to Indigenous peoples a policy to incorporate them that it has unilaterally developed, and which it offers to Indigenous peoples on a take-it-or-leave-it basis. And in point of fact (as I will discuss further below), this is how Canada acts today.[6] This is not what I mean by consent here.

I am calling the mode of consent I find applicable "proactive consent." It is the form I associate with the provisions of the 1960 United Nations Declaration on the Granting of Independence to Colonial Countries and Peoples, also known as Resolution 1514 (XV), in which the UN declared that colonized peoples have the right to self-determination that includes their establishment of independent states when these are carved out from what Resolution 1541 (XV) calls territories "of the colonial type."[7] As is seen in the implementing provisions of that resolution, here consent refers to an agreement that arises when parties engage in a mutually agreed upon project.[8]

In the case I am laying out here, that goal would be to establish a mutually agreed upon political relationship without altering the boundaries of an existing state – a form consistent with Principle 3(b) in Resolution 1541 (XV), or "free association with an independent state." But it could also legitimately result through the application of Principle 3(a), or "emergence as a sovereign independent state" in the creation of independent states (as, for example, in the break-up of Yugoslavia[9]) – a matter on which the UNDRIP is silent. So, in practical terms, the salient difference between Resolution 1514 (XV) and the UNDRIP is that, by including the option of a legitimate right to form an independent state, the former provides leverage for the colonized party in its negotiations that is not available to the Indigenous party in the latter.[10]

On Voluntary Consent

I turn now to "voluntary consent." In so doing, I rely on Jeremy Webber's paper "The Meanings of Consent,"[11] which I found to be very helpful in differentiating between different views of what voluntary consent would entail based largely on his fine-grained analysis of the abstract nature of the units (understood as Self and Other) seeking a social contract between them. Of these, the view with most relevance to my discussion he calls "consent and the relational definition of self," which he describes thusly:

> Another set of theories – theories grounded in a relational definition of the self – takes aim at the separation of self from context that is assumed in many theories of consent, where the choosing self is taken to be autonomous and self-sufficient, deciding in isolation whether or not to enter community. Relational theories emphasize the extent to which the self is necessarily fashioned in a social context, through the very process of interaction with others. Autonomy itself is a quality that is dependent on that relational context. Indeed, these theories generally have a concept of autonomy (and therefore consent) that is richer than merely the ability to make unconstrained choices, and that include the development of the capacities necessary for effective self-government in the member. Engagement in a community is not, then, the antithesis of individual agency but rather its precondition. The key question is not whether someone should join in community or not, but how one should reconstruct existing communities so that autonomy – understood as individual and collective self-determination – is maximized.[12]

Within this understanding, I will suggest that, as in classic social contract theory, "voluntary consent" is imagined in the abstract as a single act that is undertaken with urgency; for example, the agreement in Thomas Hobbes's *Leviathan* (1651) among a "multitude of men" to establish a mutually agreed upon sovereign. However, here, in Webber's reading, the reason is that political society requires the establishment of a relationship between two parties that are different from one another – that is, by the joining of Self and Other – and thus may be imagined as an initial condition rather than as a development from an earlier condition that is often described as "the state of nature."

At the same time, in contrast to Hobbes's *Leviathan*, in this formulation consent does not result from a deliberative act, but emerges as an urgent, visceral need. It is an orientation that follows a long tradition of origins of society arguments that is found prominently in the work of anthropologists and sociologists that include Émile Durkheim, Marcel Mauss, and Claude Lévi-Strauss. It is a tradition in which theorists, unlike in much of the field of anthropology, address the idea of the origins of society in abstract, theoretical terms.[13]

Here, let me put forward my interpretation[14] of the argument developed by Lévi-Strauss in his book *The Elementary Structures of Kinship*.[15] In it, he constructs a thought experiment in which he contends that society arises at the moment when consciousness of the incest taboo requires humans to find (marriage) partners from outside one's own family in order to reproduce the species. In this sense, society arises as the joining of two parties, each incomplete without the other, and each required for the success of the project to maintain a relationship of autonomy and connectedness with the other.[16] Hence, here the "transition" to humanity is coterminus with the origins of society, for both only occur when, because of the incest taboo, Self realizes that it cannot continue to exist without a rule-governed relationship with Other. For this reason, mutual consent, voluntarily given, is the essential initial condition for society, and it occurs at the very moment that society comes into existence. It is, if you will, the Big Bang.

Given that society occurs at the moment of human consciousness, it is not possible to consider "voluntary consent" as a kind of deliberative act. Rather, it would seem, given that all Selves find themselves immediately vulnerable and dependent on Others, that there is an urgency, born of necessity, that provides the motivation to enter into the consensual relationship that constitutes society. Thus, in Lévi-Strauss's thought experiment on the origins of society, as I have come to understand it, "voluntary consent, mutually given" is an urgent matter. Indeed, society cannot emerge without it.

While we are not, of course, initiating society here, I suggest that the "urgent, visceral need" is present with regard to Canada's position in its relationship with Indigenous peoples within its borders. This need, as I will discuss further below, arises from the manner in which the relationship would be comprehended by Canada and internationally were it recognized that Indigenous peoples have the same right to form independent states as is guaranteed to colonized peoples in the 1960 United Nations Declaration on the Granting of Independence to Colonial Countries and Peoples.

We are not initiating society, but we are seeking to build a relationship between two existing societies in which one seeks to permanently inhabit lands already occupied by the other. In this context, I believe that, speaking abstractly, our situation is also well-described in what Webber defines as "consent as a grounded form of life." Here, he is referring to a

> large group of theories that are heirs to the vision of consent as grounded in particular traditions or sets of practices. These theories emphasize the way in which living within a culture shapes individuals, providing them with a language which they then use to understand themselves and their society. These theories often draw, directly or indirectly, on (Ludwig)

Wittgenstein's observation that modes of understanding are embedded in particular forms of life – that linguistic formulations take their meaning from the way they are employed in social life and cannot be fully comprehended without understanding how they are used in those social practices. Language always, then, takes the form of a vernacular, local in origin and particular in its signification. In the theories of community that draw on Wittgenstein, these distinctive languages of social interaction, grounded in distinctive sets of practices, are seen to be the model for the commonality that exists in particular communities, traditions, or cultures.[17]

It is an understanding that I find reflects the idea of relationship building based on "treaty relations" as I have come to understand that concept within Indigenous political thought.

With these concepts in mind, let me turn to the role that voluntary consent might play in building the relationship between Indigenous peoples and Canada. I begin with a brief account in which I hope to clarify where Canada now stands in relationship to that process.

Canada's Sovereignty and *terra nullius*

Given the premises of social contract theory, except where a land is *terra nullius* and thus conceptualized as being previously devoid of people, it would be incumbent on new arrivals to come to an agreement with those already living in that territory (even if it arises through conquest) when asserting governing supremacy. However, as we all know, that doctrine (at least in contemporaneous accounts of our legal history) was understood to have applied here on the grounds that the people already living here were considered as sufficiently defective politically so as not to have the capacity to be in sovereign occupation of the lands where they were living. Consequently, it would, in my understanding, be beyond the realm of possibility in social contract theory for colonial authorities to gain governing authority by social contract.

That is, *terra nullius* arises as a justification for the assertion of sovereignty because it is counter to reason to imagine entering into a social contract on governance with those do not have the standing to govern. To recognize that right, then, as the Law Lords of the Privy Council opined in *In re Southern Rhodesia* with regard to property, "would make each and every person by a fictional inheritance" a member of a polity that could not exist.[18] Thus, *terra nullius* becomes the limiting case for the application of social contract theory, for here there is no party with whom to gain agreement. Or to put it another way, *terra nullius* becomes the rationale for voiding the necessity for a social contract to ground sovereignty and jurisdiction whenever a party that already is living in the state of society encounters one that is presumptively living in the state of nature.

I have argued in the past that Canada relies on the doctrine of *terra nullius* based on the understanding of that doctrine as described above. However, Canada now recognizes that Indigenous peoples were living in organized political societies when settlers first arrived, as stated in its current policy: "The Government of Canada recognizes the inherent right of self-government as an existing Aboriginal right under section 35 of the *Constitution Act, 1982*."[19] Given this recognition, it would appear as though Canada would admit, following from social contract theory, that to be legitimate its claim to sovereignty and jurisdiction requires the consent of those who were already here at the time Crown sovereignty was first asserted. Yet, it does not.

The reason may well be that Canada no longer relies on the principle of *terra nullius*.[20] However, I believe it is at least reasonable to argue that it still does, notwithstanding this admission. This is my reasoning: While "inherent rights" are expressly acknowledged, Canada completely rejects the proposition that powers that presumably flow from such recognition have any effect in the sense that they can affect the unilaterally initiated law-making authority of Canada. Instead, it limits the expression of these so-called inherent political rights to a small set of matters regarding internal governance it has predetermined to be acceptable to it,[21] and then only with respect to those Indigenous communities with whom it has reached agreements or when agreements have been established by the courts through litigation. Furthermore, the Court's assumption that it has the authority to make such determinations based on criteria it has unilaterally derived reinforces that understanding.[22]

In other words, notwithstanding its rhetorical bow to the existence of sovereign nations prior to the arrival of colonists, Canada holds that Indigenous peoples did not have sufficient political standing to withstand its unilateral assertion of sovereignty and jurisdiction in order to legitimate the project that resulted in the establishment of Canada. And that, to my mind, places Canada's contemporary justification for the legitimacy of its sovereignty and jurisdiction conceptually (and perhaps even in legal reasoning) within sphere of the doctrine of *terra nullius*.

Following from this surmise, I would suggest that the doctrine of *terra nullius* has at least two conceptual nodes. The first is the classical one, in which local inhabitants are erroneously described as living in the pre-social contract condition known in social contract theory as the state of nature. The second flows from the idea that, while local inhabitants are recognized as living in a self-governing political society (the state of political society) when colonists arrive, this standing is erased at the moment colonists first settle and establish law in their territories, thereby converting it functionally to a *terra nullius*. Thus, as with the first node, sovereignty can be legitimately asserted even without the consent of those already present. In that sense, it is akin to conquest in that a new sovereign replaces an older one. However, it differs in that an actual conquest is not required nor is the formal transfer of sovereignty. Thus, as with *terra nullius*, settlement alone is sufficient.[23] It is a proposition well-described in then Chief Justice Dickson's assertion in *R. v. Sparrow* that

> (while) it is worth recalling that while British policy towards the native population was based on respect for their right to occupy their traditional lands, a proposition to which the Royal Proclamation of 1763 bears witness, there was from the outset never any doubt that sovereignty and legislative power, and indeed the underlying title, to such lands vested in the Crown.[24]

The consequences are far reaching. By deploying this version of the doctrine, Canada can simultaneously acknowledge that Indigenous peoples were sovereign when colonists first arrived, while asserting that, in fact, this rhetorical recognition places no constraints on Canada's power to assert governing authority unilaterally. It is, if you will, a slight of hand that enables the state to concur with Indigenous peoples that they had sovereignty and jurisdiction prior to settlement, but to act as though they did not.[25]

Consent and the Right of Indigenous Peoples as Colonized Peoples to Self-Determination

The doctrine of *terra nullius* is clearly racist and colonialist, and it ought to have no place in contemporary legitimations of sovereignty and jurisdiction. It lays out a point of view that inhibits rather than fosters the possibility to build a political relationship based on mutual consent. Given its centrality to Canada's contemporary political and legal ideology, I see an urgent need to discredit and ultimately overturn the Canadian government's reliance on this doctrine as well as the representation of Indigenous peoples that it reifies to justify the occupation of Canada without the consent of Indigenous peoples as a precondition for reshaping that relationship.

Elsewhere, I offered the hope that the language in *Calder v. Attorney-General of British Columbia* affirming that Indigenous peoples were already living in a political society might be sufficient to incentivize the Government of Canada to move in that direction.[26] However, that has clearly not been the case. Here, I would like to further insist (or at least propose) that Canada accept that its political relationship with Indigenous peoples flows from the understanding that, from an objective perspective, Indigenous peoples in Canada have the same right to self-determination as do other colonized peoples, as is spelled out in relevant resolutions of the United Nations and in Resolution 1514 (XV) in particular. This right thus includes, in principle, the right to form independent states, even when this means the break-up of the state, a proposition recognized as legitimate in the case of Quebec even without the support of Resolution 1514 (XV).

I justify this argument on the following grounds. First, while it is true that the Charter of the United Nations protects the territorial integrity of member states, the famous Declaration on the Granting of Independence to Colonial Countries and Peoples guarantees the right of colonized peoples to self-determination. It thus pointedly declares the following:

1. The subjection of peoples to alien subjugation, domination and exploitation constitutes a denial of fundamental human rights, is contrary to the Charter of the United Nations and is an impediment to the promotion of world peace and cooperation.
2. All peoples have the right to self-determination; by virtue of that right they freely determine their political status and freely pursue their economic, social and cultural development.

And then, in what is clearly a repudiation of the doctrine of *terra nullius* and other colonial formulations of similar ilk used to justify unilateral assertions of sovereignty and jurisdiction, Resolution 1514 (XV) immediately goes on to state:

3. Inadequacy of political, economic, social or educational preparedness should never serve as a pretext for delaying independence.

It is a depiction of the right that is reiterated in numerous subsequent UN declarations and resolutions.[27] Thus, it is the description that I take to be the conventional understanding of the application and implications of the term "self-determination" when it is applied to colonized populations, whether internal or external to the borders of the metropolitan state in which they are found.

The ratification of Resolution 1514 (XV) by the international community, including Canada, then, raises a challenge to the UN Charter, and to the doctrine advanced by David Hume that the legitimacy of state power only requires effective control over a territory. The legitimacy of state power therefore cannot be called into question by any other party on moral, ethical, or even legal grounds, regardless of the justification a state uses to advance its claim.[28] To the contrary, Resolution 1514 (XV) outlines a specific condition, namely colonialism, under which the legitimacy of the imposition of a political relationship by one party without the express consent of the other is understood to be sufficient grounds upon which to dissolve the relationship. The application of this resolution, then, acts as counterweight to the power of the colonial state, legally, morally and potentially materially, as when sanctions are imposed on the colonial authorities. Consequently, it is clear that the UN Declaration on the Granting of Independence to Colonial Countries and Peoples represents an explicit repudiation of any justification that Canada might have to legitimately assert sovereignty and jurisdiction with respect to Indigenous peoples and their lands anywhere within its territorial boundary without their consent.

Specifically, then, I am asking that we consider for the purpose of this discussion that Resolution 1514 (XV) applies to the situation of Indigenous peoples in Canada. At the same time, I realize that, at least for the moment, I am raising a hypothetical case, for Resolution 1514 (XV) would never have been ratified by Canada and other settler states had they not found a way to exempt themselves from its provisions.[29]

What I am pointing to explicitly is this language under Principle IV in Resolution 1541 (XV) that implements the resolution: "*Prima facie* there is an obligation to transmit information in respect of a territory which is geographically separate and is distinct ethnically and/or culturally from the country administering it."[30] Called the "blue water" or "saltwater" thesis, it provides a technical exemption in the sense that in such cases evidence of colonized populations is required before the terms of Resolution 1514 (XV) are applied. And there can be no doubt that were there to be such an investigation, it would determine that Indigenous peoples in Canada constituted a colonized population. Hence, Canada is exempt from this finding only because no one will undertake such an investigation.

Nonetheless, there is a compelling moral reason for Canada to accept that Resolution 1514 (XV) applies in full to the Indigenous population within its borders: that is, it is beyond hypocritical for Canada to continue relying on the same colonial ideology to justify sovereignty and jurisdiction for itself that it so roundly and explicitly condemned with regard to others when it ratified that resolution. The fact is that Canada stands in the very same colonial relation to its colonized peoples as did Great Britain, South Africa, and other colonizing powers, differing only from them with regard to the relative size and location of the population of Indigenous peoples to that of the colonizers. That is, were the principle that, in colonial situations, the colonizer cannot impose its will over the colonized applied equally to any population colonized by Canada wherever it was located, and/or that the principle of one person, one vote could create an Indigenous majority here, I have no doubt that a dramatic transformation of political relations would have already taken place. To be here to stay necessitates a firmer foundation – one that embraces rather than elides our originating status as a colonizing power.

With this in mind, I turn now to a discussion of what the process of building consent might look like under these circumstances.

Consent and Treaty-Making

The political relationship Canada seeks with Indigenous peoples is, of course, one where a relationship is to be established between already existing political societies. Abstractly, it is one where, under originating conditions, one political society, composed of new arrivals, seeks to establish itself as a polity on territories already inhabited by other political societies. Put this way, it becomes in principle a situation of great complexity – one that evokes the kind of vulnerability on the part of all parties that reflects the incompleteness of the Self when the origins of society are conceptualized in the abstract. However, in this circumstance, care and caution in the development of relations, rather than the immediacy that results from urgent need, would appear to be the hallmark of the process. Consent here requires the strict attention to difference and the possibilities for misunderstanding it creates that are central to its definition as a "grounded form of life." Given the salience of this perspective, forging an agreement will likely be difficult, but not necessarily impossible. And given the particularly vulnerable position that the newcomers face due to Resolution 1514 (XV), it would be largely incumbent on Canada to find ways to encourage such possibilities.

In grappling to find a term to describe this process, I have found myself ultimately relying on the concept of "treaty-making." My decision to use this metaphor derives somewhat from the idea of treaty-making as it is found in Western political thought, and particularly in Immanuel Kant's *Perpetual Peace* (1795). However, it derives much more significantly from a line of thinking about relations between nations and among humans and other beings found in an important line in Indigenous political thought. It is one that I have come to better understand largely through working with the Dene Nation on building a political relationship with Canada and through other engagements.[31] I use the term "treaty" to describe this process, as that is how it is often glossed by Dene and others when explaining the process in English. At the same time, as I have developed elsewhere, the conceptual frame analogous to "treaty" is found in the work of Martin Buber and Emmanuel Levinas.[32]

As I have come to understand it, treaty-making in this context offers a process that can enable Canada to develop a political relationship with the colonized peoples within its borders that is just and enduring. The goal is to build up a consensus in a step-by-step manner that relies on mutual consent, voluntarily given. It is often reported that the first step in this process is to make a treaty of "peace and friendship" in which Canada's initial intentions have been accepted by Indigenous peoples as a truthful basis upon which to negotiate agreements to forge a political relationship. It is, for example, how Dene often describe the terms of Treaties 8 and 11, a point of view confirmed both by the oral tradition and the language of the Commissioners' reports on these two treaties.[33]

When conditions are appropriate, the intent would be to follow this first agreement with others that may well describe the relationship in more detail, and perhaps explore other avenues of connections. This is how Dene often described the intent of the so-called "land claims" agreement they were negotiating with Canada largely in the 1980s. In this process, as they described it, each step was to be carefully taken, and then only after deliberation.[34] It is a process that takes time and requires much care and attention. And, it is a relationship that must be constructed most carefully given that the objective of Canada is to inhabit this space in a manner complementary with the manner in which Indigenous peoples have cared for it – a manner that ultimately will lead to the formation of a more intimate relationship.

A Matter of History

This discussion might be sufficient were we (the newcomers) in fact new arrivals and thus about to embark on building a political relationship with Indigenous peoples who are already here. But that moment is long past. We have already been here for centuries, and through that time we have established a sorry track record of colonization and dispossession that continues up to today. We cannot presume to ignore this history and pretend that we can begin negotiations as though we were truly newcomers. Rather, it seems clear to me that taking full responsibility for the harms we have caused and still cause as well as working to rectify them must be integral to building the relationship we now seek. In other words, to inhabit the space we seek, we need to take actions to disinhibit the space we have taken over without consent.[35]

Conclusions

In sum, it is my view that "voluntary consent" in the context of relations between Canada and the Indigenous nations within Canada cannot be imagined as a simple, one-time, final act, but rather as a slow process that moves the parties along a path that only becomes more clearly delineated as they progress down it. It moves ahead more by building consensus through quotidian acts than through formalized events and ceremonies, although the latter may play a crucial role by marking key moments along the way. The sense of this process is eloquently portrayed by Lévi-Strauss when he suggests that the creation of a relationship between two formerly autonomous parties (among the Nambikwara) is developed through continuous transitions forged by ongoing exchanges. In this understanding, the goal of a close mutual political relationship becomes "the conclusion to an uninterrupted process of reciprocal gifts, which effects the transition from hostility to alliance, from anxiety to confidence, and from fear to friendship."[36]

I believe that this pathway well describes the direction we will need to follow to achieve agreement based on voluntary consent. And, if we are to faithfully follow the principles of the social contract, it is one that can logically best begin with the acceptance by newer arrivals, such as myself, of the precariousness of our presence here without first establishing that presence through the promises that we keep in the course of making it, something we have not done up to now. That, then, represents the primal challenge to achieving a political relationship based on "voluntary consent, mutually given" that we face today.

Appendix

Origins of Society in Anthropological Theory and Consent

Anthropology as a discipline found its specific voice in the wake of the revolution inaugurated by Darwin and Herbert Spencer, as informed by Hegel and Marx. That is, it was founded in evolutionary thought, both social and biological, and is still grounded by it today. Thus, the chronological sequence of evolution through which society emerged – rather than logical deductions based on abstract principles, such as thought experiments – dominates the discourse within the discipline, to the point that in the study of "origins," anthropology is more focused on "when is society" than "what is society." Nonetheless, definitional issues are still addressed, for one cannot have a "when" without at least some idea of a "what." But still, by and large, the interrogation of the "what" has been quite pedestrian, relating largely to comparisons between human society and those of primates on the grounds that, following Darwin, as our closest ancestors, primates provide a solid foundation to speculate on the "actual" or "empirical" point of departure for human society. And following from Spencer and, I am afraid, Marx and his students (largely up to today), Indigenous peoples, and particular those with "hunter-gatherer" economies or a "foraging way of life," are used as the exemplification of "human society" in its "original" condition with which comparisons to primate societies are drawn In a phrase, for many anthropologists concerned with origins, Indigenous peoples are a useful object of study because they are "our contemporary ancestors."

For the most part, these comparisons have been framed within an unacknowledged paradigm from political theory: to wit, the social contract and particularly its Hobbesian iteration.[37] There is little scope for serious enquiry into consent in all of this, nor an opening for any conversation with Indigenous peoples. And, indeed, anthropological representations derived from this model are used to confirm the appropriateness of the jurisprudential representation of First Nations as having existed in "levels" of society.

There are a good number of anthropologists, particularly here in Canada and in Australia and New Zealand, who do not subscribe to the proposition that Indigenous peoples are our contemporary ancestors. For the most part, these scholars, I would judge, subscribe to the "consent as a grounded form of life" perspective, as outlined by Webber, and see as their subject of study means to exemplify, through cross-cultural communication, the signification of these various streams of social life. It is, if you will, the subaltern position that confronts the hegemon of evolutionism with a strong humanist retort. It is a position for which I have great empathy as it offers good food for thought. It is not, however, an approach that looks into origins but rather the consequences for human relations that arise from the acceptance that societies already exist. It is for this reason that I ascribe more to the idea of "consent and the relational definition of self" category, for here anthropologists are concerned both with relatedness and with a theory to explain the relationship between this impulse and the origins of society. This is, if you will, the place where enquiry about relationships and connectedness move from a place of curiosity to one of necessity.

NOTES

* I wish to thank John Borrows and James Tully for their most helpful comments on a draft of this piece. This chapter originated in a talk I gave at the workshop entitled "Consent as the Foundation for Political Community" held at the University of Victoria in October 2004.
1 My argument assumes that a similar argument would be relevant to any settler state that relies on a liberal democratic form of government.
2 This chapter focuses on principles rather than models. I believe that a possible model could be derived from the position taken by the Dene Nation (or the Indian Brotherhood of the Northwest Territories, as it was known then) and the Métis Association of the Northwest Territories in a document called "Public Government for the People of the North" (self-pub., Yellowknife, 1981) combined with a form of consociational democracy, as that term is defined in anthropology (relations between ethnonational communities) rather than political science (elite accommodation). See Michael Asch, *Home and Native Land: Aboriginal Rights and the Canadian Constitution* (Toronto: Methuen Publications, 1984).
3 It is assumed that, in principle, the right of newcomers to remain in the territory known as Canada (and/or Quebec) depends on a successful resolution of a relationship that is based on voluntary consent.

4 I am grateful to Avigail Eisenberg for the discussion that helped clarify this distinction.
5 UN General Assembly, United Nations Declaration on the Rights of Indigenous Peoples (UNDRIP), 2 October 2007, A/RES/61/295.
6 This form of consent can, as is often the case with state and corporate development initiatives as well as governance agreements, lead to what I would call "imposed" splits in Indigenous communities, as they are forced to choose either to consent in order to obtain material and other benefits consequent to the imposition of these initiatives on them, or to refuse to give consent on grounds of principle or other such considerations.
7 UN General Assembly, Declaration on the Granting of Independence to Colonial Countries and Peoples, 14 December 1960, A/RES/1514(XV).
8 Given the foundational standing of Indigenous sovereignty, I believe proactive consent would also include initiatives on governance brought forward by Indigenous parties, and especially in the case of proposals concerning governance relations.
9 W.M. Reisman, *The Quest for World Order and Human Dignity in the Twenty-First Century: Constitutive Process and Individual Commitment* (Leiden: Brill, 2013), 247.
10 It is crucial to note that, as Adom Getachew describes, the ultimate goal of decolonization for many colonial liberation leaders was less the formation of new states than it was the development of a political and economic alliance between such newly emerged African and Caribbean states (as well as African Americans) to create "a new international economic order" that would advance the possibility of creating a post-imperial world based on economic and political equality. Nonetheless, as Getachew points out, many decolonizing thinkers and leaders, at least at the beginning, considered the gaining of political independence to be a necessary first step, if not an end in itself. See Adom Getachew, *Worldmaking after Empire: The Rise and Fall of Self-Determination* (Princeton, NJ: Princeton University Press, 2019), 15, which of course remains the focus in hegemonic strains of academic scholarship. A similar "world changing perspective" as the goal of decolonization is found as well in much Indigenous scholarship and leadership. See Glen Sean Coulthard, introduction to *The Fourth World: An Indian Reality*, ed. George Manuel and Michael Posluns (Minnesota: University of Minnesota Press, 2019), ix–xxxvi. However, the method to achieve it differs and does not necessarily include the creation of independent states.
11 Jeremy Webber, "The Meanings of Consent," in *Between Consenting Peoples: Political Community and the Meaning of Dissent*, ed. Jeremy Webber and Colin MacLeod (Vancouver: UBC Press, 2011), 3–41.
12 Ibid., 31.
13 For an abbreviated discussion of the origins of society argument and its typical counter-argument in anthropology, see the appendix to this chapter.

14 Michael Asch, *On Being Here to Stay: Treaties and Aboriginal Rights in Canada* (Toronto: University of Toronto Press, 2014).
15 Claude Lévi-Strauss, *The Elementary Structures of Kinship*, trans. James Harle Bell, John Richard von Sturmer, and Rodney Needham (Boston: Beacon Press, 1969).
16 For those initiated into anthropological jargon, this concept of society is represented most clearly in moiety structures, where the system of cross-cousin marriage creates a perpetual alliance between the sides.
17 Webber, "Meanings of Consent," 32–3. In contrast to the "consent and the relational definition of self" form, the "consent as a grounded form of life" perspective gives the impression that independent and self-contained collective Selves already exist prior to any need to enter into a relationship with Others. That is, it seems to posit that a society already exists before voluntary consent needs to be given. Thus, voluntary consent appears to play a secondary role, a position with which I have some difficulty. At the same time, the perspective on the meaning of "voluntary consent" offered by the "grounded form of life" perspective provides a set of considerations that are essential in the affairs of the real world, as when a society, having already been formed on the basis of voluntary consent between Self and Other, seeks to enter into a consensual relationship with another society. In this case, in my view, it provides an essential consideration on voluntary consent that is paramount in seeking a world in which political relations are justly based, but one, speaking from an abstract perspective, that seems to become significant as a consequence of the establishment of society. It is in this sense that I find that the concept of voluntary consent as envisioned in a relational definition of Self has priority.
18 *In re Southern Rhodesia* [1919] AC 211, at 234.
19 "The Government of Canada's Approach to Implementation of the Inherent Right and the Negotiation of Aboriginal Self-Government," Government of Canada, accessed 1 May 2023, https://www.rcaanc-cirnac.gc.ca/eng/1100100031843/1539869205136#inhrsg, part 1, para 1. In this context, "inherent" means existing prior to the arrival of Europeans.
20 As John Borrows brought to my attention, one possibility is that Canada now relies on a different legal theory – perhaps the doctrine of parliamentary sovereignty that stands outside of social contract theory. It is beyond my expertise to opine on this matter, but I am content that it does fit the facts. However, it begs the question I am addressing here: the way the legitimacy of Canadian sovereignty is reconciled with the prior existence of political societies.
21 Policy limits these to powers "in relation to matters that are internal to their communities, integral to their unique cultures, identities, traditions, languages and institutions, and with respect to their special relationship to

their land and their resources." "Government of Canada's Approach," part 1, para 1.
22 It is also unreasonable to suggest that Canada relies on voluntary consent on the part of the Indigenous parties when it comes to the so-called treaties of cession. There is little to no evidence that such consent was ever given beyond texts that have frequently proven to be unreliable. See Michael Asch, "On the Land Cession Provisions in Treaty 11," *Ethnohistory* 60, no. 3 (Summer 2013): 451–67; and *On Being Here to Stay*. Indeed, my position holds even when taken from the point of view that what transpired is erroneously represented as being an accurate account of those negotiations, for Canada presumes its unilateral assertions of sovereignty and jurisdiction are valid even in places where no such "cession" treaties were concluded. For a detailed discussion on this matter, see Kent McNeil, *Flawed Precedent: The* St. Catherine's *Case and Aboriginal Title* (Vancouver: UBC Press, 2019); and Joshua Ben David Nichols, *A Reconciliation without Recollection? An Investigation into the Foundations of Aboriginal Law in Canada* (Toronto: University of Toronto Press, 2019).
23 By personal communication, John Borrows offered a complementary possibility: that Canada is relying on the doctrine of parliamentary sovereignty.
24 *R. v. Sparrow*, [1990] 1 SCR 1075, at 30. In tracing this idea in jurisprudence, I find it advanced as one of the legal rationales for the denial of Aboriginal rights offered by Justice Davey in his judgment in *Calder v. Attorney-General of British Columbia*, [1970] 74 WWR 481 (BCCA). And, although Davies's reasons were rejected by Justice Hall at the Supreme Court of Canada, this understanding reveals itself over and over again in later Supreme Court judgments.
25 This is a play on the full box v. the empty box argument. See Michael Asch and Patrick Macklem "Aboriginal Rights and Canadian Sovereignty: An Essay on *R. v. Sparrow*," *Alberta Law Review* 29, no. 2 (1991): 498–517.
26 See Michael Asch, "Calder and the Representation of Indigenous Society in Canadian Jurisprudence," in *Let Right Be Done: Aboriginal Title, the* Calder *Case, and the Future of Indigenous Rights*, ed. Hamar Foster, Heather Raven, and Jeremy Webber (Vancouver: UBC Press, 2007) 101–10.
27 For example, the Declaration on Principles of International Law concerning Friendly Relations and Cooperation among States in accordance with the Charter of the United Nations, adopted by the General Assembly in 1970, states the following: "By virtue of the principle of equal rights and self-determination of peoples enshrined in the Charter of the United Nations, all peoples have the right freely to determine, without external interference, their political status and to pursue their economic, social and cultural development, and every State has the duty

to respect this right in accordance with the provisions of the Charter." Quoted in Edward Lawson, *Encyclopedia of Human Rights* (New York: Taylor and Francis, 1989), 1331. It also states that one of the obligations of every member state is to "bring a speedy end to colonialism, having due regard to the freely expressed will of the peoples concerned." Ibid.
28 Webber, "Meanings of Consent," 3.
29 As the relevant provisions of the UNDRIP attest, these states continue to fight successfully against extending to colonized peoples the same right of self-determination Canada so willingly recognized to colonized peoples elsewhere. Indeed, I have no doubt that Canada and other settler states will remain successful in their efforts, as its application to their situations could well lead to drastic consequences for many other member states.
30 See S. James Anaya, *Indigenous Peoples in International Law*, 2nd ed. (Oxford: Oxford University Press, 2004).
31 See Asch, *On Being Here to Stay*.
32 See Michael Asch, "Levi-Strauss and the Political: The Elementary Structures of Kinship and the Resolution of Relations between Indigenous People and Settler States," *The Journal of the Royal Anthropological Institute* 11, no. 3 (September 2005): 425–44, https://www.jstor.org/stable/3804312; "Indigenous Self-Determination and Applied Anthropology in Canada: Finding a Place to Stand," *Anthropologica* 43, no. 2 (2001): 201–7, https://doi.org/10.2307/25606035.
33 Asch, "On the Land Cession Provisions."
34 Asch, *Home and Native Land*.
35 I thank James Tully for this turn of phrase.
36 Lévi-Strauss, *Elementary Structures of Kinship*, 67.
37 Among those anthropologists concerned with questions of origins, most have taken up a modified Hobbesian view on this point, suggesting that the earliest forms of society (as exemplified by contemporaneous hunter-gatherer societies) were organized merely to avoid the war of all against all, or because the poverty of their economies demanded a degree of collectivization in the chase. A few have modelled their position from Jean-Jacques Rousseau. They suggest that Indigenous peoples do not live in society but are nonetheless cooperative. Indigenous peoples have sociability, but not society.

3 Struggles against Domestication: The United Nations Declaration on the Rights of Indigenous Peoples and Constitutional Pluralism

GORDON CHRISTIE

Introduction

In the years since the *Sparrow* decision came down from the Supreme Court of Canada,[1] different visions of the promise of that judgment have been developed. Early on, some saw in the Court's adoption of an "inherent rights" approach to Aboriginal rights an opening to the recognition and affirmation of substantive rights to Aboriginal self-government.[2] Others, more recently, see in this judgment movement towards acceptance of treaty federalism and – further developing this picture – constitutional pluralism.[3] Within Canadian law and policy, neither of these developments have come to pass; there is no indication yet that section 35 of the *Constitution Act, 1982* might be said by the Supreme Court to contain a substantive right to Aboriginal self-government, and there is no indication that section 35 itself signals that Canadian law accepts constitutional pluralism. Indeed, one might argue that the primary objective of section 35 jurisprudence has been to domesticate Aboriginal peoples' aspirations for control over who they are and how they act in the world, and to ensure further entrenchment of a monolithic constitutional order centred on state power.

Now, thirty years after *Sparrow*, we find hopes renewed that substantive rights to Aboriginal governance may emerge in Canadian law, though attention has shifted from the contents of section 35 to the promise of the United Nations Declaration on the Rights of Indigenous Peoples (UNDRIP).[4] I focus here on the promise of constitutional pluralism. To what extent might one think pulling the UNDRIP into Canadian law could open the door to the possibility of constitutional pluralism? Or, will the UNDRIP be domesticated, the constitutional order of the state reasserting what it takes to be its fundamental supremacy over all others, attempting to subsume into itself what it takes to be the remnants of Indigenous orders?

What Is Constitutional Pluralism?

We begin with a few words about the sort of constitutional pluralism we might imagine struggling to emerge. The fact is, within the geographic space marked by Canada's contemporary borders we already find ourselves living within a world marked by constitutional pluralism, if by that we acknowledge that within these borders lie multiple constitutional orders – that of the nation state alongside a multitude of Indigenous constitutional orders. Another fact, however, intrudes: the constitutional order of the state has ignored and continues to ignore the many other constitutional orders with which it has always cohabited. The question in this chapter, then, is this: How can we imagine movement to a Canada within which existing constitutional orders are driven to negotiate – and eventually reach a cooperative arrangement – such that a measure of harmony and stability are obtained?

In a recent work, Mark Tushnet defines a constitutional order as "a reasonably stable set of institutions through which a nation's fundamental decisions are made over a sustained period of time, and those principles that guide those decisions."[5] While this definition sits most easily over the modern structures of the nation state, it is possible to pull it up a degree in abstraction, producing a more widely applicable notion: a constitutional order, one might say, relates to a *people*, encompassing how it organizes itself, the order functioning through those social mechanisms by which this collectivity determines how to be and act over time, all guided by those principles and values that animate this collective. A constitutional order, then, is a fundamental manifestation of self-determination, as it represents how a collective would think of itself over time and, with this self-conception, how they then act through time and space.

Both the nation-state (narrower) form and the people-based (broader) form are distinguished from simple notions of a group or association determining its terms of union and membership (appropriate, say, to any organization) by their connections to territory. Under the Westphalian model, the nation state is essentially defined by its geographic borders (with these borders often containing or cutting across a number of distinct peoples), while under the people-focused model, we can again think of geographic borders, but these function not to define the collective but only to delimit the extent of territory connected to the people under consideration. It is in tying Indigenous peoples – as numerous collectives, each formed around common language, culture, and history – to the notion of self-constituting in relation to territory that we layer the political over the socio-cultural.

Constitutional pluralism, then, is what exists when we find in one geographic space more than one "people" (defined either nationalistically or more naturally in terms of those defined by language, culture, and history), where each collective builds, inhabits, and lives through its own constitutional order. Note, again, that this describes the nature of the socio-political complexity of human societies living in relation to the land-water mass of what is today Canada, from when settler peoples and their institutions first established colonies in Eastern Canada alongside pre-existing Indigenous polities, up to the present day in much of this country. Since at least the end of the historic treaty-making era, however, the constitutional order of the state has consistently refused to acknowledge that other constitutional orders persist.

The discourse of constitutional pluralism has been emerging in the field of international law and political philosophy over the last few decades. Much of this has been spurred on by the conceptual challenges posed by the existence of the European Union – though considerations of what some argue to be the "post-Westphalian" nature of international law have also had considerable impact.[6] In his examination of challenges faced by constitutional discourse as a result of rapid changes in how the global realm of nation states has come to be reconfigured, Neil Walker arrives at an explanatory, normative, and epistemic framework defined as constitutional pluralism. His explication of the epistemic dimension illuminates how this form of constitutional discourse would make sense of Crown–Indigenous relations in a multinational Canada:

> On this view, the very representation of distinct constitutional sites ... as distinct constitutional sites implies an incommensurability of the knowledge and authority (or sovereignty) claims emanating from these sites. That is to say, it is only possible to identify the different sites as different units if we already acknowledge that the underlying symbolic work involved in representing each of these sites as units – and so also as unities – requires a different way of knowing and ordering, a different epistemic starting point and perspective with regard to each unit(y); and that so long as these different unit(ies) continue to be plausibly represented as such, there is no neutral perspective from which their distinct representational claims can be reconciled.[7]

Translated down from the lofty heights of political theory, the notion is that within places marked by constitutional pluralism there are multiple sources of claims of authority and political understanding, where none of the sites can be said to capture a truth of the matter in some overarching sense. If, for example, one takes as seriously as one must the stance of the Haida Nation, captured in the Kunst'aa Guu – Kunst'aayah Reconciliation Protocol,[8] we see a self-contained collective – a "unity" in Walker's parlance – making a grounded claim to being a body with its own constitutional order. We then take note of another unity – the Canadian state – with its own separate claims to authority, and we end up in the world of constitutional pluralism, noting the two unities occupy one and the same geographic space, with neither able to proclaim some higher authority by which it must rule over or subsume the other into either its constitutional order or its constitutional theory.

It is not necessary from my perspective to argue that we *should* be advancing towards a state in which the multitude of constitutional orders can engage in respectful negotiations about how to peacefully coexist. Such arguments are only necessary when we engage with the point of view of those deeply vested in the commitments of the constitutional order of the nation state, as one of its central commitments is to acknowledge only its own existence and authority.[9] From the perspective of Indigenous collectives, the need to move towards constitutional pluralism does not require argumentative support, the central debate being, rather, about how to get the state to move to recognition of existing Indigenous constitutional orders.[10] We find ourselves in complex terrain when it comes to the status and possible function of various forms of arguments, and it is to that terrain that I wish to move this discussion.

The Efficacy of Arguments

While I do not attempt to make arguments directly about the need to move towards fully acknowledged constitutional pluralism, this chapter is nevertheless *about* arguments. I am interested in the *nature* and *efficacy* of arguments, which is to say I explore the different sorts of arguments people can make in the socio-political worlds we inhabit and the sorts of work these arguments can carry out. Eventually I work my way around to examining both (a) the content of arguments for and against the notion that the introduction of the UNDRIP could lead all parties in Canada to seriously attend to the fact of constitutional pluralism, and (b) the *place* and *function* of these arguments in the complex and dynamic landscape of contemporary Canada, one marked by separate and independent forms of legal and political authority. Can we reasonably expect arguments *for* this hoped-for serious consideration will lead to changes in the attitudes and ways of acting of the settler state? What role will arguments *against* this movement play in this milieu? My focus, however, is ultimately on a larger set of questions that intrude: Are there constraints on such arguments, constraints that limit us to possible argumentative moves, constraints that act to predetermine what we say about the very possibility of constitutional pluralism? Where do these constraints come from? Who controls what they might be, and why is this control exerted?

To set the stage for this examination, several preliminary explorations are carried out – first, into the nature of arguments about the social worlds we inhabit, and then second, into what happened to arguments constructed after *Sparrow* came down. Once we have some sense about what to look for in arguments in this context we can look into why, in the thirty years since *Sparrow*, there has been in Canadian law and policy a retrenchment of a monolithic form of constitutionalism, one that at best aims to *domesticate* Indigenous constitutional orders. This monolith is adamant that it will abide by no more than the opening up of the possibility that Indigenous polities might find some recognized space *within* the already tightly ordered federal structure – space that the Canadian order predefines. What role did those arguing post-*Sparrow* for constitutional pluralism or a substantive right to governance *think* their arguments could play? What roles *did* these arguments end up playing? What was the nature of the resistance to these visions of a broadened legal and political landscape? What would have had to have been the case for *Sparrow* to have actually led to movement towards constitutional pluralism?

This exploration in hand, we can then look into the currently unfolding situation concerning the UNDRIP. Are the background structuring conditions different? Are the forces resisting this movement the same? Are these forces more or less entrenched than they used to be? What should those proposing that the UNDRIP holds promise be doing besides presenting arguments (which, one seems forced to acknowledge, *in themselves* have little or no weight in making things happen)?

Arguments about Parallel Constitutional Orders

There are two levels at which arguments can arise and function when thinking about social worlds. When I stated earlier that Canada encompasses within its borders constitutional pluralism, I was making a claim about the nature of the world in which we live. Building on that, we need then think about what world we might wish to create, moving out of the world we currently inhabit. While it may be natural to think of heated arguments about the admittedly normative issue of what we *should* do, about what world we should be trying to create, arguments can, and do, also arise about the first sort of claim. There are those who disagree with the notion that Indigenous peoples continue to live within worlds structured according to their own, independent constitutional orders – indeed, to the extent Canadian authorities and courts think of such matters, they consistently dismiss or ignore the possibility that Indigenous constitutional orders persist.[11] For these parties, arguments about the second sort of matter – where to go from here – *begin* from a very different place, grounded as they are in the notion that the state of affairs at present is that of one constitutional order (which some might then go on to argue needs to better accommodate *within it* Indigenous powers of self-determination or self-government).

One might think there is a natural divide between the first sort of argument and the second, as it might seem possible (at least in principle) that a neutral and objective determination emerge as to what the world is like, while few would think such a thing is possible when thought turns to visions of the future. But while one might suppose arguments about the nature of the world can be resolved (at least in principle), actually it is not at all clear how to do so.

Consider one side of this argumentative situation – the position that there is at present just one constitutional order within the borders of Canada – and imagine how this could be reasonably held and defended. The position would have to be that constitutional orders of Indigenous peoples had to have been removed, displaced, or subsumed over time.[12] How could this have happened? Here we find ourselves in the world of arguments about how to *interpret* events in the world, as upholders of the model of monolithic order argue that the tide of history has washed over Indigenous peoples, that through the assertion of Crown sovereignty and subsequent acts pursuant to this governmental power (collectively, the gradual imposition on Indigenous nations of ever-increasing measures of state control) we no longer live in a world where an Indigenous collective lives by and through its own independent and parallel constitutional order.

But can the nation state of Canada have simply made this so over time? Note that events in history upon which this narrative rests all revolve around the notion that one people can claim authority over the lives of other collectives, and then over time exercise power over the lives of these others such that only the one authority structure remains, purportedly then the sole legitimate socio-political system. These very same events, however, can appear very differently to Indigenous peoples, who can and do read them as revolving around unjustifiable attempts to usurp authority, followed by actions over generations that were constantly and consistently resisted, such that at no time did what is essentially a foreign force gain *legitimate* authority over their lives and futures. Which account captures the true state of the world?

We might think that turning to theories of justifiable authority could assist, but here we find ourselves in a similar bind, though one that helps illuminate the nature of the argumentative problem. One might think that theories of democratic liberalism could uphold the activities of the nation state – or at least transform what would have been injustices in the past into acceptable contemporary situations.[13] But this requires that we acquiesce in accepting the normative world of the contemporary nation state as the measure by which we judge historical and contemporary activities. We could just as well, however, turn to theories of justifiable authority emanating from the worlds of Indigenous peoples, using them to judge historical and contemporary activities. The key underlying point of illumination is that this shows just how normative discourse informs how one interprets historical events in the world, which then determines how one reads the current state of the world.

An inevitable carry-over is to the world of arguments about the second sort of matter: how we think about a world to come and how to get there. If we acquiesce in the normative world built up and inhabited by the nation state and its courts, we predetermine the sorts of arguments we can make about this imagined future. This is the core matter explored herein – attempts at setting parameters of discourse by presuming that at this point in time the state of the world is x. How do such attempts look in practice, how do we spot such an attempt being made about discourse around the UNDRIP, and what might we do if we think such an attempt is being made or about to be made?

We begin by exploring what happened in the thirty years since *Sparrow* came down. We want to know how likely it is that we find section 35 domesticated as a result of this sort of move being made by those who claim control over discourse about the place of Indigenous peoples in contemporary Canada (in this case, the Supreme Court). Lessons from this analysis in hand, we can then more fruitfully consider what may well be attempted in relation to the UNDRIP. Seeing how a similar move may be (almost certainly will be) attempted – that is, the mechanics of it – can better prepare those who hold out hope that someday the high court might acknowledge constitutional pluralism as the state of the legal and political landscape in modern Canada. It may well be that simply building arguments about the need to work towards negotiated coexistence of multiple constitutional orders is insufficient if the parameters of discourse have already been set such that these arguments never really have any purchase.

What Happened to the Promise of *Sparrow*?

We begin with a basic lesson to be taken from the failed promise of *Sparrow* (and countless other settler/Crown–Indigenous situations): arguments for greater acknowledgment of existing Indigenous legal and political authority invariably carry little weight *in themselves*. Such arguments can clearly play a supporting (or justificatory) role in the context of an unfolding situation, but we cannot realistically suppose that the "right" arguments by themselves lead to change.

There are two things behind this fact. First, on a very general level we can note that while those who build arguments often seem to believe that arguments are (at least potentially) actual forces in the world, they are in fact just ordered sets of words put into speech or "on paper." Second, arguments specifically about Indigenous legal and political authority do not enter the world of discourse to do battle with other sets of arguments on a field of reason. If this were the case, we might hope that a good, persuasive argument would be able to overpower – simply in virtue of its content – weaker, faulty arguments. Tying these two points together, we should, on a simple, practical level, be able to agree that what effects change in social worlds is the *adoption* of ways of thinking by those in positions from which change can effected. On a practical level, then, we need to consider what other conditions must be obtained in order for a Canadian law or policymaker to *accede* to an argument about the continuation of Indigenous legal and political authority, to begin movement towards something like the world envisioned within the argument. What conditions lead to receptivity and action?

Keeping to the theme of how arguments actually function in social worlds, when we turn our gaze to arguments opposed to the acknowledgment of Indigenous legal and political authority, we can wonder at ways these might be meant to work and how they do actually function. Some arguments, for example, are clearly not meant to rationally persuade actors or parties but to appeal to emotional responses. For example, some arguments opposed to constitutional pluralism (or strong legal pluralism) are designed to generate fear of threats to the established ways of life of those deeply vested in the liberal capitalist world (fears tied, as well, to racism-based hatred or dislike).[14] Other arguments might be meant to be "neutral" or reason-based but actually function principally to support structures that themselves are decidedly not neutral, as when arguments based in specific liberal theories of justice function to continue to oppress or dispossess Indigenous peoples.[15]

With these thoughts in mind, let us begin to look into the arguments of some of those who saw promise in *Sparrow*. Michael Asch and Patrick Macklem read into the Supreme Court's apparent embrace of an "inherent rights" approach to section 35 in *Sparrow* the promise of the eventual emergence of a substantive Aboriginal right to governance.[16] Seeing the Court act to protect an Aboriginal (Musqueam) practice of fishing as an aspect of identity and social organization (the "inherent" aspect of the right, as identity and social organization inhere in the Aboriginal community), Asch and Macklem could see lines then extending to the protection of governance, as governance would also be essential to the continuation of identity and social organization.

Asch and Macklem also noted, however, countervailing matters that appeared in the judgment, as the Court centred its reasons on the "unquestioned" sovereignty of the Crown. Thinking about what the word "existing" might mean in section 35 of the *Constitution Act, 1982*, the Court interpreted this as requiring of a rights-claimant that they *establish* that the right claimed exists today. This, then, makes Aboriginal rights contingent on state processes (either litigation or negotiation), something that fits more naturally with a "contingent rights" approach.[17]

Time – and future case law – have shown that Asch and Macklem were correct in relatively minor matters, but that their analysis suffered from a misreading of what Aboriginal rights were meant to protect, and how this interacted with arguments around the "inherent" nature of Aboriginal rights. Key is the fact that the Supreme Court never took seriously the notion that section 35 was meant to protect "social organization." Nor, for that matter, did the Court advance a reasonable understanding of how constitutionally protecting rights could protect "identity" when this is understood in any substantive manner. In *R. v. Van der Peet*, the Court spoke of grounding Aboriginal rights in the protection of "aboriginality," but this was spelled out in terms of "practices, customs or traditions," discrete activities in which an Aboriginal community might engage. Whatever one's theory of identity might be, protecting discrete practices will have at best a very tenuous connection to the protection of identity.[18]

There are clear signs that since the time of *Calder v. Attorney-General of British Columbia* the Supreme Court has been aware of the need to acknowledge that Indigenous peoples lived in *societies* before the arrival of settlers and the Crown,[19] and in providing a purposive analysis of section 35 in *Van der Peet*, Chief Justice Lamer held that "what s. 35(1) does is provide the constitutional framework through which the fact that aboriginals lived on the land in *distinctive societies* [emphasis added], with their own practices, traditions and cultures, is acknowledged and reconciled with the sovereignty of the Crown."[20] The Court has, however, consistently pulled back from according the fact that Indigenous peoples have always constituted *politically structured societies* the constitutional significance one might think it should have. The move of the Court has been, since it began constructing section 35 jurisprudence in *Sparrow*, to equate "societies" with "cultures," and then "cultures" with discrete "practices, customs and traditions," thereby stripping out of the discourse any possibility of finding "inherent rights" that might ground substantive rights to governance or rich forms of constitutional pluralism. Asch and Macklem read into the Court's tangential discussion in *Sparrow* of Aboriginal identity and of the fact of Aboriginal existence in societies much more than was ever there, and so presented arguments that were never going to be received by the Supreme Court.

What of constitutional pluralism in Supreme Court jurisprudence? Kiera Ladner and Michael McCrossan suggest the following:

> As James (Sa'ke'j) Youngblood Henderson, Margorie Benson and Isobel Findlay argue, "the spirit and intent of section 35(1), then, should be interpreted as 'recognizing and affirming' Aboriginal legal orders, laws and jurisdictions unfolded through Aboriginal and treaty rights." In essence, Aboriginal and treaty rights are the manifestation of Indigenous constitutional orders and the means by which these orders are recognized and affirmed in the Canadian constitution.[21]

They go on to note that early jurisprudence – including *Sparrow* – supported this argument (though later jurisprudence narrowed matters down significantly). The key argument (earlier developed by Henderson, Benson, and Findlay) is that in *Sparrow*, Indigenous constitutional orders were held to exist "within the framework of constitutional supremacy."[22] That is, in recognizing and affirming Aboriginal and treaty rights in the Constitution, which proclaims in section 52(1) that it is the "supreme law" of Canada, Indigenous rights were removed from their place within imperial law and placed back where they should always have been, "vested in the Aboriginal peoples of Canada."[23]

Much hangs on the notion that with the inclusion of section 35 in a constitution that altered the fundamental nature of Canada – from a country operating through a form of parliamentary supremacy to one now functioning as a constitutional democracy – certain implications flow "logically" as a new paradigm unfolds. When Ladner makes these sorts of arguments about movement towards constitutional pluralism, she tends to alternate between normatively charged and non-normative visions. I agree with the normative claims – that courts *should* interpret section 35 as she and Henderson, Benson, and Findlay do – but I want to focus on the non-normative branch, the one that sees section 35 *already* containing the key seeds of implementation of constitutional pluralism.

In "Take 35: Reconciling Constitutional Orders," Ladner first quotes from Henderson and then unpacks the content of his argument:

> "The ultimate purpose of [the constitutional affirmation of treaty and Aboriginal rights] was to create constitutional conditions – a legal and epistemic pluralism protected by the constitutional order from pragmatic, majoritarian politics – within which Aboriginal peoples and Canadians could rediscover good relations and live together on the shared land more compatibly."
>
> In creating this "legal and epistemic pluralism," s. 35(1) constitutionalized Indigenous political orders and made them part of the Canadian constitution. In so doing it reconciled what Henderson terms provincial federalism with treaty federalism or treaty constitutionalism. To take this one step further (as Henderson and Little Bear have urged), the rights and responsibilities vested in these Indigenous constitutional orders were not only recognized and affirmed within section 35(1) but also, through the process of constitutional renewal in 1982, reconciled with those rights and responsibilities (jurisdictions) that are vested within sections 91, 92 and 93 of the Canadian constitutional order. As a result of this constitutional pluralism, and because both sets of jurisdictions exist within the (implicitly recognized or explicitly established) Canadian constitutional order, there is no need to reconcile these rights with the sovereignty of the Crown.[24]

As with Asch and Macklem's take on section 35, much hinges on how the nature of Aboriginal rights was set out in judge-made law. In the first few sections of "Take 35," Ladner sets out the sad state of this jurisprudence, detailing how in *Sparrow* and cases following in the 1990s, the Supreme Court narrowed down the promise of section 35 to the point where (as we earlier noted) Aboriginal rights were confined to customs, practices, and traditions, and the power of the state to infringe upon these rights was elevated to the point where it was unclear that constitutional protection amounted to any protection over and beyond what might otherwise have been expected of "interests" held by an ethnic group in multicultural Canada. But turning to language introduced in those earlier cases and then seemingly strengthened in key cases in the 2000s – the language of "reconciliation" and "the honour of the Crown" – Ladner then builds an argument that suggests the jurisprudence might be turning a corner, now heading towards the establishment of conditions that would facilitate the implementation of constitutional pluralism.[25]

The core argument, however, is that section 35 *already* contains constitutional pluralism within it. The picture, then, is of the high court beginning in recent years to acknowledge the true nature of section 35, moving away from its earlier illicit interpretations. But this argument rests on the notion that alongside mistaken interpretations there is a truth about the matter, and thus an objectively correct understanding of the content of section 35 – an understanding we should expect the Court to move towards and a belief that the Supreme Court will eventually have to accede to this correct view and begin to develop new jurisprudence around the core concept of constitutional pluralism.

We are now, however, nearly four decades into a domestic scene marked by constitutional supremacy. There have been no signs that the Supreme Court thinks that section 35 *requires* an understanding that constitutional pluralism has been embedded in Canada's constitution. On the contrary, the jurisprudence initiated in *Sparrow* – with its grounding in the unquestioned sovereignty of the Crown – continues to grow and deepen. To unpack why this might be so, we need to return to the task of examining how arguments are meant to function in the workings of the state and its courts, and how they do in fact function.

How Arguments about *Sparrow*'s Promise Function

We need to turn our minds to arguments that have most likely swirled in the heads of the judges of the Supreme Court since 1990 as they grappled with matters under section 35. We begin with the point made earlier – it seems clear that the state and its courts have consistently held that, and so acted as though, there is just the one constitutional order – that of the state – and that whatever constitutional orders Indigenous peoples may have created and lived by, they were all either removed or subsumed during the colonial era. Then, we need to appreciate that when we turn to arguments that likely form, however inchoately, in the minds of the justices of the high court, much of the sense and force of these arguments derive from their embeddedness in a specific normative universe of discourse. That is, Supreme Court judges come to the tasks of interpreting the nature of section 35 and placing the structures they thereby build into the world with predetermined "theories" of what the world *should* look like, what is *best* for Canadian society, and how Canadian law *should* understand and treat parties before it. In the late twentieth and early twenty-first centuries, in the context of Canada as a self-conceptualized liberal democracy, the core of this normative grounding comes from liberal democratic doctrine. As much as the Court has been careful to characterize Aboriginal rights doctrine as *sui generis*, its core is recognizable as extensions of liberal thought towards the question of how group rights could be recognized and protected in a multicultural liberal democratic society.[26]

The point is that this sets in relatively concrete terms both how the Supreme Court would have understood the *problem* before it (as it set forth to flesh out what the single sentence of section 35[1] would mean), and how it would have been able to conceive of *solutions* to this problem. Arguments about Aboriginal rights to governance and constitutional pluralism do not fit well within a world built around liberal discourse. Arguments by Asch and Macklem about substantive Aboriginal rights to governance and by Ladner (and Henderson et al.) about constitutional pluralism would, then, either (a) have been deflected away by the Court (its usual technique being to simply ignore them), or (b) have to have been (somehow) translated into the language of liberal doctrine.

Leaving aside how difficult it is to fit Indigenous (collective) rights to govern and to generate and live through their own visions of collective order into a liberal multicultural state,[27] the fact is that the Supreme Court also clearly accepts certain normatively grounded structuring elements of the world we live in that preclude the possibility of serious consideration of constitutional pluralism; they place the roots and sources of racism and oppression in the past (in colonial law and policy they see as no longer operative, such that no normative calling is *now* made upon the state and its courts), and they see the legal and political system they *now* inhabit and work in (that built around liberal doctrine) as the *best* setting within which the collective interests of Aboriginal peoples can be accommodated. We find here presumptions made about the world-as-it-is – presumptions that then contain and constrain subsequent discourse.

What can we say, then, of the actual arguments *against* constitutional pluralism that may have been in the minds of Supreme Court judges as they thought about how to give meaning to section 35? It is not hard to imagine what these may have been, and indeed some content was suggested in the previous few paragraphs; we can imagine arguments about the passage of time, about progress in social and political development, and about the soundness of liberal doctrine in dealing with all of the problems within a modern society. Further, whatever these arguments may have been, when we think of their place within a setting already predetermined in the normative world of liberal discourse, we can appreciate that (a) they need not be particularly strong, and, tied to that, (b) they function principally not to persuade parties but to justify the status quo.

Of key import, these arguments function to support the narrow model of the world-as-it-is through which the Court sees matters before it. Judges of the Supreme Court are not capable of seeing – through this lens – that Indigenous peoples enjoy continuing legal and political authority.[28] Rather, they see before them only a problem defined in terms of a need to reconcile peoples who formerly possessed independence with life under Crown sovereignty in a "just and fair" arrangement that they are properly placed to work out.

Two aspects of this model of the world-as-it-is are fundamentally important. First is the notion that colonialism (to the extent that it was harmful and problematic) took place in the long-ago, with at most reverberations echoing up into the present – echoes that Canadian society can and should acknowledge. Second is the notion that the loss of independence the Court presupposes as a pillar of the reality marking the existence of Indigenous peoples within modern Canada is not something to be undone. There is no thought of how colonial actions might be addressed, since grounding this model of the world-as-it-is in the "fact" of existence within a liberal democratic society entails that Indigenous peoples find themselves living within a social setting that is the best of all possible social worlds for any people. The way forward then is not to return to times long ago, but to work out how, in a liberal democratic setting, the interests of Indigenous peoples can be accommodated.

Turning to the United Nations Declaration on the Rights of Indigenous Peoples

In 2007, the United Nations General Assembly voted to adopt the Declaration on the Rights of Indigenous Peoples. Four countries voted against adoption – the United States, New Zealand, Australia, and Canada. Since then, all four have reversed positions, with Canada first accepting the document with qualifications in 2010 (declaring the UNDRIP to be merely "aspirational," with no legally binding force in Canada), and then accepting the UNDRIP without qualifications in 2016. In late 2019, the British Columbia legislative assembly ratified the *Declaration on the Rights of Indigenous Peoples Act*,[29] and less than two years later the federal government gave Royal Assent to the *United Nations Declaration on the Rights of Indigenous Peoples Act*.[30] These two pieces of legislation are meant to function as implementation devices, as the UNDRIP is slowly woven into both federal and British Columbia law.

Section 35 and the UNDRIP are quite different creatures. It is not just a matter of the one having its origins primarily in decades of discussions between numerous Indigenous groups representing Indigenous populations around the world while the other came out of a domestic struggle in Canada – a struggle most often fought solely between provincial premiers and top federal politicians. The two are also very different both in terms of *content* – section 35 was almost content-free when the Canadian constitution was ratified, while the UNDRIP contains an extensive perambulatory section and forty-six articles covering a wide range of matters – and in terms of *setting* – the one being embedded within the constitution of a nation state and the other a declaration within the soft law of international law.

Moves in Canada to incorporate the UNDRIP into Canadian law, however, bring the two more closely together. First, both the British Columbia and federal legislation act to pull the UNDRIP, in some sense, into provincial and federal law, pulling it over from the international arena. Second, section 35 now carries along with it over thirty years of jurisprudence that touches on all sorts of matters, many of which are likewise issues addressed in various articles of the UNDRIP. With the pulling of the UNDRIP into the domestic setting we seem now to encounter a situation similar to that faced in the 1980s and 1990s – how will Canadian governments and courts understand the impact the UNDRIP could and should have? Three paths forward seem visible: (1) the UNDRIP functions to modify section 35 law, (2) section 35 law oversees how the UNDRIP is brought into Canadian law, or (3) the two bodies of law are somehow fused together into a new hybrid approach to Crown Indigenous relations.

The question we are exploring is more focused: Can we reasonably expect that the UNDRIP will open the door to serious consideration of the project of putting constitutional pluralism into action? The threat to this movement is clear and obvious: it may well be that Canadian governments (with the assistance of their courts) will attempt to domesticate the UNDRIP. What this means in the context of constitutional pluralism (and strong legal pluralism) is also clear: if the UNDRIP is domesticated, the independent legal and political authority of Indigenous peoples in Canada would only survive under its importation as muted and controlled forces unilaterally subsumed within the sovereignty of the Crown.

It would be natural to turn, then, to arguments about what the UNDRIP seems to contain, and to arguments Canadian authorities might harbour as they eye with suspicion what they are likely to take as threats to the sovereign authority of the state. We can then more carefully think about whether the UNDRIP could be understood in some manner such that a middle ground might be found between those who see promise in the UNDRIP and those who will almost certainly aim to tame whatever radical nature it may contain.

I have already signalled, however, my concern with this approach to analysis of the situation. The thought behind such an approach would be that the "right" argument on the side of finding substantive promise of fuel for movement towards constitutional pluralism would overpower whatever arguments might exist on the side of the status quo – that is, that the battlefield on which to fight is that of arguments, the measures being that of reason and soundness. My concern is not just with the fact any such battlefield is actually tilted heavily in favour of the state and its courts, but that this is likely not a battlefield in any meaningful sense of the term. First, arguably it is a place where Indigenous peoples are sent to do relatively meaningless battle, their energies diverted so they are not put to the sort of work that might lead to substantive change. Second, to the extent something does come from expending energy on this field, it is arguable that one key hoped-for result on the part of the state is the absorption of Indigenous peoples *further* into the social-normative worlds of the state and its courts.

This, then, leads us into the approach I pursue to the question of domestication. Bearing in mind lessons we can take from thirty years of post-*Sparrow* jurisprudence, how can we make sense of the possibilities and challenges laid out before us? We begin with a brief look into the very sorts of questions and arguments we would find on a battlefield of reason and evidence, as we need to see both what promise the UNDRIP does indeed hold out in relation to constitutional pluralism and how this promise might be met with scepticism and resistance. We then turn to wonder at the actual struggles that lie ahead should Indigenous peoples hope that bringing the UNDRIP into the picture shakes the state and its courts from their firm commitment to a monolithic form of nation-state constitutionalism.

Arguments about the Promise of the UNDRIP

The UNDRIP emerged from the fact that self-determining Indigenous peoples around the world pushed for space within a global system dominated by the nation-state system. It is – it must be born in mind – a *declaration* of the *United Nations*, the product of decades of discussion *within* that system of Westphalian-defined states. Unsurprisingly, it was, then, designed to function, post-adoption, inside domestic nation-state settings as a function of the specifics attending each such setting.[31] In any such setting, in line with whatever particular history and attendant set of circumstances exist arising out of the dynamic encompassing the specific nation state and Indigenous peoples who find themselves living within it, the articles would find specific meanings.

So, given Canada has the colonial history it has in relation to Indigenous peoples now living within its borders, and given the nature and structure of the current Canadian state, how could the rights articulated in the UNDRIP, understood in light of the principles and values articulated in the preamble, manifest? Could constitutional pluralism be one way in which the self-determination of Indigenous peoples in Canada manifests as their political status within the Canadian state?

We earlier set out a sense of what is meant in referring to Indigenous constitutional orders, thinking about what this expression might mean when divorced from its usual connections to the Westphalian nation state: a constitutional order relates to a people, encompassing how it organizes itself, the order functioning through those social mechanisms by which this collectivity determines how to be and act over time, all guided by those principles and values that animate this collective. A constitutional order is a manifestation of self-determination, as it represents how collectives think of themselves over time, and with this self-conception how they then act through time and space. We are examining the UNDRIP, then, for clear indications that the rights it sets out would speak to the emergence in Canada of an understanding of Indigenous peoples' self-determination manifesting in constitutional orders protected by and coexisting with the constitutional order of the state.

Much of the UNDRIP covers rights that fall within the usual parameters of human rights – that is, rights held by individuals, usually conceptually connected to the status of humans *qua* humans. Our interest is in those articles of the UNDRIP that touch on the collective interests of an Indigenous people, and particularly those that engage with the right of self-determination (arguably a core collective right about which much of the UNDRIP spins). We begin with Articles 3, 4, and 5, which directly speak to this right and its core attributes:

- Article 3: Indigenous peoples have the right to self-determination. By virtue of that right they freely determine their political status and freely pursue their economic, social and cultural development.
- Article 4: Indigenous peoples, in exercising their right to self-determination, have the right to autonomy or self-government in

matters relating to their internal and local affairs, as well as ways and means for financing their autonomous functions.
- Article 5: Indigenous peoples have the right to maintain and strengthen their distinct political, legal, economic, social and cultural institutions, while retaining their right to participate fully, if they so choose, in the political, economic, social and cultural life of the State.

The right of self-determination covers a set of *powers*; we see these here as powers to determine political status and to pursue economic, social, and cultural development (including, particularly, as these relate to "internal and local affairs"). But as Indigenous peoples hold a *right* to self-determination, these powers are also protected – here, the powers are said to be to *freely* determine political status and to *freely* pursue economic, social, and political development, necessitating that nation states understand they are under *obligations* not to interfere with the exercise of these powers.

A number of the other articles unpack what might be included under the rubric of pursuing "economic, social and cultural development" and of exercising a right to autonomy in relation to "internal and local affairs." Article 20, for example, holds that Indigenous peoples have the right to develop their own political, economic, and social systems or institutions, while Article 12 speaks to the right of Indigenous peoples to manifest, practice, develop, and teach their spiritual and religious traditions, customs, and ceremonies.

Article 4, it must be noted, does not imply that the right to self-determination is *limited* under the UNDRIP to "autonomy or self-government in matters relating to ... internal and local affairs." Returning to Article 3, we have already noted that the right to freely pursue economic, social, and cultural development, and the pursuit of economic development, in particular, is fleshed out in other articles in such a way that it is clear the right to self-determination reaches out to matters that will intersect with the rights, interests, and powers of others.

Article 26 provides a good example of this larger reach of self-determination:

1. Indigenous peoples have the right to the lands, territories and resources which they have traditionally owned, occupied or otherwise used or acquired.
2. Indigenous peoples have the right to own, use, develop and control the lands, territories and resources that they possess by reason of

traditional ownership or other traditional occupation or use, as well as those which they have otherwise acquired.
3. States shall give legal recognition and protection to these lands, territories and resources. Such recognition shall be conducted with due respect to the customs, traditions and land tenure systems of the indigenous peoples concerned.

Article 26(2) speaks to the right not just to own but to "develop and control the lands, territories and resources ... possess[ed] by reason of traditional ownership or other traditional occupation or use." This expands rights of the community out past those of self-government (if this is conceived of solely in terms of the population of the community), as the collective rights in the UNDRIP also give power to an Indigenous people to decide how it conceives of its specific people–land relations – as we see in 26(3) – and to decide how to develop and control the lands in question.

We likewise find connections to lands and resources at the heart of Articles 25 and 32.[32] We find in these sorts of articles the connection to territory essential to the notion of constitutional orders (where earlier we broadened the notion from its narrow focus on nation states to one that encompassed the constitutional orders of *peoples* determining their existence in relation to their territories).

There are also numerous provisions that speak to the notion that under a right to self-determination Indigenous peoples are in possession of powers to determine both *who* they are – not just socially and culturally, but politically – and *how* they will think about their place in the world and so act. Article 33(1), for example, holds that "Indigenous peoples have the right to determine their own identity or membership in accordance with their customs and traditions,"[33] while Article 34 holds that "Indigenous peoples have the right to *promote*, *develop* and *maintain* [emphasis added] their institutional structures and their distinctive customs, spirituality, traditions, procedures, practices and, in the cases where they exist, juridical systems or customs, in accordance with international human rights standards."[34]

Behind all these indications that the Indigenous right to self-determination encompasses the elements necessary to uphold the maintenance and protection of Indigenous constitutional orders we find language in the preamble that clearly rests *all* this on Indigenous ways of being and thinking in the world. In the preamble, for example, we find that the UNDRIP is meant to recognize "the urgent need to respect and promote the inherent rights of indigenous peoples which *derive from* [emphasis added] their political, economic and social structures and from their cultures, spiritual traditions, histories and philosophies, especially their rights to their lands, territories and resources."[35]

If we begin with a reasonable understanding of the particular Canadian context within which the UNDRIP is supposed to unfold – acknowledging a history of not just the dispossession and oppression of Indigenous peoples but the denial of Indigenous peoples' legal and political authority, and coupling this with an understanding that in contemporary Canada a number of Indigenous peoples *continue* to live through their own constitutional orders – the radical promise of the UNDRIP emerges. One can certainly construct a strong argument to the effect that the rights of Indigenous peoples articulated in the UNDRIP could be reasonably expected to manifest in the Canadian context in calls on the state to work with Indigenous peoples to negotiate a way that the multiple constitutional orders in existence might peacefully coexist.[36]

Arguments Undercutting the Radical Promise of the UNDRIP and a Look at the State of the Struggle

In our discussion of the jurisprudence that began with *Sparrow* we noted that Canadian courts have maintained a stance that is inconsistent with – perhaps even in direct conflict with – this position, the stance that there exists just the one constitutional order of the nation state. We touched on positions that seem to lie behind this (and that arguably resulted in the domestication of section 35): the sense that colonialism is a set of events in the distant past (where racism fuelled thought and behaviour of the settler state), and the notion that in today's Canada, with the populace living within the best sort of political arrangement – that of a liberal democracy acknowledging the demands of multiculturalism – the way forward is not to return to precolonial arrangements but to reconcile the existence of Indigenous societies – understood *solely* in terms of culture – with the immovable sovereignty of the Crown. Behind these we imagined that certain arguments are meant to provide support – arguments about the effects of the passage of time, about progress in social and political development, and about the soundness of liberal doctrine.

Arguably, these very same positions and arguments would underscore the measure of scepticism and resistance fuelling those who would have trouble seeing the need to interpret the UNDRIP as requiring negotiations about constitutional pluralism. This, then, would be where we stand should we think the struggle is on the battlefield of reason and evidence. Arguments can be made that the UNDRIP should, if it is incorporated into the Canadian landscape, lead to discussions and negotiations about how to manage constitutional pluralism. The fact is, however, that the state (and its courts) are in a position whereby they exert control over how the UNDRIP ultimately restructures the dynamic between the Crown and Indigenous peoples, and the state and its courts will have in their minds thoughts about the nature of the problems faced in Crown–Indigenous relations that make it very difficult for arguments for constitutional pluralism to find purchase. Can one reasonably hold out hope that Canadian institutions might be persuaded – through reason and argumentation – to turn to how the UNDRIP could help move Canada along a path towards understanding that negotiations are required?

The problem we identified earlier is in how arguments on the side of resistance function. They are not simply arrayed *against* arguments for constitutional pluralism but rather serve to *frame* how the Court understands the problems posed in Crown–Indigenous relations, which in turn *predetermines* the sorts of solutions to these problems it can sensibly contemplate.[37] They do not function as arguments that "win over" the minds of the judges of the high court but as background arguments that only serve to justify the stance they take. One cannot, then, expect to meet them on the battlefield of reason in a contest of arguments.

Let us keep our focus on how Canadian courts – and specifically the Supreme Court of Canada, that body that ultimately determines how legal instruments are understood to function within Canada – are likely to respond to the possibility that the radical promise of the UNDRIP might seep into the Canadian legal and political landscape. They come to this possibility with the stance that there is just the one valid constitutional order, that of the state, with background arguments that do not function to rationally underscore this stance, but to justify the status quo that they operate within and under.

What we first search for, then, are signs that this time around it is different. Is there something substantially distinct between the situation that unfolded in the years after section 35 entered the scene in the early 1980s and the present situation, when the UNDRIP seems to be on the threshold of being welcomed into the Canadian arena? Will the Supreme Court persist in seeing the world solely through the lens of liberal democratic theory? Will it understand the situation the UNDRIP is meant to address as marked by acts of dispossession, oppression, and discrimination that happened generations ago (during Canada's overt colonial era)? Will it imagine, then, that with the passage of time and the development of good governance under a liberal democratic system a muted response – tied to a narrow domesticating interpretation – is all that is called for?

It is very difficult to see how all these considerations would not mark the response of the Supreme Court. While we are now thirty years post-*Sparrow*, what these years contain, on the side of Canada and its courts, is retrenchment of the sense of the "rightness" of their approach taken to Crown–Indigenous relations. We see no indication that thoughts have turned to how to respond directly to colonialism itself (rather than a deepening of their perception that the only significant matter in need of redress in multicultural Canada is the weakening of Indigenous peoples' cultures). We see no indication that thoughts have turned to investigating the appropriateness of applying liberal democratic doctrine to how the Crown–Indigenous dynamic should be understood. What we have, on the other hand, is a significant mass of jurisprudence that begins from a denial of Indigenous constitutional orders and from acceptance that the passage of time and the development of political doctrine should push concerns about what might have happened to these orders out of the consciousness of the state and its courts.

To have things move in a different direction would require that the high court recognize and accept that its thirty years of jurisprudence has been fundamentally wrong-footed. It would require it acquiesce in beginning from a different starting point when thinking of the UNDRIP, accepting fundamentally different points: first, the Court would have to begin with acknowledgment of the fact of continuing, valid Indigenous legal and political authority, and, second, it would have to accept that while Canadian authorities *believe* in the propriety of solving all social problems through the application of liberal democratic principles and processes, it cannot be *presumed* that the Crown–Indigenous situation must be understood through this one normative lens (such that "solutions," as well, are all predetermined).

Concluding Thoughts

On the one hand, this mode of assessment of the situation can understandably breed cynicism and despair. One hopes – certainly academics hope! – that arguments can have force. This hope can be given life if we acknowledge that arguments can have force, not in themselves but rather in their ability, in concert with certain conditions, to affect the thinking of those in positions from which change can emanate. This seems sensible enough: we make arguments in legal and political struggles with the hope that we can change the ways of thinking of those who exert measures of control over our individual and collective lives. But in the context of Crown–Indigenous interactions we find that those in power to effect change come to discussions about what to do with predetermined normative positions – positions that preset how they understand not just how the future should be moulded but how the past itself should be understood, and how debate should be deemed sensible. It is difficult to engage, on the level of argumentation, with those who begin by actively constraining what counts as an argument, and impossible when one sees that in fact those parties who come to arenas of engagement are not there to win debates but rather to justify their starting points.

I can say with a very high level of confidence that if the Supreme Court of Canada is given opportunities to speak to how the United Nations Declaration on the Rights of Indigenous Peoples should be understood to come into the legal and political landscape of Canada, it will do its utmost to domesticate it. I can also say that trying to fight this through nothing more than the production of reasoned arguments setting out how this is not in line with the *facts* of the world and with how things *should* play out – while important for various reasons – is futile.

But knowledge is power, and knowing this is the way of the world is valuable. This knowledge in hand, one then can appreciate, for example, how important it can be to know that one thing the state and its courts gain when Indigenous peoples engage in repeated attempts at trying to persuade these powers through reasoned argument is diffusion of the energies of resistance. One can also see clearly there is more to wonder at, behind all these machinations of the nation state and its courts. Important questions press themselves upon us: *Why* is it such that inevitably the response to the UNDRIP will be ceaseless efforts at domestication? And, is it not the case that Indigenous peoples in Canada can continue the struggle to uphold their own constitutional orders, regardless of efforts at domestication? Further, what do such continuing struggles mean to the state and its courts? Can it continue to hold out its own hope that all these struggles will themselves be eventually domesticated? Is it not the case that struggles against domestication will, in themselves, always fend off domestication?

NOTES

1 *R. v. Sparrow*, [1990] 1 SCR 1075.
2 Michael Asch and Patrick Macklem, "Aboriginal Rights and Canadian Sovereignty: An Essay on *R. v. Sparrow*," *Alberta Law Review* 29, no. 2 (1991): 498.

3 Kiera L. Ladner and Michael McCrossan, "The Road Not Taken: Aboriginal Rights after the Re-imagining of the Canadian Constitutional Order," in *Contested Constitutionalism: Reflections on the Canadian Charter of Rights and Freedoms*, ed. James B. Kelly and Christopher P. Manfredi (Vancouver: UBC Press, 2008), 263–83; Kiera L. Ladner, "Take 35: Reconciling Constitutional Orders," in *First Nations, First Thoughts: The Impact of Indigenous Thought in Canada*, ed. Annis May Timpson (Vancouver: UBC Press, 2009), 279–300; James (Sa'ke'j) Youngblood Henderson, "Aboriginal Jurisprudences and Rights," in *Advancing Aboriginal Claims: Visions, Strategies, Directions*, ed. Kerry Wilkins (Saskatoon: Purich Publishing, 2004), 67–89.
4 UN General Assembly, United Nations Declaration on the Rights of Indigenous Peoples (UNDRIP), 2 October 2007, A/RES/61/295.
5 Mark Tushnet, *The New Constitutional Order* (Princeton, NJ: Princeton University Press, 2003), 1.
6 In a 2015 article, Christian Kreuder-Sonnen and Bernhard Zangl look at the rise of the authority of international organizations – in particular, the UN security system – and locate there troubling signs of authoritarianism. The general background to their analysis, though, is the gradual emergence of multiple sites of authority in the international arena. See Christian Kreuder-Sonnen and Bernhard Zangl, "Which Post-Westphalia? International Organizations between Constitutionalism and Authoritarianism," *European Journal of International Relations* 21, no. 3 (September 2015): 568–94, https://doi.org/10.1177/1354066114548736.
7 Neil Walker, "The Idea of Constitutional Pluralism," *The Modern Law Review* 65, no. 3 (May 2002): 338, https://doi.org/10.1111/1468-2230.00383.
8 Kunst'aa Guu – Kunst'aayah Reconciliation Protocol, between the Haida Nation and Her Majesty the Queen in Right of the Province of British Columbia, 14 December 2009, https://www.haidanation.ca/wp-content/uploads/2017/03/Kunstaa-guu_Kunstaayah_Agreement.pdf.
9 James Tully works through these arguments in chapter 8 ("The Struggles of Indigenous Peoples for and of Freedom") of *Public Philosophy in a New Key*, vol. 1, *Democracy and Civic Freedom* (Cambridge: Cambridge University Press, 2008), 257–88.
10 This is the focus of Tully's analysis and argumentation in chapter 7 ("The Negotiation of Reconciliation") of *Public Philosophy*, 233–56.
11 For example, in *Mitchell v. M.N.R.*, 2001 SCC 33, at para 129, Justice Binnie, in a concurring judgment, developed his own theory about how the doctrines of continuity (from imperial law) and sovereign incompatibility contributed to the development of "merged sovereignty," the notion that in contemporary Canada, Crown sovereignty includes within itself Aboriginal sovereignty: "'Merged sovereignty' asserts that First Nations were not wholly subordinated to non-aboriginal sovereignty but over time

became merger partners. ... This updated concept of Crown sovereignty is of importance. ... If the principle of 'merged sovereignty' ... is to have any true meaning, it must include at least the idea that aboriginal and non-aboriginal Canadians *together* form a sovereign entity with a measure of common purpose and united effort. It is this new entity, as inheritor of the historical attributes of sovereignty, with which existing aboriginal and treaty rights must be reconciled."

12 Of course, some may argue these constitutional orders never existed – but note I cast the nature of constitutional orders at a level of abstraction that makes this an untenable position (though one held by certain racist parties).

13 See, for example, Jeremy Waldron, "Superseding Historic Injustice," *Ethics* 103, no. 1 (October 1992): 4; and "Supersession and Sovereignty," NYU School of Law, Public Law Research Paper No. 13–33, https://ssrn.com/abstract=2205708. See also my response to these normatively myopic arguments in Gordon Christie, "The Supersession of Indigenous Understandings of Justice and Morals," *Critical Review of International Social and Political Philosophy* 25, no. 3 (2022): 427–42, https://doi.org/10.1080/13698230.2022.2039539.

14 Reading this into arguments made and positions taken in, for example, Tom Flanagan, *First Nations? Second Thoughts* (Montreal: McGill-Queen's University Press, 2000); and Gordon Gibson, *A New Look at Canadian Indian Policy: Respect the Collective – Promote the Individual* (Vancouver: Fraser Institute, 2009).

15 See Gordon Christie, *Canadian Law and Indigenous Self-Determination: A Naturalist Analysis* (Toronto: University of Toronto Press, 2019).

16 Asch and Macklem, "Aboriginal Rights," 506–7.

17 Ibid., 507.

18 *R. v. Van der Peet*, [1996] 2 SCR 507 [hereafter *Van der Peet*], at para 46: "in order to be an aboriginal right an activity must be an element of a practice, custom or tradition integral to the distinctive culture of the aboriginal group claiming the right."

19 *Calder v. Attorney-General of British Columbia*, [1973] SCR 313.

20 *Van der Peet*, at para 31.

21 Ladner and McCrossan, "Road Not Taken," 268. Their quote is from James (Sa'ke'j) Youngblood Henderson, Marjorie L. Benson, and Isobel M. Findlay, *Aboriginal Tenure in the Constitution of Canada* (Scarborough, ON: Carswell, 2000), 432.

22 Ladner, "Take 35," 288.

23 Henderson, Benson, and Findlay, *Aboriginal Tenure*, 433.

24 Ladner, "Take 35," 294–5, quoting from Henderson, "Aboriginal Jurisprudences," 75–6.

25 Ladner, "Take 35," 292–3.
26 Much of this is detailed in Christie, *Canadian Law*, chaps. 6, 7, 8.
27 Ibid.
28 This is a particular sort of incapacity – just as the reader of this text can (I hope) see the sense in the notion of continuing independent Indigenous legal and political authority, so too could each justice of the high court. When thinking of Indigenous peoples in the context of legal issues before them as a court, however, this notion cannot enter their deliberations – their "legal imagination" cannot extend this far.
29 *Declaration on the Rights of Indigenous Peoples Act*, [SBC 2019], c 44, http://www.bclaws.ca/civix/document/id/complete/statreg/19044. In June 2020, the first report under this legislation was published: Government of British Columbia, *Declaration on the Rights of Indigenous Peoples Act: 2019/2020 Annual Report* (Victoria: Government of British Columbia, 2020), https://www2.gov.bc.ca/assets/gov/british-columbians-our-governments/indigenous-people/aboriginal-peoples-documents/dripa_annual_report_2020.pdf.
30 *United Nations Declaration on the Rights of Indigenous Peoples Act*, [SC 2021], c 14, https://canlii.ca/t/554bd.
31 The preamble notes that the UNDRIP is meant to recognize "that the situation of indigenous peoples varies from region to region and from country to country and that the significance of national and regional particularities and various historical and cultural backgrounds should be taken into consideration."
32 Article 25: "Indigenous peoples have the right to maintain and strengthen their distinctive spiritual relationship with their traditionally owned or otherwise occupied and used lands, territories, waters and coastal seas and other resources and to uphold their responsibilities to future generations in this regard."

   Article 32(1): "Indigenous peoples have the right to determine and develop priorities and strategies for the development or use of their lands or territories and other resources."
33 In furtherance of this set of powers to determine who they are politically, we find Article 35, which holds that "Indigenous peoples have the right to determine the responsibilities of individuals to their communities."
34 In furtherance of this set of powers to determine how they believe and act in the world (politically as well as socially, economically, and culturally), we find Article 18, "Indigenous peoples have the right to participate in decision-making in matters which would affect their rights, through representatives chosen by themselves in accordance with their own procedures, as well as to maintain and develop their own indigenous decision-making institutions," Article 20(1), "Indigenous peoples have the

right to maintain and develop their political, economic and social systems or institutions," and Article 32(1), "Indigenous peoples have the right to *determine* and *develop priorities and strategies* [emphasis added] for the development or use of their lands or territories and other resources."

35 The preamble also notes that the signatories welcome "the fact that indigenous peoples are organizing themselves for political, economic, social and cultural enhancement and in order to bring to an end all forms of discrimination and oppression wherever they occur" and are convinced "that control by indigenous peoples over developments affecting them and their lands, territories and resources will enable them to maintain and strengthen their institutions, cultures and traditions, and to promote their development in accordance with their aspirations and needs."

36 In the summer of 2021, a new agreement was entered into by the Haida Nation, the British Columbia government, and the federal government: the GayGahlda "Changing Tide" Framework for Negotiation, 13 August 2021, https://www2.gov.bc.ca/assets/gov/environment/natural-resource-stewardship/consulting-with-first-nations/agreements/gaygahlda_changing_tide_framework_agreement.pdf. In many respects, it signals the first visible move on the part of Canadian governments towards working out how constitutional pluralism might be acknowledged in the Crown–Indigenous context. It is, though, only an *agreement to negotiate* on the basis of certain principles, and we do not know where this might eventually lead.

37 James Tully refers to these as "hinge propositions, … around which negotiations and litigation continue to take place." His argument is that two such presumptions inform how the state thinks: first, that "exercise of exclusive jurisdiction over territories of Indigenous peoples is not only effective but also legitimate," and second, that "there is no viable alternative." See Tully, *Public Philosophy*, 276–7.

PART TWO

Decolonizing Constitutionalism

4 Politicizing Indigenous Self-Determination: The UNDRIP and Legal and Political Constitutionalism

YANN ALLARD-TREMBLAY

Introduction

Declarations of universal human, political, and social rights constitute a political tradition that can be interpreted as the paradigmatic political manifestation of a style of rationalist discourse that bloomed during Western modernity and that focuses on identifying and affirming universal norms to structure, limit, and guide politics everywhere and at any time. Despite not being legally binding, the rights, principles, and commitments affirmed by declarations are meant to be authoritative, in the sense that they cannot easily and without solid political justification be ignored and acted against. They are to some extent *politically* binding. It thus makes sense to refer to the tradition to which they belong as a universal constitutional tradition.

Indeed, just as written national constitutions are meant to provide clear norms and rules to structure, limit, and direct the exercise of political power within the modern state, declarations consist of the proclamation of fundamental rights and norms that should structure, limit, and direct the exercise of political power across the globe, and that should eventually give rise to conventions or be incorporated into national laws. There are clear differences between constitutionalism at the state level and at the global level, yet both are strongly committed to the idea of providing clear normative standards held to be essential for politics to be minimally right or just. Despite the differences, it is appropriate to speak of two variants of the same general constitutional tradition.

It is in light of this tradition that I want to approach the United Nations Declaration on the Rights of Indigenous Peoples (UNDRIP).[1] The relevance of this discourse to the UNDRIP is made clear by considering how the UNDRIP is described on the website of the United Nations:

> [T]he Declaration is the most comprehensive international instrument on the rights of indigenous peoples. It establishes a universal framework of minimum standards for the survival, dignity and well-being of the indigenous peoples of the world and it elaborates on existing human rights standards and fundamental freedoms as they apply to the specific situation of indigenous peoples.[2]

The relevance of this discourse is further supported when we consider, in the Canadian context, the current discussions about the best ways to give legal force to the UNDRIP through its incorporation or legal implementation into the domestic legal system, and about how to make other federal and provincial laws coherent with this declaration and with the terms of its implementation.

A central claim of this chapter is that the UNDRIP, along with the project of its implementation, can be associated with a legal constitutional discourse about governance – one that emphasizes the importance of clear fundamental legal rules and norms to properly direct the exercise of political power. This is a discourse that favours forms of civic conduct that support and enhance constitutional governance through legal measures, as opposed to political actions.

Yet, despite the broad global uptake of this discourse, it is essential to recognize the extent to which it nevertheless belongs to a specific historical-cultural tradition that conceives the political project of bringing formal political power under control – constraining it to prevent drifts towards arbitrary power and subjecting it to moral principles – through the affirmation of universal and binding legal rights, norms, and principles. But there are other ways of thinking about how political actions can enable the goods pursued by the UNDRIP. As Quentin Skinner explains about traditions of thought and normative concepts, "it is easy to become bewitched into believing that the ways of thinking about them bequeathed to us by the mainstream of our intellectual traditions must be *the* ways of thinking about them."[3] Similarly, it is easy to believe that the right or best way to limit, structure, and direct political power is found in the tradition of declarations and constitutions, and that Indigenous self-determination should be pursued through this form of legal constitutionalization. It would thus appear natural to implement the UNDRIP by seeking to incorporate it into Canadian domestic law, and preferably Canadian constitutional law.

As such, there is a risk that this specific manner of protecting Indigenous self-determination through (domestic) legal implementation will be mistaken as the whole and complete way to secure self-determination. There is a further and more serious risk that the legal terms by which Indigenous self-determination will be acknowledged through implementation may be mistaken for self-determination itself. In what follows, I will argue that there are serious limits to making the mistake Skinner warns us against, that is, mistaking the specific historical-cultural solution that the UNDRIP is for the embodiment and guarantee of Indigenous self-determination. My main objective is to highlight that Indigenous self-determination cannot be captured fully and completely by any legal standards. Instead, Indigenous self-determination is ultimately a political manifestation and process as opposed to a legal guarantee.

To make this point, I propose to look, in the first and second sections, at the UNDRIP, along with the project of legal implementation, as an exemplar of the modern constitutional tradition and to consider it in light of the ideas of legal and political constitutionalism. This will allow me, in the third section, to link two criticisms of the UNDRIP with these broader strands of theoretical reflection on constitutional politics and thus to achieve greater clarity on what is deeply at stake with these criticisms. I will ultimately contend, in the fourth section, that engaging with the position offered by political constitutionalism may be more fruitful for those concerned with enabling and safeguarding Indigenous self-determination. This is because it better appreciates the diversity and multiplicity of forms that Indigenous self-determination may take – a diversity and multiplicity that the legal implementation of the UNDRIP, in a political irony, may actually undermine, even as its formal aim is to support these ends.

The UNDRIP and Legal Constitutionalism

The UNDRIP affirms that Indigenous peoples have the right to self-determination (Article 3), and it affirms their autonomy from the settler states with regard to internal matters and local affairs (Article 4). Various articles of the declaration then expand on what self-determination and autonomy entail in political, legal, economic, social, and cultural terms with regard to land, and with regard to the relationship between Indigenous peoples and the settler states. Notably, the declaration puts forward the principle that states should seek free, prior, and informed consent from Indigenous peoples with regard to political decisions that concern them. Along with the right of self-determination, the UNDRIP also maintains the right of Indigenous peoples to fully participate in the life of the state (Article 5). Ultimately, however, it appears to limit the self-determination of Indigenous peoples by reaffirming the primacy of "the territorial integrity or political unity of sovereign and independent States" (Article 46),[4] and by emphasizing the reach of their autonomy to be limited to local and internal affairs.[5]

Leaving aside the content of the declaration, I focus on its form. The UNDRIP sets forth broad and abstract norms and principles that should guide the political conduct of states claiming authority over Indigenous peoples, lands, and bodies. That is, it provides a normative framework of universal normative political standards meant as elaborations of "existing human rights standards and fundamental freedom"[6] for the specific context of persistent and durable settler colonialism found in states like Canada and the US. It can thus be seen both as the expression of "a common understanding" of what human rights and freedoms entail in this specific context, and as the promulgation of "a common standard of achievement" on the basis of which the performance of states can be measured.[7]

The UNDRIP is not in the proper sense of the term a constitution, but it remains a type of constitutional document. It sets overarching norms and principles that should guide the conduct of regular politics. This is why it is seen as requiring legal implementation, where the terms of implementation would occupy a fundamental position in the legal system, and where the rest of the legal system would need to be made coherent with the terms of the implementation of the UNDRIP.[8] As such, it can be associated with the broad constitutional tradition. This claim might be obvious to some, but it is nevertheless useful to consider and highlight the extent to which this approach to UNDRIP implementation belongs to this tradition, and to understand what views of political theory lie underneath this constitutional discourse, with its universalizing pretensions. Eventually, this will allow us to disclose the extent to which the criticisms of the declaration I consider hit at something more profound than the declaration itself. Indeed, I believe that the issues identified by some critics of the UNDRIP can be traced back to the tradition of legal constitutionalism, and ultimately back to the universalist and rational morality informing it.

I start by considering what is generally meant by a constitution and by legal constitutionalism. I then make clear the sense in which the UNDRIP – and more specifically, the project of implementation into domestic law – participates in this mode of governance. Constitutions are generally understood as foundational documents that structure, limit, and direct the exercise of political power within a state. They structure political power by describing the institutions through which political power will be exercised. They limit political power by defining the reach of the authority of political institutions and by setting out (negative) rights that ought to be respected. They direct political power by setting out principles and (positive) rights that political institutions should strive to realize.

In order to function as foundational documents that can structure, limit, and direct political power, constitutions require certain features. Andrei Marmor lists six such features.[9] First, a constitution needs to hold normative supremacy, which means it has to frame the rest of the political and legal system: inferior laws should be compatible with the constitution, and if an inconsistency is found, the inferior law should be changed. Moreover, day-to-day politics is bound by the elements of the constitution. Second, a constitution generally requires judicial review to enforce the supremacy of the constitutional requirements on the rest of the legal and political system. Third, a constitution should have longevity; that is, it is intended to be in place in a manner that is not transitory or fleeting. Fourth, a constitution should be rigid in the sense that it should not easily be modified, notably by the day-to-day political process precisely in order to check drifts towards arbitrary power and to ensure that politics can be subjected to those constitutionalized moral principles. Fifth, a constitution should provide norms defining and governing both the structure of the state and the negative and positive rights of citizens (and more broadly of those subjected to the power of the state). Sixth, the norms contained in a constitution should be general and abstract so as to apply to a great variety of situations and to garner broad agreement.

Civil associations have not always used constitutions to structure, limit, and direct their power; and they might not always be used. Constitutions especially make sense as instruments within this specific formalized and juridical understanding of the relationship between politics and certain rights and norms – and thus of the allowable reach of political actions – that can be referred to as legal constitutionalism. Legal constitutionalism highlights the centrality of constitutions to the conduct of politics and the importance of constraining political conduct in light of superior norms and principles.[10] It holds it as rightful, as Marmor says, "to remove certain important moral/political decisions from the ordinary business of lawmaking" and to rely on the power of the courts to protect these decisions.[11] The idea that certain decisions can be removed from regular politics can be grounded on various reasons. As Richard Bellamy writes, this is generally because it is believed that "we can come to a rational consensus on the substantive outcomes that a society committed to the democratic ideals of equality of concern and respect should achieve. These outcomes are best expressed in terms of human rights and should form the fundamental law of a democratic society."[12] Another reason to remove considerations from regular politics would be an incompletely theorized agreement; that is, an agreement that some vague norm should be protected in a relatively permanent manner, though we leave out the details of its specification to regular politics or to the courts.[13] A final reason to remove certain considerations from regular politics would be if we held these norms to be self-evident and therefore beyond reasonable disagreement.[14] In sum, legal constitutionalism makes sense if we assume that some shared understanding of fundamental norms can be achieved and promulgated in a fundamental legal instrument that will allow them to escape the political world and offer standards by which politics should be assessed and guided.[15]

These constitutional rights and norms become some sort of "hinge propositions"[16] around which the political and legal debate orbit. They structure the conduct of politics by setting out the standards that should be respected and to which political actors can appeal, including the limitation of the exercise of power by other actors. Politics within the legal constitutionalist understanding is then largely concerned with seeking to get others – especially judges and justices – to share our precise understanding of these abstract and broad fundamental rights and norms, or with seeking to get some actor, process, or object protected from interference on the basis of constitutional norms and rights. Put differently, politics within a legal constitutionalist framework can be largely associated with the practice of affirming and claiming constitutional rights, or with political acts and decisions that assume and take for granted the bounds of these constitutionally affirmed rights.

As should be clear, the UNDRIP, as such, is not a perfect example of legal constitutionalism or of constitutions, most notably due to the absence of enforceability and judicial review.[17] Yet, we should not take the absence of legal enforceability as negating the fact that the UNDRIP fits in the logic of legal constitutionalism. Although the absence of legal enforceability is significant from a legal point of view, it is less so from a political theoretical or normative point of view. This is because the core of the constitutional tradition is that political conduct should be structured, limited, and directed by promulgated fundamental norms that are beyond the reach of and external to regular politics. The normative significance of these norms, just like the articles of the UNDRIP, does not depend on legal enforceability. As Michael Perry explains, "Even if courts are not empowered to protect them (and, indeed, even if courts are so empowered), constitutionally entrenched human rights – qua 'maxims of political morality' – can serve as shared, fundamental grounds of political-moral judgement in a political community."[18]

On this view, the UNDRIP is an exemplar of legal constitutionalism: it is a statement of a supposedly shared understanding of what is entailed by human rights – as specifically developed for Indigenous peoples in the context of settler states – over which there is meant to be some fundamental and widely shared agreement, and it is meant to set a standard for the conduct of political affairs that is itself somewhat external to politics. Another way of stating this is to say that, like other constitutional documents, the UNDRIP represents a highly formalized, institutionalized tool of moral-normative persuasion. This becomes even clearer when we consider the expectation that it will be incorporated within the domestic legal system and become enforceable against the Crown; indeed, through incorporation or implementation, the UNDRIP would surely end up meeting most if not all of the six features of constitutions offered by Marmor.

Hence, though not a constitution, the UNDRIP and the project of implementation clearly participate in the logic of legal constitutionalism. This is in fact one of the central reasons why the UNDRIP is often held to be useful in furthering the self-determination of Indigenous peoples. Its strength lies precisely in setting out the hinge propositions in light of which settler states and Indigenous peoples' political relationships should be structured and thought about. It also sets forth – and even more so were it to be incorporated or implemented – clear rights and principles to which political actors can appeal to justify and support political claims and actions advancing Indigenous self-determination.

Legal Constitutionalism, Modern Political Theory, and Rationalism

Legal constitutionalism should not be separated from the broader underlying assumptions about political theorizing that accompany it. These assumptions can justify and make sense of the type of civic conduct recommended by legal constitutionalism. In this section, I contend that a close relationship can be established between legal constitutionalism and what can be called the modern mode of political theorizing and rationalism in political theory.[19]

First, the modern mode of political theorizing can be defined primarily by what it considers to be its ideal object. This ideal object is generally considered to be the sovereign power, the supreme authority and the hierarchical structure of a political organization representing a relatively united and coherent political entity vested with self-determination, located on a defined territory.[20] The paradigmatic example here is the nation state – the state being the political organization of a sovereign nation. This focus on the uniform state is supported by an assumption that self-determination should be understood as independent sovereign autonomy. As Richard Day writes, quoting E.J. Hobsbawm, "Within European political thought, self-determination refers to the right of a 'people' to determine its own destiny independent of external interference. After the French and American revolutions, it was assumed that the only way in which such a right could be exercised was through an attachment to 'a separate, sovereign, independent state.'"[21] This sovereign independent autonomy requires both the absence of external interference and the absence of internal division.[22] This last claim is central to the reflections of various modern European political theorists, such as Hobbes and Pufendorf, for whom internal coherence was a required condition of stability and political agency.[23] On their view, there cannot be stable agency when the state is internally divided and pulled in various directions by the worms in its entrails,[24] such that self-determination is held to require a significant level of unity and coherence.

Following these assumptions about the object of political theorizing, we can make sense of the logic of legal constitutionalism. A constitution would then be a document founding "an independent and self-governing nation state with a set of uniform legal and representative political institutions,"[25] with the six features discussed by Marmor allowing this document to secure unity and coherence by setting out the structure, the limits, and the direction of the political power of this self-determining political entity.

The UNDRIP extends a similar logic to a context where absolute sovereign autonomy is held to not be possible for both the colonial states and Indigenous peoples. It can first be interpreted as seeking to realize to the largest extent possible the idea of autonomous self-governing entities on defined territories by emphasizing the territorial and political unity and integrity of the sovereign colonial state and thus limiting the legitimate extent of internal division. Second, by affirming Indigenous peoples as distinct peoples and recognizing their right to self-determination and their right to land, yet emphasizing their local and internal autonomy, the UNDRIP challenges the sovereign right and autonomy of colonial states, but it does so by reproducing the modern logic of independent autonomous territorial political entities for Indigenous peoples. Third, in subjecting the interferences of the settler states to the free, prior, and informed *consent* of Indigenous peoples, it seeks to ensure that those interferences can be seen to result from the autonomous choice of Indigenous peoples.

Moreover, legal constitutionalism can also be associated with rationalism in political theory, which has been well-characterized and explained by Michael Oakeshott.[26] On his view, rationalism in political theory relies both on doubts about what is not rationally grounded and on optimism that a universal human reason is sufficient to understand the world and resolve the problems we face. In this sense, political problems need to be approached through rational reflection, as opposed to negotiations, struggles, or appeals to tradition or emotions. It is through rational reflection that justified and valid solutions will be identified such that, correlatively, what warrants the implementation of these solutions is their rational justification. More generally, rationalism in political theory is marked by "the politics of perfection" and the "politics of uniformity." To all political problems there must be a rational solution, and "the 'rational' solution of any problem is, in its nature, the perfect solution." Rationalism is not concerned with pragmatic solutions or with what is expedient but rather with what is fully right or just. And, as Oakeshott further explains, "from this politics of perfection springs the politics of uniformity" since perfection is not contextual.[27] Once a fully right or just solution has been identified, it should be applied universally.[28]

Broadly, what rationalism in political theory means for political conduct is that it should be subjected to rationally justified requirements. This can be seen, for instance, in the approaches that consider political philosophy to be a subcategory of moral philosophy. On this view, political actions are entirely subjected to the rational requirements of morality. In the present case, I contend that legal constitutionalism can be interpreted as a form of rationalist political theorizing. It consists in removing from day-to-day politics certain considerations that should bind the rest of the legal and political systems. On this view, the whole of society should be structured by these norms that cannot easily be contested. There can be various degrees of "rationalism" with the various versions of legal constitutionalism. A version that relies on broad consensus on constitutional norms is much less rationalist than one that relies on self-evident truths. Nonetheless, all of these versions of legal constitutionalism share the feature of "depoliticizing constitutional values"[29] and, as such, exemplify the politics of perfection and uniformity. Similarly, we can see the same logic at play with declarations like the UNDRIP. These declarations seek to formulate norms and principles that will have universal validity and that should guide political conduct in all contexts. They seek to subsume political conduct to the norms they affirm. As such, the UNDRIP and the project of implementation also exemplify the politics of perfection and uniformity in depoliticizing the relationship between Indigenous peoples and settler states and setting this relationship on grounds that are presented as rationally supported by universally valid human rights norms.[30]

Tying Criticisms of the UNDRIP with Legal Constitutionalism

The UNDRIP seems to be a useful tool to further the goods it seeks to protect, notably by offering hinge propositions that structure the political landscape. Yet, there are objections that have been raised against this declaration, often by Indigenous critics supporting Indigenous self-determination. In this section, I discuss two main objections, and I trace the issues they raise back to the modern and rationalist mode of political theorizing that undergirds the UNDRIP as a form of legal constitutionalism.

The first criticism relates precisely to the context that renders a declaration of the rights of Indigenous peoples relevant: the persistence of settler colonialism. According to this criticism, despite seeking the freedom of Indigenous peoples from colonial oppression and domination, the UNDRIP ironically offers a way to legitimate the domination of the political, legal, and social orders of the settlers and the position of Indigenous peoples as ethnic, cultural, and political minorities. To understand this criticism, it is essential to appreciate the nature of settler colonialism.

Settler colonialism refers to the complex organization of political, legal, social, and cultural institutions, structures of power, and systems of ideas that enables the ongoing process of the domination of native populations and the replacement of their own political, legal, social, and cultural institutions by those of the settlers. As Patrick Wolfe puts it, "settler colonizers come to stay: invasion is a structure not an event."[31] Settlers do not come to stay and integrate; they come to stay and secure the dominance of their own political, social, legal, and cultural orders. Their "staying" depends on the displacement, dispossession, and elimination of the natives. As Nick Estes succinctly puts it, "Indigenous elimination, in all its orientations, is the organizing principle of settler society."[32]

This elimination can take various forms, as is reflected in the policy options considered by members of the Colonial Office of the United Kingdom concerning the Indigenous populations in British North America: "In 1841, [Herman] Merivale pointed out that four alternatives had been put forward to address the 'native question': extermination, slavery, insulation and amalgamation."[33] As is obvious, none of these seek to enable the flourishing, continued existence of Indigenous peoples as distinct peoples. Today, none of these options are even conceivable as legitimate state policies towards Indigenous peoples, albeit they remain subjected to the power of the settler states. Faced with this conundrum of persistent settler colonialism and Indigenous resilience, the idea of eliminating the natives has given way to the idea of reconciling the distinct self-determining existence of Indigenous peoples with the sovereignty of the settler state.[34]

Critics argue that this apparent substantive transformation in policy should be interpreted as merely a change of gear for settler colonialism. Indeed, if we follow Elizabeth Strakosch and Alissa Macoun, these political projects of reconciliation should not be interpreted as pursuing decolonization but rather in light of the "vanishing end point of settler colonialism."[35] In their words, this refers to "the moment of colonial completion. That is when the settler society will have fully replaced Indigenous societies on their land, and naturalized this replacement."[36] On this view, the elimination of the natives is still the guiding idea of settler colonialism, but rather than being observable in policies of actual elimination, it now takes the form of political projects that eliminate Indigenous political and legal difference by subsuming it under, and thereby legitimating, the authority of the state. These political projects can be seen in agreements or treaties defining the legitimate scope of Indigenous peoples' political authority within the overarching sovereign settler state. In settling the terms of Indigenous peoples' political and legal difference, they transform internally divided and contested political entities into united and harmonious ones. In other words, through these agreements, the "colonial relationships will dissolve themselves and settler authority will be naturalized" and fully legitimated.[37] Although this full legitimation may remain elusive and ever only partially realized, it remains the end point in the light of which we should interpret current political projects of reconciliation.

On this view, the legitimation of settler institutions is often a by-product of solutions aiming to enable Indigenous self-determination, whether they come from states granting forms of self-government arrangements to Indigenous peoples or from Indigenous peoples seeking legal recognition from the state as self-determining entities. As Martin Papillion explains, even though the Canadian policy concerned with Indigenous self-government does extend self-government capacities to certain Indigenous groups, it remains "firmly anchored in federalism," in that it states the supremacy of the Canadian constitution and the need for Indigenous governments to "work in harmony" (read: unity and coherence) with the other jurisdictions of the federation.[38] Similarly, and broadly following Glen Coulthard[39] and Jeff Corntassel,[40] it can be argued that in seeking the legal recognition of their political and legal difference from the state and following the terms set out by it, or in seeking to claim legally defined rights against the state, Indigenous peoples would precisely be naturalizing and legitimating the power of the state and hindering their capacity to define the terms of their self-determination by themselves.

A similar concern can be addressed to the UNDRIP and its implementation. It can be interpreted as providing rights and principles that should be respected and followed in order to regularize and legitimate the relationship between Indigenous peoples and settler states. On this account, what the UNDRIP offers is not decolonization; what it offers is limited self-determination within the overarching structure of the settler state. As Hayden King explains, "practicing the politics of recognition [associated with the UNDRIP] forces Indigenous peoples to accept their colonization and seek limited 'rights' as redress within the colonial framework. This ultimately affirms the legitimacy of the Settler state and the discourses through which it articulates itself."[41] Hence, even if the UNDRIP recognizes "the urgent need to respect and promote the inherent rights of indigenous peoples,"[42] it nevertheless works to incorporate these inherent rights – through implementation – into a new, now rightly ordered and thus no longer objectional, overarching political association on the basis of universally valid principles, where colonialism is transcended and the political autonomy of Indigenous peoples is limited to local and internal affairs.[43]

If we consider this objection closely, we will see that it is not fundamentally raised against the terms of the UNDRIP or with any specific terms of implementation. True, this objection opposes the limitation of Indigenous self-determination within the bounds of the settler state. But what allows the UNDRIP to limit Indigenous self-determination in such a way is the assumption that it can be above and beyond politics, that it can provide a complete blueprint for justice and the complete terms of realization for Indigenous self-determination. In other words, this objection is fundamentally against the underlying modern and rationalist features of the legal constitutionalist discourse that can be associated with the UNDRIP. It is against the idea that the UNDRIP and the terms of its implementation can set out universally valid rights and principles to which political conduct should be subordinated and in light of which political conduct should be framed in order to be just. In sum, what the objection seeks to remind us of is that the justice of the relationship between Indigenous peoples and settler states is not guaranteed by compliance with any specific terms or formulation included in a fundamental constitutional document; settler colonialism is not transcended merely by acting in accordance with the terms of implementation of the UNDRIP.

The second criticism of the UNDRIP I discuss is, again, not concerned with the content of the declaration but with its form. It is concerned with the consequences, for political self-determination, of relying on fundamental legal documents to structure and limit political conduct. According to this objection, the legal terms by which the UNDRIP would be implemented would necessarily tend to become (1) the focal point of political actions and claims; (2) the terms around which political contentions would be formulated; and (3) the terms by which the political imaginary would be limited. This is because the UNDRIP and the terms of its implementation, as fundamental constitutional considerations, would tend to function as hinge propositions around which and through which politics would be structured. As discussed above, constitutional politics tends to be framed around the claiming of constitutional rights. This is the same dynamic referred to here.

This means that Indigenous peoples seeking to exercise their self-determination would often be institutionally led to seek the recognition of their rights as they are specified by the UNDRIP, or as they are formulated in the terms of implementation. In other words, they would be directing their political energies to lead others to recognize their fundamental rights. Jeff Corntassel has criticized precisely this focus on what he labels the "Indigenous-rights discourse," since it leads Indigenous peoples to seek recognition of their "'human rights' from colonial institutions."[44] As he argues, rather than directing their energies towards claiming self-determination from the settler state and trying to fit into and realize the specified terms of Indigenous self-determination, Indigenous peoples should focus on "local, indigenous-centered responsibility-based movements."[45] The issue here is that this framing of the political contention and the focalization of political energies towards the institutions of the settler state prevent us from seeing the extent to which the pursuit of self-determination also requires that the focus be directed inwards – on living individually and collectively a self-determining existence.

Similarly, in specifying the legal terms of Indigenous self-determination, there is a further risk that the political imaginary would be limited. Indigenous self-determination is meant to be acknowledged and recognized by the UNDRIP, not created and defined. There is, nevertheless, a risk that Indigenous self-determination may become subjected to its specified legal form, both practically and conceptually. Practically, it may wholly become an object of legal contention and legal decisions. As Matthew Palmer explains with regard to the Treaty of Waitangi, "If the Treaty is outside the law its moral and normative power can continue untouched, as a reference point for political agitation. Inside the law, it becomes an instrument of the legal system and a plaything for lawyers and judges."[46] On this view, in giving legal form to Indigenous self-determination and in implementing the UNDRIP, the law would become the primary vessel for the realization and protection of Indigenous self-determination. It would also grant the law the capacity to resolve contentions about Indigenous self-determination. Furthermore, the terms by which it would be legally specified may risk becoming the complete and whole terms by which it is understood and envisioned, such that Indigenous self-determination may also be conceptually subjected to its legal form; Indigenous social and legal orders should, however, be understood on the basis of their own respective epistemic foundations.[47] Without a transition to strong legal and political pluralism,[48] the current vehicle of state law may not be able to acknowledge these various incommensurable foundations, and it may be limited in what it recognizes and envisions as possible by its own terms of specification.

In sum, the second objection is that the reliance on fundamental legal documents to pursue and secure Indigenous self-determination has the potential to depoliticize Indigenous self-determination. What is objected is the potential of legal constitutional discourses to structure, direct, and limit political conduct, whereas the affirmation of Indigenous peoples' self-determination is meant to empower and broaden their political agency. In implementing the UNDRIP and giving it a fundamental legal form, we appear to disempower Indigenous peoples by limiting their inherent rights to the terms set out in the declaration or, even worse, to those by which the UNDRIP would be implemented. When we combine this with the first objection, we appear to crystalize the inherent rights of Indigenous peoples and to disqualify further contention when the terms by which the declaration is implemented have been met.

These worries are not too far from those expressed by James (Sa'ke'j) Youngblood Henderson:

> Our apprehension was that the colonizing states would attempt to appropriate our inherent rights or dilute them in their attempt to implement our human rights. Inherent human rights belong to the people, not to the will of the sovereign, states or governments. All aspects of our inherent human rights belong to and serve our distinct and diverse knowledge systems,

languages and laws, rather than the artificial settler states or their Eurocentric legal traditions of civil or common law. The Indigenous peoples' view was that none of our human rights affirmed in the conventions and declarations could be delegated to any states or their institutions through consultation and cooperation. They could only be recognized and promoted by the state with our cooperation for the purposes of preventing violence or discrimination against, or assimilation of, Indigenous peoples in our full enjoyment and effective exercise of our humanity.[49]

These considerations were clear for those who help draft the Declaration and, I believe, *are* clear for many of those who today work for its implementation. Indeed, the content of the UNDRIP and how it should be implemented are generally understood in ways that seek to booster the *sui generis* self-determination of Indigenous peoples and avoid this appropriation and dilution by settler states.[50] Yet, I remain concerned that the dynamics of legal constitutionalism that underlie the project of implementation of the UNDRIP and the associated project of seeking fundamental legal protection for Indigenous self-determination may inadvertently lead to precisely this form of appropriation and dilution. This is why I speak of a political irony when I say that the UNDRIP and its implementation may end up limiting the very same inherent rights they seek to protect.

Political Constitutionalism and the Effective Manifestation of Self-Determination

At the core of the objections discussed above are two key concerns. The first is that the specified legal form of the inherent rights affirmed and recognized in the UNDRIP may end up being taken for the complete and full realization of these inherent rights. The second is that the legal venue of implementation may appear as the primary vessel of realization for Indigenous self-determination. These concerns make sense when the relationship between politics and law is theorized following the assumptions I associated with the modern and rationalist mode of political theorizing. On this view, politics is subordinated to law, and law should be a reflection of universally valid norms. Realizing Indigenous self-determination in the context of persistent settler colonialism would mean something akin to implementing a well-defined rational plan rooted in universal moral norms and principles.

To dampen these concerns, we have to move to a distinct understanding of the relationship between law and politics – one that would avoid making Indigenous self-determination the creature and ward of the law. I contend that we need to politicize our understanding of how Indigenous self-determination can be realized and secured, which means that we need an approach to political theorizing that centres political conduct in the task of achieving just relationships. This different conception would see political conduct not as something to be fully structured and directed, but as itself the way to realize and protect self-determination.

The point here is related to the one made by Joshua Nichols in his discussion of "two possible approaches to implementation." As he explains, we can see, on the one hand, implementation as a project of giving legal form to the UNDRIP through "section 35 of the *Constitution Act, 1982*" and thus as a project of specifying the UNDRIP "as [a] set of Charter-like rights." This is what I see as belonging to a legal constitutionalist discourse. On the other hand, we can see implementation "as jurisdictional in nature,"[51] or as consisting in the recognition of distinct, potentially conflicting and overlapping "rights to jurisdiction."[52] On this view, the inherent rights affirmed and recognized by the UNDRIP are not respected through some form of coherent and perfect legal construction but through the effective realization of a nation-to-nation relationship where distinct political entities can engage one another on equal terms in the negotiation of terms of governance and of the terms of their interactions.[53] Centring the recognition of jurisdictions, or political conduct more broadly, as key to the realization of Indigenous self-determination leads to the recognition that its implementation does not entail coherence and order; on the contrary, it entails a complex political order marked by political and legal pluralism, by the centrality of negotiations, and by the potential for agonistic contentions in the affirmation and protection of distinct jurisdictional orders.[54] This understanding of self-determination sees Indigenous self-determination as something effectively manifested through political conduct rather than as something guaranteed by law.

We can centre political conduct in such a way once we recognize that law is the child of politics, not of objective reason. Various theorists working on agonistic politics, such as James Tully[55] and Andrew Schaap,[56] have argued that law is always a partial convention that can never completely and fully account for the complexity of human experience. It is and should always be open for revision and contestation, and, furthermore, the very same terms by which politics is carried out are and should themselves be open for contestation. This entails a change of perspective about what justice consists of. A just political order, rather than being understood as a well-defined and structured political order, should be seen as a negotiated one, sustained by those subject to it. As James Tully has argued, to recognize that laws and political settlements should be the results of negotiations by those subject to them is not to give in to power, but to recognize that a just peace is precisely a negotiated peace.[57] Once this is recognized, we can start appreciating the relevance of seeing self-determination as something that should effectively and concretely be manifested in the continuous structuring and negotiating of political relationships, where the law is subject to these continuous negotiations.

In pursuing this centring of political conduct to the realization and protection of Indigenous self-determination, I contend that we should look to the political constitutionalist discourse.[58] It is, in fact, a central objective of this chapter to invite those engaged in thinking about the UNDRIP and its implementation to consider this constitutional discourse. This is because the understanding of constitutionalism offered by it – and thus the ways in which it allows us to envision implementation – focuses on political conduct and political contentions, as opposed to legal instruments, to secure rights and freedom. Considering the worries raised earlier about fundamental legal instruments, this view of constitutionalism would be less likely to lead to an appropriation and dilution of Indigenous self-determination.

In more detail, political constitutionalism denies that law is independent from politics. It denies that there can be an understanding of rights that is universally accepted and sufficiently detailed to completely structure, limit, and direct the conduct of politics. Following this discourse, fundamental legal instruments seeking to secure rights are not legitimate because rights are, instead, "contestable, political claims" that "should be recognized and labelled as such."[59] Rather than conceiving of a constitution as a fundamental legal instruments, we should start seeing it as the political organization of any civic association that enables claims and conflicts to be made explicit, but also to be negotiated and resolved, and that, through this process, safeguards the political agency of political actors. The constitution is political, as opposed to legal, because rights are not protected through legal instruments but through political institutions and forums that allow political actors to contest, debate, and negotiate. More broadly, the focus of a political constitution is to ensure that governance is under the joint control of those subject to it,[60] through venues that enable their effective political agency as opposed to their formal and legalistically formulated agency.

A political constitution recognizes that political settlements and the terms by which they are achieved are all open for negotiation and contestation:

> Absent a set of fundamental laws, justiciable and enforceable in the courts, that impose restraints on political institutions and the political process more generally, a political constitution is conceived as a direct expression of ordinary political activity operating within and across political institutions. Critically, a political constitution is conceived in a way that makes explicit the possibility of adaptation, and even radical adaptation, through such ordinary, day-to-day political activity.[61]

In sum, political constitutions should be "conceived as institutional mechanisms for preserving the civic freedom of citizens to negotiate different views of rights and justice and reach collective agreements that avoid mutual domination."[62] For those favouring the political constitutionalist discourse, this centring of political agency in the claiming and defining of rights is both how self-determination is enabled and safeguarded.[63]

What this means for Indigenous self-determination is that we should recognize that no constitutional provision seeking to recognize Indigenous self-determination and no term of legal implementation will ever completely account for it. Indigenous self-determination will always exceed, supersede, and transcend any legal form applied to it or seeking to account for it. Indigenous self-determination is not reducible to formalization in law but is something that is realized in practice through the ability of Indigenous peoples to bring terms of governance under their joint control.[64]

Moreover, envisioning the inherent right to self-determination in light of political constitutionalism and agonistic politics means that the law is not the measure of self-determination, but either an outcome of the effective expression of self-determination or a limit set by others on the self-determination of some. This entails that self-determining political entities can always put into question the terms through which political contentions take place, and that they have the authority to bring into question the legal limits imposed on their self-determination. Ultimately, we need to recognize the extent to which conflict is central to the affirmation of self-determination and to the contestation of the terms of self-determination recognized by others. Despite our best efforts at securing political structures for negotiations, conflicts and disagreements are bound to arise. Indeed, as Roger Merino discusses in chapter 5 of this volume, self-determination is often realized and secured through everyday acts of resistance, such that on his view, a decolonizing constitutionalism should not be seen as a rational abstract construction but as an everyday praxis that can take the form of direct actions, such as the "creation of autonomous governments." The potential for conflict in the direct exercise of self-determination is not something to be lamented, for it is a direct consequence of the essence of self-determining entities, which is to ongoingly define and delineate the reach of their authority. As Robert Odawi Porter writes, "A hallmark attribute of the right of self-determination possessed by any people is their ability to interpret the scope of their own authority."[65]

In fact, Porter has clearly argued, through his use of the concept of "tribal disobedience," that the conflicts that may arise around the affirmation of self-determining authority are those most likely to enable and preserve self-determination, more than would any rational, normative, or legal scheme we could implement or conceive. As he explains, tribal disobedience is an advocating strategy that "allows for the preservation and regeneration of uniquely Indigenous conceptions of self-determination."[66] Tribal disobedience is a form of civil disobedience in which Indigenous peoples disobey or transgress some laws of the settler state on the basis of their own understanding of their laws, rights, and authority. For instance, the settler state might affirm its authority to build pipelines on a given territory while Indigenous peoples deny this right and thus refuse to obey injunctions to grant free passage to their land and in place seek to enforce their own injunctions, as we recently observed on the land of the Wet'suwet'en people.[67] Through these actions, Indigenous peoples are not merely opposing and contesting a law or a decision because they disagree with it or do not like it; they are also engaging in the more profound and significant affirmation of their status as self-determining political entities through the affirmation that the laws they are disobeying or transgressing are *ultra vires* and inconsistent or contrary to their own laws.

In disobeying the laws of the settler state on the basis of their own laws, Indigenous peoples are also thereby affirming their own political authority, along with their own *sui generis* understanding of the foundations of their authority,[68] and their own authority to determine the scope of their authority. Their inherent right to self-determination is not seen as something enabled or defined by some external legal instruments but as something coming from within and understood in its own idiom. Their disobedience is both an enactment and the means of safeguarding their self-determining status and their own understanding of their social, legal, and political orders. In sum, self-determination is realized in the affirmation of jurisdiction, which may lead to incommensurable conflict, such as those exemplified by tribal disobedience.[69]

And here we return to where we started this section: the implementation of Indigenous self-determination requires the recognition of distinct overlapping and potentially conflicting jurisdictions, each propped up by its distinct epistemic foundations. My claim is that this recognition makes the most sense when our understanding of constitutionalism moves from the legal to the political, and when we fully acknowledge and accept the centrality of political conduct in the enactment and safeguarding of self-determination.

Conclusion: Politicizing the UNDRIP

As I wrote at the beginning of this chapter, the ways we have been led to think about certain concepts by the intellectual tradition might not be the only or the most useful ways to think about these concepts. More specifically, we generally tend to think of fundamental legal instruments like declarations and constitutions as key to the enactment and safeguarding of rights. On this account, notions like treaty federalism or declarations like the UNDRIP, which are meant to enable the joint governance and interactions of distinct *sui generis* political entities, may end up being conceived as requiring some definite and binding legal implementations. As I argued, the underlying modern and rationalist discourse we can associate with this legal constitutionalist discourse tends to imagine itself as providing a blueprint for the just resolutions of all claims and conflicts, and ultimately to reduce the inherent right of self-determination of Indigenous peoples to its legal form.

In contrast, I have argued that we need to infuse our thinking about Indigenous self-determination with a dose of agonistic politics. This does not mean that there is no room for declarations or fundamental legal documents. It means, rather, that we need to remain conscious of the centrality of politics, and that there often will be no clear and definite answers, including juridically, to political conflicts and contentions between self-determining entities. Allowing political contentions to play a more significant role in our understanding of the enactment and safeguarding of Indigenous self-determination ensures that the legal terms of implementation of the UNDRIP will not be seen as the final and complete terms of Indigenous self-determination, precisely because it acknowledges the fundamental indeterminacy of treaty federalism and of the UNDRIP. Furthermore, it also ensures that we will remain conscious that any rational scheme of implementation we can come up with will always be transcended by Indigenous self-determination.

NOTES

1. UN General Assembly, United Nations Declaration on the Rights of Indigenous Peoples (UNDRIP), 2 October 2007, A/RES/61/295.
2. UN Department of Economic and Social Affairs, "United Nations Declaration on the Rights of Indigenous Peoples," accessed 12 May 2023, https://www.un.org/development/desa/indigenouspeoples/declaration-on-the-rights-of-indigenous-peoples.html, para 2.
3. Quentin Skinner, *Liberty before Liberalism* (Cambridge: Cambridge University Press, 1998), 116. On critical political theorizing, see James Tully, *Public Philosophy in a New Key*, vol. 1, *Democracy and Civic Freedom* (Cambridge: Cambridge University Press, 2008), 16–17.
4. The actual limiting effect of Article 46 is questionable. See Paul Joffe, "Self-Determination and Territorial Integrity," Assembly of First Nations, 11 October 2020, https://www.afn.ca/wp-content/uploads/2020/11/Joffe_paper_ENG.pdf.
5. Thanks to Elaine Coburn for emphasizing this.
6. UN Department of Economic and Social Affairs, "United Nations Declaration on the Rights of Indigenous Peoples," para 2.
7. UN General Assembly, Universal Declaration of Human Rights, 10 December 1948, A/RES/217(III), https://www.un.org/en/universal-declaration-human-rights.
8. Kerry Wilkins's discussion of various challenges in making the UNDRIP enforceable against the Crown helps to clarify why domestic implementation is generally seen as requiring constitutional implementation: statutory rights do not have the same binding legal implications on the rest of the legal system as constitutional ones and as such are not constraining enough. See Kerry Wilkins, "Strategizing UNDRIP Implementation: Some Fundamentals," in *UNDRIP Implementation: More Reflections on the Braiding of International, Domestic and Indigenous Laws* (Waterloo, ON: Centre for International Governance Innovation, 2018), 121.
9. Andrei Marmor, "Are Constitutions Legitimate?," *Canadian Journal of Law and Jurisprudence* 20, no. 1 (2007): 71–2.
10. John Laws, "Law and Democracy," *Public Law* (1995): 72–93.
11. Marmor, "Are Constitutions Legitimate?," 70.
12. Richard Bellamy, *Political Constitutionalism: A Republican Defence of the Constitutionality of Democracy* (Cambridge: Cambridge University Press, 2007), 3.
13. Grégoire C.N. Webber, *The Negotiable Constitution: On the Limitations of Rights* (Cambridge: Cambridge University Press, 2009), 1; Cass R. Sunstein, "Incompletely Theorized Agreements," *Harvard Law Review* 108, no. 7 (May 1995): 1733–72, https://doi.org/10.2307/1341816.

14 This is why, for instance, John Laws can write the following: "Such principles are not matters of policy. They are logically prior to the institution of democratic government. The constitutional role of the courts is to act as their guardians." John Laws, "The Constitution: Morals and Rights," *Public Law* (1996): 629.
15 The account I offer builds on prevalent views about legal constitutionalism and is distinctively modern. Those who prefer other accounts of legal constitutionalism, drawing from other traditions, can at least recognize that the issues I raise apply to the modern account presented. Graham Gee and Grégoire C.N. Webber, "What Is a Political Constitution?," *Oxford Journal of Legal Studies* 30, no. 2 (Summer 2010): 284, https://doi.org/10.1093/ojls/gqq013.
16 As explained by James Tully, "propositions which play the hinge role in a society – of being presupposed by and legitimising its routine way of political and economic life – are relatively immune from direct criticism. They are background norms of the daily operation and criticism of the institutions and practices, not objects of criticism – the riverbed, not the river." James Tully, "The Struggles of Indigenous Peoples for and of Freedom," in *Political Theory and the Rights of Indigenous Peoples*, ed. Duncan Ivison, Paul Patton, and Will Sanders (Cambridge: Cambridge University Press, 2000), 58. On challenging hinge propositions, see chapter 9 by Robert Hamilton in this volume.
17 For similar reasons, and due to their unwritten features, the Constitutions of the UK and of New Zealand, for instance, have sometimes been presented as examples of political constitutions.
18 Michael J. Perry, *The Political Morality of Liberal Democracy* (Cambridge: Cambridge University Press, 2010), 161.
19 Yann Allard-Tremblay, "The Modern and the Political Pluralist Perspectives on Political Authorities," *The Review of Politics* 80, no. 4 (Fall 2018): 675–700, https://doi.org/10.1017/S0034670518000517.
20 Richard Day, "Who Is This We That Gives the Gift? Native American Political Theory and the Western Tradition," *Critical Horizons* 2, no. 2 (2001): 188, https://doi.org/10.1163/156851601760001300.
21 Ibid., 183.
22 This does not mean that federalism is entirely excluded, but it is an exception to the paradigmatic and ideal case that needs to be justified.
23 James Tully, *Strange Multiplicity: Constitutionalism in an Age of Diversity* (Cambridge: Cambridge University Press, 1995), 84.
24 Thomas Hobbes, *Leviathan; or, the Matter, Forme, and Power of a Common Wealth Ecclesiasticall and Civill* (London: Andrew Crooke, 1651), chap. 29.
25 Tully, *Strange Multiplicity*, 41.

26 Michael Joseph Oakeshott, *Rationalism in Politics and Other Essays* (London: Hertford and Harlow, 1962).
27 Ibid., 5–6.
28 As Elaine Coburn pointed out to me, the UNDRIP might be rejected by rationalism since it seeks to elaborate what universal human rights require in the *imperfect* circumstances of settler colonialism. In a sense this is accurate. But rationalism is an idealized account of modes of political theorizing; in practice, political discourses will vary in how they exemplify the features of rationalism. I am not claiming that the UNDRIP perfectly exemplifies rationalism – only that the features associated with rationalism can be read in the political discourse surrounding the UNDRIP.
29 Bellamy, *Political Constitutionalism*, 146.
30 I recognize how the UNDRIP can also be read as requiring a strong form of legal pluralism where its implementation would need to be the result of negotiations. In that sense, the UNDRIP may not entirely depoliticize (as the objections discussed below argue) the relationship between Indigenous peoples and the state. See Gordon Christie, "Indigenous Legal Orders, Canadian Law and UNDRIP," in *UNDRIP Implementation: Braiding International, Domestic and Indigenous Laws* (Waterloo, ON: Centre for International Governance Innovation, 2017), 48.

   This pluralism, however, is limited and does not extend to the UNDRIP itself, which is still conceived in light of a universal morality: "like all human rights, self-determination derives from common conceptions about the essential nature of human beings, and it accordingly applies universally and equally to all segments of humanity. Third, as a human right, self-determination cannot be viewed in isolation from other human rights norms, but rather must be reconciled with and understood as part of the broader universe of values and prescriptions that constitute the modern human rights regime." James S. Anaya, "Self-Determination as a Collective Human Right under Contemporary International Law," in *Operationalizing the Right of Indigenous Peoples to Self-Determination*, ed. Pekka Aikio and Martin Scheinin (Turku, FI: Institute for Human Rights, Åbo Akademi University, 2000), 5–6.
31 Patrick Wolfe, "Settler Colonialism and the Elimination of the Native," *Journal of Genocide Research* 8, no. 4 (2006): 388, https://doi.org/10.1080/14623520601056240.
32 Nick Estes, *Our History Is the Future: Standing Rock versus the Dakota Access Pipeline, and the Long Tradition of Indigenous Resistance* (London: Verso, 2019), 89.
33 David T. McNab, "Herman Merivale and Colonial Office Indian Policy in the Mid-Nineteenth Century," *The Canadian Journal of Native Studies* 1, no. 2 (1981): 280.

34 *Delgamuukw v. British Columbia*, [1997] 3 SCR 1010; *R. v. Van der Peet*, [1996] SCR 507.
35 Elizabeth Strakosch and Alissa Macoun, "The Vanishing Endpoint of Settler Colonialism," *Arena Journal* 38–39 (January 2012): 40–62.
36 Ibid., 42.
37 Ibid., 52.
38 Martin Papillon, "Adapting Federalism: Indigenous Governance in Canada and the United States," *Publius: The Journal of Federalism* 42, no. 2 (2011): 302. See also Christopher Alcantara and Greg Whitfield, "Aboriginal Self-Government through Constitutional Design: A Survey of Fourteen Aboriginal Constitutions in Canada," *Journal of Canadian Studies* 44, no. 2 (Spring 2010): 130, https://doi.org/10.3138/jcs.44.2.122.
39 Glen Sean Coulthard, *Red Skin, White Masks: Rejecting the Colonial Politics of Recognition* (Minneapolis: University of Minnesota Press, 2014).
40 Jeff Corntassel, "Toward Sustainable Self-Determination: Rethinking the Contemporary Indigenous-Rights Discourse," *Alternatives: Global, Local, Political* 33, no. 1 (2008): 105–32, https://doi.org/10.1177/030437540 803300106; "Re-envisioning Resurgence: Indigenous Pathways to Decolonization and Sustainable Self-Determination," *Decolonization: Indigeneity, Education, and Society* 1, no. 1 (2012): 86–101.
41 Hayden King, "The Problem with 'Indigenous Peoples': Re-considering International Indigenous Rights Activism," in *More Will Sing Their Way to Freedom: Indigenous Resistance and Resurgence*, ed. Elaine Coburn (Winnipeg: Fernwood Publishing, 2015), 176.
42 UNDRIP, preamble.
43 See Kiera Ladner, "Proceed with Caution: Reflections on Resurgence and Reconciliation," in *Resurgence and Reconciliation: Indigenous–Settler Relations and Earth Teachings*, ed. Michael Asch, John Borrows, and James Tully (Toronto: University of Toronto Press, 2018), 245.
44 Corntassel, "Toward Sustainable Self-Determination," 122.
45 Ibid., 122.
46 Matthew S.R. Palmer, "Constitutional Realism about Constitutional Protection: Indigenous Rights under a Judicialized and a Politicized Constitution," *Dalhousie Law Journal* 29, no. 1 (2006): 31.
47 James (Sa'ke'j) Youngblood Henderson, "Ayukpachi: Empowering Aboriginal Thought," in *Reclaiming Indigenous Voice and Vision*, ed. Marie Battiste (Vancouver: UBC Press, 2000), 248; Kiera Ladner, "Up the Creek: Fishing for a New Constitutional Order," *Canadian Journal of Political Science* 38, no. 4 (December 2005): 923–53, https://doi.org/10.1017/S0008423905040539; "Governing within an Ecological Context: Creating an Alternative Understanding of Siiksikaawa Governance," *Studies in Political Economy* 70, no. 1 (2003): 125–50.

48 Christie, "Indigenous Legal Orders."
49 James (Sa'ke'j) Youngblood Henderson, "The Art of Braiding Indigenous Peoples' Inherent Human Rights into the Law of Nation-States," in *UNDRIP Implementation: Braiding International, Domestic and Indigenous Laws* (Waterloo, ON: Centre for International Governance Innovation, 2017), 14.
50 See the Centre for International Governance Innovation's two special reports on the UNDRIP implementation: *UNDRIP Implementation: Braiding International, Domestic and Indigenous Laws* (Waterloo, ON: Centre for International Governance Innovation, 2017); and *UNDRIP Implementation: More Reflections on the Braiding of International, Domestic and Indigenous Laws* (Waterloo, ON: Centre for International Governance Innovation, 2018). See also the contributions in the present volume.
51 Joshua Nichols, "UNDRIP and the Move to the Nation-to-Nation Relationship," in *UNDRIP Implementation: More Reflections on the Braiding of International, Domestic and Indigenous Laws* (Waterloo, ON: Centre for International Governance Innovation, 2018), 96.
52 Ibid., 99.
53 See chapter 1 in this volume by James (Sa'ke'j) Youngblood Henderson on treaty federalism.
54 See Ladner, "Up the Creek," 924; Shiri Pasternak, *Grounded Authority: The Algonquins of Barriere Lake against the State* (Minneapolis: University of Minnesota Press, 2017).
55 Tully, *Strange Multiplicity*.
56 Andrew Schaap, "The Absurd Proposition of Aboriginal Sovereignty," in *Law and Agonistic Politics*, ed. Andrew Schaap (Burlington, VT: Ashgate Publishing Company, 2009), 209.
57 Tully, *Strange Multiplicity*, 211.
58 Bellamy, *Political Constitutionalism*; Gee and Webber, "What Is a Political Constitution?"
59 Gee and Webber, "What Is a Political Constitution?," 279.
60 James Tully, *On Global Citizenship: James Tully in Dialogue* (London: Bloomsbury, 2014).
61 Gee and Webber, "What Is a Political Constitution?," 288.
62 Richard Bellamy, "Constitutive Citizenship versus Constitutional Rights: Republican Reflections on the EU Charter and the Human Rights Act," in *Sceptical Essays on Human Rights*, ed. Tom Campbell, K.D. Ewing, and Adam Tomkins (Oxford: Oxford University Press, 2001), 16; *Political Constitutionalism*, 8.
63 Legal and political constitutionalism lead to different institutional mechanisms and opportunities that can be associated with distinctive goods. These goods can be balanced against one another: for instance,

some may favour the finality of decisions afforded by judicial review despite its partial depoliticization of right claims. This is a well-trodden debate, and it should not detain us. In turning to political constitutionalism, the essential point I am making is that the goods secured by legal constitutionalism should not be confused with self-determination.

64 Accordingly, we should see in a positive light the suggestion made by Robert Hamilton in chapter 9 of this volume: that constitutionalism and federalism should be thought of in a dialogical and dialectical manner.
65 Robert Odawi Porter, "Tribal Disobedience," *Texas Journal of Civil Liberties and Civil Rights* 11 (2006): 284.
66 Ibid., 172.
67 Unist'ot'en Camp, "No Pipelines," Unist'ot'en: Heal the People, Heal the Land, 2017, https://unistoten.camp/no-pipelines. On similar "tribal disobedience" against the Dakota Access Pipeline, see Estes, *Our History*. See also Pasternak, *Grounded Authority*.
68 See Ladner, "Governing"; Wahpimaskwasis (Little White Bear) and Janice Alison Makokis, "Nehiyaw iskwew kiskinowâtasinahikewina – paminisowin namôya tipeyimisowin: Learning Self Determination through the Sacred," *Canadian Woman Studies/Les Cahiers de la Femme* 26, no. 3 (2008): 39–51.
69 Tribal disobedience may be met by repressive violence from the settler state. Though not a safe conduit for Indigenous self-determination, this use of force may nevertheless serve to lay bare the illegitimate foundations of settler colonialism and its reliance on unmediated violent imposition.

5 A Theory of Decolonial Constitutionalism: Insights from Latin America

ROGER MERINO

Introduction

Indigenous self-determination is the basis of the current international infrastructure of Indigenous rights, which include, among others, the 2007 United Nations Declaration on the Rights of Indigenous Peoples (UNDRIP), the 2016 American Declaration on the Rights of Indigenous Peoples, the International Labour Organization (ILO) Convention 169 of 1989, and landmark decisions of international tribunals such as the Inter-American Court of Human Rights. Indigenous self-determination has challenged classical views of state sovereignty[1] and has meant advances in titling of Indigenous land; the implementation of the free, prior, and informed consent standard; and the respect of Indigenous cultures and traditional knowledge.

However, the recognition of Indigenous self-determination has not meant meaningful transformations of governmental structures since states still monopolize power over Indigenous territories and subsoil resources. Under national sovereignty, nation states still adhere to free trade agreements that liberalize Indigenous territories as free areas for exploitation. They enact laws for promoting transnational investments in extractive industries and infrastructure within Indigenous land. They create protected areas that exclude Indigenous groups. In the end, these measures produce new social conflicts and disputes on the meaning of self-determination in the Global North and the Global South.

In Latin America, scholars have discussed how multicultural and plurinational constitutions recognize some degrees of autonomy to Indigenous peoples.[2] In common law countries, the emerging field of Indigenous, postcolonial, or tribal constitutionalism[3] starts from the premise that Indigenous nations possess a set of precolonial principles, values, and laws that sustains self-government. From these perspectives, by practising their own ancestral traditions, Indigenous nations are constitutionalists[4] and negotiate their incorporation into state constitutional arrangements. These perspectives highlight Indigenous constitutional practices and interactions with state institutions, although further reflections are needed on the potential of plurinational political projects to reconfigure state structures and the limitations to Indigenous aspirations posed by the political economy of resource extraction.

This chapter delineates a theory of decolonial constitutionalism to enlarge our understanding of constitutionalism from Indigenous perspectives, including those factors missed in the current literature: the political economy and Indigenous political aspirations expressed in everyday social struggles. By critically dialoguing with the Marxist critique of the political economy and the critique of modernity by postcolonial studies, Latin American social scientists and philosophers have formulated "decolonial theory."[5] In this theory, the colonization of the Americas inaugurated a pattern of power dynamics based on two global processes: a global process of labelling (the creation of Indigenous, Black, and mestizo identities as inferiors to European white identities), and a global process of accumulation (the exploitation of labour and extraction of raw material from the South to the North). These two global processes have survived in postcolonial nation states even though Indigenous peoples are legally conceived as equals citizens with cultural rights. Thus, formal colonialism no longer exists, but the power dynamics subjacent to colonial logics remain under what is called "coloniality of power."[6] In this context, state sovereignty over natural resources has meant the power of the state to grant the exploitation of raw materials to transnational corporations, which have massively expanded their activities over Indigenous territories and natural ecosystems. Legal provisions allow the state to remove Indigenous populations by exception and repress them if opposing to massive resource extraction.

A decolonial approach to constitutional theory allows for a critical assessment of current constitutional frameworks for Indigenous rights' recognition. This entails unravelling the patterns of colonial continuities in legal forms and discourses and acknowledging the structural limitations to make Indigenous jurisdiction effective. These limitations relate to the extractive political economy complemented by racialized state forms and approaches to Indigenous peoples that allow repression, displacement, pollution, or marginalization. A decolonial approach also allows re-elaborating the meaning of self-determination. The analysis of everyday practices of resistance as a form of reimagining and transforming constitutional structures allows exploring the building of plurinationality as an unfinished struggle to re-enact self-determination as a foundational right able to push a new constitutional consensus.

Latin America provides an inspiring field of analysis because this region has advanced in innovative ways the institutionalization of Indigenous self-determination in recent years. Most Latin American constitutions and legal frameworks recognize some degree of autonomy and collective territorial rights for Indigenous peoples. Two Latin American countries – Bolivia and Ecuador – are the first in the world to implement a state model of plurinationalism based on Indigenous perspectives. However, the region is still the site of massive protests around territorial rights and the meaning and scope of Indigenous self-determination. Based on the analysis of constitutional texts, legal instruments, and official reports, as well as official and Indigenous movements' declarations around social conflicts in Peru, Colombia, Bolivia, and Ecuador, this chapter problematizes current understandings of Indigenous constitutionalism and delineates a decolonial approach to constitutional theory.

Varieties of Indigenous Constitutionalism

In Latin America, socio-legal theory focuses on Indigenous peoples mainly under the scholarly sub-field of legal pluralism, as the recognition of Indigenous peoples' own legal systems within nation states.[7] Most discussions on legal pluralism have not deepened the implications of Indigenous rights' recognition for legal and constitutional structural changes and, on the contrary, have reinforced the idea that Indigenous rights must be accommodated within the constitutional structures of liberal multiculturalism.

Classical approaches in Latin America thus engage with a "weak" version of legal pluralism, conceiving Indigenous law as traditional or consuetudinary law, a second-level source of law that governments recognize within the specific territorial boundaries inhabited by Indigenous communities. These communities might solve conflicts of interests over these specific territorial jurisdictions, but when their consuetudinary norms contradict the "official law," the state denies Indigenous norms and practices or deploys paternalistic measures, such as the exoneration of criminal responsibility for culturally conditioned criminal offences. Another practical consequence of this approach is that Indigenous authority over their own territory is very limited. States advance extractive and infrastructure projects over Indigenous territories appealing to the "national interest," and Indigenous communities are simply consulted as stakeholders or participants, not as owners of the land.

Recent approaches to legal pluralism in the region focus on the power dynamics among systems of law to define legality and illegality. In this view, formal law and those systems based on legal pluralism (including global standards and Indigenous law) generate fragmented and overlapping sovereignties, which are both *de jure* and *de facto*, legal and illegal.[8] As a consequence, the key socio-legal problem in the region is not how to "accommodate" Indigenous law within petrified state structures, but how to rethink and re-elaborate the foundational idea of sovereignty over the whole territory.

Constitutional theory has not engaged with this critical approach to legal pluralism when addressing the constitutional transformations in Ecuador (2008) and Bolivia (2009). Constitutional scholars conceive of those constitutions as the expression of the "New Latin American Constitutionalism." Many include within this term comprehensive constitutional reforms of the 1980s and the first half of the 1990s, as well as the constitutions born from the "Left turn" since the end of the 1990s.[9] The term thus includes both multicultural and plurinational constitutions, although they are very different.

Multicultural constitutions such as the Constitutions of Colombia (1991) and Peru (1993) designate their respective countries as "pluricultural" and, apart from a long list of standard civil and political rights, incorporate environmental and cultural rights and explicit provisions for the respect of ethnic minorities and their customs and autonomy within their collective land. All these provisions coexist with strong free market principles, including explicit provisions to protect property rights, freedom of contract, and international investor's rights. Plurinational constitutions, such as the ones of Ecuador (2008) and Bolivia (2009), designate their respective countries as plurinational and Indigenous peoples as Indigenous nations rather than ethnic minorities. Indigenous land entitlements are not recognized as collective property under civil law provisions but as Indigenous territories inserted in the territorial governance of the state. In the case of Bolivia, it has also entailed the redistribution of political power by establishing designated seats for Indigenous representation in the Congress and the Constitutional Court. In the case of Ecuador, the Constitution incorporates strong environmental provisions, including the rights of Mother Earth. In both cases, plurinationalism coexists with strong post–neo-liberal principles, establishing a robust role of the state for regulating and limiting the free market economy.

Most authors agree that plurinational constitutions question the dominant forms of legal knowledge and consider seriously Indigenous peoples.[10] Rubén Martínez Dalmau considers that both constitutional texts have a popular basis and have contributed to improving the living conditions of their respective societies, but with weak democratic control, becoming a kind of populist constitutionalism.[11] Other authors focus on specific achievements of the new constitutions. For Mauricio Garcia Villegas, these are "aspirational constitutions" full of proclaims and social compromises.[12] Roberto Gargarella questions how power organization in both constitutional texts still relies on classic elitist and authoritarian structures of the liberal–conservative consensus in which Latin American republics were born.[13] First, their organic part (power distribution section) still relies on power structures politically concentrated and territorially centralized. Second, their dogmatic part (rights section) still declares a large, generous, and robust list of rights. In this view, whereas Bolivian and Ecuadorian Constitutions have enlarged the right's section, they would have not substantially transformed the organic part.

The debate about Indigenous constitutionalism in Latin America has focused on the constitutional texts or specific constitutional outcomes achieved in plurinational experiences. Less attention has been paid to the relationship between Indigenous politics and constitutional practice and change, and how structural conditions establish limitations to plurinational projects. This perspective risks also neglecting Indigenous constitutional practices where no plurinational constitutions have been yet enacted, such as in Peru, Chile, or Colombia.

In common law, an important branch of literature has another perspective on Indigenous constitutionalism. The focus is not on constitutional texts but on the specific constitutional practices of Indigenous peoples and the interactions between Indigenous self-determination and legal techniques deployed by the state to incorporate Indigenous groups into the state governance. In this view, constitutionalism is deeply embedded in long-standing Indigenous understandings of social organization; therefore, most Indigenous nations, by entangling their constitutional structures with their broader lifeways, are constitutionalists.[14] Before European invasion, Indigenous peoples governed their territories and, although they did not have written constitutions, shared a group of principles or values that gave stable shape to a polity, organized the processes of governing, and recognized a distribution of rights and duties. The organization and exercise of authority typically rested on a body of law, unwritten but known, shared, and transmitted orally from generation to generation, that ordered processes of decision-making and both individual and collective action.[15]

As Indigenous peoples possess distinct legal traditions, even more clearly defined when measured against European and colonially derived constitutional law,[16] they struggle to regain self-governing power over their lands, communities, and affairs. In the process, they face the organizational legacies of colonialism, in particular, the institutional mechanisms established by national governments. Different legal techniques of incorporation, such as the tribal governing systems in the United States (established under the *Indian Reorganization Act* of 1934) or the governing structures over the First Nations in Canada (established by the *Indian Act* of 1876), were impositions that reflected Western expectations, needs, and convenience.[17] The juridification of what Westerners conceived of as "native customs" rather than "native laws" was ultimately controlled by state bureaucrats and did not express Indigenous self-constitution.[18]

In fact, today the different means of recognition have severe limitations. In Australia, New Zealand, and Canada, Indigenous nations are obliged to prepare written constitutions or codes as a condition of the granting of official status. In these experiences, the so-called tribal constitutionalism requires the accommodation within the regulatory frame of the state for the operation of tribal jurisdictions, but the extent of tribal formal authority varies across the countries. As Kirsty Gover notes, North American tribes "govern bounded reserved lands ('reserves' in Canada, and 'reservations' in the United States) and are able to control access to, and residence on, tribal territory. This is not the case for Australian and New Zealand tribes, whose jurisdictions are defined by reference to the boundaries of their traditional territories, but whose governance authority is narrowly confined to the management of tribal property" from the settlement of historic land claims.[19]

The challenge for Indigenous nations, then, is to give new meanings to current legal and constitutional arrangements.[20] This entails rethinking the constitutional pillars of the countries in which they live, including their conceptions of sovereignty. This does not mean that Indigenous constitutional views are static or that they advocate the revival of precolonial arrangements; rather, Indigenous constitutionalism and governance is fluent, relational, and an unfinished work. Indigenous constitutional arrangements continued to develop after Europeans contact and keep renewing today.[21]

In both Latin American and common law experiences, what most Indigenous peoples aim to achieve by using current arrangements or proposing new institutions is self-determination. This political goal does not mean, in general, the creation of new states. There are of course some exceptions, such as the radical proposals of the Native American scholar Ward Churchill, who calls for the constitution of an Indian Nation independent from the United States, or the radical proposals of the Indigenous leader Felipe Quispe in Bolivia for the constitution of an independent Aymara Nation. However, most academic and political proposals range from some degree of autonomy through administrative decentralization within a dominant nation, such as the model of multicultural constitutionalism, to political projects that recognize Indigenous nations within the state, such as the project of multinational federations,[22] treaty federalism,[23] or the plurinational state of Bolivia and Ecuador.

However, the right to self-determination continues to be undertheorized by the different versions of Indigenous constitutionalism. Self-determination is often understood through the way it has been recognized in constitutional texts or legal techniques of incorporation. Less attention has been put on the theoretical and empirical implications of truly recognizing Indigenous jurisdiction. This entails conceiving self-determination not simply as a collective right to govern specific land units but as a sovereignty principle able to reconfigure the state's territorial governance and the distribution of political power within the country. Conceiving of self-determination in these terms also obliges us to reflect on the challenges of implementing such ambitious arrangements. Particularly important in this regard is the role of the political economy of resource extraction in conditioning and limiting the transformative potential of Indigenous sovereign aspirations to govern their territories. A more detailed focus on Latin American processes of constitutional transformation will assist in reconceptualizing self-determination as the basis of another constitutional paradigm.

Indigenous Rights in Latin America: The Constitutional Challenge

Latin American countries achieved independence from the Spanish and Portuguese Empires in the first quarter of the nineteenth century. The huge Indigenous population was a challenge for the *criollo* national elites who tried to build a European-inspired nation state.[24] These elites promoted policies for either assimilation or exclusion, which implied forced conversion to Christianity, compulsory use of Spanish, or physical genocide.[25] National elites also appealed to international law to legally support this process by using racialized standards of civilization to claim being part of the international community while denying native legalities.[26]

Agrarian reforms in the region between the 1950s and 1960s for the first time recognized Indigenous peoples as political agents, but this process gave them socio-economic rights under a peasant identity, not as autonomous Indigenous nations.[27] The ILO Convention 107 of 1957 consolidated this trend by promoting the inclusion of Indigenous peoples within the larger society through education and economic assistance.[28]

The second half of the twentieth century also saw the growth of international Indigenous organizations. Peasant unions in Left-oriented governments, ethnic federations in the Amazon, and Indian movements, mainly in Bolivia,[29] used the concept of self-determination as the material basis of statehood[30] since it was key in international politics for African decolonization[31] and within the United Nations Charter.[32] In 1960, the UN General Assembly adopted the Declaration on the Granting of Independence to Colonial Countries and Peoples,[33] conceiving of self-determination as a right to independence from a colonial authority.[34]

The international community nuanced this notion of self-determination in the following years by differentiating between external and internal self-determination: the former as a right to independence and the latter as a right to maintain some degrees of autonomy under the nation-state authority.[35] Even though Indigenous peoples struggled for a broad recognition of self-determination as included in Article 3 of the UNDRIP of 2007,[36] Articles 4 and 46.1 seem to refer to internal self-determination.[37] These articles were added after the conclusion of negotiations as a way to ensure the UNDRIP had a chance of passing a vote at the General Assembly. Internal self-determination excludes more comprehensive notions of "indigenous sovereignty"[38] as parallel sovereignty to that of the state.[39] Rather than being rooted in a decolonial framework based on resistance to colonization, it is based on the human rights framework under the paradigm of the unitary nation state.[40] It consolidates, then, the multicultural state, which recognizes the "autonomy" of Indigenous communities as ethnic minorities.

In the late 1980s, constitutions in the region started to become multicultural[41] with the growing importance of ILO Convention 169, decisions by the Inter-American Court of Human Rights, and the soft law of global institutions such as the World Bank, the Inter-American Development Bank, the World Intellectual Property Organization, and various UN offices, forums, and programs.[42] Global institutions concerned with persistent poverty in the region also started recording the size of the Indigenous population. Recent data shows between 42 to 45 million Indigenous persons in the region, representing an estimated 8 to 12 per cent of the total population.[43]

Multicultural constitutions incorporated Indigenous collective rights, including land rights, customary norms, language rights,[44] and some degree of autonomy (limited territorial control and systems of justice). These constitutions recognized the cultural diversity in Latin American countries but had no real incidence in state territorial governance and power relations. For example, these constitutions did not establish provisions for Indigenous representation in their respective parliaments or territorial rights over entire Indigenous jurisdictions and their resources. Rather, they recognize Indigenous peoples as ethnic minorities that should be "tolerated." Indigenous collectives are only able to govern themselves within the boundaries of limited land units and are subjected to the use of the land by the state on behalf of the "national interest." In practice, this has meant the imposition of extractive and infrastructure projects within Indigenous territories.

Multicultural Constitutionalism in Peru and Colombia

Peru and Colombia each possess a multicultural constitutional framework and a neo-liberal political economy. Both recognize Indigenous rights under legal arrangements inspired by colonial institutions: the community in Peru and the *resguardo* in Colombia. In both cases as well, Indigenous organizations struggle to enlarge their rights and obtain more degrees of self-determination vis-à-vis the expansion of extractive and infrastructure projects.

In Peru, 25 per cent of the population considers themselves as having Indigenous origins.[45] The state officially recognizes fifty-five groups of Indigenous peoples, fifty-one from the Amazon and four from the Andes,[46] which are legally organized in 3,029 peasant communities and 2,558 native communities. Legislation and the political Constitution of 1993 recognize the "autonomy" of these communities and their land rights (as collective property), cultural norms, and jurisdiction (power to solve internal disputes within their collective land). No formal definition of Indigenous territory or Indigenous peoples exists in the Constitution. This omission is important because the notion of "community" is very different from that of "peoples."

The communities are the expression of the colonial legal arrangement known as *reducciones*, which served to organize Indigenous groups for taxing, forced work, and religious indoctrination during Spanish colonization. These arrangements, however, also helped Indigenous subjects maintain their cultural identities and cultural norms. The 1920 Constitution for the first time recognized these peoples as "indigenous communities" with the aim of reducing social unrest in the highlands against Spanish descendants who were landowners of huge extensions of land (*hacendados*). The state, however, did not eliminate the abuses of *hacendados* in the Andes and in the Amazon; for example, it not only allowed but also promoted the rubber industry, which enslaved and tortured hundreds of Indigenous groups. Years later, the military government in the 1960s and 1970s recognized land rights to ancestral peoples as peasant communities (in the Andes) and native communities (in the Amazon). The subjacent idea was that the term "indigenous" or "Indian" was derogatory; the government also held the view that these groups had to be modernized. In the Andes, it was held that the Indians should become peasant cooperatives that contribute to the national economy. The legislation only kept the term "native" for those Indigenous peoples of the Amazon, a region considered an inhospitable territory.

The multiculturalism of the 1990s kept the terms peasant and native communities and granted protection to communal property, but this property does not include the forest, rivers, or subsoil resources, which are subjected to the "national interest" as understood by national elites. The community is, moreover, an institutional arrangement that does not recognize the character of nation of ancestral peoples. This is a private law institution even regulated in the Civil Code. For this reason, when the Right to Prior Consultation Law (Law No. 29785) was enacted in 2011, including for the first time in Peruvian legislation the term "Indigenous peoples," many refused to consider peasant communities as Indigenous.

The Right to Prior Consultation saw the creation of a Database of Indigenous Peoples and triggered a bunch of pro-Indigenous policies, such as intercultural health and education, and a language rights legal regime. Indigenous peoples, however, keep struggling to defend their rights. As more than 4,000 communities lack collective property titles,[47] and those with title have not been able to stop the expansion of extractive activities in their territories, Indigenous organizations are pursuing two strategies: demanding more consultations and land rights through litigation and mobilization, and exerting direct autonomy. The first strategy entails engaging with formal institutions such as litigation at the Courts of Justice, administrative petitions, or attendance at national and international forums. The second strategy is exemplified by the creation of autonomous governments, such as the Wampis Nation. This Amazonian people declared in 2017 to be the first autonomous government in Peru. The Wampis are governed by their own statute – what they consider their own political constitution that defines their ancestral territory, government structure, the election of their representatives, and development goals, among other things. Other Amazonian peoples are enacting their own institutional arrangements to be recognized as autonomous, although the state has not taken any steps to formally recognize this type of autonomy.

In Colombia, the 2018 national census found that 4.4 per cent of the population (1,905,617 inhabitants) is Indigenous and they belong to one of the 115 Indigenous peoples of the country.[48] They are organized in Indigenous *resguardos*. The *resguardos* have colonial origins as they were created by the Spanish Crown between the end of the sixteenth and beginning of the seventeenth centuries. The aim of creating these territorial units was to control Indigenous forced work and taxation and, in general, to manage the Indigenous population. Unlike previous colonial legal models, such as *reducciones*, the *resguardos* allowed Indigenous peoples to keep their land and organize themselves through *cabildos*, or popular elections, in which they elected their leaders.

Colombian legislation (Decreto 2164/1995) defines *resguardos* as special legal and socio-political institutions formed by one or more Indigenous communities holding a collective property title to possess and govern their territory. The National Agency of Land states that by April 2019 there were 767 Indigenous *resguardos* occupying 32,653 hectares. However, there are pending many petitions for recognizing or enlarging *resguardos*, and Indigenous organizations accuse authorities of privileging the formalization of oil blocks and other economic activities. *Resguardos* also overlap with protected areas since 53.4 per cent of the tropical forests are located in Indigenous territories.[49]

The political Constitution of 1991 recognized territorial rights to "ethnic groups," including within this category to Indigenous peoples, Black communities, Afro-descendants, *raizales*, *Palenqueras*, and the Rom people (Directiva Presidencial 01/2010). Communal land and *resguardos* cannot be sold (Art. 63) and are granted in perpetuity as territorial entities (Art. 286). They have, then, the autonomy to be governed by their own authorities and to manage their own resources (Art. 287) through councils created and operated according to their own traditions (Art. 330). These rights have been reinforced and expanded by the Constitutional Court in landmark decisions.[50]

The government's decision to expand Indigenous lands through *resguardos* over almost 30 per cent of the country's territory was a pragmatic policy to delegate governance over remote regions. It did not derive from multicultural provisions but rather, in the first place, from state failures of expanding the agricultural frontier and commoditizing land, and second, from the failure of governmental entities to win the international "war on drugs" and combat guerrilla groups.[51] This strategy of control also fostered the assimilation of Indigenous peoples and lands into a model of economic development based on resource extraction. Natural resources, including subsoil resources, are controlled by the state (Arts. 102 and 332). Under neo-liberal multiculturalism, the government is not there to provide funds or social services, but to help strengthen the capacity of Indigenous authorities to provide these services themselves.[52]

As a result, the multicultural constitutional regimen has not challenged the prioritization of extractive activities. Colombian governments have also designed policies, plans, and programs aimed at positioning Colombia as a "mining country." Mineral exports reached US$39 billion between 2000 and 2009, and between 2004 and 2011 the number of mining claims rose from 2,056 to 5,903. Many Indigenous communities have conflicts with mining companies exploiting strategic mining areas approved by the executive branch. Indigenous peoples Arhuaco, Kogui, Wiwa, and Kankuamo from Sierra Nevada of Santa Marta initiated protests in December 2017 against 132 mining titles granted over their ancestral territory, despite the Constitutional Court (decision T-766/2015) stating that it is compulsory to make prior consultation with Indigenous communities when mining activities are intended to be developed in their territories. Similar conflicts emerged with the oil industry, such as the long judicial and social dispute between EcoPetrol and the U'wa people.[53]

As in the case of Peru, Indigenous leaders from Colombia subverted a colonial legal institution, making this a means to fortify their identities around their rights to territory, initiating processes of land recovery, collective organization, and the construction of Indigenous authority over an important part of the country.[54] As in Peru as well, Indigenous organizations have included within their claims tenure security[55] but also legal arrangements that overcome current *resguardo* legality, such as the recognition of "ancestral territories."[56]

In Peru and Colombia, multicultural constitutionalism has recognized cultural rights but at the same time has legitimized state interventions within Indigenous territories. Indigenous aspirations to be recognized as sovereigns over their ancestral territories seek to transcend current multicultural arrangements.

Plurinational Constitutionalism in Bolivia and Ecuador

To overcome neo-liberal multiculturalism, the Ecuadorian Constitution of 2008 and the Bolivian Constitution of 2009 have constitutionalized a state model of plurinationalism. By transforming the state's multilevel governance through territorial rearrangements and (in Bolivia) also by granting Indigenous peoples representation in the legislative branch and the Constitutional Court, plurinationalism seeks to remove the foundations of a historically racialized state.

However, classical notions of property, resources, and national interest coexist with plurinational proclamations in both constitutions. In Ecuador, the Indigenous population accounts for 8 per cent of the total population.[57] The 2008 Constitution fostered by the Left-oriented government of Rafael Correa was the first in the world to grant rights to nature or Mother Earth (*Pachamama*) and establish plurinationality as a state model. The Constitution conceives of nature as a subject of specific rights, such as conservation and restauration (Arts. 71 and 72). Under the principle of plurinationality, Indigenous nations have the right to communal property and to possess their ancestral territories (Art. 57), which are included within the political-administrative organization of the country as Indigenous Territorial Circumscriptions (Art. 242). These are special regimes of decentralized autonomous governments that manage ancestral territories. Ecuador subnational units (*parroquias*, *cantones*, and provinces) formed mostly by Indigenous communities might adopt this special regimen after a referendum approved by at least two-thirds of the valid votes of the electoral registry of the circumscription. The criterion for delimiting territories responds not to the boundaries of ancestral territories but to the formal administrative frontiers established by the state.

Moreover, the Constitution states that natural resources, subsoil resources, and biodiversity pertain to the state and are exclusively managed by the central government (Arts. 1, 261, and 317). In addition, the state completely controls strategic sectors such as energy sources, natural resources, hydrocarbons, biodiversity, and water (Art. 313). This framework promotes extractive activities under a Western notion of resources that conflicts with the rights of nature and Indigenous territorial rights.

Therefore, the development model inspired in Indigenous *cosmovisions* of *buen vivir* coexists with classical developmental strategies. For example, the state has the latent power to exploit resources on behalf of the national interest. The Constitution states that Ecuador is free of genetically modified organisms (GMOs) but, by exception and on behalf of the national interest alleged by the president and approved by the National Assembly, GMOs might be introduced (Art. 401). Similarly, extractive activities of non-removable resources in protected areas are prohibited, but, by exception, these resources might be exploited if proposed by the president and if the National Assembly declares it of national interest. This conflicts with the plurinational character of the state (Art. 1).

Conflicts around the Yasuní National Park in the Amazon, a 982,000-hectare area in which the Huaroni possess their ancestral territory, illustrate this situation. The government of former president Rafael Correa estimated that the park possessed 920 million barrels of oil, but instead of exploiting hydrocarbons, in 2007 Correa proposed the Yasuní Initiative before the United Nations. In exchange for fighting climate change by strictly protecting the park's biodiversity, the Ecuadorian government asked for $3.6 billion in compensation from the international community over twelve years. However, arguing lack of international support, the government gave up the Yasuní Initiative in 2013 and approved investments for $18.3 million.[58] The civil society collective Yasunidos denounced the government's decision, citing that six oil blocks operate in around 79 per cent of the park, harming biodiversity and risking the survival of Indigenous peoples in voluntary isolation.[59]

Mining expansion has also triggered strong resistance from Indigenous communities.[60] For example, in 2012 the Proyecto Mirador, located in the south of the Cordillera del Condor, was tendered for thirty years to EcuaCorriente S.A., a mining company of Chinese capitals, for a project of large-scale open-pit copper and gold extraction. This project was not subjected to a prior consultation even though it overlaps territories of Shuar and Kichwas peoples.[61] Indigenous organizations also denounced EcuaCorriente for blackmailing locals into selling their land and has claimed that the company uses the police to criminalize Indigenous leaders.

Bolivia has followed a similar path. The last national census found that the Indigenous population has reached 47.7 per cent of the total population. The government of the first Indigenous president of the country, the Aymara Evo Morales, fostered the approval of the 2009 Constitution, which establishes the plurinational, social, and unitarian nature of the state (Art. 1). Consequently, it recognizes ancestral territories and self-determination to Indigenous nations (Arts. 2 and 30) and rights over the natural resources of their territories (Arts. 30.6 and 403).

The Bolivian Constitution and the Autonomy and Decentralization Framework Law of 2010 establish that municipalities might become First Peoples' Peasant Autonomies through the majority vote of the local population in a referendum. Two or more converted municipalities might also become Regional Indigenous Autonomies. These processes, however, apply only to rural Indigenous communities, which by some estimations represent half of the total Indigenous population.[62]

Moreover, autonomies' boundaries remain the same as those of the municipalities already created.[63] As in the case of Ecuador, the legal framework does not respect precolonial territorial frontiers, which cover areas much larger than contemporary municipalities, but restricts Indigenous autonomies to much smaller areas based on formal state boundaries.[64]

At the same time, the constitutional regimen establishes that natural resources pertain to the Bolivian people, are administered by the state, and are strategic and of public interest (Art. 348). It also promotes the industrialization of natural resources to overcome the dependency of raw material exports. In general, the Constitution states that all economic activity must contribute to fortifying the country's economic sovereignty (Art. 312). Thus, as national sovereignty is invoked to justify extractivist and infrastructural projects,[65] plurinationality becomes more an aspiration than a concrete practice.

The conflict around an infrastructure project over the ecological area Isiboro Sécure National Park and Indigenous Territory (TIPNIS) is illustrative. The project, funded by the Brazilian Development Bank, intended to build a highway over the TIPNIS to connect the Cochabamba tropics to the Brazilian border, fostering trade with Brazil and increasing the prosperity of lowland peoples. Opponents of the project argued that the highway would generate significant environmental impacts. Other local Indigenous communities defended the project because it would bring access to cities, markets, and public services. This shows how national narratives of autonomy and sovereignty have different local articulations to Indigenous communities.[66]

Because of the conflict, national Indigenous organizations once allied with the government started opposing President Morales. They promoted the first march in 2011, obtaining international attention because of the strong police repression. Protestors received massive support when they arrived in La Paz, and Morales declared the park a protected area (untouchable) and ordered an ex post facto consultation on the project. The consultation process, which was strongly criticized for not providing enough information to the communities, ended with the approval of the highway. However, conflicts continued with accusations of leaders' co-optation by the government party and the creation of parallel organizations, and the government accusing protesters of being obstacles to national development.[67]

These conflicts explain an intrinsic tension in Bolivian and Ecuadorian experiences: on the one hand, plurinational governments try to unify the people around the "national interest" of developing extractive industries and infrastructure projects; and on the other, they attempt to recognize ethno-political differences that often challenge the transnational exploitation of local resources. Because these governments depend heavily on extractive industries such as oil and gas production and mining, they formulate a discourse of "nationalism" based on the argument that revenues derived from extractive exploitation are crucial for economic development and justified by the interest of "the nation." This, ultimately, perpetuates the practical existence of the nation-state model.[68]

A Theory of Decolonial Constitutionalism

The Constitutions of Bolivia and Ecuador contain promises for decolonizing the state. These promises are ineffective not because no changes or attempts at changes in the formal distribution of political power exist in both texts. They both include constitutional provisions for restructuring the state territorial governance and, in Bolivia, a criterion of proportional representation of Indigenous peoples in the Parliament (Art. 146) and the Constitutional Court (Art. 197.1). Rather, these promises are ineffective because power still materially depends on the political economy of resource extraction. This political economy has not been removed from the basis of constitutional regimens and makes them share with the Peruvian and Colombian constitutional frameworks the intrinsic tension between exalting social inclusion as a major political goal and expanding extractive activities that often affect the natural environment and Indigenous territories.

This tension has colonial roots. After liberalizing from colonial powers, national elites built a racialized nation state and continued subalternazing Indigenous populations by subjecting them to two options: (1) be included in the legal, political, and socio-cultural logic of a European-inspired state, losing territorial and self-determination rights but gaining formal citizenship and property entitlements; or (2) be excluded from the nation state by being subjected to slavery, deprivation, and genocide. Some countries prioritized either inclusion or exclusion. For instance, Argentina, Brazil, and Chile openly excluded their Indigenous populations. In those countries where Indigenous populations occupied large areas of the territory, such as in Peru, Bolivia, and Ecuador, national elites fostered both inclusion and exclusion at different moments depending on political and social conditions.[69]

This paradox remains active in today's legal and social relationships between Indigenous peoples and the state. On the one hand, the state promises social inclusion by granting Indigenous peoples rights to collective property titles, intercultural health, and education. On the other hand, Indigenous peoples live in constant material deprivation and abandonment until an extractive or infrastructure project based on the national interest is planned in the area. At this moment, consultation arrangements are aimed at legitimizing the projects, and when opposition continues, Indigenous protestors are criminalized and their rights suspended under state of emergency decrees.

A theory of decolonial constitutionalism must address this inclusion/exclusion paradox by enlarging our understanding of constitutional processes beyond legal texts. The constitutional ontology must include everyday struggles of Indigenous nations for decolonizing the matrix of extractive power. When indigenous movements oppose state policies and projects or decide to practise direct autonomy in their territories, they are exerting constitutional-making processes beyond the nation state. When they recur to national and international litigation to claim for consultation and land rights, they are using the liberal legal system as a vehicle to struggle for self-determination. This is a struggle in the (liberal) law and beyond the (liberal) law.

By limiting Indigenous constitutionalism to legal outcomes, scholars focus on the extension of so-called cultural, social, or economic rights, such as titling of collective land and language rights, among others. Under a human rights discourse, each "constitutional moment" or tensions and conflictive interaction between the state and Indigenous peoples is solved by the incorporation of further "fundamental rights" in constitutional and legal texts, most of them aligned with the needs for participation in economic and public affairs.

This view of Indigenous constitutionalism obscures the struggle for recognizing "foundational rights," a type of rights that needs socio-economic structural transformation, not solely the granting of social rights or even political representation. Empirically, foundational rights entail the recognition of the right to territory and self-determination; consequently, they call for transforming current constitutional structures and territorial governance, reconfiguring the ownership of natural resources, and ensuring Indigenous power of decision at all state levels. Theoretically, foundational rights aim at transcending the inclusion/exclusion paradox; they are the basis of a whole legal, political, and economic system rooted in non-Western ontologies and epistemologies.[70]

Foundational rights break the logic of rights recognition under national and international Western and liberal systems. For example, self-determination and territoriality support the right of free, prior, and informed consent not as a "right to veto," because it does not derive from a special power in the democratic and liberal system (as is the case with the presidential veto power), but as an expression of Indigenous peoples' self-determination as nations. Self-determination also supports the right to use and obtain direct benefits from the land, and the right of peoples to establish their own views of development, among others. They are different from new Indigenous rights that have been recognized in the last decades by international standards.[71] Many of these new rights build on Western logic: the right of consultation (Arts. 6(1), 6(2), and 15(2) of ILO Convention 169) assumes, for example, that affecting Indigenous territories is unavoidable, and it is therefore important to collect the communities' opinion; the right to participate in economic benefits obtained by extractive industries (Art. 15(2) of ILO Convention 169) assumes that companies are exploiting (or are going to exploit anyway) Indigenous territories. This does not mean that there is not some recognition of foundational rights at the international level (e.g., the ILO Convention 169 timidly recognizes the right to territory, and the UNDRIP recognizes a weak version of the right of self-determination), or that many Indigenous peoples might not engage strategically with the discourse and practice of the new rights (such as consultation and economic benefits). But it does mean that foundational rights are crucial to understanding Indigenous political aspirations.

Under a decolonial approach to constitutionalism, the first step to recognize foundational rights is the explicit inclusion of the character of nations of Indigenous peoples in constitutional provisions. But nominally transforming the state into a plurinational state with Indigenous nations and territorial rights is not enough. The transformation needs to establish concrete measures to rebuild Indigenous territories and provide practical governance over them beyond the "national interest." This means addressing the political economy of resource extraction, the factor missed in the Bolivian and Ecuadorian constitutional experiences.

Therefore, constitutional theory needs to engage with both social struggles and the national and global political economy if it wishes to grasp the possibilities and limitations of Indigenous self-determination. To decolonize constitutional structures, it is crucial to imagine (and struggle for) an alternative future where Indigenous lives and territories are not subjected to transnational economic processes.

NOTES

1 Steven Wheatley, "Conceptualizing the Authority of the Sovereign State over Indigenous Peoples," *Leiden Journal of International Law* 27, no. 2 (June 2014): 371–96, https://doi.org/10.1017/S092215651300037X;

Federico Lenzerini, "Sovereignty Revisited: International Law and Parallel Sovereignty of Indigenous Peoples," *Texas International Law Journal* 42 (2006–7): 155–83; Jeff J. Corntassel and Tomas Hopkins Primeau, "Indigenous 'Sovereignty' and International Law: Revised Strategies for Pursuing 'Self-Determination,'" *Human Rights Quarterly* 17, no. 2 (May 1995): 343–65, https://doi.org/10.1353/hrq.1995.0015.

2 David Bilchitz, "Constitutionalism, the Global South, and Economic Justice," in *Constitutionalism of the Global South: The Activist Tribunals of India, South Africa, and Colombia*, ed. Daniel Bonilla Maldonado (Cambridge: Cambridge University Press, 2013), 41–94; Daniel Bonilla Maldonado, "Introduction: Toward a Constitutionalism of the Global South," in *Constitutionalism of the Global South: The Activist Tribunals of India, South Africa, and Colombia*, ed. Daniel Bonilla Maldonado (Cambridge: Cambridge University Press, 2013), 1–40; Felipe Curcó Cobos, "The New Latin American Constitutionalism: A Critical Review in the Context of Neo-Constitutionalism," *Canadian Journal of Latin American and Caribbean Studies* 43, no. 2 (2018): 212–30, https://doi.org/10.1080/08263663.2018.1456141; Antonio Carlos Wolkmer and Samuel Radaelli, "Refundación de la Teoría Constitucional Latinoamericana: Pluralidad y Descolonización," *Derechos y Libertades* 37 (June 2017): 31–50, https://doi.org/10.14679/1046; Rodrigo Uprimny, "The Recent Transformation of Constitutional Law in Latin America: Trends and Challenges," *Texas Law Review* 89 (2011): 1586–609.

3 John Borrows, "Indigenous Constitutionalism: Pre-existing Legal Genealogies in Canada," in *The Oxford Handbook of the Canadian Constitution*, ed. Peter Oliver, Patrick Macklem, and Nathalie Des Rosiers (Oxford: Oxford University Press, 2017), 13–44, https://doi.org/10.1093/law/9780190664817.003.0002; *Freedom and Indigenous Constitutionalism* (Toronto: University of Toronto Press, 2016); Pranoto Iskandar, "Indigenizing Constitutionalism: A Critical Reading of 'Asian Constitutionalism,'" *Oxford University Comparative Law Forum* 2 (2017); Kirsty Gover, *Tribal Constitutionalism: States, Tribes, and the Governance of Membership* (Oxford: Oxford University Press, 2010), 67–107; Duncan Ivison, "Decolonising the Rule of Law: Mabo's Case and Postcolonial Constitutionalism," *Oxford Journal of Legal Studies* 17, no. 2 (1997): 252–79.

4 Stephen Cornell, "'Wolves Have a Constitution': Continuities in Indigenous Self-Government," *The International Indigenous Policy Journal* 6, no. 1 (2015), https://doi.org/10.18584/iipj.2015.6.1.8.

5 Anibal Quijano and Michael Ennis, "Coloniality of Power, Eurocentrism, and Latin America," *Neplanta* 1, no. 3 (2000): 533–80; Enrique Dussel, *1492 – El encubrimiento del otro: Hacia el origen del mito de la modernidad* (La Paz: Plural Editores, 1994); Walter D. Mignolo, *The Darker Side of*

Western Modernity: Global Futures, Decolonial Options (Durham, NC: Duke University Press, 2011).
6 Quijano and Ennis, "Coloniality of Power."
7 Sally Engle Merry, "Legal Pluralism," *Law and Society Review* 22, no. 5 (1988): 869–96, https://doi.org/10.2307/3053638; Marcela Velasco, "Multiculturalism, Legal Pluralism and Local Government in Colombia: Indigenous Autonomy and Institutional Embeddedness in Karmata Rúa, Antioquia," *Journal of Latin American Studies* 50, no. 3 (August 2018): 517–47, https://doi.org/10.1017/S0022216X17001183; Rachel Sieder and Anna Barrera, "Women and Legal Pluralism: Lessons from Indigenous Governance Systems in the Andes," *Journal of Latin American Studies* 49, no. 3 (August 2017): 633–58, https://doi.org/10.1017/S0022216X16002273.
8 Rachel Sieder, "Legal Pluralism and Fragmented Sovereignties: Legality and Illegality in Latin America," in *The Handbook of Law and Society in Latin America*, ed. Rachel Sieder, Karina Ansolabehere, and Tatiana Alfonso (New York: Routledge, 2019), 51–65.
9 Bilchitz, "Constitutionalism"; Bonilla Maldonado, "Introduction"; Curcó Cobos, "New Latin American Constitutionalism"; Wolkmer and Radaelli, "Refundación"; Uprimny, "Recent Transformation."
10 Ramiro Ávila Santamaría, *La utopía del oprimido: Los derechos de la Pachamama (naturaleza) y el Sumak Kawsay (Buen Vivir) en el pensamiento crítico, el Derecho y la Literatura* (Mexico City: Akal, 2019); Daniel Bonilla Maldonado, "El constitucionalismo radical ambiental y la diversidad cultural en América Latina: Los derechos de la naturaleza y el buen vivir en Ecuador y Bolivia," *Revista Derecho del Estado* 42 (2019): 3–23.
11 Rubén Martínez Dalmau, "¿Han funcionado las Constituciones del nuevo constitucionalismo latinoamericano?," *Revista Derecho & Sociedad* 51 (2018): 191–205.
12 Mauricio García Villegas, "Constitucionalismo aspiracional," *Araucaria: Revista Iberoamericana de Filosofía, Política y Humanidades* 15, no. 29 (2013): 77–97.
13 Roberto Gargarella, "Sobre el 'Nuevo Constitucionalismo Latinoamericano,'" *Revista Uruguaya de Ciencia Política* 27, no. 1 (2018): 109–29.
14 Cornell, "Wolves"; Borrows, "Indigenous Constitutionalism."
15 Cornell, "Wolves," 4.
16 Borrows, "Indigenous Constitutionalism," 15.
17 Cornell, "Wolves," 9.
18 Gover, *Tribal Constitutionalism*, 80–104.
19 Ibid., 104.
20 Cornell, "Wolves," 13.
21 Borrows, "Indigenous Constitutionalism," 38.
22 For James Tully, the dominant constitutional system that emphasizes the unity of nation states should be supplemented by a project of just

recognition through multinational federations. Tully finds that the Western common law system can serve as a model for a federal system that includes Indigenous nations, since prior to colonization, Indigenous populations were formed by political units that negotiated among themselves the access and entitlement to resources. James Tully, *Strange Multiplicity: Constitutionalism in an Age of Diversity* (Cambridge: Cambridge University Press, 1995).

23 See chapter 1 by James (Sa'ke'j) Youngblood Henderson in this volume.

24 J. Fernando Galindo, "Cultural Diversity in Bolivia: From Liberal Interculturalism to Indigenous Modernity," in *The Sustainability of Cultural Diversity: Nations, Cities and Organizations*, ed. Maddy Jassens, Myriam Bechtoldt, Arie de Ruijter, Dino Pinelli, Diovanni Prarolo, and Vanja M.K. Stenius (Cheltenham, UK: Edward Elgar, 2010), 110–25; Rodolfo Stavenhagen, "Challenging the Nation-State in Latin America," *Journal of International Affairs* 45, no. 2 (Winter 1992): 421–40, https://www.jstor.org/stable/24357364; Felipe Arocena, "Multiculturalism in Brazil, Bolivia and Peru," *Race & Class* 49, no. 4 (April 2008): 1–21, https://doi.org/10.1177/0306396808089284.

25 Douglas Sanders, "The UN Working Group on Indigenous Populations," *Human Rights Quarterly* 11, no. 3 (1989): 406–33, https://doi.org/10.2307/762100.

26 Liliana Obregón, "Between Civilisation and Barbarism: Creole Interventions in International Law," *Third World Quarterly* 27, no. 5 (2006): 815–32, https://www.jstor.org/stable/4017780; Luis Eslava, Michael Fakhri, and Vasuki Nesiah, "Introduction: The Spirit of Bandung," in *Bandung, Global History and International Law: Critical Pasts and Pending Futures*, ed. Luis Eslava, Michael Fakhri, and Vasuki Nesiah (Cambridge: Cambridge University Press, 2017), 3–31; Jorge Esquirol, "Alejandro Álvarez's Latin American Law: A Question of Identity," *Leiden Journal of International Law* 19, no. 4 (December 2006): 931–56, https://doi.org/10.1017/S0922156506003700; Carl Landauer, "A Latin American in Paris: Alejandro Álvarez's *Le droit international américain*," *Leiden Journal of International Law* 19, no. 4 (December 2006): 957–81, https://doi.org/10.1017/S0922156506003712; Stavenhagen, "Challenging the Nation-State."

27 Arocena, "Multiculturalism."

28 Sanders, "UN Working Group"; Dean B. Suagee, "Human Rights of Indigenous Peoples: Will the United States Rise to the Occasion?," *American Indian Law Review* 21, no. 2 (1997): 365–90; Elsa Stamatopoulou, "Indigenous Peoples and the United Nations: Human Rights as a Developing Dynamic," *Human Rights Quarterly* 16, no. 1 (February 1994): 58–81, https://doi.org/10.2307/762411; R. Pitty, "Indigenous Peoples, Self-Determination and International Law," *The International Journal of Human Rights* 5, no. 4 (2001): 44–71, https://doi.org/10.1080/714003733.

29 Richard Smith, "Lo transnacional, instrumento y desafío para los pueblos indígenas," in *Los indígenas amazónicos suben al escenario internacional: Reflexiones sobre el accidentado camino recorrido*, ed. Françoise Morinand and Roberto Santana (Ecuador: Abya-Yala, 2003), 203–42.
30 Daniel Philpott, "In Defense of Self-Determination," *Ethics* 105, no. 2 (January 1995): 352–85, https://doi.org/10.1086/293704; Abdulgaffar Peang-meth, "The Rights of Indigenous Peoples and Their Fight for Self-Determination," *World Affairs* 164, no. 3 (Winter 2002): 101–14, https://www.jstor.org/stable/20672633.
31 Rose Parfitt and Matthew Craven, "Statehood, Self-Determination and Recognition," in *International Law*, ed. Malcolm D. Evans, 3rd ed. (Oxford: Oxford University Press, 2018), 203–51.
32 Val Napoleon, "Aboriginal Self Determination: Individual Self and Collective Selves," *Atlantis* 29, no. 2 (2005): 1–21.
33 UN General Assembly, United Nations Declaration on the Granting of Independence to Colonial Countries and Peoples, 14 December 1960, A/RES/1514(XV).
34 Andrea Muehlebach, "What Self in Self-Determination? Notes from the Frontiers of Transnational Indigenous Activism," *Identities: Global Studies in Culture and Power* 10, no. 2 (2003): 241–68, https://doi.org/10.1080/10702890304329.
35 Paul Oldham and Miriam Anne Frank, "'We the Peoples…': The United Nations Declaration on the Rights of Indigenous People," *Anthropology Today* 24, no. 2 (2008): 5–9; Stavenhagen, "Challenging the Nation-State"; Stefania Errico, "The Draft UN Declaration on the Rights of Indigenous Peoples: An Overview," *Human Rights Law Review* 7, no. 4 (August 2007): 741–55, https://doi.org/10.1093/hrlr/ngm023 .
36 Article 3: "Indigenous peoples have the right to self-determination. By virtue of that right they freely determine their political status and freely pursue their economic, social and cultural development."
37 Article 4: "Indigenous peoples, in exercising their right to self-determination, have the right to autonomy or self-government in matters relating to their internal and local affairs, as well as ways and means for financing their autonomous functions."

  Article 46(1): "Nothing in this Declaration may be interpreted as implying for any State, people, group or person any right to engage in any activity or to perform any act contrary to the Charter of the United Nations or construed as authorizing or encouraging any action which would dismember or impair, totally or in part, the territorial integrity or political unity of sovereign and independent States."
38 Wheatley, "Conceptualizing the Authority," 377.
39 Lenzerini, "Sovereignty Revisited," 155–83.

40 Karen Engle, "On Fragile Architecture: The UN Declaration on the Rights of Indigenous Peoples in the Context of Human Rights," *European Journal of International Law* 22, no. 1 (February 2011): 141–63, https://doi.org/10.1093/ejil/chr019; Peter Fitzpatrick, "Necessary Fictions: Indigenous Claims and the Humanity of Rights," *Journal of Postcolonial Writing* 46, no. 5 (2010): 446–56, https://doi.org/10.1080/17449855.2010.517045; Roger Merino, "Law and Politics of Indigenous Self-Determination: The Meaning of the Right to Prior Consultation," in *Indigenous Peoples as Subjects of International Law*, ed. Irene Watson (London: Routledge, 2017), 120–40.

41 The constitutions enacted included those of Brazil (1988), Colombia (1991), Paraguay (1992), Peru (1993), Guatemala (1993), Bolivia (1995), Ecuador (1998), and Venezuela (1999), whereas Mexico (1992) and Argentina (1994) made significant constitutional reforms. Rachel Sieder, ed., *Multiculturalism in Latin America: Indigenous Rights, Diversity and Democracy* (New York: Palgrave Macmillan 2002).

42 S. James Anaya, "International Human Rights and Indigenous Peoples: The Move Toward the Multicultural State," *Arizona Journal of International and Comparative Law* 21, no. 1 (2004): 13–61.

43 World Bank, *Indigenous Latin America in the Twenty-First Century* (Washington, DC: World Bank Group, 2015); International Work Group for Indigenous Affairs (IWGIA), *The Indigenous World 2016* (Copenhagen: IWGIA, 2016); United Nations Economic Commission for Latin America and the Caribbean (ECLAC), *Guaranteeing Indigenous People's Rights in Latin America* (Santiago, CL: ECLAC, 2014).

44 Lynn Horton, "Contesting State Multiculturalisms: Indigenous Land Struggles in Eastern Panama," *Journal of Latin American Studies* 38, no. 4 (2006): 829–58.

45 Instituto Nacional de Estadística e Informática (INEI), *Perú: Perfil Sociodemográfico – Informe nacional* (Lima: INEI, 2018).

46 Ministerio de Cultura (MINCUL), *Indigenous and Native Peoples of Peru* (Lima: MINCUL, 2020).

47 Instituto del Bien Común (IBC), *Tierras Comunales: Más que preservar el pasado el asegurarse el futuro. El estado de las comunidades indígenas en el Perú* (Lima: IBC and Territorios Seguros para las Comunidades del Perú, 2016).

48 National Administrative Department of Statistics (DANE), *Población Indígena de Colombia: Resultados del Censo Nacional de Población y Vivienda 2018* (Bogotá: DANE, 2019).

49 Departamento Nacional de Planeación (DNP) de Colombia, *Plan Nacional de Desarrollo 2018–2022* (Bogotá: DNP, 2019).

50 Constitutional Court of Colombia, decision T-693/2011 on the rights that include territorial governance; decision SU-123/2018 on the rights over the territory resources.

51 Pablo Rueda-Saiz, "Indigenous Autonomy in Colombia: State-Building Processes and Multiculturalism," *Global Constitutionalism* 6, no. 2 (2017): 265–97.
52 Ibid.
53 David Hill, "Colombian Tribe Scores 'Historic' Victory versus Big Gas," *The Guardian*, 26 March 2015, https://www.theguardian.com/environment/andes-to-the-amazon/2015/mar/26/colombian-tribe-scores-historic-victory-versus-big-gas; German Gomez, "Los U´was No Quieren a Ecopetrol en sus Territorios Ancestrales," *El Espectador*, 18 July 2016, https://www.elespectador.com/economia/los-uwas-no-quieren-a-ecopetrol-en-sus-territorios-ancestrales-article-644102.
54 Rueda-Saiz, "Indigenous Autonomy."
55 Organización Nacional de los Pueblos Indígenas de la Amazonia Colombiana (OPIAC), "Los Pueblos indígenas y un PND 2018–2022 Justo," 11 February 2019, https://www.ambienteysociedad.org.co/los-pueblos-indigenas-y-un-pnd-2018-2022-justo.
56 Interview with Kasokaku Busintana, "No hablamos de resguardo, sino de territorio ancestral," *Semana*, 21 October 2011, https://www.semana.com/enfoque/enfoque-principal/articulo/no-hablamos-resguardo-sino-territorio-ancestral/248249-3.
57 Secretaría Nacional de Planificación y Desarrollo (SENPLANDES), *Ecuador: Informe nacional sobre el avance en la implementación del consenso de Montevideo sobre población y desarrollo* (2017).
58 "Correa: 'El mundo nos ha fallado' con Yasuní," BBC Mundo, 16 August 2013, https://www.bbc.com/mundo/ultimas_noticias/2013/08/130815_ultnot_ecuador_correa_yasuni_mena_lav.
59 Yasunidos, "Preguntas frecuentes," accessed June 2018, https://sitio.yasunidos.org/es/yasunidos/preguntas-frecuentes.
60 Murat Arsel, "Between 'Marx and Markets'? The State, the 'Left Turn' and Nature in Ecuador," *Tijdschrift voor Economische en Sociale Geografie* 103, no. 2 (2012): 150–63, https://doi.org/10.1111/j.1467-9663.2012.00709.x; Anthony Bebbington, "The New Extraction: Rewriting the Political Ecology of the Andes?," *NACLA Report on the Americas* 5, no. 42 (2009): 12–40, https://doi.org/10.1080/10714839.2009.11722221; Matt Finer, Clinton N. Jenkins, Stuart L. Pimm, Brian Keane, and Carl Ross, "Oil and Gas Projects in the Western Amazon: Threats to Wilderness, Biodiversity, and Indigenous Peoples," *Plos One* 3, no. 8 (August 2008): 1–9, https://doi.org/10.1371/journal.pone.0002932.
61 Milton López, "Ecuador: Pueblo indígena Shuar exige respeto a consulta previa en proyectos mineros," Observatorio de Conflictos Mineros de América Latina (OCMAL), 24 March 2017, https://www.ocmal.org

/ecuador-pueblo-indigena-shuar-exige-respeto-a-consulta-previa-en-proyectos-mineros.
62 Benjamen Franklen Gussen, "A Comparative Analysis of Constitutional Recognition of Aboriginal Peoples," *Melbourne University Law Review* 40 (2017): 867–904.
63 Jason Tockman and John Cameron, "Indigenous Autonomy and the Contradictions of Plurinationalism in Bolivia," *Latin American Politics and Society* 56, no. 3 (2014): 46–69, https://doi.org/10.1111/j.1548-2456.2014.00239.x; Edwin Cruz Rodríguez, "Redefiniendo la nacion: Luchas indígenas y Estado Plurinacional en Ecuador (1990–2008)," *Nomadas: Revista Crítica de Ciencias Sociales y Jurídicas* (2013): 469–91.
64 Tockman and Cameron, "Indigenous Autonomy."
65 Nancy Postero, *The Indigenous State: Race, Politics, and Performance in Plurinational Bolivia* (Oakland: University of California Press, 2017).
66 Nancy Postero, "Indigenous Development in Latin America," in *The Routledge Handbook of Latin American Development*, ed. Julie Cupples, Marcela Palomina-Schalsch, and Manuel Prieto (London: Routledge, 2018), 43–53.
67 Ibid.
68 Roger Merino, "Reimagining the Nation-State: Indigenous Peoples and the Making of Plurinationalism in Latin America," *Leiden Journal of International Law* 31, no. 4 (December 2018): 773–92, https://doi.org/10.1017/S0922156518000389.
69 Roger Merino, "An Alternative to 'Alternative Development'? *Buen vivir* and Human Development in Andean Countries," *Oxford Development Studies* 44, no. 3 (2016): 271–86, https://doi.org/10.1080/13600818.2016.1144733.
70 Ibid.
71 Ibid.

6 The UNDRIP, the Treaty of Waitangi, and the Developing Constitution of Aotearoa New Zealand

CARWYN JONES

Introduction

As the settlement of historical claims based on breaches of the Treaty of Waitangi are concluded, attention in Aotearoa New Zealand is now turning to the role that the Treaty of Waitangi ought to play in further developing constitutional relationships. There exists significant potential to transform the constitution of Aotearoa New Zealand so that it gives effect to the relationship established by the Treaty of Waitangi. The United Nations Declaration on the Rights of Indigenous Peoples (UNDRIP) is an increasingly important component of the Treaty of Waitangi discourse in Aotearoa and can be used to support a shift to constitutional relationships based on the treaty partnership and principles of Māori constitutional thought and practice. The Treaty of Waitangi claims settlement process illustrates some of the potential that exists to rethink the Māori–Crown relationship and implement a partnership based on mutual recognition and respect for different spheres of authority, akin to a federal model, but framed by a treaty relationship.

There are two main parts to this chapter. The first part examines the role of Te Tiriti o Waitangi (the Treaty of Waitangi) in framing the Indigenous rights discourse in Aotearoa New Zealand. This includes the role of Te Tiriti in the constitution of Aotearoa New Zealand and the development and application of "Treaty principles," particularly through the Waitangi Tribunal process established to inquire into breaches of those principles. The interpretation and implementation of Treaty principles has been criticized by some scholars as watering down the terms of Te Tiriti itself.[1] However, if these principles are understood within the context of the Māori legal order and international recognition of Indigenous rights, it is possible to perceive potential for restructuring the Māori–Crown relationship to transcend the Treaty principles framework and rebuild a just treaty partnership.

The second part of the chapter considers the role of the UNDRIP in that restructuring and rebuilding. The UNDRIP is increasingly being deployed to strengthen and expand upon rights in the Treaty of Waitangi, and linking the UNDRIP to Treaty of Waitangi rights in the context of constitutional reform is particularly significant. Some important developments in the Treaty of Waitangi claims settlement process suggest that the use of the UNDRIP to enhance the constitutional dimension of these settlements may provide a significant opportunity to positively restructure the relationship between *iwi* (Māori nations) and the New Zealand state.

Constitutional Framework of Aotearoa New Zealand

Aotearoa New Zealand is formally a unitary state, and its institutions are not oriented towards federalism. However, the discussion of Māori rights and Te Tiriti o Waitangi has always engaged deeply with ideas of pluralism, coexisting sovereignties, and multiple spheres of authority. In this section, I outline some key aspects of Aotearoa New Zealand's constitutional framework to sketch the basic backdrop against which this discussion of Indigenous rights plays out. This framework presents both opportunities and challenges for recasting the constitutional relationship between the many Māori nations and the New Zealand state.

The Cabinet Manual provides a useful summary of the main features of New Zealand's constitution:

> The New Zealand constitution is to be found in formal legal documents, in decisions of the courts, and in practices (some of which are described as conventions). It reflects and establishes that New Zealand is a constitutional monarchy, that it has a parliamentary system of government, and that it is a democracy. It increasingly reflects the fact that the Treaty of Waitangi is regarded as a founding document of government in New Zealand. The constitution must also be seen in its international context, because New Zealand governmental institutions must increasingly have regard to international obligations and standards.[2]

Aotearoa New Zealand has a highly centralized system of government. It does not have a federal system, having abolished provincial government in 1876,[3] though there remains a system of local government with city, district, and regional councils delegated functions and authority by statute. Legislative authority is further concentrated in New Zealand's unicameral Parliament. The Legislative Council, which had previously operated as the upper house of the New Zealand Parliament, was abolished in 1951.[4] Since that time, the House of Representatives has been the sole legislative chamber.

New Zealand is also one of the few countries in the world that does not have a written constitution. Many aspects of New Zealand's constitution exist in a written form, including Te Tiriti o Waitangi, which is addressed in more detail below. New Zealand also has the *Constitution Act, 1986* and the *Bill of Rights Act, 1990*, although neither of these operate as supreme law. Other legislation includes constitutional matters, such as the *Electoral Act, 1993*, which includes provisions relating to voting and representation, some of which are entrenched (requiring a supermajority of MPs to amend). Since 1996, MPs have been elected under a system of proportional representation known as the Mixed Member Proportional system, or MMP. The introduction of MMP has had a significant impact on political representation and governing arrangements.

Te Tiriti o Waitangi (The Treaty of Waitangi)

Te Tiriti o Waitangi, signed in 1840 by Māori leaders and the British Crown, is central to any discussion of Māori rights. The Treaty, therefore, provides the framework and context for the application of the UNDRIP in Aotearoa New Zealand. At the same time, the recognition of the UNDRIP provides opportunities to strengthen the treaty relationship and demands that the treaty partners give greater consideration to the constitutional dimensions of that relationship.

Te Tiriti o Waitangi is a constitutional instrument. It directly addresses the exercise of public power in Aotearoa. However, Te Tiriti is not independently, directly enforceable in the domestic courts.[5] But there are numerous references to Te Tiriti and Treaty principles in New Zealand legislation, and there are other ways in which the courts can give effect to Te Tiriti indirectly (for example, as a mandatory relevant consideration in administrative law).[6] Te Tiriti is a relatively brief document, comprising a preamble, three brief written articles, and a fourth article agreed upon as part of the discussions at the signing at Waitangi in 1840. There is an English text and a Māori text of Te Tiriti. There are some significant differences between the meanings conveyed by the two different language texts.[7] In Article 1 of the English text, Māori ceded "sovereignty" to the British Crown. However, in the Māori text, the authority that is granted to the Crown is *kāwanatanga*, which translates as "government." In what is perhaps the most thorough examination of the meaning of Te Tiriti to those who signed it, the Waitangi Tribunal's report, *He Whakaputanga me Te Tiriti – The Declaration and the Treaty*, finds that Māori did not, in fact, cede sovereignty by entering into Te Tiriti o Waitangi.[8] The Tribunal determined that the grant of kāwanatanga was a grant of governmental authority over the settler population only and was understood by the Māori who signed to not derogate from their own independence and the self-determination of Māori communities.[9]

This interpretation is further supported by Article 2 of Te Tiriti, which guarantees Māori rights. In the English text, those guaranteed rights are largely cast as property rights. The Māori text again conveys a somewhat different meaning. The guarantee in the Māori text is to *tino rangatiratanga*, the authority of Māori leaders and their communities, which today is commonly translated as "self-determination." Furthermore, Article 2 of Te Tiriti records that this authority is to be guaranteed in relation to *taonga katoa*, that is, all things that are highly valued. This covers much more than rights to tangible property, including, for example, rights in relation to the Māori language.[10] Article 2 rights clearly go beyond property rights and include political and constitutional rights. Article 3 provides that Māori will have "all the rights and privileges of British subjects." There is no substantive difference in meaning between the English and Māori texts in relation to this article. The fourth article that forms part of the treaty agreement is effectively a protection of the right to religious freedom.

The status of Te Tiriti and the constitutional relationship between Māori and the Crown has continued to evolve since the signing of Te Tiriti in 1840. References to the Treaty of Waitangi have appeared in legislation and in judgments of the New Zealand courts since the nineteenth century. However, it was not until the latter years of the twentieth century that New Zealand's state legal institutions began to recognize the principles of the Treaty as providing some constraints on the exercise of public power. The *Treaty of Waitangi Act, 1975* established the Waitangi Tribunal, a standing commission of inquiry to hear claims based on Crown breaches of the principles of the Treaty. As discussed in more detail below, the Waitangi Tribunal has played an important role in helping to reshape the relationship between Māori and the Crown – a relationship that continues to be framed by Te Tiriti o Waitangi but is also being shaped by the numerous treaty settlement agreements concluded between Māori communities and the Crown.[11]

The Waitangi Tribunal is charged with making recommendations to the government of the day, but from the mid-1980s, the concept of Treaty principles was given legal effect through significant pieces of legislation and the application of statutory Treaty principles provisions by the ordinary courts. Major reforms of the public sector began in the 1980s, and references to the principles of the Treaty of Waitangi were included in statutes such as the *State-Owned Enterprises Act, 1986*, the *Conservation Act, 1987*, the *Resource Management Act, 1991*, and the *Crown Minerals Act, 1991*. Litigation based on such legislative incorporations of Te Tiriti and its principles has helped to give further definition to the Māori–Crown relationship. In applying those provisions, the New Zealand courts have also helped to shape the treaty settlement process, which, as described further below, continues to play an important role in recasting relationships between Māori nations and the Crown.

The application of Treaty principles in Aotearoa suggests ways in which the relationship between Māori and the New Zealand state can be reframed to better give effect to the relationship established in Te Tiriti o Waitangi. There is no authoritative list of the principles of the Treaty of Waitangi. The concept of Treaty principles is widely used in New Zealand law. Given that the concept has been deployed in the Waitangi Tribunal and the courts for nearly fifty years, there exists a significant body of jurisprudence on this subject. So, although there is a degree of flexibility that is deliberately built into the concept of Treaty principles (it is not, after all, a reference to the specific terms or articles of Te Tiriti), there is, today, a high degree of certainty as to how the courts and the Waitangi Tribunal will apply those principles.

Recognized Treaty principles are closely aligned with the characteristics of the type of relationship between states and Indigenous peoples that James Tully describes as a "treaty relationship" (in contrast to a "colonial relationship").[12] Tully uses the concept of an idealized treaty relationship to describe nation-to-nation relationships between states and Indigenous peoples that are respectful and consensual, that recognize the authority of Indigenous peoples, and that are framed by negotiation. It is important to note that the existence of a historic treaty is not a precondition for this type of relationship. Conversely, although Tully uses the label of a "treaty relationship," the existence of a historic treaty does not necessarily mean that the state and Indigenous peoples are currently in a mutually respectful relationship – or have ever been so. In both Canada and Aotearoa New Zealand, historic treaties exist between the Crown and Indigenous peoples, yet in neither of those countries could the relationships between Indigenous peoples and the state be seen to conform with qualities Tully ascribes to a treaty relationship.

Treaties between states and Indigenous peoples have often been entered into in less-than-ideal conditions and have not properly recognized Indigenous self-determination nor been based on free negotiation and consent. Even where initial interactions between states and

Indigenous peoples have genuinely respected Indigenous rights, a colonial relationship, characterized by oppression and domination, can be imposed by actions of the state party and/or by settler institutions. In such circumstances, even the interpretation and application of existing treaties can be transformed. It is not the existence of a treaty that defines a just relationship between Indigenous peoples and states but rather the maintenance of particular qualities within the relationship that is important. Tully identifies five principles that underpin just relationships between Indigenous peoples and states: mutual recognition, intercultural negotiation, mutual respect, sharing, and mutual responsibility. These principles align with principles of the Treaty of Waitangi that have been recognized in Aotearoa New Zealand and the articles of the UNDRIP, as discussed below.

According to a Māori worldview, the Treaty of Waitangi ought to be understood as the foundation of an ongoing reciprocal relationship. Reciprocity is a key aspect of both Tully's abstract "treaty relationship" and the application of the principles of the Treaty of Waitangi in Aotearoa New Zealand. Mutuality is a core thread of Tully's principles – mutual recognition, negotiation, mutual respect, sharing, and mutual responsibility. These ideas are also reflected in the Treaty principles of partnership and good faith, mutual benefit and obligation, requiring the partners to Te Tiriti to act reasonably towards each other. Indeed, the nature of a treaty relationship is such that one would expect to see some give and take, an exchange of some kind, as the basis for a treaty agreement. The implication of maintaining a treaty relationship is that this mutuality, this reciprocity, will continue to be a feature of the relationship. As Michael Asch notes in his contribution to this volume, the expectation, at least from the Indigenous parties entering into treaties with the Crown, would have been that the treaty relationship would be reflected by ongoing processes of exchange. Asch suggests that settler societies, such as Canada and Aotearoa New Zealand, should seek constitutional relationships that are based on "mutual consent, voluntarily given." Asch also notes that "voluntary consent," in the context of relationships between Indigenous peoples and settler polities, ought not to be understood as a single act but instead as a process that is continually being refined.[13]

This is also an important dimension of the relationship that was given formal expression in Te Tiriti o Waitangi. The Treaty set up a relationship that was to be implemented and maintained through an ongoing series of reciprocal transactions. The Waitangi Tribunal, in its Te Paparahi o Te Raki inquiry,[14] heard evidence about the expectations of the original signatories to Te Tiriti. Some of this evidence related directly to the conceptualization of Te Tiriti as effectively setting the framework for an ongoing series of reciprocal exchanges.

Historian Anne Salmond gave evidence to the Waitangi Tribunal about how the principle of *utu* (reciprocity) shaped Māori understandings and expectations of the relationship that was established by Te Tiriti o Waitangi. That is, the relationship is not conceived of as being wholly contained within the articles of Te Tiriti, but instead Te Tiriti established enduring obligations on the treaty partners to continually respond to exchanges within the framework of that relationship. Salmond points to Māori expectations that the relationship established by Te Tiriti would be continually reconfirmed through further engagements, transactions, and agreements with the Crown. This suggests an ongoing recognition of distinct spheres of authority and the continuing evolution of governance models and constitutional forms to give effect to the relationship in Te Tiriti while responding to changing circumstances over time.[15] That approach is now overlaid and supported by the articulation of Indigenous self-determination in the UNDRIP.

The UNDRIP and the Constitution of Aotearoa New Zealand

As noted above, the constitutional relationships in Aotearoa New Zealand and Māori and Crown spheres of authority are framed by Te Tiriti o Waitangi. The UNDRIP supports that framework through its articulation of Indigenous rights and internationally accepted standards. This section considers the recent, and more specific, advice from the UN's Expert Mechanism on the Rights of Indigenous Peoples, which directly addresses the need to transform the constitutional relationship between Māori and the Crown to effectively recognize Indigenous peoples' rights in Aotearoa New Zealand.[16] In particular, the Expert Mechanism noted that the UNDRIP could be used to support the restructuring of the relationship between Māori and the New Zealand state that the Treaty of Waitangi claims settlement process can open up.

In 2019, a delegation from the Expert Mechanism on the Rights of Indigenous Peoples (EMRIP) visited Aotearoa New Zealand. Members of EMRIP had been invited by the government of New Zealand to provide advice on the development of a national plan to implement the UNDRIP. The advisory note provided by EMRIP following the delegation's visit pointed to the use of Te Tiriti o Waitangi as a framework for structuring the relationship between Māori and the state and recommended strengthening the settlement process so as to better deliver the constitutional transformation necessary to give effect to the rights recognized in the UNDRIP.

The UNDRIP, the Treaty of Waitangi, and the Developing Constitution   149

The EMRIP advisory note observes the existing mechanisms that are intended to give effect to Māori rights, beginning with Te Tiriti itself and emphasizing the apparatus that has developed from that framework. This includes the Waitangi Tribunal, the various agreements that have been reached between Māori and the Crown to settle claims of historical breaches of Te Tiriti, and the recent establishment of the Office of Māori Crown Relations – Te Arawhiti, which now has the responsibility of settling historical claims, alongside ensuring that the Crown fulfils its commitments arising from those settlements, and supporting government agencies to proactively enhance the Māori Crown relationship, centred around the partnership set out in Te Tiriti, across all functions of government. EMRIP noted that the existing apparatus will be central to developing a national plan of action to implement the UNDRIP.

EMRIP also noted that the UNDRIP is being referred to with increasing frequency in the Waitangi Tribunal and in the New Zealand courts. Decisions from the courts have suggested that the courts themselves recognize that the UNDRIP ought to influence the development of New Zealand common law, consistent with the importance of recognizing the collective nature of the rights of Indigenous peoples. The Waitangi Tribunal's discussion of the alignment between principles of Te Tiriti and key articles of the UNDRIP is addressed above. In addition, EMRIP pointed to more general comments made by the Waitangi Tribunal about the relevance of the UNDRIP ["the Declaration"] for Māori, including that the

> Waitangi Tribunal has indicated that the Declaration is "perhaps the most important international instrument ever for Māori people" and carries "great moral and political force," "valuable guidance on those issues [collective and individual rights in terms of culture, identity, education, health and so forth] and reflects in many ways the spirit of the principles of the Treaty of Waitangi." Another Waitangi Tribunal report refers to the Declaration, as a "base standard" and considered that, to the extent that Declaration rights may be recognised consistent with the jurisdiction of the Tribunal, the Tribunal should apply them. Most extensively, the Waitangi Tribunal has stated that the Crown "accepts that the UNDRIP articles are relevant to the interpretation of the principles of the Treaty. Because the New Zealand government has now affirmed the Declaration, the obligations described in its articles are a circumstance we can take into account in assessing the Crown's actions."[17]

The EMRIP advisory note includes specific consideration of the right to self-determination, which is of particular relevance to the nature of the constitutional relationship between Māori and the Crown. The advisory note highlights the central importance of the right to self-determination, describing it as "a foundational right upon which all other rights of indigenous peoples are dependent."[18] The right to self-determination is recognized in Article 3 of the UNDRIP and is the same right as guaranteed to other peoples in the International Covenant on Civil and Political Rights and the International Covenant on Economic, Social and Cultural Rights. Therefore, Indigenous Peoples, like all peoples, "are entitled to participate equally in the constitution and development of the governing institutional order."

Furthermore, UNDRIP makes explicit that Indigenous peoples have the right to autonomy or self-government in matters relating to their internal affairs and the right to maintain their own political, legal, economic, social, and cultural systems and institutions as well as the right to fully participate in the political, economic, social, and cultural life of the country in which they live.[19] This has important implications for the way in which the constitutional relationship between Indigenous nations and states ought to be structured. In particular, it requires that the way in which self-determination is given effect in practice must be "implemented through partnership and full and effective participation of indigenous peoples themselves," working through their own political institutions.[20] The Cabinet paper in which the New Zealand government committed to developing a national plan of action included a commitment to "contribute to enhancing the self-determination of Māori as the indigenous peoples of Aotearoa/New Zealand."[21] The EMRIP delegation noted that the Cabinet paper also recognized that a plan to implement the UNDRIP would need to identify actions "representing the mutual priorities of government and Māori."[22]

EMRIP, therefore, advised both Māori and the Crown to:

- Ensure that the plan makes explicit reference to the Declaration, the relevant articles of the Declaration, and uses the language of the Declaration wherever possible.
- Ensure respect for the self-determination of Māori, as expressed above, during the process of developing a national plan of action, including through their full participation (see below).
- Ensure that the priorities established in the plan are priorities for Māori as much as the government.
- Consider how to engage with Māori on implementing their right to autonomy or self-government in matters relating to their internal and local affairs within the context of the State.[23]

EMRIP also adverted to the role played by treaties and other agreements with states in recognizing and implementing the rights of Indigenous peoples.[24] The preamble of the UNDRIP identifies that "treaties, agreements and other constructive arrangements, and the relationship they represent, are the basis for a strengthened partnership between indigenous peoples and States." Article 37 of the UNDRIP reinforces the role of treaties in structuring relationships between States and Indigenous peoples:

1. Indigenous peoples have the right to recognition, observance and enforcement of treaties, agreements and other constructive arrangements concluded with States or their successors and to have States honour and respect such treaties, agreements and other constructive arrangements.
2. Nothing in this Declaration may be interpreted as diminishing or eliminating the rights of indigenous peoples contained in treaties, agreements and other constructive arrangements.

EMRIP has previously recognized that in interpreting treaties between states and Indigenous peoples, it is important to "emphasise and assert indigenous peoples' own understanding of the treaties negotiated by treaty nations, as documented and evidenced by indigenous people's oral histories, traditions and the concepts expressed in their own languages."[25]

The EMRIP advisory note recognizes the particular constitutional issues that exist in relation to the full recognition of Indigenous rights in Aotearoa New Zealand.[26] These issues relate primarily to the absence of a supreme law constitution and the consequently somewhat precarious constitutional position of Te Tiriti. EMRIP, therefore, considered that further work on constitutional structures was necessary to effectively implement Indigenous rights in accordance with the UNDRIP. EMRIP recommended that the Crown and Māori:

- Continue to develop, and take measures to ensure, the interpretation of the Treaty of Waitangi, and other relevant legislation, consistent with the rights in the Declaration, in particular article 37, to ensure consistency. This approach could contribute to resolving disagreements over interpretations of the Treaty of Waitangi.
- Review domestic laws/policies and strategies to ensure consistency with the Declaration and the Treaty of Waitangi.

- Establish measures to ensure that new legislation conforms to the rights in the Declaration and the Treaty of Waitangi and makes explicit reference to Declaration rights.
- Consider enhancing the role of the Waitangi Tribunal to include: binding rather than recommendatory decisions; the power to assess policies against the Treaty; and the provision of additional human and financial resources.
- Pursue the constitutional reform or transformation discussions with all New Zealanders, in light of the recommendations of the Constitutional Advisory Panel Report, the Matike Mai report [see below] and the outcome of the process by the Office of Māori Crown Relations – Te Arawhiti.[27]

The EMRIP advisory note is further illustration of the importance for the recognition of Indigenous rights of power-sharing arrangements established through agreement. The advice from EMRIP also shows the way in which the UNDRIP can encourage further evolution of constitutional relationships between Indigenous peoples and states within an overarching treaty framework.

The Matike Mai report that was referenced by EMRIP was produced by a Māori group that was convened to address Māori constitutional aspirations. Matike Mai Aotearoa (literally, "rise up, Aotearoa New Zealand") was the name adopted by the Independent Working Group on Constitutional Transformation. This group was established by a national Māori leadership organization, the National Iwi Chairs Forum. The group was led by a senior academic and community leader, Margaret Mutu, and a prominent legal and constitutional scholar, Moana Jackson. Other members of the group were put forward by their iwi or invited to participate because of relevant expertise or experience.

The central purpose of Matike Mai was to

> develop and implement a model for an inclusive Constitution for Aotearoa based on *tikanga* and *kawa* [Māori law and social practices], He Whakaputanga o te Rangatiratanga o Niu Tireni of 1835 [the 1835 Declaration of Independence], Te Tiriti o Waitangi of 1840, and other indigenous human rights instruments which enjoy a wide degree of international recognition.[28]

In 2016, Matike Mai produced a report that proposed a range of indicative constitutional models that could reflect the relationship between Māori and the Crown, as envisaged by Te Tiriti o Waitangi.[29] This report was based on hundreds of public meetings with Māori community groups and organizations and on more focused interviews addressing particular elements of constitutional design. The report is framed as a discussion document, aimed at taking the constitutional conversation further. The high-level constitutional models offered in the report are presented as "indicative" only in the sense that they point to the range of ways in which a relationship between Māori and the Crown might be structured to give effect to aspirations of self-determination and recognize different spheres of authority consistent with Te Tiriti, tikanga Māori, and international human rights instruments. By focusing on the relationships between Māori and Crown spheres of authority, the report implicitly invites consideration of innovative models of federalism that could push the kinds of mechanisms developing in treaty settlement agreements into a more constitutionally transformative space.

Following the advisory note from EMRIP, the New Zealand Government established a working group in late 2019 to develop a national plan and an engagement process strategy to realize the UNDRIP in Aotearoa. This working group was made up of four government officials and five non-state representatives. The working group produced a report, entitled *He Puapua*, which was released by the Minister of Māori Development in 2021.[30] *He Puapua* builds on both the EMRIP advisory note and the Matike Mai report to set out a vision for the progressive implementation of Indigenous rights in Aotearoa to achieve shared authority consistent with Te Tiriti o Waitangi and the UNDRIP by 2040, the bicentennial year of the signing of Te Tiriti. This vision suggests that the UNDRIP can help to realize the potential of the treaty claims and settlement process to significantly reshape constitutional relationships between Māori and the Crown.

The Waitangi Tribunal, Claims, and Settlements

Treaty settlement agreements derive from a staged process of negotiation between the Crown and defined Māori communities. This process is aimed at agreeing redress packages that will settle historical claims of breaches of the Te Tiriti o Waitangi. It is a political process, though grounded in legal and constitutional rights. A key body in the settlement process is the Waitangi Tribunal. Although the Waitangi Tribunal does not settle treaty claims, it inquires into and reports on those claims, producing findings and recommendations. Its work, therefore, provides the basis for the current treaty settlement process.

The *Treaty of Waitangi Act, 1975* established the Waitangi Tribunal as a standing commission of inquiry that could hear claims alleging breaches of "the principles of the Treaty of Waitangi" by the Crown.[31]

The *Treaty of Waitangi Act* does not define "the principles of the Treaty" but requires the Tribunal to have regard for the two different language texts of the Treaty in exercising its functions and gives the Tribunal "exclusive authority to determine the meaning and effect of the Treaty as embodied in the two texts and to decide issues raised by the differences between them."[32] The key functions of the Tribunal are to inquire into and make recommendations on claims submitted to it. If the Tribunal determines that a claim of treaty breach is well-founded, it may "recommend to the Crown that action be taken to compensate for or remove the prejudice or to prevent other persons from being similarly affected in the future."[33]

Since its establishment, the Waitangi Tribunal has heard and reported on claims covering a wide range of subjects. These include claims relating to Te Reo Māori (the Māori language), environmental protection, allocation of radio frequencies, intellectual property and traditional knowledge, fisheries management, *kohanga reo* (early childhood Māori language immersion centres, literally "language nests"), Māori land reforms, and the Trans-Pacific Partnership Agreement.[34] However, until recent years, the bulk of the Tribunal's work was focused on historical claims, addressing the period in which much of the large-scale alienation of land and natural resources took place. Initially, the Tribunal heard individual claims as they were received. However, with the increased volume of claims that began to come in once historical claims were allowed, the Tribunal looked for ways to adapt its process. In 1993, the Waitangi Tribunal commissioned a series of research reports as part of the Rangahaua Whānui program. These reports provided an overview of historical grievances by district and themes and culminated in the publication of a three-volume *National Overview* report in 1997. The Rangahaua Whānui reports enabled the Tribunal to plan its historical inquiry program to hear and report on historical claims grouped together by geographical district. This also assisted the Crown in developing a systematic approach to the settlement of historical claims of breaches of the Treaty.

Since the establishment of the treaty settlement process, the Waitangi Tribunal has also reported on claims alleging that actions that the Crown has taken as part of the process have themselves been in breach of the principles of the Treaty.[35] In recent years, the Tribunal has also been asked to make recommendations for specific remedies where the settlement process has failed to deliver outcomes sought by the claimants.[36]

The treaty settlement process is currently managed by Te Kāhui Whakatau (the treaty settlement group) within the Office of Māori Crown Relations – Te Arawhiti. Although the treaty settlement process has evolved significantly since the mid-1990s, the basic framework developed through the negotiations of the commercial fisheries ("Sealord"), Ngai Tahu, and Waikato-Tainui settlements has largely been maintained. In the second half of this chapter, I examine components of treaty settlement packages that are reshaping relationships between Māori nations and the Crown and that, I suggest, have the potential to contribute to a more fundamental reconceptualization of those relations within a federal model. This reconceptualization could be grounded in a more expansive understanding of Treaty principles, supported by the application of Māori law understandings of the treaty relationship, and enhanced by the articulation of rights in the UNDRIP.

Whaia te Mana Motuhake (In Pursuit of Self-Determination)

While Māori understandings of constitutional relationships and Treaty principles underpin the framework of Te Tiriti, there is also an increasingly explicit connection between the claims and settlement processes in Aotearoa and the international Indigenous rights framework recognized in the UNDRIP.

The Waitangi Tribunal, in its report *Whaia te Mana Motuhake* on the reform of the *Māori Community Development Act, 1962*, examined the link between the principles of the Treaty of Waitangi and the UNDRIP. The claim was brought by the New Zealand Māori Council, a body established under the *Māori Community Development Act* itself. The New Zealand Māori Council argued that recognition of the right to self-determination required that the Council, not the New Zealand government, lead the reform of this legislation. The Waitangi Tribunal examined the principles of the Treaty of Waitangi in the light of the rights recognized in the UNDRIP and concluded that any reform in this area ought to be led by the Council and negotiated with the Crown. The Tribunal described the connection between treaty rights and the UNDRIP as follows:

> Our jurisdiction is to assess Crown actions against the principles of the Treaty. It is not our role to make findings on whether the Crown has acted inconsistently with UNDRIP.
>
> However, both the claimants and the Crown accept that the UNDRIP articles are a circumstance we can take into account in assessing the Crown's actions. UNDRIP is therefore relevant to the manner in which the principles of the Treaty of Waitangi should be observed by Crown officials.
>
> This is particularly the case where the UNDRIP articles provide specific guidance as to how the Crown should be interacting with Māori or recognising their interests.[37]

The Tribunal explains how articles of the UNDRIP are relevant to understanding the application of Treaty principles. In particular, the Tribunal identifies the overlap in content between the UNDRIP and the recognized Treaty principles of:

- kāwanatanga (government);
- active protection;
- informed decision-making;
- equity and equality; and
- the right to development.

The Tribunal then went on to connect specific, recognized Treaty principles with key articles of the UNDRIP.

Kāwanatanga refers to the role of the Crown to govern the State of New Zealand, while also requiring it to act towards Māori with utmost good faith. This principle recognizes that the Crown exercises powers of government, but that the scope of those governmental powers is constrained by the rights of Māori. In the context of Te Triti o Waitangi, this principle reflects the duty held by both Māori and the Crown to act towards each other reasonably and in good faith. The Crown must consult Māori on matters that will affect Māori rights and interests. At the same time, Māori do not have any right to unreasonably frustrate the government's policy program.

The Tribunal noted that the principle of kāwanatanga addressed many of the central concerns of Articles 19, 38, 39, and 46 of the UNDRIP. These articles, like the principle of kāwanatanga, recognize the functions and responsibilities of government that are exercised in New Zealand by the Crown. They point to the role that the Crown has in developing law, public policy, and administrative arrangements that provide support for Māori communities. Yet these articles also recognize the need for the Crown to exercise its functions collaboratively with Māori communities. The Tribunal notes that these specific articles of the UNDRIP are consistent with the Treaty principle of kāwanatanga because they recognize that a responsible Crown must exercise its right to govern in a way that respects Māori rights and demonstrates utmost good faith.

The Tribunal notes that these articles also speak to the right of states to govern, but that the state also has a role to play in ensuring that Indigenous peoples participate in collaboratively developing legislation or administrative measures and providing support for this to occur. Furthermore, in exercising its governing role, the state has an obligation to protect the rights of all citizens, including Indigenous peoples. These articles also make it clear that the rights recognized in the UNDRIP are to be interpreted and implemented in accordance "with principles of justice, democracy, respect for human rights, equality, non-discrimination, good governance and good faith."[38] This, the Tribunal finds, is consistent with the Treaty principle of kāwanatanga and in fact reinforces and assists with our understanding of that principle.

The Tribunal undertakes a similar analysis of the recognized Treaty of Waitangi principles of partnership, active protection, equity and equal treatment, and the right to development in the context of specific articles of UNDRIP. This contributes to the Tribunal's assessment of the Crown's compliance with Treaty principles in the development and implementation of policy. The Tribunal also sees articles in the UNDRIP as being supportive of the principle of rangatiratanga.[39]

There are articles in the UNDRIP that explicitly recognize Indigenous peoples' right to self-determination in both a general political sense but also specifically in the context of internal self-government; distinct political, legal, economic, social, and cultural institutions; rights to determine group membership and identity; and the right to maintain and develop distinctive customs and traditions, including in relation to juridical systems. The Tribunal describes the connection with rangatiratanga as follows:

> All these articles are consistent with the notion that Māori should have authority and local self-government over their own spheres of influence and affairs. ... these articles reflect a consistent scheme in UNDRIP that recognises that indigenous peoples should not have outcomes imposed upon them by Governments. The principle of rangatiratanga operates in practice with the same effect.[40]

Just as the guarantee of tino rangatiratanga sits alongside the grant of kāwanatanga in Te Tiriti, so the recognition of Indigenous peoples' self-determination sits besides the UNDRIP's recognition of the role that state parties have in exercising functions of government. These articles of the UNDRIP reflect the document's central theme of Indigenous self-determination. As with the Treaty principle of tino rangatiratanga, these articles affirm that Indigenous peoples should exercise authority within their own spheres of influence and ought not to have outcomes imposed upon them by the government of the state party.

If kawanatanga and tino rangatiratanga are the two big concepts at the heart of what the Treaty of Waitangi has to say about the exercise of public power, it is now an established part of the public discourse to speak of the relationship between those two spheres of authority as the principle of partnership. This principle has been central to the articulation and application of rights under the Treaty of Waitangi in the Waitangi Tribunal as well as in the ordinary courts. In *Whaia te Mana Motuhake*, the Tribunal situates the principle of partnership alongside provisions of the UNDRIP that recognize Indigenous peoples' right to participate in decision-making in accordance with their own processes and institutions. In particular, the requirement that the Treaty "partners must make every *effort to reach agreement* through a spirit of compromise"[41] appears to reflect the principle of free, prior, and informed consent that is woven throughout the UNDRIP.

Linking the UNDRIP to Te Tiriti o Waitangi in this way creates significant opportunities to give better effect to the constitutional dimensions of Te Tiriti. As discussed above, Te Tiriti provides the key organizing framework for the relationship between Māori and the Crown. The adoption of the UNDRIP, and New Zealand's eventual endorsement of it, has made much more visible the context of international Indigenous rights, in which Te Tiriti sits. This has also provided support for the development of Treaty principles and a treaty relationship that is grounded in Indigenous understandings and based on mutual recognition and respect. The modern agreements arising from the settlement of historical claims have the potential to extend and implement this kind of relationship. Framed by the original agreement in Te Tiriti o Waitangi, a settlement agreement establishes a specific set of measures for recognizing past harm to a particular community that has been caused by Crown actions and provides a platform from which the relationship between the particular community and the Crown can be restored and can develop in ways that are mutually beneficial. If these agreements can give effect to principles of mutual recognition and respect, and to Māori understandings of maintaining and nurturing constitutional relationships, there is scope to develop an Indigenous form of federalism.

The Treaty of Waitangi claims settlement process provides an opportunity to restructure the relationship between iwi and the New Zealand state. This can be seen in some of the settlement redress that relates to environmental governance and the delivery of social services. The settlement agreements that are reached through a process of negotiation are ostensibly aimed at providing redress for the Crown's historical breaches of Te Tiriti in relation to a specified Māori community. However, settlement agreements inevitably contain content that is effectively directed more at mechanisms for future engagement and a vision for how the relationship between the settling community and the Crown will develop into the future. These can, slowly, begin to transform the series of relationships that Māori communities have with the Crown within the overarching framework of Te Tiriti o Waitangi.

Environmental Governance

Environmental governance is the area of law and policy in which the reframing of the relationship between Māori and the New Zealand state has perhaps been most visible in recent years. Virtually all settlement packages that have been agreed upon under the process for the settlement of historic Treaty of Waitangi claims have included measures relating to environmental governance. These measures are often implemented in the form of detailed relationship agreements with agencies such as the Department of Conservation, the Ministry for the Environment, or relevant local authorities. They may include mechanisms that provide for general participation in environmental management within the settling group's area of interest and/or processes or values that are applied to specific sites.

The recognition of legal personality of landscape features has been one novel and visible component of restructuring the Māori–Crown relationship in the context of environmental governance. The Crown has agreed to recognize the legal personality of landscape features in three instances. These are Te Urewera (formerly a national park),[42] Te Awa Tupua (formerly the Whanganui River),[43] and Ngā Maunga (formerly Egmont National Park, including Mount Taranaki/Egmont).[44] Each of these recognitions has been agreed upon as part of the settlement of historical claims based on breaches of Te Tiriti and are part of the process of resetting the Māori–Crown relationship consistently with the Treaty principles. It is important to note that these arrangements are not primarily focused on giving effect to the "rights of nature" or to promoting environmental concerns. The driver, in each of these cases, is the aim to better reflect the relationship that the local Māori community has or wishes to have with the particular landscape feature, whether it is a forest, or a river, or a mountain. The recognition of legal personality is part of more closely approximating the relationship as it is understood in the Māori world. Similarly, restoring and protecting the health and well-being of these aspects of the natural environment are central to these agreements because that is also necessary for the relationship with the Māori community and their exercise of self-determination. This is obviously central to how the arrangement of constitutional relationships between Māori communities and the Crown are conceptualized.

Each of these settlements put in place different mechanisms that reflect the legal personality of particular landscape features and implement new governance arrangements. I focus here on the Te Awa Tupua (Whanganui River) settlement as an example of the type of restructuring of the relationship between Māori and the Crown (and the natural environment) that could be further developed using the framework of Te Tiriti.

The settlement in relation to Te Awa Tupua was given legal effect by the *Te Awa Tupua (Whanganui River Claims Settlement) Act, 2017*. The Act itself was one of the outcomes of an agreement reached between the Crown and Whanganui Iwi (the Indigenous people that historically exercised rights and responsibilities in relation to the river). That agreement settled all the historical claims of Whanganui Iwi in relation to the river. It was negotiated as part of the systematic treaty settlement process, as described above. Whanganui Iwi had sought to have their rights to the river recognized within the settler legal system since the nineteenth century. The settlement reflects the particular long-standing concerns of Whanganui Iwi in the context of Te Awa Tupua. The settlement recognizes Te Awa Tupua as "an indivisible and living whole, comprising the Whanganui River from the mountains to the sea, incorporating all its physical and metaphysical elements."[45] Te Awa Tupua is also declared to be a legal person with "all the rights, powers, duties, and liabilities of a legal person."[46] Another central part of the settlement is the recognition of four intrinsic values for which those exercising powers and functions in relation to Te Awa Tupua must provide. These values are:

- *Ko Te Kawa Tuatahi*
    a. *Ko te Awa te mātāpuna o te ora*: the River is the source of spiritual and physical sustenance:

    Te Awa Tupua is a spiritual and physical entity that supports and sustains both the life and natural resources within the Whanganui River and the health and well-being of the iwi, hapū, and other communities of the River.

- *Ko Te Kawa Tuarua*
    b. *E rere kau mai i te Awa nui mai i te Kahui Maunga ki Tangaroa*: the great River flows from the mountains to the sea:

    Te Awa Tupua is an indivisible and living whole from the mountains to the sea, incorporating the Whanganui River and all of its physical and metaphysical elements.

- *Ko Te Kawa Tuatoru*

    c. *Ko au te Awa, ko te Awa ko au*: I am the River and the River is me:

    The iwi and hapū of the Whanganui River have an inalienable connection with, and responsibility to, Te Awa Tupua and its health and well-being.

- *Ko Te Kawa Tuawhā*

    d. *Ngā manga iti, ngā manga nui e honohono kau ana, ka tupu hei Awa Tupua*: the small and large streams that flow into one another form one River:

    Te Awa Tupua is a singular entity comprised of many elements and communities, working collaboratively for the common purpose of the health and well-being of Te Awa Tupua.[47]

The settlement provides for two people to be appointed to act as guardians, to be the human voice for Te Awa Tupua. These two people are supported by an advisory group. A strategy group comprised of representatives from a range of communities of interest, including representatives of local and central government, has a significant role under the statute in developing, monitoring, and reviewing plans to advance the health and well-being of Te Awa Tupua.

It is still too early to evaluate the effectiveness of these changes and the implementation of the settlement and governing legislation. However, it is clear that the legal framework in relation to the environmental governance of Te Awa Tupua has been fundamentally transformed. In particular, the legal relationships between Māori (specifically, Whanganui Iwi), government, and Te Awa Tupua have been restructured. The values that now govern the management of Te Awa Tupua require different kinds of relationships between people as much as they do a reconceptualized relationship with Te Awa Tupua itself. It is notable that these changes are the result of negotiations between Māori and the Crown that were framed by Te Tiriti o Waitangi and the Treaty principles developed by the courts and the Waitangi Tribunal. Treaty settlement negotiations are by no means perfect. In fact, I consider that the process contains some serious flaws.[48] Essentially, these flaws arise from the fact that the Crown-dominated negotiations fail to give full effect to either Te Tiriti or Tully's principles of ideal treaty relationships. This places constraints on the ability of the process to effectively deliver Māori self-determination. Yet, examples such as Te Awa Tupua provide glimpses of the possibilities that exist to reshape Māori–Crown relationships, and which can be strengthened through centring Indigenous self-determination as recognized in the UNDRIP.

Social Policy

Treaty settlements are also prompting a restructuring of the relationship between Māori and the Crown in the areas of social policy and the delivery of social services. A number of groups who have entered settlement agreements with the Crown have agreed to new arrangements that aim to embed tikanga Māori (Māori law and values) within the broad area of state social policy. There are a range of examples of the way in which Māori communities pursue these objectives through the treaty settlement process, including the Te Hiku Social Accord and the Tūhoe Services Management Plan. For the purpose of this chapter, I will briefly outline the approach that is being pursued by my own community through the Wairoa Social and Economic Revitalisation Strategy (SERS).

The SERS forms a part of the cultural redress set out in the Deed of Settlement agreed between the Crown and the iwi and hapū of Te Rohe o Te Wairoa in 2016. The primary goal of this strategy is to positively transform the social and economic circumstances of Te Rohe o Te Wairoa to ensure that the people are well-housed, have good ongoing health and great education, and that they are provided with employment and economic development opportunities to move towards the collective vision of Mana Motuhake. The parties responsible for this strategy are:

- Tātau Tātau o Te Wairoa (the post-settlement governance body for the iwi);
- Ministry for Primary Industries;
- Ministry of Business, Innovation and Employment;
- Ministry of Education;
- Ministry of Social Development; and
- Te Puni Kōkiri (Ministry of Māori Development);

The main overarching objectives of the strategy include:

1. Providing a framework for the Crown to partner with iwi and hapū of Te Rohe o Te Wairoa to identify and fulfil opportunities to promote economic and social well-being objectives;
2. Enabling iwi and hapū of Te Rohe o Te Wairoa to support and contribute to social and economic developments; and

3. Developing and implementing a plan for the transformation of the social and economic circumstances of the iwi and hapū of te Rohe o Te Wairoa.

The shared principles guiding the relationships between the parties are *mana motuhake* (respect for the authority, autonomy, relationships, and mandates of the parties), *kanohi e kitea* (the importance of engaging with the community), *kōrero pono* (open, honest, and transparent communication), and *anga whakamua – kia puāwai, kia tutuki ngā wawata* (looking to the future, to the realization of our aspirations).

The basic mechanics of this agreement are that, for as long as the SERS is in place, the parties will agree on priorities and specific goals every five years. The Crown, in consultation with iwi and hapū of Te Rohe o Te Wairoa, will prepare an annual plan with specific actions and progress. The annual report will provide progress towards specific goals identified in the five-year plan, identify obstacles in achieving those goals and solutions for overcoming these obstacles, and provide disaggregated data relevant to the social and economic circumstances of the iwi and hapū of Te Rohe o Te Wairoa.

However, perhaps the most significant, and indeed radical, aspect of the SERS is the commitment by Crown agencies for the relationship with the iwi and hapū of Te Wairoa to be underpinned by Māori legal principles. This begins to reflect the type of mutual respect and recognition inherent in good treaty relationships and even allows for the existence of different spheres of authority, which suggests something of a federalist inflection. Just as the settlement in relation to Te Awa Tupua pointed to the potential of treaty settlement processes to radically reframe authority and jurisdiction in environmental governance, agreements such as the SERS demonstrate that governance of social policy can also be recast to move towards models of constitutional power-sharing consistent with Indigenous self-determination recognized in the UNDRIP.

Conclusion

There exists significant potential to transform the constitution of Aotearoa New Zealand so that it recognizes the spheres of authority of both Māori and the Crown and gives effect to the relationship established by the Treaty of Waitangi. Glimpses of that potential can be seen in the evolution of the Treaty of Waitangi claims settlement process. This process, as currently conceived, has significant limitations, but, as each settlement agreement is reached, the Māori–Crown relationship is changed. Although these settlements are ostensibly aimed at providing redress for historical breaches of Te Tiriti o Waitangi, a substantial component of each settlement focuses on setting relationships with government departments and other agencies that better give effect to the guarantee of tino rangatiratanga (self-determination) in Te Tiriti. This approach can be seen in novel arrangements for environmental governance and delivery of social services. It is framed by Te Tiriti o Waitangi and further supported by the UNDRIP. Articulating the broader context of Indigenous rights, the UNDRIP, and the broader institutions of international Indigenous rights can strengthen the application of the Te Tiriti o Waitangi and support the developing constitution of Aotearoa New Zealand to implement a treaty partnership that is grounded in Indigenous constitutionalism and based on mutual recognition and respect.

NOTES

1 See, for example, Moana Jackson, "The Treaty and the Word: The Colonization of Māori Philosophy," in *Justice, Ethics and New Zealand Society*, ed. Graham Oddie and Roy Perrett (Auckland: Oxford University Press, 1992), 1; Carwyn Jones, "Tawhaki and Te Tiriti: A Principled Approach to the Constitutional Future of The Treaty of Waitangi," *New Zealand Law Review* 25, no. 4 (2013): 703.
2 Cabinet Office, *Cabinet Manual 2017* (Wellington: Cabinet Office, Department of the Prime Minister and Cabinet, 2017), 1.
3 *Abolition of the Provinces Act, 1876*.
4 *Legislative Council Abolition Act, 1950*.
5 *Te Heuheu Tukino v. Aotea District Maori Land Board*, [1941] NZLR 590.
6 See, for example, *Huakina Development Trust v. Waikato Valley Authority*, [1987] 2 NZLR 188; *Attorney-General v. New Zealand Maori Council*, [1991] 2 NZLR 129.
7 See, for example, Matthew S.R. Palmer, *The Treaty of Waitangi in New Zealand's Law and Constitution* (Wellington: Victoria University Press, 2008), 31–81; Margaret Mutu, "Constitutional Intentions: The Treaty of Waitangi Texts," in *Weeping Waters: The Treaty of Waitangi and Constitutional Change*, ed. Malcom Mulholland and Veronica Tawhai (Wellington: Huia, 2010), 13.
8 Waitangi Tribunal, *He Whakaputanga me te Tiriti – The Declaration and the Treaty: The Report on Stage 1 of the Te Paparahi o Te Raki Inquiry* (Wellington: Legislation Direct, 2014).
9 Ibid.
10 Waitangi Tribunal, *Report of the Waitangi Tribunal on the Te Reo Māori Claim* (Wellington: Waitangi Tribunal, 1986).

11 All publicaly available settlement documents are available to access via the New Zealand Government's settlement website: https://www.govt.nz/treaty-settlement-documents.
12 James Tully, *Public Philosophy in a New Key*, vol. 1, *Democracy and Civic Freedom* (Cambridge: Cambridge University Press, 2008), 225–8.
13 See chapter 2 by Micahael Asch in this volume.
14 Waitangi Tribunal, *He Whakaputanga me te Tiriti*.
15 Carwyn Jones, "Māori and State Visions of Law and Peace," in *Indigenous Peoples and the State: International Perspectives on the Treaty of Waitangi*, ed. Mark Hickford and Carwyn Hones (Oxford: Routledge, 2019), 13–29.
16 See UN Office of the High Commissioner for Human Rights, The Expert Mechanism on the Rights of Indigenous Peoples (EMRIP), Country Engagement Mission (8–13 April 2019) – New Zealand, Advisory Note, 14 July 2019, https://www.ohchr.org/sites/default/files/Documents/Issues/IPeoples/EMRIP/Session12/EMRIPAdvisroyNoteNZ2019.docx [hereafter UN, "Advisory Note"].
17 Ibid., para 9.
18 Ibid., para 14.
19 UN General Assembly, United Nations Declaration on the Rights of Indigenous Peoples (UNDRIP), 2 October 2007, A/RES/61/295, Articles 4 and 5.
20 UN, "Advisory Note," para 15.
21 Office of Te Minita Whanaketanga Māori, "Developing a Plan on New Zealand's Progress on the United Nations Declaration on the Rights of Indigenous Peoples," 28 February 2019, para 21.
22 UN, "Advisory Note," para 16.
23 Ibid., para 24.
24 Ibid.
25 "Report of the United Nations Seminar on Treaties, Agreements and Other Constructive Arrangements between States and Indigenous Peoples," A/HRC/EMRIP/2010/5, para 22.
26 UN, "Advisory Note," para 25.
27 Ibid., para 27.
28 Quoted in Working Group on Constitutional Transformation, "He Whakaaro Here Whakaumu mō Aotearoa: The Report of Matike Mai Aotearoa – The Independent Working Group on Constitutional Transformation," Network Waitangi Ōtautahi, 25 January 2016, https://nwo.org.nz/resources/report-of-matike-mai-aotearoa-the-independent-working-group-on-constitutional-transformation.
29 Ibid.
30 Claire Charters, Kayla Kingdon-Bebb, Tamati Olsen, Waimirirangi Ormsby, Emily Owen, Judith Pryor, Jacinta Ruru, Naomi Solomon, and Gary

Williams, *He Puapua: Report of the Working Group on a Plan to Realise the UN Declaration on the Rights of Indigenous Peoples in Aotearoa/New Zealand* (Wellington: Te Puni Kokiri, 2019).
31 "The Crown" tends to be used in the context of treaty claims and settlement to describe the New Zealand state, encompassing all government agencies.
32 *Treaty of Waitangi Act, 1975*, s 5(2).
33 Ibid., s 6(3).
34 Waitangi Tribunal reports are available at https://www.waitangitribunal.govt.nz/publications-and-resources/waitangi-tribunal-reports.
35 See, for example, Waitangi Tribunal, *The Ngāti Maniapoto/Ngāti Tama Settlement Cross-Claims Report* (Wellington: Legislation Direct, 2001); *The Tāmaki Makaurau Settlement Process Report* (Wellington: Legislation Direct, 2007); *The East Coast Settlement Report* (Wellington: Legislation Direct, 2010); *The Port Nicholson Block Urgency Report* (Wellington: Legislation Direct, 2012); *The Ngāpuhi Mandate Inquiry Report* (Wellington: Legislation Direct, 2015); *The Ngātiwai Mandate Inquiry Report* (Wellington: Legislation Direct, 2017); and *The Hauraki Settlement Overlapping Claims Inquiry Report* (Wellington: Legislation Direct, 2020).
36 See Waitangi Tribunal, *The Ngāti Kahu Remedies Report* (Wellington: Legislation Direct, 2013); and *The Mangatū Remedies Report* (Wellington: Legislation Direct, 2014).
37 Waitangi Tribunal, *Whaia te Mana Motuhake* (Wellington: Legislation Direct, 2015), 38–9, https://forms.justice.govt.nz/search/Documents/WT/wt_DOC_85007148/Maori%20Council%20ReportW.pdf.
38 UNDRIP, Article 46(3).
39 Waitangi Tribunal, *Whaia te Mana Motuhake*, 40–1.
40 Ibid., 41.
41 Ibid., 42.
42 *Te Urewera Act, 2014*.
43 *Te Awa Tupua (Whanganui River Claims Settlement) Act, 2017* [hereafter *Te Awa Tupua*].
44 "Te Anga Pūtakerongo mo Nga Maunga o Taranaki, Pouakai me Kaitake: Record of Understanding for Mount Taranaki, Pouakai and the Kaitake Ranges," New Zealand Government, 20 December 2017, https://www.govt.nz/assets/Documents/OTS/Taranaki-Maunga/Taranaki-Maunga-Te-Anga-Putakerongo-Record-of-Understanding-20-December-2017.pdf.
45 *Te Awa Tupua*, s 12.
46 Ibid., s 14.
47 Ibid., s 13.
48 See Carwyn Jones, *New Treaty, New Tradition: Reconciling New Zealand and Māori Law* (Vancouver: UBC Press, 2016).

PART THREE

Plurinational Federalism

7 Treaty Federalism, the *Canadian Charter of Rights and Freedoms*, and Section 25 as a Bridge across Legal Cultures

AMY SWIFFEN

Introduction

This chapter considers the meaning of the *Canadian Charter of Rights and Freedoms*[1] in the context of the implications of the concept of treaty federalism for Canadian constitutional law. It begins by reviewing the current case law and legal scholarship on the application of section 25 of the *Charter*, which guarantees nothing therein will "abrogate or derogate from any aboriginal, treaty or other rights or freedoms that pertain to the aboriginal peoples of Canada."

Despite the seeming simplicity of this statement, case law and jurisprudence on the provision's meaning and application, especially in the context of Indigenous/Aboriginal self-government rights, remain quite inconclusive. As discussed below, various applications of section 25 have been put forward, but no general approach has been articulated by the courts. There is relatively little case law on the meaning of the section, and the jurisprudence is not that well developed.[2] However, recent cases concerning the right to self-government are putting it on the table. This chapter looks at the decision by the Court of Appeal of Yukon in *Dickson v. Vuntut Gwitchin First Nation*[3] in the context of the discussion of the meaning of section 25 of the *Charter of Rights and Freedoms*. The *Dickson* case engages many important legal issues,[4] including the application of section 25 in the context of a self-governing First Nation. The chapter concludes by drawing attention to how the issues that emerged from the *Dickson* case relate to the constitutional jurisdiction of Indigenous nations and how the ongoing process of decolonization should factor into the application of section 25. I suggest section 25 could be a key part of incorporating Indigenous jurisdiction, which has always existed, into Canadian federalism. With this in mind, the chapter sets out to develop an application of section 25 that anchors Indigenous jurisdiction in the *Charter*.

Case Law on Section 25 Is Inconclusive

To reflect on section 25, some brief background regarding the case law is useful. One reason the jurisprudence is limited is that since the enactment of the *Constitution Act, 1982*,[5] most Aboriginal rights claims have been brought before the courts within the context of section 35.[6] There have been fewer cases that involve section 25. It is the only explicit reference to Indigenous/Aboriginal rights in the *Charter*. It reads:

> The guarantee in this Charter of certain rights and freedoms shall not be construed so as to abrogate or derogate from any aboriginal, treaty or other rights or freedoms that pertain to the aboriginal peoples of Canada including
>
> (a) any rights or freedoms that have been recognized by the Royal Proclamation of October 7, 1763; and
> (b) any rights or freedoms that now exist by way of land claims agreements or may be so acquired.[7]

At the time the *Charter* was drafted, among the perceived threats to Aboriginal rights were the individual equality provisions contained in section 15, in particular, whether a guarantee of individual equality could undermine government actions that aim to protect collective Aboriginal rights.[8] It is generally understood that section 25 was incorporated into the *Charter* to serve as direction for the judiciary not to apply the latter's provisions in ways that undermine the rights of Indigenous peoples.[9] Jane Arbour points to other sections of the *Charter* to bolster this view, such as the corresponding provisions in sections 26 to 29 that indicate the legislature intended to increase and protect rights and freedoms with section 25.[10] This seems to be reflected in the words of Deputy Minister of Justice Roger Tassé, who described section 25 as "a rule of construction for the *Charter* in its application to the rights of Aboriginal peoples."[11] Former Justice Minister Jean Chrétien framed things in a slightly different manner, emphasizing that section 25 would not create new rights but merely protect Aboriginal rights deriving from elsewhere by preventing the *Charter* from infringing upon them.[12] This suggests the provision was intended more as a shield to protect Aboriginal rights after an infringement has been found.

Since that time, it has proven difficult for courts to figure out what section 25 means in practice. One reason is the nature of Aboriginal law in general in Canada, which is complex and lacks coherence due to the inheritance of flawed precedents grounded in empirically inaccurate and racist assumptions about Indigenous peoples.[13] Nonetheless, it is possible to discern trends in the judicial reasoning. One of these is the idea that the purpose of section 25 lies in ensuring that the rights of Indigenous/Aboriginal peoples exist apart from the *Charter* and are not diminished by its application. For instance, in the *Reference re Secession of Quebec*, the Supreme Court of Canada cites section 25 as an example underscoring the constitutional principle of protection for minority rights.[14] In *R. v. Redhead*, Justice Oliphant states that "section [25] does not confer new rights upon aboriginal people. It merely confirms certain rights held by aboriginal people."[15] Different views have been expressed in relation to how this principle translates into legal protection. For example, in *Campbell v. British Columbia*, the Court stated that "the section is meant to be a 'shield' which protects aboriginal, treaty, and other rights from being adversely affected by provisions of the *Charter*."[16] In *Shubenacadie Indian Band v. Canada*, however, the Court added that section 25 "can only be invoked as a defence if it had been found that the appellant's conduct had violated subsection 15(1) of the *Charter*."[17] This suggests it may not be a solid shield so much as a justificatory provision that is relevant once an infringement has been found. Furthermore, *Shubenacadie* is a case about section 15, and the context of the discussion was the impact of equality rights, which suggests the Court was likely thinking of how section 25 would work in the case of section 15(1) specifically, and not in relation to other *Charter* rights.

The most recent Supreme Court case to comment on section 25 was *R. v. Kapp* in 2008, where a majority of the Court found that federal Aboriginal fishing licence regulations contained in the Aboriginal Fisheries Strategy violated section 15(1) of the *Charter* but were saved by section 15(2).[18] Kapp was a non-Aboriginal person accused of salmon fishing in an area of British Columbia contrary to Aboriginal communal fishing licence regulations created by the federal government pursuant to the *Fisheries Act, 1985*.[19] The area in which Kapp was fishing was closed for a twenty-four-hour period during which only members of three First Nation bands – Musqueam, Tsleil-Waututh (formerly known as Burrard Indian Band), and Tsawwassen – could fish.[20] Kapp challenged these regulations on the grounds that they violated his equality rights under section 15 of the *Charter*. As a result of the section 15(2) save, however, the Court found it unnecessary to analyse the meaning of section 25 in the context of the case.

In concurring reasons, Justice Bastarache also found that the provisions were saved but arrived at the conclusion differently from the majority. He stated that the purpose of section 25 is "protecting the rights of aboriginal peoples where the application of the *Charter* protections for individuals would diminish the distinctive, collective and cultural identity of an aboriginal group."[21] Bastarache found this to mean that in cases involving Indigenous/Aboriginal rights there is only a need to do a *prima facie* section 15(1) analysis before section 25 is engaged.[22] Justice Bastarache is not saying that section 25 completely shields Aboriginal rights from *Charter* scrutiny. Rather, he places section 25 at a halfway point in the *Charter* analysis, after an infringement is found but before arriving at a section 1 analysis of whether the infringement is justified.[23]

In this case, the majority of the Court did not analyse the meaning of section 25 because it found it could decide the appeal by more ordinary means and did not need to consider the relatively uncharted provision. Thus, many questions pertaining to section 25 remain unresolved, including what ultimately falls within its scope, how it could work outside of the section 15 context, and whether it should be applied as a shield, a justificatory provision, or even possibly as "an interpretive provision informing the construction of potentially conflicting *Charter* rights."[24]

How *Dickson* Puts Section 25 on the Table

The decision of the Court of Appeal of Yukon in *Dickson v. Vuntut Gwitchin First Nation* is the most recent proceeding to put the meaning of section 25 on the table. The Vuntut Gwitchin First Nation (VGFN) is part of the Gwitchin Nation, whose territory covers an area of northern Yukon, Alaska, and the Northwest Territories. The VGFN government is based in a settlement called Old Crow, which is a small community in the Yukon. About half of VGFN citizens live in Old Crow and about half live elsewhere, including the applicant, Cindy Dickson, who lives in Whitehorse. In 1993, the VGFN, Yukon, and Canada signed the Vuntut Gwitchin First Nation Final Agreement and the Vuntut Gwitchin Self-Government Agreement (SGA). The Final Agreement is equivalent to a modern treaty for the purposes of section 35, but the SGA is not.[25] Under the SGA, the VGFN enacted its own Constitution, which provides that a candidate for chief or councillor who wins an election must relocate to the Old Crow settlement within fourteen days.[26] The VGFN had rejected Dickson's nomination to run for council because she would not commit to leaving Whitehorse if she won the election. The reasons cited in the court documents are her employment and her son's health needs. Dickson argued the residency requirement was in violation of her equality rights in section 15(1) of the *Charter*. She lost the case at trial when the chambers judge found that, apart from the "within 14 days" time limit, the residency requirement did not infringe upon section 15(1). Dickson appealed the decision, as did the VGFN.

The Court of Appeal of Yukon (YKCA) heard the case and it disagreed with the chambers judge, finding that the residency requirement did infringe upon section 15(1), but before looking to section 1 and an infringement analysis it turned to section 25. To reiterate, section 25 states that rights and freedoms in the *Charter* "shall not be construed so as to abrogate or derogate from any aboriginal, treaty or other rights or freedoms that pertain to the aboriginal peoples of Canada." The YKCA characterized the purpose of section 25 as protecting collective Indigenous/Aboriginal rights from being diminished by the rights and freedoms in the *Charter*. It found that in the context of a self-governing First Nation, a residency requirement for elected officials can be an expression of the community's self-government rights, and as such is shielded from *Charter* scrutiny by section 25. Connected to this is the broader idea that the *Charter* applies to self-governing Indigenous groups, but when the exercise of self-government rights conflict with *Charter* rights, the government power may be shielded from the Oakes test by section 25. Dickson applied for leave to appeal to the Supreme Court of Canada, which was opposed by the VGFN. The application was granted and is now awaiting a decision by the Supreme Court.

In a sense, the *Dickson* and *Kapp* cases are similar. At stake is a section 15 challenge to a government action that makes a distinction among individuals based on potentially discriminatory grounds with the objective of protecting Indigenous/Aboriginal rights. However, the cases are different in at least two connected ways. Unlike in *Kapp*, where the challenge came from a non-Aboriginal individual, *Dickson* involves a challenge by a citizen of the community to a provision contained in the constitution of a self-governing First Nation on the grounds that it violates individual equality rights in section 15(1) of the *Charter*. Thus, the residency requirement in *Dickson* represents an internal restriction and not an external restriction, as is the case in *Kapp*.[27] In this sense, the Court's decision in *Kapp* does not offer a clear precedent.

A comparison of the *Campbell* and *Dickson* cases is also illuminating. *Campbell* involved a *Charter* challenge to an election code created by the Nisga'a government. One of the arguments raised in the case was that the provisions that prevented non-Nisga'a from voting in Nisga'a elections violated section 3 of the *Charter*. The Court determined that the *Charter* applied to the actions of the Nisga'a government because it operates under the authority of the Nisga'a Treaty.[28] However, it found that section 25 protected the limited right of self-government enshrined in the Nisga'a Final Agreement and implementing legislation. Thus, it rejected the argument that the self-government provisions of the Final Agreement and implementing legislation had to be struck down for violating *Charter* rights. This is similar to the finding of the YKCA. *Campbell*, however, differs from *Dickson* in two ways. In the former, the challenge is by a non-member of the Nisga'a community and was made primarily under section 3.[29] In contrast, *Dickson* involves a challenge to an internal restriction by a VGFN citizen and was made in light of the equality rights in section 15. Thus, *Campbell* also does not offer a clear precedent.

In reaching its decision, the YKCA drew on Justice Bastarashe's concurrence in *Kapp* more than the majority decision. It linked this application of section 25 to jurisprudence on minority language rights where "collective rights are clearly prioritized in terms of protection … [and] individual equality rights have typically given way."[30] The YKCA characterizes section 25 as a shield for rights that pertain to Aboriginal persons.[31] Speaking to the context where "the 'collective' is a first nation that has survived years of paternalism and the suppression of its culture," the YKCA found that section 25 means that the collective right should prevail undiminished by other rights in the *Charter*.[32] It states: "in the circumstances, to apply 15(1) would impermissibly derogate from VGFN's right to govern themselves in accordance with their own particular values and traditions."[33] However, the YKCA determined that section 25 may shield an action from the Oakes test only after being subjected to a 15(1) *prima facie* analysis. Thus, the *Charter* applies to the actions of the VGFN government, and section 25 shields the residency requirement from some scrutiny under section 15.

The YKCA made the point that it "would not be appropriate to suggest any general rule" about the application of section 25 based on its decision.[34] This echoes the Supreme Court's last words on the matter in *Kapp*, where it stated the questions raised by the application of section 25 are of such complexity that they "are best left for resolution on a case-by-case basis as they arise before the Court."[35] So far, therefore, the courts have alternately suggested that section 25 become relevant only if an infringement cannot be saved by section 1, or that it shield a provision from the Oakes test after a *prima facie* infringement is found.[36] The Supreme Court has not yet been tasked with applying section 25 in a scenario like that in *Dickson*.[37]

Colonial Legal Hierarchies

The scholarly commentary on section 25 can roughly be categorized into two perspectives, one that sees the section as a lens for interpreting and applying the Charter and another that sees it as more of a shield to stop the Charter from undermining collective Aboriginal and treaty rights. These perspectives mirror the case law to some extent but also articulate different possibilities. On the one hand, there are those who describe section 25 as a rule of construction that directs courts to characterize *Charter* rights in ways that do not undermine Aboriginal rights/Indigenous difference.[38] William Pentney was possibly the first to argue section 25 should be seen as "an interpretive guide and not as an independently enforceable guarantee of aboriginal and treaty rights."[39] This implies section 25 is relevant at the outset of a *Charter* analysis in characterizing the right before an infringement analysis has taken place. This directs the courts to protect Indigenous/Aboriginal rights by choosing the interpretation of a *Charter* right "that is the least intrusive on aboriginal rights."[40] However, Pentney also stipulates that in the case of actual conflict where an Aboriginal right and a *Charter* right cannot be reconciled, the *Charter* right should be given effect. Thus, he proposes that section 25 is a rule of construction with a hierarchy prioritizing *Charter* rights over Aboriginal rights in the last instance.

David Milward has tried to develop a contextual approach to section 1 that draws on section 25 as requiring balancing rights instead of trading them off.[41] He draws on the Supreme Court decision in *Dagenais v. Canadian Broadcasting Corp*[42] and precedents in administrative law to suggest that section 25 directs courts to use culturally sensitive modes of interpretation in order to accomplish this balancing in the context of Aboriginal rights and *Charter* rights. From this perspective, section 25 would protect Aboriginal rights by directing the courts to interpret the *Charter* in ways that are compatible with Indigenous cultural meanings. Such culturally sensitive interpretation would mean that *Charter* rights would apply to the actions of Indigenous governments in "limited" or "modified" form.[43] With this formulation, however, the onus in a proportionality analysis remains on the Indigenous government. This means that in a section 25 case, the burden is on the Indigenous government to justify its action, as opposed to the state having to show its infringement of Aboriginal rights is justified by the *Charter*.

Patrick Macklem has offered an elaborate approach to section 25 that argues that the language of the provision means that it protects all "federal, provincial and Aboriginal initiatives" that make a distinction between Aboriginal and non-Aboriginal people with the goal "to protect [Indigenous] interests associated with culture, territory, sovereignty, and the treaty process."[44] This means laws that make a distinction between Aboriginal and non-Aboriginal people and infringe the

Charter would have to be justified under section 25 by the objective of protecting Indigenous difference. Importantly, Macklem makes a distinction between "external protections," which are government actions that impact non-community members, and "internal restrictions," which are actions that place restrictions on citizens/community members. Examples of external protections would be the provisions in the *Fisheries Act* in *Kapp* and the Nisga'a government's restriction on the voting rights of residents who are non-Nisga'a citizens. Macklem argues that section 25 means such external protections should be shielded from scrutiny under section 15 of the *Charter*.

However, Macklem suggests that the courts use a different approach in a case of an internal restriction. This is closer to what is at stake in *Dickson*. The first step is the same as with an external restriction, which is for the judiciary to adopt interpretations of a *Charter* right "in which the restriction does not violate the *Charter*."[45] When this is not possible, however, an internal restriction must be justified under section 25 by the purpose of protecting Indigenous difference. This involves first assessing whether Aboriginal rights are engaged and whether the government action in question is an external or internal protection. If an internal restriction is involved, Macklem echoes Pentney in suggesting that section 25 plays an interpretive role. If there are multiple possible interpretations of a *Charter* right – one in which the internal restriction violates the *Charter* and one in which it does not – "the judiciary ought to adopt the latter interpretation."[46] However, if there is no plausible interpretation other than one that results in a *Charter* violation, "section 25 should give way and the restriction should be regarded as a violation and require justification under section 1."[47] In this scenario, however, instead of assessing infringement in relation to a section 1 analysis, it is assessed in relation to protecting Indigenous difference and whether the deleterious consequences for some community members bear a close relation to interests associated with Indigenous difference.[48]

The hierarchy of rights in Pentney's interpretation is to be found here as well, though in an attenuated form. In the case of an internal restriction, the onus is on Indigenous governments to justify their actions under a test developed in the settler legal system and potentially to have their actions rendered void by the courts. Kerry Wilkins captures the problem in his discussion of the characterization of section 25 advanced by the Royal Commission on Aboriginal Peoples; he states that section 25 protects Aboriginal rights – including self-government – "from 'unreasonable' or 'disproportionate' derogation at the hands of the *Charter*." Wilkins points out how "the burden rests on the communities having such rights to show that any derogation would be disproportionate or unreasonable."[49] *Charter* rights and freedoms take precedence over Aboriginal rights in the last instance and position Indigenous legalities as a lesser form of legal authority.

Others have suggested the colonial legal hierarchy could be entirely reversed in the last instance. For example, Bruce Wildsmith argues the purpose and effect of section 25 "to maintain the special position of Canada's aboriginal peoples unimpaired by the *Charter*" means Aboriginal rights must be completely unabridged by the *Charter*.[50] In a situation of "irreconcilable conflict between *Charter* rights or freedoms and section 25 rights or freedoms, section 25 rights or freedoms prevail."[51] Brian Slattery agrees, arguing that section 25 means where "a *Charter* right impinges on a section 25 right, the latter must prevail."[52] Arbour also agrees, arguing that section 25 means Indigenous/Aboriginal rights must be prioritized in the last instance.[53] However, she contends there is one exception, which is sex-based equality. This is grounded in section 28 of the *Charter*, which is a stand-alone "directive to the courts to interpret the scope of *Charter* rights in a manner consistent with the equality of the sexes," which along with subsection 35(4) of the *Constitution Act*[54] "stand as clear indicators that the interpretation and application of the *Charter* (including section 25) and the determination of the existence and scope of Aboriginal and treaty rights must be consistent with the important constitutional value of the equality of men and women."[55]

Kent McNeil has developed a strong version of a shield approach. He argues that the "obvious" purpose of section 25 "is to prevent the *Charter* from being interpreted in a way that infringes on any rights or freedoms that aboriginal peoples may have," and to accomplish this it must shield the actions of Indigenous/Aboriginal governments without exception.[56] Thus, it is not only in cases of actual conflict between *Charter* rights and Aboriginal rights that *Charter* rights give way. In McNeil's view, section 25 must grant a broader *Charter* immunity to Indigenous governments. Wilkins agrees, opining that "from a legal standpoint ... the *Charter* has no application to inherent-right communities in the exercise of their self-government right."[57]

James (Sa'ke'j) Youngblood Henderson's conception of treaty federalism implies perhaps the strongest shield of all. It is grounded in the idea that the jurisdiction of Indigenous governments exists outside and independent of the settler colonial Constitution. As part of that Constitution, the *Charter* represents a settler rights paradigm that never legitimately applied to Indigenous peoples.[58] Henderson argues that the *Charter* was about imposing a rule of law on the power of provincial and federal governments over Canadians, but that it does not apply to the actions of Indigenous governments whose jurisdiction is pre-existing and outside the *Charter*. From this perspective, section 25 explicitly marks "a protective zone from the colonialists' rights paradigm" that the pre-existing Indigenous jurisdiction implies.[59] From this perspective, the relationship between Aboriginal and *Charter* rights is not a hierarchy but a plurality of legalities. Section 25 – or any section of the *Charter* – is not relevant to Indigenous peoples unless they meaningfully choose to engage with the settler rights paradigm.

Overall, legal scholarship on section 25 reads the provision either as granting immunity to Aboriginal governments, or as some form of justificatory framework designed to balance Aboriginal rights and *Charter* rights while allowing one or the other to take precedence in the last instance. It is relevant to note that all of the shield interpretations presume an irreconcilability and a hierarchical relationship, even if they differ on which term in the relation is to be prioritized. Thus, while the shield approaches that prioritize Aboriginal rights are truer to the wording of section 25 in not abrogating or derogating from Aboriginal rights, Milward's reading is the least hierarchical in that he articulates an interpretive application of section 25 that calls for a culturally sensitive interpretation of *Charter* rights to ensure the protection of Aboriginal rights. In this approach, however, there remains a hierarchy of a lesser sort reflected in the direction of the onus in the balancing exercise. It is only Henderson's treaty federalism approach that does not posit a relation of hierarchy of rights because Aboriginal rights are based on the constitutional jurisdiction of Indigenous nations outside and independent of the *Charter*. However, such an account could present its own challenges.

Which Governments Are Engaged by Section 25?

The Supreme Court of Canada's approach to the *Dickson* case may depend on the type of government entity that is involved. Distinctions between delegated vs. inherent governments on the question of *Charter* application could be seen as formalistic. However, it is significant that the case law discussed above mainly pertains to challenges to laws and actions of the Canadian state in one form or another, often in the form of provisions in federal legislation designed to give priority to Aboriginal rights. There is no case law in the context of an action of an Indigenous government with jurisdiction that is not assumed to be derived or delegated from the Crown in a legal sense. Once we try to apply the current framework to such a scenario, we see it presents challenges.

One issue to address is which government actions are being understood as falling within the scope of section 25. So far in this discussion this category has been assumed, but it is quite complex and contested in ways that could be relevant to the approach taken to section 25. Candidates for section 25 protection include those based on negotiated treaties and self-government agreements, such as the Nisga'a government. In addition to treaty governments, Indigenous communities that have negotiated partial sectoral self-government arrangements would also fall under the protection of section 25, at least in some contexts.[60] Another scenario is an Indigenous government that is based on an Aboriginal self-government right recognized under section 35. The latter is not likely given the Court's tendency to read down claims of self-government to particular rights and activities historically integral to a distinctive Indigenous culture.[61] Thus, while the assertion of a right to self-government under section 35 might be possible in theory, it would be very difficult to enact under the current framework.[62]

Another possibility are self-government rights claimed as incidental to an Aboriginal title recognized under section 35. Aboriginal title is held communally and cannot be held by individual Aboriginal persons. As explained by the Supreme Court in *Delgamuukw v. British Columbia* and affirmed in *Campbell*, it is "a collective right to land held by all members of an aboriginal nation. Decisions with respect to that land are also made by that community."[63] The collective nature of Aboriginal title necessarily implies a collective mechanism for management and decision-making regarding the land. Thus, self-government rights could be argued to be incidental to Aboriginal title by virtue of its collective character. Such rights flow naturally from the nature of Aboriginal title. Unlike the self-government rights under section 35, self-government rights incidental to Aboriginal title would include uses of the land beyond traditional uses. As McNeil explains, "any use of the land that is encompassed by Aboriginal titleholders' 'right to exclusive use and occupation' should ... be subject to their decision-making authority."[64] This includes uses of the land involving extraction of natural resources, as was held in *Delgamuukw*, as well as other direct uses such as hunting, fishing, farming, building, and so on. As noted by McNeil, "Not all activities that take place on land are necessarily a use of the land," and he suggests the right "would probably be limited to activities that can properly be classified as uses of the land, rather than as encompassing all activities that might take place on the land."[65] In this sense, the possibility of Aboriginal self-government rights as incidental to Aboriginal title would be somewhat more expansive than as articulated in the section 35 framework. However, it is still limited.

Another possibility of an entity that could trigger section 25 is an Aboriginal self-government falling under the "other rights and freedoms" protected by section 25. Currently, there are three possible sources for these such rights: statute, case law, and inherency. In *Corbiere v. Canada*, Justice L'Heureux-Dubé suggested that rights created by statute could qualify under section 25.[66] One question is whether the *Indian Act* could be such a statute. The *Indian Act* originally imposed the band council regime without the voluntary consent of Indigenous peoples and disregarded traditional Indigenous governments. Some band councils continue to operate under procedures created by the Act. However, could the custom election and membership codes created by some band councils constitute Aboriginal rights for the purposes of section 25? As discussed below, the answer so far has been no, and actions of band councils are treated as a form of delegated federal authority.

Another source of "other" Aboriginal rights under section 25 could be inherency.[67] Patricia Monture-Angus makes the point that the application of the *Indian Act* has been taken by courts to have extinguished any Indigenous rights that may have preceded it. However, the concept of extinguishment implies the existence of something that can be extinguished. Thus, the reasoning for subjecting band councils to the *Charter* assumes the prior existence of Indigenous self-government. For this reason, she argues, groups who did not come under the jurisdiction of the *Indian Act* continue to have self-government rights, and those who have come under the *Indian Act* are understood to have possessed such rights at one time.[68] Moreover, the process by which Indigenous communities came under the *Indian Act* cannot be said to entail "voluntary consent, mutually given" to abdicate the capacity for self-government.[69] These arguments have an affinity with the treaty federalist approach that Indigenous nations have an inherent constitutional jurisdiction. This idea is discussed more below, but understanding how, thanks to the current framework, the concept of "aboriginal governments" is actually a diverse set of legal entities is important for understanding how courts have applied (or avoided applying) section 25 in contexts involving Indigenous governments so far.

External Protections vs. Internal Restrictions

As evident above, the scholarly commentary seems to be settling on the idea that section 25 provides protection in both the context of "external" and "internal" restrictions of an Indigenous government, though there is disagreement as to how much protection should be given and how to hierarchize the relationship between Aboriginal rights and *Charter* rights in a conflict situation.[70] Most of the existing case law on section 25 pertains to external protections deriving from federal authority or that are directed to non-Aboriginal individuals.[71] It remains to be seen what will happen in *Dickson*, which involves a *Charter* challenge to an internal restriction of an Indigenous government by a community member.

None of the conflict rules proposed would seem a good fit for such a scenario as all assume that individual rights and Aboriginal rights can be separated, either for balancing or for protecting the latter. Either *Charter* rights are not protected in cases where they might be most relevant – when government actions conflict with individual rights – or political autonomy is diminished in the name of *Charter* rights. One cannot be traded off without forcing individuals to trade off one dimension of self-determination for another. However, the case of an internal restriction brings to the fore how they are joined in individuals whose capacity to participate in the political community is not separable from a collective right to self-government. In this context, it is worth considering the idea of self-determination as it has developed in international law, which incorporates both individual and collective dimensions. This understanding is reflected in the United Nations Declaration on the Rights of Indigenous Peoples, which articulates a conception of self-determination that includes, among other things, that peoples and individuals be able to freely participate in the social and political life of their communities, as well as the capacity of Indigenous peoples to collectively self-govern their territories.[72] While we can conceptually separate *Charter* rights and Aboriginal rights for the purposes of a legal analysis, they are organically linked in the individuals making up a people.

Conversely, the issue remains that what may look from the outside like discrimination might mean something else from an internal point of view. For example, a group could have a traditional rule that only men can be chiefs, but that it is the women who decide who is qualified to be chief and, after enough warnings, when it is time for a chief to be recalled.[73] If this rule is challenged by a female member of the community who wants to be chief, how is such a scenario assessed and from whose perspective? In such a scenario, are the approaches to section 25 developed so far are attuned to discerning between discrimination and cultural difference? Even if section 25 were applied as favoured by Milward, the result would be a culturally sensitive interpretation of *Charter* rights and freedoms – but does this imply the creation of two sets of *Charter* rights? Does it still repeat a colonial imposition and hierarchy of legal cultures by requiring Indigenous government jurisdiction be balanced against the *Charter*? These questions reflect how the current section 25 framework is underdeveloped. But they beg the question: Is there another way?

Aboriginal Governments as Delegated Authority

Insofar as Aboriginal governments have until now been framed as equivalent to delegated authority, they have no stand-alone constitutional status or inherent jurisdiction. Indeed, they have mostly been regarded as administrative entities and creatures of federal power. For example, in *Orr v. Peerless Trout First Nation*,[74] the Alberta Court of Queen's Bench dismissed a claim by a member of the Peerless Trout First Nation (PTFN) alleging that the Nation's Customary Election Regulations were unconstitutional. The court described PTFN as "a self-governed First Nation" in the Treaty 8 territory of Northern Alberta operating under section 74(1) of the *Indian Act*.[75] The court assumed without deciding that the *Charter* applied to the actions of the PTFN by virtue of the fact that its government was constituted under the *Indian Act*.[76] Section 25 was not addressed because there were no Aboriginal or treaty rights at issue: the Indigenous government involved was a delegated federal power. However, the court did not review the reasons for applying the *Charter* in the factual matrix of the *Orr* case. Instead, it assumed the holding from *Taypotat v. Taypotat*, in which a Federal Court of Appeal held that while a First Nation is "clearly a *sui generis* government entity," a band council "exercises government authority within the sphere of federal jurisdiction under the *Indian Act* and other federal legislation."[77]

Taypotat concerns the Kā-kīwistāhāw First Nation in Saskatchewan and a community election code adopted by the band council under section 74(1) of the *Indian Act*. In the code, eligibility for the position of chief was restricted to persons who had at least a grade 12 education or equivalent. This excluded seventy-four-year-old Louis Taypotat, who had attended residential school until grade 10, though he had previously served as chief for a total of twenty-seven years. Taypotat challenged the eligibility provision and election results under section 15(1) of the *Charter*. At the Federal Court hearing, he argued the election code discriminated on the basis of education, which is analogous to race and age.[78] The education requirement adversely impacted older band members and residential school survivors. The Federal Court rejected this, finding education requirements related to "merit and capacities" and "deal with personal attributes rather than characteristics based on association with a group."[79] However, the Federal Court of Appeal reversed this and found that while the education requirement did not directly engage a protected ground of discrimination under section 15(1), it resulted in adverse effects that were discriminatory based on age and Aboriginality-residence.[80] The Court of Appeal declared the eligibility provision unconstitutional and ordered new elections without it.[81] This was reversed again, however, by the Supreme Court in a unanimous judgment that held that the adverse effects claim was not established by the evidence.[82]

The Supreme Court did not comment on section 25 in *Taypotat*. However, the Federal Court and the Court of Appeal did. Similar to *Orr*, the courts applied the *Charter* without deciding as it regarded the government action as a form of delegated authority. In *Taypotat*, the courts referred to *Crow v. Blood Band*, a case from 1996 in which the Federal Court was asked to decide whether section 3 applied to customary band election procedures implemented outside of the *Indian Act*. Again, the court avoided directly deciding and resolved the complaint without recourse to section 25:

> This is a complex matter which involves, *inter alia*, the application of section 32 of the *Charter* as well as the interpretation and possible application of section 25 the *Charter*. However, given the conclusion that I have reached with respect to the infringement of the Plaintiff's *Charter* rights in this case, it is unnecessary for me to reach a conclusion on this issue. Accordingly, for the purposes of the ensuing discussion, I have assumed, without deciding, that the *Charter* does apply to the Band's Custom Election Bylaw.[83]

All of the case law on the applicability of section 25 to band council customary codes has assumed that since band councils are created by federal legislation, the government authority is delegated federal authority. It would seem that no Canadian court has actually broached the question of the application of the *Charter* to an Indigenous government as a jurisdictional entity in any context.

Here it is useful to note the Government of Canada's current policy regarding the Aboriginal right to self-government, which it characterizes as an inherent right.[84] This framing is consistent with the 1983 report of the Special Committee on Indian Self-Government, which interprets the Royal Proclamation of 1763 as acknowledging that Aboriginal societies were self-governing.[85] The Special Committee, chaired by Keith Penner, found the Royal Proclamation established a nation-to-nation relationship between the Crown and First Nations, and recommended the acknowledgment of Indigenous jurisdictions as a distinct order of government within federalism.[86] Similarly, the Charlottetown Accord of the early 1990s proposed a constitutional amendment to acknowledge an inherent right of self-government of Indigenous peoples in Canada. In the wake of the failure of that accord, the federal government began to take various measures to move from direct administration of "Aboriginal affairs" to a more indirect and hands-off approach. This involves creating delegated self-government arrangements and agreements with Indigenous communities. For example, section 74 of the *Indian Act* provides the Minister of Indigenous and Northern Affairs the discretion to impose an election system on band council governments. However, under section 74(1), this order can be rescinded so a band government may be "reverted" by the minister to a custom code for electing its chief and members of the council.[87] A federal policy known as the Conversion to Community Election System Policy[88] sets a basic framework for such custom election and leadership selection processes.

This arrangement falls short of the true constitutional jurisdiction envisioned by treaty federalism and the report of the Special Committee on Indian Self-Government. At most, these governments have constitutional status akin to municipalities. This is apparent in *Scrimbitt v. Sakimay Indian Band Council*.[89] Mary Scrimbitt was denied the right to vote in a band election because she was a Bill C-31 Indian and not considered a member of the community according to its election code. A Federal Court applied the *Charter* on the basis of the link to the *Indian Act*. Thus, it did not consider how the *Charter* would apply if the government had jurisdiction in its own right. Similarly, in *Horse Lake First Nation v. Horseman*,[90] when a group of women occupied a band office and the band applied for a court order to evict them, the Alberta Court of Queen's Bench held that the *Charter* should apply to the decision of the band because it was a creature of federal statute. This administrative end route means there is no case law on the question of the relationship between the *Charter* and Aboriginal governments with constitutional jurisdiction.

Governments and Peoples

Many have pointed to the potential of *Charter* claims to undermine self-government through challenges to traditional leadership selection practices, limitations on mobility rights, and the right to sell land.[91] Some see *Charter* rights as culturally incompatible with Indigenous legal cultures. Mary-Ellen Turpel argues that the *Charter* and surrounding case law embody cultural values that are "too individualistic and European" to deliver responses that reflect the needs of Indigenous peoples.[92] The discourse of *Charter* rights can be "elitist and culturally specific" and the court system "adversarial and impersonal"; these legal and political structures are "unknown among Aboriginal peoples."[93] Patricia Monture-Angus shares these sentiments, calling the *Charter* a "narrow instrument" incapable of addressing the discrimination faced by Indigenous women.[94] She argues that a set of legal rights like those found in the *Charter* "may actually result in harm and reinforce injustice and inequality when applied to a system that operates on different assumptions."[95] In acknowledgment of these points, I am interested if there is a way to think of the relationship between Indigenous jurisdiction and the *Charter* that is cognizant of such difference. And what is the role of section 25 in doing that? To explore some answers, we have to look outside of the realm of legal doctrine and consider some relevant sociological concepts. For instance, the concepts of governments and peoples are not synonymous, and at times might be in different states of tension. Arguably, such tension is greatest when the actions of governments differentiate between segments of the community and infringe on the rights of some members.

Joyce Green and Val Napoleon discuss how Indigenous women's interests tend to be invisible to male political leadership – an exclusion that stems from "the difference between male and female experience in relation to oppression."[96] Settler colonialism impacts people differently depending on their sex, and its specific impacts on women risk being missed. As Joanne Barker writes, "although there was certainly much violence and discrimination directed at Indian men within Canada," Indigenous women experience sex-specific harms as "the social roles and responsibilities of heterosexual Indian men within bands and on the reserves were systematically elevated over that of women and non-heterosexuals by the institutions of Christianity, capitalism, sexism, and homophobia."[97] The assimilationist *Indian Act*, for instance, had sexist provisions that targeted female persons and their descendants in ways that entrenched inequality in some communities. Several band council governments did not oppose the disenfranchisement of women by the *Indian Act*, and some joined the Government of Canada in supporting it in court, with various forms of internal sex-based restrictions contining today.[98] Green and Napoleon point out the discussion of Indigenous women's issues in the final report of the Royal Commission on Aboriginal Peoples does not address "the vicious reprisals inflicted on Aboriginal women who are politically active as women, or who contest male power, or who identify as feminist."[99]

In this context, it is instructive to consider the call of the Native Women's Association of Canada (NWAC) for the *Charter of Rights and Freedoms* to apply to all forms of Indigenous governments, including those based on treaties and inherency.[100] The NWAC's intervention in the *Corbiere* case argued that section 25 should only shield external protections while *Charter* challenges to actions of Indigenous/Aboriginal governments should be allowed when launched by citizens, as this provides a means for individual women to address oppression by male-dominated leadership.[101] Indigenous women have used the *Charter* as a tool to try to advance equality in their communities.[102] The NWAC also used the *Charter* during the Charlottetown Accord discussions to challenge their exclusion from the process.[103] It initiated two court cases to gain equal participation. The controversy surrounding the NWAC's position is echoed in the contemporary discussions of how Indigenous communities wish to relate to the Canadian government.[104] Teressa Nahanee argues that Indigenous women have benefited from the *Charter*, as its strategic use has led to reduced sex discrimination in areas such as membership entitlement provisions.[105] In a similar vein, John Borrows has argued that the NWAC's actions helped to highlight the sex-based inequality Indigenous women may face within their communities.[106] Sharon McIvor discusses the strategic use of *Charter* litigation by Indigenous women when their challenges were opposed by male leadership within their communities.[107] These thinkers argue that the *Charter* can be a mechanism Indigenous people can use to undo patriarchal systems and structures associated with colonization and to recapture the strength of legal principles that past colonial governments have eroded.[108] This resonates with the understanding of self-determination discussed above, which entails the ability of individuals to fully participate in the social and political life of their communities. If there are sex-based barriers created by governments, the conditions for collective self-determination might not be met.[109]

These debates demonstrate that the meaning of section 25 is not strictly a legal question but a deeply political one. Moreover, the debates over the use of the *Charter* by Indigenous women shows the relationship between governments and peoples is not straightforward, and that contemporary discourses of self-government must involve a developed perspective on individual and collective self-determination.

Section 25 as a Reversed Cognizability Requirement

The rest of this chapter explores possible approaches to section 25 of the *Charter* that do not instantiate a hierarchy of jurisdiction. Instead, I suggest that section 25 can be seen as a tool for bridging or even weaving legal cultures by understanding section 25 as imposing a duty of cognizablility that flows from Canada's nation-to-nation relationship with Indigenous peoples. Section 25 should be seen along with sections 35 and 91(24) as offering the possibility of a framework for a reimagined federalism that includes the jurisdiction of Indigenous legalities. This means the courts would be required to arrive at constitutional interpretations that are cognizable with Indigenous legal cultures, not the other way around. The direction of this duty is centred on undoing the settler colonial hierarchy that haunts the current jurisprudence while acknowledging the jurisdiction of Indigenous nations within federalism.[110] While others have argued compellingly for Indigenous/Aboriginal control in different areas – for instance, over some criminal matters – focusing only on an area of law and not the root of jurisdiction in the Constitution can only carve out pockets within the settler legal system.

It is important to distinguish the reversed duty of cognizability from the idea of "translation" proposed in *R. v. Marshall* and *R. v. Bernard*, which has been critiqued as an exercise of hierarchical extinguishment (i.e., if the common law cannot understand it, then it does not exist). Such an approach is inconsistent with reconciliation with Indigenous jurisdiction. Rather, section 25 could allow for dialogue across legal cultures so as to make it possible to weave together interpretations. Sovereignty is not assumed to be a unitary power but is relational and plural.[111] Section 25 supports a plurinational understanding of the *Charter* because it has a juridical quality. The duty of cognizability acknowledges this jurisdiction of Indigenous legalities.

Gordon Christie makes some interesting arguments in regard to section 25 as a tool for decolonization, which is a process that unfolds in time. He argues that the application of section 25 should adapt and change as well. This can be conceptualized in two phases. First, section 25 could be a tool for Indigenous peoples in removing unjust power structures within their communities. In this sense, Christie agrees with the NWAC that section 25 could be a "strong hedge" around Indigenous/Aboriginal rights, but "in the absence of viable community-based alternative governing structures grounded in traditional principles and values, it would not protect Aboriginal governments from member-initiated challenges based on *Charter* principles."[112] In other words, internal restrictions would not be shielded by section 25 unless there are "internally determined institutions [that] are operational" to address such challenges.[113] Christie associates this with a second phase of decolonization as Indigenous communities reconstruct governing institutions that reflect their identities. In this phase, section 25 could be extended to "protect traditional ways of living from identity-challenging intrusions (both externally and internally)."[114] The two-fold approach is interesting in that it is flexible and could allow for *Charter* challenges by community members when it makes sense.

However, it begs the question of who decides on the "viability" of community-based alternatives. Given the current composition and structure of the Canadian courts it would most likely be judges without knowledge of Indigenous legal cultures making the determination. And who bears the burden of proof when the inquiry is happening? It is worth noting that Ms. Dickson had been prepared to make alternative arguments under the VGFN Constitution, as article 4 sets out rights that are similar to section 15 of the *Charter*.[115] Section 7, the equality clause, states the following:

> Every individual is equal before and under the laws of the Vuntut Gwitchin First Nation and has the right to the equal protection an[d] equal benefit of Vuntut Gwitchin First Nation law without discrimination.

However, neither court considers this possibility.[116] The YKSC has found that the VGFN Constitution "did not oust the *Charter*" and was more similar to a provincial charter of rights than a constitutional document – and the YKCA agreed.[117] The VGFN Constitution foresees the establishment of a VGFN court, and perhaps the Canadian courts would rule differently once this happens. This highlights a final issue. A strict shield application of section 25 may limit possibilities for the constitutional expression of Indigenous legalities.

Conclusion

Henderson argues that Indigenous nations have a jurisdiction that exists outside the Canadian Constitution and the *Charter*. This is true, but it does not mean that the *Charter* can have no relationship to Indigenous governments. There is the legitimate objection that the Canadian judiciary is not equipped to interpret and apply Indigenous laws in the way the proposal would require. Admittedly, considerable expertise in relevant Indigenous legal traditions is needed, and not many currently have it. However, it is overly pessimistic to discount the idea on this basis alone. Expertise exists and is developing. Law schools in Canada are intensifying efforts to develop Indigenous legal traditions.[118] The capacity will grow over time. There are also other jurisdictions that we can look to for guidance, including the US and New Zealand.[119] Thus, while doubts about the ability of the Canadian courts to integrate Indigenous legalities are justified, I believe section 25 could hold the promise of a plurinational federalism.

NOTES

1 *Canadian Charter of Rights and Freedoms*, Part 1 of the *Constitution Act, 1982*, being Schedule B to the *Canada Act, 1982* (UK), 1982, c 11 [hereafter *Charter*].

2 One of the only cases to give sustained consideration of section 25 is *R. v. Kapp*, 2008 SCC 41 [hereafter *Kapp*].
3 *Dickson v. Vuntut Gwitchin First Nation*, 2021 YKCA 5 [hereafter *Dickson*].
4 See Amy Swiffen, ed., "*Dickson v. Vuntut Gwitchin First Nation* Case," special issue, *Constitutional Forum* 31, no. 2 (2022), https://doi.org/10.21991/cf29440.
5 *Constitution Act, 1982*, being Schedule B to the *Canada Act, 1982*, s 35 [hereafter *Constitution Act, 1982*].
6 Jane Arbour, "The Protection of Aboriginal Rights within a Human Rights Regime: In Search of an Analytical Framework for Section 25 of the *Charter of Rights and Freedoms*," *Supreme Court Law Review* 21, no. 1 (2003): 43. See also Celeste Hutchison, "Case Comment on *R. v. Kapp*: An Analytical Framework for Section 25 of the *Charter*," *McGill Law Journal* 52, no. 1 (2007): 173.
7 *Charter*, s 25.
8 Section 15(1) of the *Charter* reads: "Every individual is equal before and under the law and has the right to the equal protection and equal benefit of the law without discrimination and, in particular, without discrimination based on race, national or ethnic origin, colour, religion, sex, age or mental or physical disability." See Arbour, "Protection of Aboriginal Rights," 43; Hutchison, "Case Comment," 173.
9 Arbour, "Protection of Aboriginal Rights," 43; Hutchinson, "Case Comment."
10 Arbour, "Protection of Aboriginal Rights," 36–7.
11 Canada, Parliament, Minutes of Proceedings and Evidence of the Special Joint Committee of the Senate and of the House of Commons on the Constitution of Canada, 32nd Parl, 1st Sess, No 49 (30 January 1981), 94.
12 Amy Swiffen, "Constitutional Reconciliation and the *Canadian Charter of Rights and Freedoms*," *Review of Constitutional Studies* 24, no. 1 (June 2019): 85; Hutchison, "Case Comment," 178.
13 Kent McNeil shows how biological anthropology and racism of the nineteenth century influenced judicial interpretations of fact in the area of Aboriginal law; see Kent McNeil, *Flawed Precedent: The St. Catherine's Case and Aboriginal Title* (Vancouver: UBC Press, 2019). Joshua Nichols gives similar treatment to section 91(24) of the *Constitution Act, 1867*; see Joshua Nichols, *A Reconciliation without Recollection? An Investigation of the Foundations of Aboriginal Law in Canada* (Toronto: University of Toronto Press, 2019).
14 *Reference re Secession of Quebec*, [1998] 2 SCR 217, at para 82.
15 *R. v. Redhead*, [1995] 103 Man R (2d) 269, at para 83. The current wording of section 25(b) includes reference to rights that exist from land claim agreements and those that may be so acquired. Thus, Oliphant's statement

should be understood as meaning only that new Aboriginal rights are not recognized by section 25.
16 *Campbell v. British Columbia (Attorney General)*, [2000] BCSC 1123 [hereafter *Campbell*], at para 156. Another point of variance is the breadth of what is included in the protection, with some cases suggesting that only Indigenous/Aboriginal rights of a constitutional nature are protected, while others argue the protection is more broad and extends to other rights and interests as well.
17 *Shubenacadie Indian Band v. Canada (Human Rights Commission)*, [2000] 187 DLR (4th) 741, at para 43.
18 The trial judge found that the communal fishing license regulations discriminated on the basis of race. However, the British Columbia Court of Appeal dismissed the challenge (majority and concurring minority), finding the provisions were saved by section 15(2). In the course of its decision, the majority of the BC Court of Appeal commented that section 25 was only applicable if a *Charter* violation is established in the context of Aboriginal rights. In other words, it adopted a weaker version of the shield approach that sees section 25 as a justificatory provision that is relevant after an infringement has been found. In the case at issue, however, the Court found there was no infringement by drawing on subsection 15(2). Because section 15(2) saved the communal fishing license provisions, the Court concluded that section 25 was inapplicable and not necessary to analyse within the facts of the case. See also Hutchison, "Case Comment," 176.
19 Hutchison, "Case Comment," 176.
20 Ibid., 175–6. The licenses were created pursuant to the Aboriginal Communal Fishing Licenses Regulations, SOR/1993-332.
21 *Kapp*, at para 89.
22 Ibid., at para 111.
23 Naiomi Metallic, "Checking Our Attachment to the *Charter* and Respecting Indigenous Legal Orders: A Framework for *Charter* Application to Indigenous Governments," *Constitutional Forum* 31, no. 2 (2022): 3–16, https://doi.org/10.21991/cf29441.
24 *Kapp*, at paras 63–4.
25 *Dickson*, at para 11. This is something that the YKCA stresses.
26 *Vuntut Gwitchin First Nation Constitution*, last modified 10 August 2019, 12, https://www.vgfn.ca/pdf/constitution.pdf.
27 One might think the *Corbiere* case represented an earlier example, but it involved membership restrictions created by a band council, which is a creature of the *Indian Act* and was understood by the Court as delegated federal authority. In this sense, the membership restrictions in *Corbiere* derive from the authority of the *Indian Act*, whereas the claim by the

VGFN are based on the inherent/constitutional right to self-government. See *Corbiere v. Canada (Minister of Indian and Northern Affairs)*, [1999] 2 SCR 203 [hereafter *Corbiere*], at para 52.
28 As per section 9 of the Nisga'a Final Agreement, "the *Canadian Charter of Rights and Freedoms* applies to Nisga'a Government in respect of all matters within its authority, bearing in mind the free and democratic nature of Nisga'a Government as set out in this Agreement."
29 *Campbell*, at paras 163–4. The plaintiffs also based their challenge on sections 7 and 15(1), but they "did not press these submissions in oral argument."
30 *Kapp*, at para 89.
31 *Dickson*, at paras 143–4.
32 Ibid., at para 144.
33 Ibid., at para 4. The YKCA made a point of saying the self-government agreement that gave rise to the VGFN Constitution is not a Treaty. Thus, section 25 will be applicable to the VGFN self-government right as an "aboriginal" right under section 35, or as an "other" right.
34 Ibid., at para 151. At paragraph 4 the YKCA states that while the "case at bar could have been resolved by an analysis of s. 25 without a full equality analysis under ss. 15(1) … [i]t would not be appropriate to suggest at this point any general rule that s. 25 should be considered and applied only after a court has determined that a *Charter* right or freedom has been breached."
35 *Kapp*, at para 65.
36 *Dickson*, at para 177. The YKSC did not apply section 25 because it found no infringement of section 15(1). However, it stated that if section 25 did apply to "shield" the residency requirement it would be relevant after a determination of a breach that cannot be saved by section 1.
37 See Jennifer Koshan and Jonnette Watson Hamilton, "Kahkewistahaw First Nation v Taypotat: Whither Section 25 of the *Charter*?," *Constitutional Forum* 25, no. 2 (2016): 39. Koshan and Hamilton argue the Court missed an opportunity to consider section 25 in *Kahkewistahaw First Nation v. Taypotat*, 2015 SCC 30. Louis Taypotat challenged his community's election code that stipulates members running for election as Chief or Councillor must have a grade 12 education or equivalent. The Court resolved the case without recourse to section 25, but Koshan and Hamilton argue it presented an opportunity to explore whether Bastarache's approach in *Kapp* applies to actions of an Indigenous self-government when one of its members brings a challenge.
38 See Royal Commission on Aboriginal Peoples (RCAP), *Bridging the Cultural Divide: A Report on Aboriginal People and Criminal Justice in Canada* (Ottawa: RCAP, 1996), 467–8. See also David Milward, *Aboriginal Justice*

and the Charter: Realizing a Culturally Sensitive Interpretation of Legal Rights (Vancouver: UBC Press, 2012), 66–9; Timothy Dickson, "Section 25 and Intercultural Judgement," *University of Toronto Faculty Law Review* 61, no. 2 (2003): 157–8.

39 William Pentney, "The Rights of the Aboriginal Peoples of Canada and the Constitution Act, 1982: Part I: The Interpretive Prism of Section 25," *UBC Law Review* 22, no. 1 (1988): 28.
40 Thomas Isaac, "*Canadian Charter of Rights and Freedoms*: The Challenge of the Individual and Collective Rights of Aboriginal People," *Windsor Yearbook of Access to Justice* 29, no. 1 (2002): 436.
41 David Milward, *Aboriginal Justice and the Charter: Realizing a Culturally Sensitive Interpretation of Legal Rights* (Vancouver: UBC Press, 2012), 71.
42 *Dagenais v. Canadian Broadcasting Corp.*, [1994] 3 SCR 835.
43 Milward, *Aboriginal Justice*, 71.
44 Patrick Macklem, *Indigenous Difference and the Constitution of Canada* (Toronto: University of Toronto Press, 2001), 225. This is a broad reading of the scope of section 25.
45 Ibid., 225.
46 Ibid.
47 Ibid., 232.
48 Ibid., 231.
49 Kerry Wilkins, "... But We Need the Eggs: The Royal Commission, the Charter of Rights and the Inherent Right of Aboriginal Self-Government," *University of Toronto Law Journal* 49, no. 1 (Winter 1999): 114, https://doi.org/10.2307/826053.
50 Bruce Wildsmith, *Aboriginal Peoples and Section 25 of the Canadian Charter of Rights and Freedoms* (Saskatoon: Native Law Centre, University of Saskatchewan, 1988), 2.
51 Ibid., 23.
52 Brian Slattery, "The Constitutional Guarantee of Aboriginal and Treaty Rights," *Queen's Law Journal* 8, no. 1–2 (1982): 239.
53 See Arbour, "Protection of Aboriginal Rights," 62.
54 *Constitution Act, 1982*, s 35(4) reads: "Notwithstanding any other provision of this Act, the aboriginal and treaty rights referred to in subsection (1) are guaranteed equally to male and female persons."
55 Arbour, "Protection of Aboriginal Rights," 62.
56 Kent McNeil, "The Constitutional Rights of the Aboriginal Peoples of Canada," *Supreme Court Law Review* 4, no. 1 (1982): 262.
57 Wilkins, "... But We Need the Eggs," 119. From this perspective, there may be no need to resort to section 25 of the *Charter* if the *Charter* does not apply. Section 32 of the *Charter* defines which governmental bodies are covered by the *Charter*. It is not clear that Indigenous government actions that are

grounded in Indigenous laws, and not delegated by federal or provincial laws, would be caught by the *Charter*, given the language in section 32. However, in a recent decision the Yukon Court of Appeal held that "the Vuntut Gwitchin First Nation government is based on both an inherent right" and has been "validated by Canada and Yukon legislation and thus part of the *Constitution Act, 1982*. ... [Further,] the *Charter* applies to the VGFN Constitution, and laws pursuant to s. 32 of the *Charter* as the VGFN acts as a government and exercises government activities." *Dickson*, at para 40.

58 James (Sa'ke'j) Youngblood Henderson, "Empowering Treaty Federalism," *Saskatchewan Law Review* 58, no. 2 (1994): 286.
59 Ibid. See also chapter 1 by James (Sa'ke'j) Youngblood Henderson in this volume.
60 An example of this is the *First Nations Land Management Act*, SC 1999, c 24.
61 In the case of a right to self-government these aspects of the test are especially problematic. See John Borrows, "Frozen Rights in Canada: Constitutional Interpretation and the Trickster," *American Indian Law Review* 22, no. 1 (1997–8): 37–64, https://doi.org/10.2307/20068838. See also Russel Lawrence Barsh and James (Sa'ke'j) Youngblood Henderson, "The Supreme Court's Van der Peet Trilogy: Naïve Imperialism and Ropes of Sand," *McGill Law Journal* 42, no. 1 (1997): 993–1009; Catherine Bell, "New Directions in the Law of Aboriginal Rights," *Canadian Bar Review* 77, no. 1–2 (1998): 44–50.
62 Kent McNeil, "Judicial Approaches to Self-Government since *Calder*: Searching for Doctrinal Coherence," in *Let Right Be Done: Aboriginal Title, the* Calder *Case, and the Future of Indigenous Rights*, ed. Hamar Foster, Heather Raven, and Jeremy Webber (Vancouver: UBC Press, 2007), 129.
63 *Delgamuukw v. British Columbia*, [1997] 3 SCR 1010 [hereafter *Delgamuukw*], at para 115.
64 McNeil, "Judicial Approaches," 138.
65 Ibid., 143. McNeil further points out that "in municipal law, authority to make by-laws regulating use of land does not include authority to regulate businesses operating on the land and *vice versa*." McNeil, "Judicial Approaches," 249n88. In addition, Aboriginal title is subject to an internal limit that prevents the land from being used in ways that are irreconcilable with the collective interest in the land that forms the basis of the title: *Delgamuukw*, at paras 125–32. See also Kent McNeil, "The Post-Delgamuukw Nature and Content of Aboriginal Title," in *Emerging Justice? Essays on Indigenous Rights in Canada and Australia*, ed. Kent McNeil (Saskatoon: Native Law Centre, University of Saskatchewan, 2001), 116–22.
66 *Corbiere*, at para 52. L'Heureux-Dubé: "mere reference to aboriginal people in a statute, on its own, is not sufficient to bring the statute or the reference within the scope of section 25."

67 See Darlene Johnston, "The Quest of the Six Nations: Confederacy for Self-Determination," *University of Toronto Faculty of Law Review* 44, no. 1 (1986): 1–32.
68 Patricia Monture-Angus, *Journeying Forward: Dreaming of First Nations' Independence* (Halifax: Fernwood Publishing, 1999), 150.
69 See chapter 2 by Michael Asch in this volume.
70 See Swiffen, "*Dickson v. Vuntut Gwitchin First Nation* Case."
71 Justice Bastarache mentions the distinction in passing as one of the contextual factors to be considered in applying section 25. *Kapp*, at para 99.
72 See Val Napoleon, "Aboriginal Self Determination: Individual Self and Collective Selves," *Atlantis* 29, no. 2 (2005): 31–46.
73 See Darlene M. Johnston, "The Quest of the Six Nations Confederacy for Self-Determination," *University of Toronto Faculty Law Review* 44, no. 1 (1986): 8–9. Johnston cites Bruce Johansen, *Forgotten Founders: Benjamin Franklin, the Iroquois and the Rationale for the American Revolution* (Ipswich, MA: Gambit, 1982), chap. 1.
74 *Orr v. Peerless Trout First Nation*, 2015 ABQB 5.
75 Ibid., at para 4.
76 Other cases involving judicial review of band council actions have followed the same logic. See *Lafond v. Muskeg Lake First Nation*, 2008 FC 726, at para 17, where the court cites jurisprudence that has "consistently found Councils to be acting as 'federal board[s], commission[s] or other tribunal[s],' and thus subject to judicial review pursuant to section 2 of the *Federal Courts Act*." See Francis v. Mohawk Council of Kanesatake (T.D.), 2003 FCT 115 at 13. See also *Minde v. Ermineskin Cree Nation*, 2006 FC 1311.
77 *Taypotat v. Taypotat*, 2013 FCA 192, at para 36.
78 *Taypotat v. Taypotat*, 2012 FC 1036, at para 54.
79 Ibid., at para 59.
80 *Taypotat v. Taypotat*, 2013 FCA 192, at para 45.
81 Ibid., at para 66.
82 *Kahkewistahaw First Nation v. Taypotat*, 2015 SCC 30.
83 *Crow v. Blood Band*, 1996 CarswellNat 53, at para 20.
84 See Senate Canada, *First Nations Elections: The Choice Is Entirely Theirs* (Ottawa: Senate, 2010), 39, https://publications.gc.ca/collections/collection_2011/sen/yc28-0/YC28-0-403-3-eng.pdf. This is defined practically as the "establishment of governing structures, internal constitutions, elections, [and] leadership selection processes."
85 House of Commons of Canada, *Minutes of Proceedings of the Special Committee on Indian Self-Government* (Ottawa: Queen's Printer, 1983).
86 Ibid., 3.
87 Canadian Human Rights Commission, *Section 1.2 of the Canadian Human Rights Act: Balancing Collective and Individual Rights and the Principle*

of Gender Equality (Native Women's Association of Canada, 2010), 14, https://www.chrc-ccdp.gc.ca/sites/default/files/publication-pdfs/section1-2_article1-2_eng.pdf. See also Wayne Daughtery and Dennis Madill, *Indian Government Under Indian Act Legislation, 1868–1951* (Ottawa: Department of Indian and Northern Affairs, 1980); Royal Commission on Aboriginal Peoples (RCAP), *Report of the Royal Commission on Aboriginal Peoples*, vol. 1, *Looking Forward, Looking Back* (Ottawa: Supply and Services Canada, 1996), chap. 9; Vic Satzewich and Linda Mahood, "Indian Affairs and Band Governance: Deposing Indian Chiefs in Western Canada, 1896–1911," *Canadian Ethnic Studies* 26, no. 1 (1994): 40–58.

88 Indigenous Services Canada, "Conversion to Community Election System Policy," last modified 1 June 2015, Government of Canada, https://www.sac-isc.gc.ca/eng/1433166668652/1565371688997.
89 *Scrimbitt v. Sakimay Indian Band Council*, 1999 CarswellNat 2176.
90 *Horse Lake First Nation v. Horseman*, 2003 ABQB 152.
91 See Dan Russell, *A People's Dream: Aboriginal Self-Government in Canada* (Vancouver: UBC Press, 2000), 104; Will Kymlicka, *Liberalism Community and Culture* (New York: Oxford University Press, 1989), 152.
92 Mary Ellen Turpel, "Aboriginal Peoples and the *Canadian Charter*: Interpretive Monopolies, Cultural Differences," *Canadian Human Rights Yearbook* 6, no. 1 (1989–90): 3. See also Mary Ellen Turpel, "Patriarchy and Paternalism: The Legacy of the Canadian State for First Nations Women," in *Women and the Canadian State*, ed. Caroline Andrew and Sandra Rodgers (Montreal: McGill-Queen's University Press, 1997), 64–78; "Aboriginal Peoples and the *Canadian Charter of Rights and Freedoms*: Contradictions and Challenges," *Canadian Woman Studies* 10, no. 2 (1989): 149–57.
93 Mary Ellen Turpel, "Aboriginal Peoples and the *Canadian Charter*: Interpretive Monopolies, Cultural Difference," in *Canadian Perspectives on Legal Theory*, ed. Richard Devlin (Toronto: Emond Montgomery Publications, 1991), 513.
94 Monture-Angus, *Journeying Forward*, 150. See also Patricia Monture-Angus, *Thunder in My Soul: A Mohawk Woman Speaks* (Halifax: Fernwood Publishing, 1995), 142–5.
95 Patricia Monture-Angus, *Community Governance and Nation (Re)Building: Centering Indigenous Learning and Research* (Vancouver: National Centre for First Nations Governance, 2004), 35.
96 Joyce Green and Val Napoleon, "Seeking Measures of Justice: Aboriginal Women's Rights Claims, Legal Orders, and Politics" (paper presented at the Meeting of the Canadian Political Science Association, Saskatoon, SK, 29 May–1 June 2007), 3.

97 Joanne Barker, "Gender, Sovereignty, and the Discourse of Rights in Native Women's Activism," *Meridians* 7, no. 1 (2006): 133, https://www.jstor.org/stable/40338720. See also Kim Anderson, *A Recognition of Being: Reconstructing Native Womanhood* (Toronto: Sumach Press, 2000); Joyce Green, ed., *Making Space for Indigenous Feminism* (Black Point, NS: Fernwood Publishing, 2007); Renya Ramirez, "Race, Tribal Nation, and Gender: A Native Feminist Approach to Belonging," *Meridians* 7, no. 2 (2007): 22–40, https://www.jstor.org/stable/40314242; Sylvia Van Kirk, "Toward a Feminist Perspective in Native History," in *Papers of the Eighteenth Algonquian Conference*, ed. William Cowan (Ottawa: Carleton University, 1987), 377–89.

98 Green and Napoleon, "Seeking Measures of Justice," 4. See also Lilianne Krosenbrink-Gelissen, "The Canadian Constitution, the *Charter* and Aboriginal Women's Rights: Conflicts and Dilemmas," *International Journal of Canadian Studies* 7–8 (1993): 208; Bill Rafoss, "The Application of the *Canadian Charter of Rights and Freedoms* to First Nations' Jurisdiction: An Analysis of the Debate" (MA thesis, University of Saskatchewan, 2005), 39; John Borrows, "Contemporary Traditional Equality: The Effect of the *Charter* on First Nations Politics," in *Charting the Consequences: The Impact of the Charter of Rights on Canadian Law and Politics*, ed. David Schneiderman and Kate Sutherland (University of Toronto Press, 1997), 182.

99 Green and Napoleon, "Seeking Measures of Justice," 10–11. They continue: "This is unfortunate, as it avoids documenting or critiquing the extent to which patriarchal power is used to subordinate contemporary indigenous women, and the ways in which Aboriginal organisations, governments, and the colonial state support these processes. It suggests rather that the existing power relations in Aboriginal politics are unconflicted; are about resistance to the oppressor state and responsiveness to the consequences of colonialism. This avoids looking at the fundamentalist and oppressive practices that subordinate women as women, and further dignifies these practices as beyond critique because they are expressions of Aboriginal traditions."

100 It argued that provisions in the *Human Rights Act* that exempted Indigenous governments be repealed for similar reasons. Native Women's Association of Canada (NWAC), *Statement on the Canada Package* (Ottawa: NWAC, 1992). See also Canadian Human Rights Commission, *Balancing Collective and Individual Rights*; Quebec Native Women's Association, *Brief Presented by the Quebec Native Women's Association to the Royal Commission on Aboriginal Peoples: Taking Our Rightful Place* (Montreal: Quebec Native Women's Association, 1993), https://data2.archives.ca/rcap/pdf/rcap-539.pdf. The Quebec Native Women's

Association also rejected the availability of section 33 to Aboriginal governments.
101 *Corbiere*, at para 51.
102 At the Charlottetown Accord, the NWAC stated:
> Aboriginal Women are human beings and we have rights which cannot be denied or removed at the whim of any government. These views are in conflict with many Aboriginal leaders and legal theoreticians who advocate for recognition by Canada of sovereignty, self-government and collective rights. It is their unwavering view of the Aboriginal male leadership that the "collective" comes first, and that it will decide the rights of individuals.... Stripped of equality by patriarchal laws which created "male privilege" as the norm on reserve lands, Aboriginal women have a tremendous struggle to regain their social position. We want the *Canadian Charter of Rights and Freedoms* to apply to Aboriginal governments.

Quoted in Karena Shaw, *Indigeneity and Political Theory: Sovereignty and the Limits of the Political* (New York: Routledge, 2008), 94.
103 Canadian Human Rights Commission, *Balancing Collective and Individual Rights*. The NWAC supported the repeal of the exemption for band governments from the *Canadian Human Rights Act*. See also Mary Eberts, Sharon McIvor, and Teressa Nahanee, "Native Women's Association of Canada v. Canada," *Canadian Journal of Women and the Law* 18 (2006): 67–119.
104 See Barker, "Gender," 138: "If bands did indeed possess 'sacred rights,' then Canada dared not play, even in jest, with the only law that preserved them. Indian women, by implication, were likewise put on notice. By challenging the Indian Act, they were undermining not only the rights of bands but also the sacred character of bands as sovereigns."
105 Teressa Nahanee, "Indian Women, Sex Equality and the *Charter*," in *Women and the Canadian State*, ed. Caroline Andrew and Sanda Rodgers (Montreal: McGill-Queen's University Press, 1997), 89–103.
106 Borrows writes:
> While I am aware that NWAC was not representative of all Aboriginal women, and their tactics pose significant challenges to the consensus and public support needed to facilitate self-government, at the bottom of my assessment of their actions is an appreciation that a discrete and specific group of people were suffering and that their leaders were being ignored by those with greater access to power and resources. While it would have been my wish that "rights" discourse could have had a more political, rather than legal, impact, as was the case with the Constitutional and Indian Act amendments, I cannot dispute with these people for pressing their claims in the courts. Again, it is no different than what other First

Nations have done in combatting Crown failures to consider and protect their lands and culture. Why should this group of First Nations women be prevented from exercising the same liberties that other First Nations organizations regularly utilize?
John Borrows, "Contemporary Traditional Equality: The Effect of the Charter on First Nations Politics," *University of New Brunswick Law Journal* 43, no. 1 (1994): 44.

107 Sharon McIvor, "Aboriginal Women Unmasked: Using Equality Litigation to Advance Women's Rights," *Canadian Journal of Women and the Law* 16, no. 1 (2004): 128. In her account of how Indigenous women were discriminated against by Canadian governments and Indigenous men's groups during the Charlottetown Accord negotiations, McIvor writes, "For the women, to stand up in court is to be subject to the harshest treatment from their own communities locally, regionally, and nationally – be they Indian, Inuit, or Métis." Ibid., 111.

108 See also John Borrows, *Freedom and Indigenous Constitutionalism* (Toronto: University of Toronto Press, 2016).

109 As seen in *Dickson*, the question of the application of section 25 is relevant in circumstances outside of sex discrimination and will involve sections other than section 15. One possible idea inspired by Jane Arbour's proposal is that the shielding function of section 25 in the context of sex-based discrimination must be taken together with section 28 of the *Charter* and section 35(4) of the *Constitution Act*, which means that sex-based equality cannot be abridged by section 25. Another way of thinking of this is that taken together, 28 and 35(4) suggest that sex-based discrimination could potentially be addressed via section 28 instead of section 15 when section 25 is engaged. See Swiffen, "*Dickson v. Gwitchin First Nation* Case."

110 See John Borrows, *Canada's Indigenous Constitution* (Toronto: University of Toronto Press, 2010), 152–3.

111 See Bruce Clark, *Native Liberty, Crown Sovereignty: The Existing Aboriginal Right of Self-Government in Canada* (Montreal: McGill-Queen's University Press, 1990). See also Borrows, *Canada's Indigenous Constitution*; James Tully, *Strange Multiplicity: Constitutionalism in an Age of Diversity* (Cambridge: Cambridge University Press, 1995); Nichols, *A Reconciliation without Recollection?*

112 See Gordon Christie, "Aboriginal Citizenship: Sections 35, 25 and 15 of Canada's *Constitution Act, 1982*," *Citizenship Studies* 7, no. 4 (2003): 491, https://doi.org/10.1080/1362102032000134994.

113 Ibid., 491. Christie suggests that as communities reconstruct governing institutions that reflect their identities, they should be able to opt for an extended application of section 25 that would "protect traditional

ways of living from identity-challenging intrusions (both externally and internally)." Ibid., 495.
114 Ibid., 495.
115 *Dickson*, at para 104, states that "Ms. Dickson can have her application addressed under the VGFN Constitution, which incidentally she pled as an alternative remedy."
116 *Dickson*, at para 157, states that "the chambers judge's order made no reference to the claim under Article IV having been pursued before him," but as mentioned in *Dickson*, at para 104, the YKSC did note that Dickson had plead it as an alternate remedy. *Dickson*, at para 5, also notes that "the pleadings of both parties also addressed the VGFN counterpart to s. 15(1) of the *Charter*, article 4(7) of the First Nation's constitution, which guarantees equality rights to VGFN citizens. However, that part of the pleadings was not addressed by the court below and remains outside the scope of this appeal."
117 *Dickson*, at paras 119–20. Perhaps once the VGFN court is established, a Canadian court would make a different determination. See Ryan Beaton, "Doctrine Calling: Inherent Indigenous Jurisdiction in *Vuntut Gwitchin*," *Constitutional Forum* 31, no. 2 (2022): 39–52, https://doi.org/10.21991/cf29444.
118 The University of Victoria offers a joint law degree in common law and Indigenous legal orders. The Wahkohtowin Law and Governance Lodge at the Faculty of Law at the University of Alberta supports research on Indigenous laws and governance principles.
119 See Raymond Austin, *Navajo Courts and Navajo Common Law: A Tradition of Tribal Self-Governance* (Minneapolis: University of Minnesota Press, 2009); Carwyn Jones, *New Treaty, New Tradition: Reconciling New Zealand and Maori Law* (Vancouver: UBC Press, 2016).

8 Positivism and Pluralism: The Legal Imagination of Sovereignty in Indigenous–State Relations

RYAN BEATON

Law's exile of moral, philosophical, and religious insight about the nature of its own meaning-making metaphysics sustains a dangerous lack of self-reflexivity.
– John Borrows, "Origin Stories and the Law"[1]

The dominant experience over constitutional history in Canada has been of a constitution as compact and political compromise.
– Benjamin Berger, "Children of Two Logics"[2]

Conquest gives a title which the Courts of the conqueror cannot deny, whatever the private and speculative opinions of individuals may be, respecting the original justice of the claim which has been successfully asserted.
– John Marshall, *Johnson v. M'Intosh*[3]

Introduction

In July 1867, the three British colonies of Canada, New Brunswick, and Nova Scotia were united as the four Canadian provinces of Nova Scotia, New Brunswick, Quebec, and Ontario. At the time, there was a vast expanse of territory to their north and west known, on British maps, as Rupert's Land and the North-Western Territory. Rupert's Land was territory under royal charter to the Hudson's Bay Company (HBC). The North-Western Territory was, from a European perspective, unorganized territory over which the British Crown asserted sovereignty, but in which it had little real presence apart from aspects of the fur trade under *de facto* control or influence of the HBC. At the time, the majority of inhabitants across Rupert's Land and the North-Western Territory were Indigenous peoples. Estimates suggest "there were 25–35,000 Indians in the western interior in 1870, and another 10,000 metis [sic], and fewer than 2,000 Europeans or Canadians."[4]

The founding document of confederation was the *British North America Act, 1867* (the *BNA Act, 1867*),[5] a statute passed by the British imperial Parliament that set the basic terms of the new federal system and its executive, legislative, and judicial components. The Act established the Dominion Parliament and divided all legislative powers granted by the Act between that Dominion Parliament and the provincial legislatures.

The final two sections of the *BNA Act, 1867* provided for the "Admission of Other Colonies" into confederation. In particular, section 146 specified that it would be "lawful for the Queen … on address from the Houses of the Parliament of Canada to admit Rupert's Land and the North-Western Territory, or either of them, into the Union, on such Terms and Conditions" as contained in the address from the Parliament of Canada "and as the Queen thinks fit to approve." If the Queen (in effect, her imperial Privy Council) issued the Order-in-Council to admit such territory, the provisions of her Order would "have effect as if they had been enacted by the Parliament of the United Kingdom of Great Britain and Ireland."

The young Dominion was eager to welcome the vast area of Rupert's Land and the North-Western Territory (collectively, the "Territory") into confederation. Already in December 1867, the Parliament of Canada sent an address (the *"1867 Address"*)[6] to the Queen requesting that the entire Territory be admitted into the Union. In the *1867 Address*, the Parliament of Canada promised that it would respect the "legal rights of any corporation, company, or individual" in the Territory. The specific content of that promise ultimately became a focus of argument before the Supreme Court of Canada in 2015 in *Caron v. Alberta*,[7] which is examined below.

Britain in 1867 was not prepared, however, to accede to Canada's request in the absence of an agreement with the HBC. Canada therefore entered into negotiations with the HBC, and, agreement in hand, the Parliament of Canada issued another address to the Queen in May 1869 (the *"1869 Address"*),[8] providing details of that agreement and again requesting that the Territory be annexed to Canada.

To that point, no one had sought the input of the Territory's inhabitants, but reports of imminent annexation had begun to circulate and "led to unrest … particularly in the major population centre of the Red River Settlement."[9] Led by Métis leader Louis Riel, part of the population took up arms in November 1869, seizing Fort Garry, a crucial military outpost, thereby establishing control over access to the settlement. On 8 December, Riel proclaimed the establishment of a provisional government through a "Declaration of the People of Rupert's Land and the North West" (the "Declaration") that echoed the American Declaration of Independence of 1776 in structure and rhetorical style, though embodying a considerably more moderate assertion of political and legal independence.[10]

While the Declaration has been fairly characterized as the Declaration of Métis Independence, it was expressly made "in the name of the people of Rupert's Land and the North West," apparently including "the neighbouring tribes of Indians who are now in friendly relations with us." The Declaration also characterized the provisional government it proclaimed as "the only and lawful authority now in existence in Rupert's Land and the North West which claims the obedience and respect of the people."[11]

In general terms, the Declaration asserted the inherent liberty of a people "to establish any form of government it may consider suitable to its wants, as soon as the power to which it was subject abandons it or attempts to subjugate it without its consent to a foreign power."[12] In specific terms, the Declaration laid out the case that the HBC had abandoned the people of the Territory and acted "contrary to the law of nations" when it "surrendered and transferred to Canada all the rights which it had or pretended to have" in the Territory.[13]

As a result, "from the day on which the Government [i.e., the HBC] we always respected abandoned us – by transferring to a strange power the sacred authority confided to it – the people of Rupert's Land and the North West became free and exempt from all allegiance to the said Government." Interestingly, while the Declaration thus invokes notions of popular liberty and "refuse[s] to recognise the authority of Canada," it also asserts "our rights and interests as British subjects."[14]

The Declaration did not insist on permanent independence from Canada, stating rather that "we hold ourselves in readiness to enter into negotiations with the Canadian Government as may be favourable for the good government and prosperity of this people."[15] In this respect, the Declaration obviously had much more modest aims than the American Declaration of 1776. The Métis provisional government wanted, in essence, to negotiate the terms on which annexation of the Territory to Canada would take place. The Declaration nonetheless forcefully proclaimed the inherent lawful authority of the people of the Territory to determine their own political fate in the absence of an effective government acting in the people's interests.

In any event, Canada would not risk military confrontation without British support, and the British, for their part, pressured Canada to negotiate. The Métis provisional government drew up a bill of rights, in several iterations, for Canada to guarantee as a condition for the provisional government's acceptance of annexation. In early 1870, Canada sent a delegation to Red River. The Canadian delegation was headed by Donald Smith, who recognized the authority of the Métis provisional government, after it had been restructured and confirmed by a convention of the entire Red River Settlement, with Riel now officially recognized as head of the provisional government.

Donald Smith reviewed a version of the bill of rights drawn up by the provisional government and discussed the contents in detail with representatives of that government. That draft bill of rights included demands that the Territory enter confederation as a province and that all laws for the new province be published in both French and English. This demand for a guarantee of legislative bilingualism was at the heart of *Caron* almost a century and a half later.

Following the negotiations at Red River, the Métis provisional government in turn sent a delegation to Ottawa in the spring of 1870, with the aim of working out the details of an agreement with Canada on the terms of annexation. The provisional government informed its delegates that they did not have authority to conclude a binding final agreement; any agreement they reached with Canada would have to be ratified by the provisional government. The idea, at least from the perspective of the provisional government, seems to have been that these were negotiations conducted on behalf of distinct legal authorities, and that formal ratification by both parties was required to give binding force to any final agreement.

The parties did reach an agreement in Ottawa that was subsequently approved by the provisional government in Red River and by the Dominion Parliament through the *Manitoba Act, 1870*,[16] which created the new province of Manitoba out of a (very small) fraction of the Territory upon the Territory's annexation to Canada. These developments paved the way for the *Rupert's Land and the North-Western Territory Order* (hereafter the *1870 Order*) of the Queen-in-Council annexing the Territory to Canada, effective 15 July 1870, pursuant to section 146 of the *BNA Act, 1867*.

Of course, these negotiations were radically asymmetric in terms of the military and political power and population size governed by these respective legal orders, with the Red River Settlement (and arguably the inhabitants of the Territory more broadly) represented in improvised fashion by the Métis provisional government on the one side, and the Dominion of Canada together with imperial Britain (and arguably, in a more diffuse sense, European colonial power and authority) on the other.

In the decades that followed the 1870 agreement, the Métis population at Red River was largely dispersed and overwhelmed by migrants from the east, particularly Ontario. The Métis population suffered considerably from Canada's failure to effectively survey and grant the 1.4 million acres of land it promised to set aside for the Métis.[17] By contrast, Canadian institutions became more stable and self-assured with the westward sweep of settlement.[18] The outcome of the negotiations between Canada and the Métis provisional government was embedded, on the Canadian and British side, in various legal and constitutional instruments, notably the *Manitoba Act, 1870*, adopted by the Dominion Parliament, the *1870 Order* of the Queen-in-Council, and the *British North America Act, 1871* (the *BNA Act, 1871*),[19] adopted by the imperial Parliament in order to confirm the Dominion Parliament's authority to create new provinces. The *BNA Act, 1871* thus shored up the validity of the *Manitoba Act, 1870*.

Over the next few decades, the Dominion Parliament adopted further legislation adjusting provincial and territorial borders in the annexed Territory, and in 1905 it created two new provinces, Alberta and Saskatchewan, across parts of the Territory.[20] The Métis provisional government, for its part, did not leave any comparable institutional legacy or set of legal instruments ratifying and implementing its 1870 agreement with Canada.

This extremely cursory review of a striking episode in Canadian history will have to suffice for purposes of setting up the central question of this chapter: How should a Canadian court today approach and resolve disputes about the legal and constitutional force attaching to promises made in historic agreements between Canada and Aboriginal peoples? That question is at the heart of the clash between the interpretive approaches of the majority and dissent in *Caron*, which respectively exemplify the approaches described in this chapter as *institutional positivism* and *historically grounded pluralism*.

While *Caron* was not argued or decided specifically as a matter of Aboriginal law, the judgment is helpful in isolating and teeing up questions about the proper judicial approach to interpreting historic agreements between representatives of the Canadian state and representatives of Aboriginal peoples within Canada's asserted territory. The term "Aboriginal peoples" is used here with reference to its definition in section 35 of the *Constitution Act, 1982*, which recognizes and affirms existing Aboriginal and treaty rights in Canada and explicitly affirms that Métis are Aboriginal peoples within the meaning of that section.[21]

Caron can also be read more generally as a case dealing with the relationship between a state legal order and state assertions of sovereignty on one side, and peoples within the asserted territory of the state who claim their own inherent legal authority independent from the state on the other. Such relationships raise legal issues for all nation states,[22] but those issues are particularly acute in the context of Indigenous–state relations in settler states like Canada.

This chapter explores institutional positivism and historically grounded pluralism as distinct interpretive orientations, drawing out their respective characteristics. The chapter is divided into two principal parts. The first section examines *Caron* in detail, placing side by side a handful of key contrasting interpretive steps taken by the majority and dissent in that case. The second section then provides some philosophical, legal-historical, and jurisprudential reflection on the contrasting interpretive approaches found in *Caron*.

There are a number of reasons for beginning with a particular court judgment before turning to the broader discussion. Most important, institutional positivism and historically grounded pluralism, as understood and examined here, are not concepts or theories of adjudication but *interpretive approaches*, built from specific interpretive and rhetorical manoeuvres, including statements about such things as the role of domestic courts and legislatures, the constitution as a statement of the will of the people, principles relating to separation of powers and provincial sovereignty, and so on. Judges use interpretive and rhetorical manoeuvres to arrange the materials before them into sets of reasons that "resolve" the case at hand. The materials to be arranged include legal materials (e.g., statutes, regulations, judicial precedent, constitutional provisions, treaties, international conventions) and legal arguments put forward by the parties, sometimes with academic commentary and citations to foreign or international courts, as well as factual evidence relating to the particular dispute before the court. Judicial interpretation, so understood, is best explained through concrete examples, supplemented by discussion that draws on those concrete examples.

A second reason for beginning directly with *Caron* is to have a concrete touchstone to help ground the broader discussion that follows. That discussion will draw on foundational cases of Canadian Aboriginal law, notably the Marshall trilogy of decisions issued by the Supreme Court of the United States between 1823 and 1832, which have had great influence in Canadian law as well.[23]

Throughout this chapter, the aim is to move back and forth between, on the one hand, the more concrete level of legal dispute and doctrinal evolution in the case law and, on the other hand, the more theoretical level of legal philosophy and legal historical development, in a fashion that is mutually illuminating for these intertwined levels. That said, this approach accords a certain priority to (or adopts a certain parochialism[24] towards) concrete legal context and doctrinal development as the material for legal philosophical reflection and discussion (with the understanding that such reflection is never purely descriptive, as it is necessarily informed by partisan[25] commitments).

One final note before diving into *Caron*: I am not an historian, and this chapter does not pretend to be a historical study of the events summarized above and discussed below. The central aim of this chapter is to make sense of the divergent approaches to legal interpretation illustrated in the majority and dissenting reasons of *Caron*, and to relate these interpretive approaches more generally to the Canadian case law on Indigenous–state relations. I largely present the historical events in question through the Court's reading of them, though I will occasionally clarify or amend certain historical statements made by the Court where I am aware of shortcomings.

Caron: How to Interpret the 1870 Agreement between Canada and the Métis?

Caron had its humble beginnings in traffic offences charged to Gilles Caron and Pierre Boutet in Alberta. The two defendants conceded the relevant facts but challenged the applicable provincial law and regulation as unconstitutional on the grounds that they had not been enacted or published in French as well as in English. They argued that Alberta had a constitutional obligation to "enact, print, and publish its laws and regulations in both French and English."[26] In other words, they claimed a right to legislative bilingualism in Alberta.

Caron turned on the Court's interpretation of the negotiations and resulting agreement in 1870 between representatives of Canada and of the Métis provisional government, established at Red River to represent inhabitants of Rupert's Land and the North-Western Territory (the "Territory"). The Court had to decide whether the outcome of those negotiations included a guarantee of legislative bilingualism throughout the entire Territory following annexation to Canada, such that the guarantee remained constitutionally binding on Alberta subsequent to that province's creation in 1905. By a count of six justices to three, the Court said no.

The majority in *Caron* drew on features of the Canadian constitutional order – notably, modern understandings of provincial sovereignty, minority language rights, and constitutional entrenchment – in order to interpret the content of the agreement between Canada and the Métis provisional government. In effect, the majority circumscribed the legal significance of that agreement by requiring consistency with modern elements of Canadian constitutionalism, parliamentary sovereignty foremost among them. John Borrows has observed that this approach is common in treaty interpretation: "Parties engaged in treaty interpretation often act as if post-hoc national structures mirror historical circumstances."[27] Conversely, the dissent laid primary emphasis on historical context in first determining the content of the negotiated agreement, in order then to ask how the relevant constitutional provisions might be interpreted to give effect to the agreement.

Oversimplifying greatly (and unfairly to both majority and dissent), we might say that the majority interpreted the historic agreement instrumentally for consistency with parliamentary sovereignty and modern constitutional structure more generally, while the dissent interpreted relevant constitutional provisions instrumentally to fulfil the actual historic agreement. The discussion of *Caron* below begins by providing a somewhat more detailed overview of the historical background relevant to the case, before adding nuance to the oversimplified characterization just given of the majority and dissent's respective interpretive approaches.

Overview of the Historical Events before the Court in Caron

As explained above, in December 1867 the Canadian Parliament sent its first address to the Queen requesting annexation of the Territory. After the Queen declined to act on that request, Canada negotiated an agreement with the HBC for the surrender of the HBC's royal charter to Rupert's Land, and then sent a second request for annexation to the Queen in May 1869, including the terms of that agreement. While neither British nor Canadian representatives had to that point discussed annexation with inhabitants of the Territory, reports of imminent annexation were circulating. The situation escalated:

> In November 1869, a group of inhabitants blocked the entry of Canada's proposed Lieutenant Governor of the new territory. Shortly thereafter, a group of Métis inhabitants, including Louis Riel, seized control of Upper Fort Garry in the Red River Settlement. Riel summoned representatives of the English- and French-speaking parishes. These representatives and others subsequently formed a provisional government.[28]

The provisional government issued at least three "Lists of Rights" between December 1869 and March 1870, demands "that Canada would have to satisfy before they would accept Canadian control."[29]

These Lists of Rights included a demand for legislative bilingualism throughout the Territory, as well as a demand that the entire Territory enter confederation as a province. Both the majority and dissent in *Caron* accepted the findings of the trial judge that legislative bilingualism was already the *de facto* reality under HBC rule.

Confronted with Métis resistance, Canada suggested to Britain that the transfer be delayed. In the meantime, however, the HBC had surrendered its royal charter to the British Crown, who opposed the delay and pressured Canada to negotiate with the provisional government. As a result, Canada sent a delegation to Red River to negotiate:

> Canadian representative Donald Smith met with Riel and members of the provisional government in early 1870 to discuss their concerns. ... Canada subsequently invited a delegation to Ottawa to present the demands of the settlers. Three delegates from the provisional government travelled to Ottawa in April 1870 to negotiate. ... They met and negotiated with Prime Minister John A. Macdonald and the Minister of Militia and Defence, George-Étienne Cartier.[30]

While the majority stated (and the dissent did not dispute) that "there is little evidence regarding the substance of [the] negotiations" that took place in Ottawa,[31] the negotiations between Smith and the provisional government at Red River are well documented in the record that was before the Court. Notably, responding specifically to demands presented in one of the Lists of Rights, "Smith assured the inhabitants of their right to legislative bilingualism, stating: '... I have to say, that its propriety is so very evident that it will unquestionably be provided for.'"[32]

When the provisional government sent its delegates, in turn, to Ottawa in April 1870 to pursue further negotiations, it advised those delegates in a letter of instruction that the demand for legislative bilingualism was peremptory.[33] It also "informed the delegates that they were not empowered to conclude final arrangements with the Canadian government; any agreement entered into would require the approval of and ratification by the provisional government."[34] There seems to be no record of what, if anything, was said specifically about the "peremptory" demand for legislative bilingualism in the course of the negotiations in Ottawa between the representatives of the provisional government and Minister Cartier. (Prime Minister Macdonald was "indisposed" and absent from negotiations from 28 April until 2 May, leaving Minister Cartier to lead the negotiations on behalf of Canada.[35])

However, one undisputed outcome of the negotiations is that in May 1870 the Parliament of Canada adopted the *Manitoba Act, 1870*. The *Manitoba Act, 1870* created, upon annexation of the Territory as a whole, a new province out of only a small portion of the Territory. The Territory as a whole was formally annexed to Canada in July 1870 by the *1870 Order* of the Queen-in-Council. The *Manitoba Act, 1870* included a guarantee of legislative bilingualism in the newly created province.[36] The remainder of the Territory admitted into the Union came under federal jurisdiction – in particular, under the legislative authority of Parliament, which had a constitutional obligation of legislative bilingualism under section 133 of the *BNA Act, 1867*.[37]

What to make of this situation? The Métis provisional government was, it seems, unsuccessful in pressing its demand that the entire Territory enter the Union as a province. (Though it is worth noting that Father Ritchot, who was, in effect, the lead negotiator in Ottawa on behalf of the Métis provisional government, considered this outcome not inconsistent with the demand that the Territory become a province of Canada.[38] He accepted Canada's proposal for the immediate creation of Manitoba as a province, with the creation of further provinces out of the remaining territory to follow at a later date.)

Was the provisional government also unsuccessful in its demand that legislative bilingualism be guaranteed throughout the Territory? Perhaps the most that can be said without controversy is that the newly admitted Territory was formally split under two legislative authorities: that of Manitoba (in matters of provincial jurisdiction) in the new province and that of Parliament in the remainder of the Territory, both of which had constitutional obligations of legislative bilingualism. But did that amount to a lasting constitutional entrenchment of legislative bilingualism across the entire Territory? Perhaps the most that can be said here without controversy is that when the provinces of Alberta and Saskatchewan were later formed from parts of the Territory, those new provinces assumed that the federal obligation of legislative bilingualism did not pass to their legislatures. The Supreme Court of Canada seemed to confirm this assumption in *R. v. Mercure*.[39]

However, the Court in *Mercure* did not consider in any detail the constitutional significance of the 1870 negotiations and agreement between Canada and the Métis provisional government, nor how that agreement may have been entrenched through the *1870 Order*, which belongs to Canada's Constitution by virtue of being listed (Item 3) in the Schedule to the *Constitution Act, 1982*. In turn, the *1867 Address* and the *1869 Address* are attached as schedules to the *1870 Order*, which became the focus of constitutional interpretation in *Caron*. The majority and dissent both accepted that the promise in the *1867 Address* to protect the "legal rights of any corporation, company, or individual" was the most plausible textual hook on which to hang the appellants' argument that Canada's promise to ensure legislative bilingualism throughout the Territory had been entrenched in the constitutional provisions through which Canada gave effect to the 1870 agreement with the Métis provisional government.

Institutional Positivism and Historically Grounded Pluralism in Caron

There are, of course, many additional elements to be drawn from the historical context that might be relevant to the dispute in *Caron*. The aim here is not to relitigate the case, nor to argue that either the majority or the dissent was right in its respective disposition of the case. Rather, the purpose of subsections (1) to (5) below is to highlight key points of contrast in the interpretive approaches taken by the majority and the dissent, in order to begin fleshing out the meaning of *institutional positivism* and *historically grounded pluralism* as interpretive approaches taking shape in Canadian Aboriginal law today.

As *Caron* also illustrates, significant constitutional cases tend to allow for – in fact, require – a great deal of legal imagination and creativity in the crafting of judicial resolution. This is evidently true for cases in which legal interpretation includes an important dimension of historical interpretation, for example, assessments of historical relationships between the state, settlers, Métis, Indigenous peoples, and of various institutions and practices that shaped these relationships. These cases present the courts – and legal imagination more generally – with a great deal of room to manoeuvre. That is not a defect of these cases or of the legal system; it is simply the reality of any attempt to render complex historical, social, and political relationships in the language of law in order to draw precise legal conclusions about disputes arising from the context of these relationships.

The historical, social, and political contexts at issue in *Caron* also present a great deal of legal uncertainty, which animates this chapter's overarching question: How should a Canadian court today interpret a historic agreement between Canada and the government of an Aboriginal people asserting legal authority independent of the state? The majority and the dissent in *Caron* adopt contrasting interpretive approaches in answering this question. The interplay between these two approaches in *Caron* offers a particularly clear illustration of a dynamic resonating across Canadian Aboriginal law and throughout the Court's recent efforts to help "reconcile pre-existing Aboriginal sovereignty with assumed Crown sovereignty," "prior Aboriginal occupation with *de facto* Crown sovereignty," and Canadian state law with "pre-existing systems of aboriginal law."[40]

These phrases highlight the fact that reconciliation, the "ultimate purpose of the honour of the Crown,"[41] which the Court has placed at the heart of section 35, requires the courts to grapple with Canada's history of legal pluralism arising from Indigenous–state relations. In what follows, *Caron* is used to introduce five key interpretive manoeuvres deployed by the courts in that task of grappling with Canada's legal pluralism, and to illustrate how sequences of such manoeuvres may be linked together to produce contrasting legal outcomes, in what I am describing as institutional positivist and historically grounded pluralist modes, respectively.

(1) OPENING SALVOS: TO FRAME HISTORY WITH LAW, OR LAW WITH HISTORY?

The opening paragraphs of the majority and dissenting reasons are a study in contrasting frames. The majority's opening sentence places us immediately within Canadian constitutional concerns: "These appeals sit at a contentious crossroads in Canadian constitutional law, the intersection of minority language rights and provincial legislative powers."[42] The majority reasons repeatedly draw on constitutional principles relating to minority language rights and provincial legislative powers to interpret the outcome of negotiations in 1870 between Canada and the Métis provisional government.

In contrast, the first paragraph of the dissenting reasons immediately foregrounds the historic negotiations and agreement, insisting that the question before the Court "requires us to go back to the country's foundational moments, to its 'constitution' in the most literal sense. More precisely, at the heart of this case are the negotiations regarding the annexation of Rupert's Land and the North-Western Territory to Canada."[43] The dissent closes its first paragraph by stressing that the negotiations and resulting historic compromise were the necessary foundation for any constitutional moment to emerge: "It is common ground that [the negotiations] unequivocally resulted in a historic political compromise that permitted the annexation of those territories."[44]

(2) ARE WE ASKING WHICH RIGHTS WERE *GRANTED* OR *AGREED UPON*?

Having placed the interpretation of the historic agreement within the frame of Canadian constitutional principles, the majority naturally turns to the question of what the Constitution *granted*. The majority is interested in what *Canada and Britain intended* to give or create through the legal instruments they used to implement the 1870 agreement. The majority focuses on intent through the lens of concerns internal to Canadian and British legal systems and practices, rather than through the lens of the negotiations between Canada and the Métis provisional government. In particular, the majority finds an insurmountable obstacle to the appellants' argument in the fact that the *1870 Order* did not explicitly address legislative bilingualism. The majority finds it "inconceivable that such an important right, if it were *granted* [emphasis added], would not have been *granted* [emphasis added] in explicit language."[45]

The dissent, for its part focusing on the historical context and negotiations, does not ask what the Constitution granted, but what the parties agreed upon. The dissent ultimately concludes that an obligation of legislative bilingualism binds Alberta today "on the basis that the historic agreement between the Canadian government and the inhabitants of Rupert's Land and the North-Western Territory contained a promise to protect legislative bilingualism."[46] In other words, the dissent builds its reasons on a foundation of historical evidence, finding that a commitment to legislative bilingualism was part of the historic agreement. That historical finding then grounds the dissent's interpretation of the commitments that Canada entrenched through formal legal instruments. On this basis, the dissent accepts "the appellants' argument that that [historic 1870] agreement is constitutionally entrenched by virtue of the *1867 Address*."[47]

The dissent thus places greater emphasis on what was agreed in negotiations between Canadian representatives and representatives of the provisional government, interpreting Canada's own legal instruments accordingly. By contrast, the majority places greater emphasis on what Canada intended through these legal instruments and is less prepared to interpret that intent in light of historical evidence about what was jointly agreed in negotiations.

It is worth underscoring, again, that these contrasting emphases are matters of degree and orientation, not conceptual binaries. This point is examined further below. Nonetheless, although the contrast highlighted in each pair of interpretive manoeuvres discussed here may be a matter of degrees, the two series of interlinking manoeuvres (in the majority and dissenting reasons, respectively) ultimately produce the opposing legal outcomes favoured by the majority and dissent, respectively. Over a series of cases across an area of law, interpretive approaches made from such building blocks (i.e., interpretive manoeuvres differing by degrees or orientation from opposing counterparts) may acquire a rough consistency and recognizable pattern of interpretive use.

(3) OKAY, BUT DIDN'T THE *1867 ADDRESS* PRECEDE THE NEGOTIATIONS?

The majority quite sensibly points out that the *1867 Address*, including its promise that the "legal rights of any corporation, company, or individual" in the Territory would be assured after annexation, preceded by more than two years any negotiations between Canada and the Métis provisional government. Even if it were possible to overlook the fact that the *1867 Address* nowhere explicitly mentions legislative bilingualism or language rights, how could anyone think that it entrenched a promise of legislative bilingualism made years later? The majority finds it simply cannot build a constitutional guarantee of legislative bilingualism from "broad and uncontroversial generalities" or "infus[e] vague phrases with improbable meanings."[48]

Once again, the dissent counters with a focus on the political and historical context. The meaning of the promise in the *1867 Address*, for purposes of resolving the legal dispute in *Caron*, has to be understood not solely with reference to Parliament's intent in 1867, but with reference also to the subsequent events that paved the way for annexation through the *1870 Order* and, therefore, also for the constitutional entrenchment of the words of the *1867 Address* as a schedule to the *1870 Order*.

True, when Parliament issued the *1867 Address*, it had not turned its mind specifically to guaranteeing legislative bilingualism in the territory to be annexed. Yet, as events unfolded, the British Crown refused to issue the order requested in the *1867 Address* and again in the *1869 Address* until Canada had reached a settlement with the provisional government at Red River. In this context, Parliament's promise in the *1867 Address* to protect the "legal rights of any corporation, company, or individual" in the Territory was transformed into "a forward-looking undertaking that was shaped by subsequent negotiations. The meaning of its terms must therefore be informed by those negotiations."[49] By the time the *1867 Address* was attached to the *1870 Order, subsequent* to the conclusion of negotiations, it is clear, in the dissent's view, that the "legal rights" actually negotiated in the interim included the right to legislative bilingualism.

These contrasting readings of the *1867 Address* are where the clash of interpretive approaches in *Caron* really comes to a head. The majority is dismissive of "the complex web of instruments, vague phrases, political pronouncements and historical context on which the appellants' claims depend."[50] The majority's position is understandable in light of its focus on parliamentary intent as the most important factor controlling the meaning of the *1867 Address*. For no legal alchemy based on subsequent events can transform what Parliament intended in 1867.

214   Ryan Beaton

For the dissent, however, the majority's interpretive approach is both inaccurate and unjust, *precisely because* its interpretation of Parliament's words ignores the crucial "socio-political context" of events *subsequent* to Parliament's initial pronouncement of those words:

> The British government was applying significant pressure on Canada to negotiate reasonable terms for the transfer. This was the socio-political context in which the negotiations and the promises made to the inhabitants by the Canadian government must be understood. *An interpretation that does not account for this context is not only inaccurate, but also unjust* [emphasis added].[51]

The dissent supports its interpretation of the legal effect of the negotiations and promises with a constitutional principle of its own – the nature of the Constitution as an expression of the will of the people:

> The Constitution of Canada emerged from negotiations and compromises between the founding peoples, and continues to develop on the basis of similar negotiations and compromises. Such compromises are achieved when parties to the negotiations make concessions in pursuit of a mutual agreement and reach a meeting of the minds. *Therefore, our reading of constitutional documents must be informed by the intentions and perspectives of all the parties, as revealed by the historical evidence* [emphasis added]. It is in this context that we will apply the third interpretive principle regarding the nature of a constitution as a statement of the will of the people.[52]

The dissent's appeal to constitutional principle here is another useful reminder that nuance must be brought to the contrast drawn between majority and dissent at the outset of this chapter – that is, to the oversimplified view that the majority interprets the historic agreement instrumentally for consistency with the Constitution, while the dissent interprets the Constitution instrumentally for consistency with historic agreement. Clearly, both approaches interpret the Constitution (including constitutional text, principles, and structure) and historical events in mutually informing ways, but there remains an undeniable difference in emphasis. Even when the dissent draws on the "interpretive principle regarding the nature of a constitution as a statement of the will of the people," it puts flesh on the bones of this constitutional principle by focusing on the historic agreement itself, and on the need to account for the perspective not just of Canadian representatives and institutions but also of those who entered into agreement with Canada:

> [I]n assessing the historical context of the promise contained in the *1867 Address*, due weight must be given to the perspective of the people who, through their representatives, concluded a historic compromise that resulted in the peaceful entry of their territories into Canada. As the historical record discussed above demonstrates, they had every reason to believe that they had secured the right to legislative bilingualism as a condition for their entry into union.[53]

And in more general terms:

> The story of our nation's founding therefore cannot be understood without considering the perspective of the people who agreed to enter into Confederation. If only the Canadian government's perspective is taken into account, the result is a truncated view of the concessions made in the negotiations.[54]

In case there was any doubt as to the driving force in the dissent's analysis, its closing paragraphs stress that the historical context "*dictates* [emphasis added] an interpretation of 'legal rights' that recognizes this promise" of legislative bilingualism.[55]

The interpretive orientation found in the dissent's reasons sees constitutional provisions, at least those used to implement foundational historic agreements, *first* as vehicles for implementing the historic agreement and only *second* as elements of a self-structuring (or "autopoietic"[56]) constitutional system. The majority's interpretive orientation is generally the reverse.

Both the majority and dissenting reasons are necessarily embedded within the broader social and political imaginaries of the present day. Note, however, that the dissent's emphasis on historical context – to the point of stating that this context *dictates* the proper interpretation of relevant constitutional provisions – opens greater space for a transformed reading of historical context to have a transformative impact on present-day constitutional interpretation. By contrast, the majority's approach – hewing more tightly (1) to the intention of state institutions and actors at the time they adopted relevant constitutional provisions and (2) to existing internal constitutional principles and institutional structures – insulates constitutional interpretation to a degree from transformations in our social and political imaginaries that compel revisions in our readings of history.

(4) DIDN'T THEY KNOW HOW TO ENTRENCH LANGUAGE RIGHTS?

The majority places great stock in the notion that Parliament knew how to entrench language rights if it wanted to. Thus, "[t]he words in the *1867 Address* cannot support a constitutional guarantee of legislative bilingualism in the province of Alberta. Parliament knew how to entrench language rights and did so in the *Manitoba Act, 1870* but not in the *1867 Address*."[57] As noted in sections (2) and (3) above, this focus on what Parliament intended flows from the majority's framing of the case in terms of what rights were "granted" to the inhabitants of the Territory. Even setting that point aside, the majority's emphasis on Parliament knowing how to entrench language rights in 1870 is anachronistic for at least two reasons.

First, Parliament did not really know how to entrench anything at the time. On basic principles of parliamentary sovereignty derived from Britain, no parliament could entrench an act against itself. It is doubtful, at the very least, that the *Manitoba Act, 1870* was entrenched against the Parliament of Canada, which had passed that Act into law. Or, to put the point somewhat differently, it is unclear whether the Parliament of Canada had the power to create new provinces within the federal structure of Canada established by the *BNA Act, 1867*.

It is hard to assess the historical legal situation with certainty, since the *BNA Act, 1867*, adopted by the imperial Parliament, was undoubtedly entrenched against the Parliament of Canada and divided powers between that Parliament and the provincial legislatures. Arguably, then, the *Manitoba Act, 1870*, once adopted by the Parliament of Canada, achieved a measure of entrenchment insofar as the new province's jurisdictional powers were protected under the *BNA Act, 1867*. Yet precisely such a result – the Parliament of Canada successfully entrenching an Act against itself – conflicts with British notions of parliamentary sovereignty and raises questions about the power of the Parliament of Canada to create new provinces.

At a minimum, this situation is hardly a model of clarity. Indeed, this state of uncertainty led the imperial Parliament to enact the *BNA Act, 1871* to address "doubts ... respecting the powers of the Parliament of Canada to establish Provinces in territories admitted, or which may hereafter be admitted, into the Dominion of Canada."[58] If implementation of the historic agreement between Canada and the provisional government was to stand or fall with Parliament's know-how for constitutional entrenchment, it was on shaky ground.

Second, as the dissent in *Caron* explained, the *Manitoba Act, 1870* and the *1870 Order* "are not really comparable, as they did not come from the same legislative authorities – the *Manitoba Act, 1870* was passed by the Canadian Parliament, while the *1870 Order* was issued by Imperial authorities."[59] Moreover, "the annexed territories fell under federal authority. It was therefore guaranteed pursuant to s. 133 of the *Constitution Act, 1867* that federal Acts applicable to the territories would be printed and published in both languages as a consequence of their being Acts of the Parliament of Canada."[60] Arguably, the protection for legislative bilingualism in 1870 would have appeared stronger in the portion of the annexed Territory under federal authority than in the new province of Manitoba, since there was no doubt that section 133 was entrenched against the Parliament of Canada.

(5) CAN WE STILL PRIVILEGE PARLIAMENT'S WORDS, IF NOT ITS INTENTIONS?

Despite all the points highlighted above, the majority insists that it is not privileging Parliament's intentions:

> Of course, this is not to suggest that the intentions of Parliament occupy a position of privilege over those of the territorial inhabitants negotiating three years later in 1870. On the contrary, the understanding and intention of the representatives and negotiators also informs the context of the negotiations in 1870. However, there is no evidence that they used the words "legal rights" from the *1867 Address* in the broad manner suggested by the appellants.[61]

The majority here says that it is not privileging the intentions of Parliament but is also taking into account the meaning that the territorial inhabitants' representatives attached *to words used by Parliament*. This reveals how deeply anchored the majority's approach is in the perspective of Parliament, or at least in a perspective grounded by the legal instruments of Parliament.

By contrast, the dissent does not focus on the meaning that representatives of the Métis provisional government might have attached to words *used by Canada and Britain* to give effect to the historic agreement. Rather, the dissent focuses on the words used by the Métis representatives themselves in negotiations leading to the 1870 agreement. The dissent then uses its conclusions about the content of the negotiated agreement to ground its interpretation of the words found in the constitutional instruments that gave effect to the agreement.

On each of the five points addressed above, the majority and dissent made contrasting interpretive manoeuvres. In broad terms, the contrast reflects the dissent's primary emphasis on historical evidence and context (as read through present-day social and political imaginaries) and the majority's primary emphasis on (1) the historical intent of state institutions and actors as governed by (2) internal constitutional principles and structure flowing from state authority.

In *Caron*, these two series of interpretive manoeuvres ultimately led to opposite conclusions about the proper resolution of the specific legal dispute before the Court. The majority concluded that the appellants had failed to establish that Alberta was bound by an obligation of legislative bilingualism and dismissed the appeal. The dissent concluded that the appellants had established this obligation and would have allowed the appeal. In the result, then, no constitutional obligation of legislative bilingualism is enforced on Alberta today.

The specific legal dispute in *Caron* arose under traffic safety legislation adopted by the provincial legislature of Alberta and, insofar as the dispute was adjudicated in Canadian courts, this forced parties involved in the litigation to mobilize a host of technical legal aspects of the Canadian legal system in order, first, to present the dispute over traffic tickets as a constitutional issue and, second, to develop legal arguments about the proper resolution of the constitutional issue once raised. The forum thus forced the parties to debate, through the same medium of technical legal argument, issues of pressing social and political importance today, including the meaning and binding authority of historic agreements between the state and Aboriginal peoples.

The majority and dissenting reasons in *Caron* provide a snapshot of positivist and pluralist approaches to the Court's interpretive task. Both approaches draw together commitments grounded in the country's legal history to justify a binding legal outcome today. In the ways detailed above, however, they adopt distinct orientations to the task, characterized by contrasting interpretive manoeuvres. The remainder of this chapter traces some of the roots of these contrasting interpretive orientations through foundational Aboriginal law cases, and explores legal philosophical implications and issues raised by the contrast.

The Roots of Positivism and Pluralism in Canadian Aboriginal Law and in the Marshall Trilogy

The Disagreement in Caron as a Dispute about the Sources of Law

In an article addressing treaty interpretation in Canada and New Zealand, John Borrows makes the following observations:

> Indigenous issues in Canada and New Zealand also raise metaphysical questions. "Where do we come from?" is a fundamental inquiry in

the treaty field. The answer to this question structures subsequent legal analysis. Law's origin is a big deal. If we believe our primary laws come from Britain, this will produce different normative obligations from those laws which originate on Indigenous shores. Thus, we should not overlook law's "in the beginning" inquiries. When we identify law's source, we can learn more about in whose image it was created. Origins matter. Or to use a scientific analogy: origins *are* matter; they spawn the elements from which legal worlds are subsequently formed.[62]

One way of reading the underlying disagreement between majority and dissent in *Caron* is in terms of the origins of Canadian law. The majority looks to the institutions and legal instruments of imperial Britain and the Canadian state as the primary sources of law in framing the case. The dissent leans more heavily on the negotiations and agreement between Canada and the Métis, as established by the historical evidence before the Court.

Again, it bears emphasizing that this contrast is a matter of degrees. The majority certainly does not ignore the content of the negotiations when interpreting the legal instruments used by Canada and Britain. The dissent, for its part, accepts that those legal instruments are key to the case: the appellants must establish that those legal instruments can plausibly be read as implementing a negotiated guarantee of legislative bilingualism. Yet the majority's approach fits more naturally within a picture of the Canadian constitutional order as a political project founded on the assertion of Crown sovereignty on North American soil. The project must adapt to local conditions in order to take root, but it traces its political legitimacy and lawful authority to the assertion of Crown sovereignty and to the institutions founded on that assertion.

By contrast, the dissent's approach fits most naturally within a picture of our constitutional order as a political project founded by commitments made between distinct communities and political powers born of local social, political, and historical relationships within Canadian territory. Yes, the courts must interpret constitutional texts and institutional contexts that spring, as a matter of historical fact, from the assertion of Crown sovereignty and the establishment of Canadian confederation, but the political legitimacy and lawful authority of any such interpretation must be grounded in the commitments made between peoples on Canadian soil and in the relationships established between them.

Consider, in this respect, the constitutional status of the *1870 Order*. No party before the Court in *Caron* disputed that the *1870 Order* annexing the Territory to Canada had the force, in Canadian law, of a statute passed by the imperial Parliament in Britain, as stated in section 146 of the *BNA Act, 1867*, and, since 1982, of a constitutional document listed in the Schedule to the *Constitution Act, 1982*.[63] The *1870 Order* is therefore constitutionally entrenched against the Parliament of Canada and the provincial legislatures.[64] These are basic aspects of how the *1870 Order* functions as a legal instrument within the Canadian legal system. The appellants in *Caron* did not ask the Court to revisit these technical features of the *1870 Order* as an entrenched legal instrument in Canadian law; on the contrary, their argument depended on these technical features as the medium through which Canada implemented the guarantee it made (according to the appellants) to entrench legislative bilingualism across the annexed Territory. In this sense, there was widespread agreement before the Court, and between the justices, about such technical aspects of the Canadian legal system.

Yet, as we saw in the first part of this chapter, the dissent placed much greater emphasis than the majority on the historic negotiations and agreement as a *source* of the legal content that instruments such as the *1870 Order* and the *Manitoba Act, 1870* implemented in the newly annexed Territory. The historic negotiations and agreement were, for the dissent, a crucial source of the content (the "matter") that these legal instruments organized through their technical legal form.

From this angle, we can see the disagreement in *Caron* as a disagreement about the source of the law – about *where lawful authority flows from* and where the Court derives its own authority to declare what the law is. The dissent looks to historical events and relationships as a key source of law; the majority looks to the authority and practices of Canadian and British political institutions. The perspective taken by the majority might be defended on the grounds that the Canadian constitutional order, like the British (indeed, as an offspring of the British), is founded on Crown sovereignty as the ultimate source of all lawful power. On this view, domestic courts, as arbiters of lawfulness within this constitutional order, must trace the validity of any legal proposition to some authority flowing ultimately from Crown sovereignty.

In certain cases, the distinction may seem subtle. Suppose, for instance, that all justices in *Caron* had agreed that the negotiations and historic agreement of 1870 included a commitment to legislative bilingualism and that, on a plain reading, the instruments used by Canadian and British Parliaments entrenched that commitment across the Territory with continuing legal validity today. Would it matter if one group of justices located "the source" of that legal validity in the historical negotiations and agreement, while another group located it instead in the legal instruments used by Canada and Britain to implement the agreement?

Certainly, in cases where the positivist and pluralist orientations converge on a common outcome, it may be uninteresting to argue too deeply about their relative merits. But *Caron* gives us a case in which the orientations diverge in terms of acceptable legal outcomes. Other recent landmark decisions, including *Mikisew Cree II*, *Uashaunnuat*, and *Nevsun*, offer further examples.[65] The point is not that positivism and pluralism, taken as theoretical approaches to legal interpretation, drive these divergent outcomes. Rather, the divergent legal outcomes favoured by majority and dissent are, in each of these cases, heavily context-dependent, resting on (sometimes only slightly) differing visions of historical relationships, political context, the role of domestic courts, and the legal significance of these factors.

Across a series of cases, however, these different ways of seeing and interpreting may emerge as recognizably distinct legal orientations or "philosophies" and may be progressively refined by identifiable judicial or legal camps. There is a continuous back and forth in this process between the factual contexts of particular legal disputes and partial theorizing about the legal concepts and interpretive approaches used to resolve those disputes.

Relating Institutional Positivism as a Judicial Approach to Theories of Legal Positivism

Of course, the point of describing the *Caron* majority's interpretive approach *as institutional positivism* is that such an interpretive approach resonates with theories of legal positivism. The following pages explore that resonance with accounts of legal positivism developed by H.L.A. Hart and his followers, while pointing to the seeds of institutional positivism found in the Marshall trilogy as taken up in Canadian law. However, the Marshall trilogy also contains the seeds of a more pluralist approach, sensitive to the local context of social and political relationships. These seeds suggest a different direction in which Canadian Aboriginal law may yet branch out.

According to positivists in the tradition shaped by Hart, a modern legal system must have both primary and secondary rules.[66] Primary rules require or prohibit particular actions (e.g., driving faster than a set speed limit on a given highway, or entering a public building without wearing a mask during a pandemic), while secondary rules contain the criteria of legal validity for primary (and sometimes other secondary) rules. Secondary rules thus include, for example, the procedural requirements that must be followed for a legislature to validly adopt bills into law. The ultimate criteria of validity in a legal system are those secondary rules that are accepted by legal officials without needing validation through any further secondary rules. In a legal system with a written constitution, the rules enshrined in its provisions are obvious candidates for ultimate criteria of validity. But these criteria may come in other forms as well, such as unwritten constitutional principles and case law precedent.[67] The ultimate criteria of legal validity within a given legal system, taken all together, make up what Hart called the "rule of recognition" of that legal system.

Legal positivism is largely defined by the line it draws between law and politics (and, in a related sense, between law and morality), on the basis of this notion of a rule of recognition. Legal positivists insist that it is a matter of socio-political fact whether there exists sufficient consensus within a political community, notably among its legal officials, on the ultimate criteria of legal validity (i.e., on the rule of recognition). Acceptance (or not) of the rule of recognition by legal officials (including, importantly, judges) is a question of fact, sharply distinguished from questions of legal validity *under* the rule of recognition. It would be a category mistake to ask whether the ultimate criteria themselves are valid or invalid; rather, they are either accepted (at least, by a critical mass of legal officials applying them) or they are not, in which case there is no functioning legal system. As Hart stated, his theory requires "that the existence and authority of the rule of recognition should depend on its acceptance by the courts."[68] (Of course, there can be borderline cases, in which it is debatable whether the legitimacy of a constitution is accepted by a critical mass of legal officials. That would, however, remain a question of social or political fact, on the positivist view, not a question of legal validity.)

For domestic legal systems of modern states, the state's assertions of sovereignty over its territory may be the quintessential ultimate criterion of legal validity, with all legal validity within the domestic legal order resting ultimately on the acceptance of the legitimacy of the state's assertions of sovereignty. On this view, domestic judges must, by virtue of their office, *accept* the legitimacy of state assertions of sovereignty, and thus cannot *reason* about the legality or legitimacy of these assertions. Such reasoning simply cannot be understood or intelligibly cognized from within the domestic legal order. From this positivist perspective, state assertions of sovereignty are what first open a space of legal reasoning for domestic courts. Legal validity flows ultimately from sovereign intent.

Moreover, the judicial channels through which legal validity flows outward from the fact of sovereign intent are, on the positivist view, also determined through "social facts."[69] In particular, judges should not engage in moral reasoning to assess legal validity.[70] Rather, they must determine, to the extent possible, the fact of sovereign intent through criteria found in the rule of recognition. For instance, a positivist perspective on the Canadian legal system would find that it belongs to (or flows immediately from) the rule of recognition that the federal Parliament (more technically, the Crown-in-Parliament) is the seat of sovereign legislative power in matters of federal jurisdiction, and that federal bills become legally valid statutes once adopted by majority vote in three readings in both the House of Commons and Senate and receiving royal assent. The legal validity of a statute flows from the acceptance of this law-making power of Parliament and the fact that the statute was adopted according to the accepted legislative procedures. When disputes inevitably arise about the proper interpretation of various statutory provisions, judges should resolve them by attempting to determine sovereign legislative intent. Such analysis may legitimately draw on the broad factual context in and through which such intent is expressed – examining, for instance, the legislative history of the statute, the institutional design of the legislature (including, for example, the role of subcommittees and drafting committees), relevant political conventions, and so on – in order to provide the most accurate factual reconstruction of legislative intent.

The point, in essence, is that the rule of recognition is established as a matter of socio-political fact, and judges must determine how legal validity flows from the rule of recognition as a matter of "social pedigree" – that is, they must assess the validity of a legal proposition according to the factual context described above. When interpreting the law, judges may engage in moral reasoning only if directed or authorized to do so by some element of the rule of recognition or by some other legal authority factually validated by the rule of recognition.[71] They may also engage in moral reasoning to fill in gaps in the law, but then they are not technically engaged in *legal* interpretation, even if they themselves state and believe that they are.

That said, the focus on sovereign legislative intent is not entirely so narrow in the view of Hart and his followers as the paragraphs above may suggest. As already noted, many legal positivists, including Hart, allow room in the rule of recognition not only for criteria of sovereign intent but also for such things as judicial precedent and unwritten constitutional principles that need not themselves flow from sovereign intent or constitute criteria for determining sovereign intent. From a historical perspective, however, such allowance looks like a compromise position resulting from Hart's insistence that his theory of law is a matter of "descriptive sociology" as opposed to a prescriptive account of how law ought to function. Given the deep common law tradition of the British legal system that Hart was (primarily) looking at, he could not plausibly have developed a descriptive account narrowly focused on sovereign legislative intent as the source of all legal validity.

David Dyzenhaus, in diagnosing what he calls "judicial positivism," helpfully draws the genealogy of legal positivism in Anglo-American thinking back to the legal reform projects of Hobbes and Bentham.[72] These reform projects aimed at eliminating the pernicious – for Hobbes and Bentham – reality that common law judges *are* constantly engaging in political and moral reasoning under the guise of developing the common law. As Dyzenhaus writes:

> Positive law, properly so called, is not merely law whose existence is determinable by factual tests but law whose content is determinable by the same sort of tests, here tests which appeal only to facts about legislative intent. ... The very values that underpin the design of the legal order which Hobbes and Bentham favour are supposed to issue in non-evaluative legal reasoning by judges, reasoning which does not involve moral deliberation. That judges will have to engage in at least some measure of moral deliberation is not denied, but as soon as they do they are, from the positivist perspective, no longer engaged in legal reasoning. As I will now argue, the stance that I call judicial positivism comes about because there are judges who accept some version of Hobbes's or Bentham's political theories, but find themselves working in a legal order which is not designed along the right lines.[73]

Hobbes and Bentham wanted to eliminate, to the extent possible, moral deliberation from the judicial task of interpreting the law. Judges ought to interpret the law based on factual tests, and in particular factual tests about legislative, or sovereign, intent. Moreover, judicial interpretation should not have force of law beyond the case being decided; limiting judicial authority in this way would thereby limit the consequences of any judicial moral reasoning to the case at hand.

Hobbes and Bentham were clear, of course, that they were engaging in reform projects, not descriptive analysis. Their reform projects confronted a legal system with a deep common law tradition that did not conform to their positivist visions. Dyzenhaus describes the contrasting style of legal reasoning anchoring this common law tradition:

> The common law style of reasoning is exemplified in the reasoning of judges within the conceptual space of the common law tradition. Such judges suppose – and thus aim to show in their judgments – that the law (which includes both statutes and their judgments) – is a repository of

inexhaustible legal reasons. As long as they go about reasoning in the right way – searching for the reason of the law – they will be able to solve any problem of interpretation by working out what the best understanding of relevant legal material requires. That solution is both fully determined by the law and the result of reason.[74]

I find the formulation "fully determined by the law and the result of reason" somewhat misleading once we discard the positivist barrier between law and morality (and, in a related way, between law and politics, law and history), because it may suggest a questionable independence of the law from morality, politics, and history. However, given Dyzenhaus's subsequent elaboration of "legal reason," this may be a matter of semantics rather than a substantial disagreement:

> Reason here is "artificial" in that it is not unconstrained "natural" reason but constrained legal reason – reason immanent in already existing legal material. But it is reason nonetheless, which is to say moral, practical reason, reason which sustains conclusions about what the law both morally and legally requires. *But the morality does not come from a source extrinsic to law. It does not have to be injected into the law by some authority* [emphasis added]. Rather, morality emerges through judges engaging in the common law style, through their bringing to the surface the fundamental principles already immanent in the law.[75]

My characterizations of institutional positivism and historically grounded pluralism, as styles of judicial reasoning exemplified by the majority and dissent in *Caron*, closely track Dyzenhaus's characterizations of judicial positivism and common law reasoning. Dyzenhaus admittedly does not mention pluralism. Yet historically grounded pluralism is the natural response of common law reasoning to the kind of historical, social, and political context found in *Caron* and in Indigenous–state relations in North America more broadly. In the remainder of this chapter, I begin to illustrate this point using the Marshall trilogy of cases.

Before turning to the Marshall trilogy, it is worth quoting Dyzenhaus at some length on the dilemma Hart faced because of his commitment to a descriptive account of the law. Dyzenhaus's characterization of this dilemma nicely captures an unresolved tension running through positivist theories of law that is also reflected in the institutional positivist approach found in the case law:

> Hart found himself caught in a dilemma between his tradition and its politically motivated opposition to the common law style theory and an a-political description of that style which concedes too much, perhaps

almost everything to it. The first horn of this dilemma consists of the attempt to describe the conceptual space of the common law by using positivist, legislative language. Such language implies that the space in which the judge operates is unconstrained by law and offers political reasons for adopting this implication – the avoidance of the childish fiction.[76] Since that implication seems false and since Hart wishes to avoid putting legal theory on a political, prescriptive foundation, he moves at other times in the direction of the other horn. On this second horn, not only is the space very much filled by law, but the more natural description – from the inside – is the common law one in which judges are drawing out the best solution from the inexhaustible stock of legal reasons. But to adopt the second horn is also to go some considerable distance to adopt the common law style of reasoning.[77]

Dyzenhaus is a critic of legal positivism in both prescriptive and descriptive forms, but he is particularly biting in his criticism of the descriptive tradition shaped by Hart, which renounces (or represses) the "politically motivated opposition" to common law reasoning of earlier positivists. In "judicial positivism" today, Dyzenhaus sees a "neo-Benthamite" revival that "argues on democratic grounds for a legal order in which Parliament has a virtual monopoly on law-making. It resists constraints on ultimate legal authority that go beyond the constraints of manner and form required to make it possible to identify both Parliament's laws and their content."[78] Although Dyzenhaus is critical of judicial positivism, he applauds the openness with which it embraces its prescriptive roots and seeks to draw from them today.

The institutional positivism of the majority in *Caron* may not go quite so far as to argue for "a legal order in which Parliament has a virtual monopoly on law-making." But it does tend towards the position that sovereign legislative intent is the ultimate source of law by focusing its legal interpretation on instruments of the Dominion Parliament (the *Manitoba Act, 1870*), the British Crown (the *1870 Order*), and the British Parliament (the *BNA Act, 1867*), and by treating sovereign legislative intent as governing the meaning of the provisions found in each of those instruments. While the dissent also interprets these same instruments, it looks primarily to the historic negotiations and agreement between Canada and the Métis provisional government as the source of meaning and lawful authority for the relevant provisions found in those instruments.

Recent decisions by the Supreme Court of Canada sharpen the institutional positivist focus (often in dissenting or concurring reasons) on state sovereignty as the ultimate source of law in the Canadian legal order. The dissenting reasons in both *Uashaunnuat*, and *Nevsun* are illustrative. The majority reasons in these same two cases adopt variations on the pluralist orientation explored here. Yet other cases, notably *Tsilhqot'in Nation*[79] and *Sparrow*,[80] awkwardly incorporate aspects of both the positivist and pluralist approaches within a single set of reasons.

This ongoing partial schizophrenia of the judicial interpretation of Indigenous–state relations is not surprising, given the historical situation. The colonial project in North America involved extensive assertions of Crown sovereignty over Indigenous territories and peoples. Domestic courts in the US and Canada today – and comparably in the other British settler states of Australia and New Zealand – gained *de facto* judicial authority within the territories claimed by their respective states through the state's acquisition of *de facto* sovereignty. In other words, whatever one thinks about the legitimacy or legal validity of Crown assertions of sovereignty over Canadian territory, the state has gradually and effectively extended its *de facto* control over land and resources within this territory. As Canadian governments and courts now acknowledge, the state did not thereby extinguish Indigenous legal orders, but it did severely constrain their ability to develop free of state interference and domination. Clearly, if the Canadian state had not extended its *de facto* control in this manner, then the courts established and maintained by the state would not enjoy the *de facto* authority they now do, with vast state powers at their disposal to enforce their orders and thus to give effect to their legal reasons.

It is not hard to understand, given this broad context, how domestic court judges might view state sovereignty as the foundation of their own lawful authority and jurisdiction. At the same time, it is also not hard to see how this context raises questions about the legitimacy and legality of state assertions of sovereignty. Judges working in a common law tradition – which does not see sovereign or legislative intent as the sole source of law but draws instead on "a repository of inexhaustible legal reasons"[81] thoroughly imbued with moral reasoning, with respect for existing customs and practices, with historical and judicial precedent, and with reasoning by analogy – have the interpretive resources with which to tackle such questions *as legal questions*.

Institutional positivism responds to this possibility by focusing on the place of domestic courts within the state institutional context. Institutional positivism is *positivist* insofar as it understands (implicitly or explicitly) sovereign intent as the ultimate source of law. It is *institutional* insofar as it highlights the position of domestic courts as institutions whose own (*de facto*) authority depends on (*de facto*) successful assertion of state sovereignty. Of course, institutional positivism, in good positivist fashion, does not accept that *de facto* and *de jure* can be peeled apart in this context. State assertion of sovereignty is at the heart of the rule of recognition and is not the kind of thing that can be legally valid or invalid; rather, it is accepted, or it is not.[82]

The Positivist and Pluralist Roots Found in the Marshall Trilogy

In this respect, consider the following statement from Chief Justice John Marshall of the United States Supreme Court in his 1823 opinion in *Johnson v. M'Intosh*, a foundational case in US federal Indian law: "Conquest gives a title which the Courts of the conqueror cannot deny, whatever the private and speculative opinions of individuals may be, respecting the original justice of the claim which has been successfully asserted."[83] Questions about the legal validity or *de jure* status ("the original justice") of a state's assertions of sovereignty cannot be entertained by that state's courts. From the perspectives of such courts, what matters is the *de facto* status of state sovereignty – that is, whether that sovereignty has been "successfully asserted." Successful assertion establishes, *as a matter of fact*, the authority of the state's domestic courts to declare the law of the land.

The following discussion uses the term "*M'Intosh* exclusion" to refer to this exclusion of legal questions about state assertions of sovereignty from review by state domestic courts. (In the language of US, English, and Australian courts – language that the Supreme Court of Canada has excised from Canadian law – the *M'Intosh* exclusion is a branch of the "act of state" doctrine, prohibiting domestic courts from adjudicating categories of state action deemed too political for review.[84])

The *M'Intosh* exclusion has been adopted, in the blunt technical language of modern law, by the High Court of Australia in cases dealing with Aboriginal title claims. In *Coe v. Commonwealth of Australia*, for instance, Justice Jacobs of the High Court stated that a challenge to state sovereignty was "not cognisable in a court exercising jurisdiction under that sovereignty which is sought to be challenged."[85] In *Mabo v. Queensland (No. 2)*, the High Court upheld the proposition that "[t]he acquisition of territory by a sovereign state for the first time is an act of state which cannot be challenged, controlled or interfered with by the courts of that state."[86]

The Supreme Court of Canada has taken a more ambiguous position on the *M'Intosh* exclusion. In *Sparrow*, the Court unanimously endorsed the following statement: "Section 35 calls for a just settlement for aboriginal peoples. It renounces the old rules of the game under which the Crown established courts of law and denied those courts the authority to question sovereign claims made by the Crown."[87] Yet in the very same judgment the Court also wrote the following, relying on the authority of *M'Intosh*:

> It is worth recalling that while British policy towards the native population was based on respect for their right to occupy their traditional lands, a proposition to which the Royal Proclamation of 1763 bears witness, there was from the outset never any doubt that sovereignty and legislative power, and indeed the underlying title, to such lands vested in the Crown; see *Johnson v. M'Intosh* (1823), 8 Wheaton 543 (U.S.S.C.).[88]

We find the same basic ambiguity, or unresolved tension, in the unanimous Supreme Court of Canada decision in *Tsilhqot'in Nation* issued a quarter century after *Sparrow*.[89] In other cases, however, the Court has acknowledged competing state and Indigenous sovereign claims, highlighting the importance of reconciling "pre-existing Aboriginal sovereignty with assumed Crown sovereignty";[90] has characterized Crown sovereignty as *de facto* in at least some areas of the country;[91] has found that Aboriginal rights and title have a source in Indigenous legal systems that existed prior to, and survived, assertions of Crown sovereignty;[92] and has held that the Crown is under a binding legal obligation to negotiate treaties to resolve claims grounded in pre-existing Indigenous sovereignty and rights to the land (at least in certain circumstances).[93] These are all striking statements for a domestic court to make.

The reasons of Chief Justice Marshall in *M'Intosh* – characterized by the Supreme Court of Canada as "the *locus classicus* of the principles governing aboriginal title"[94] – are worth unpacking in greater detail. The analysis below reveals that while Chief Justice Marshall held that US courts could not directly question the legitimacy or legality of US assertions of sovereignty, he also forcefully asserted judicial authority to determine the legal significance and content of state sovereignty. The *M'Intosh* exclusion is thus Janus-faced: one face obediently accepts successful state assertions of sovereignty; the other face declares what that sovereignty amounts to, legally speaking. The second face speaks particularly loud in the two subsequent cases in the Marshall trilogy, *Cherokee Nation* and *Worcester*,[95] as explained below.

M'Intosh dealt with the validity of private purchases, made prior to the American Revolution, of Indigenous territory north of the Ohio River where the British Crown claimed sovereignty. Chief Justice Marshall held that US courts could not uphold these purchases, on the grounds (1) that the doctrine of discovery, as he called it, gave the discovering European nation the exclusive power to acquire territory from Indigenous peoples by purchase or conquest, and (2) that the Royal Proclamation of 1763 prohibited purchases of Indigenous lands except by the British Crown at a public meeting with appropriate Indigenous representatives. Following the American Revolution, according to Chief Justice Marshall, the newly sovereign US nation stepped into the shoes of the British Crown for purposes of the doctrine of discovery and of the sole right to purchase Indigenous lands under the Royal Proclamation of 1763.

As discussed above, there is a plausible legal positivist reading of Chief Justice Marshall's famous statement that conquest gives a title that cannot be questioned in the courts of the conqueror. Beyond the concerns of legal theory, however, the *M'Intosh* exclusion is undoubtedly an expression of the political and social imaginary in which Chief Justice Marshall and the Supreme Court of the United States were embedded at the time. Throughout the nineteenth and the first half of the twentieth centuries, as settler state offspring of the British Empire embraced the colonial project and a vision of civilizational hierarchy, European assertions of sovereignty over Indigenous territories were accepted as a matter of course within the social and political imaginaries of governing elites. The *M'Intosh* exclusion is an expression, in legal doctrinal form, of this acceptance of state assertions of sovereignty over territories in the New World. As Antony Anghie has argued, the very notion of sovereignty in modern international law largely developed *out of* the colonial encounter.[96] The imaginary of imperial expansion and colonization inevitably found legal articulations that justified imperial assertions of sovereignty.

The *M'Intosh* exclusion holds, in positivist fashion, that such justifications are beyond the concern of domestic courts, as matters settled in the realm of politics or the international legal order. Thus, domestic courts are in principle precluded from assessing the validity or the justice of state assertions of sovereignty over Indigenous territories and peoples. However, given that the *M'Intosh* exclusion itself sprang from the social and political imaginary of imperial expansion, it is not surprising to find *M'Intosh* giving voice to this imaginary and its justifications for imperial assertions. Consider the following passage:

> On the discovery of this immense continent, the great nations of Europe were eager to appropriate to themselves so much of it as they could respectively acquire. Its vast extent offered an ample field to the ambition and enterprise of all, and the character and religion of its inhabitants afforded

an apology for considering them as a people over whom the superior genius of Europe might claim an ascendency. The potentates of the old world found no difficulty in convincing themselves that they made ample compensation to the inhabitants of the new by bestowing on them civilization and Christianity in exchange for unlimited independence.[97]

Chief Justice Marshall here gives voice to the imperial imaginary without necessarily endorsing its "apology" for imperial expansion or its assertion of "unlimited independence" in the New World. Nine years later in *Worcester*, the chief justice takes a caustic view of the "extravagant and absurd idea" that European rulers could unilaterally convey "legitimate power" (let alone unlimited independence) over the lands and peoples of the New World. He says the following in reference to the charters issued by the British Crown in "planting colonies in America":

> The first of these charters was made before possession was taken of any part of the country. They purport, generally, to convey the soil from the Atlantic to the South Sea. This soil was occupied by numerous and warlike nations, equally willing and able to defend their possessions. The extravagant and absurd idea that the feeble settlements made on the sea coast, or the companies under whom they were made, acquired legitimate power by them to govern the people, or occupy the lands from sea to sea did not enter the mind of any man. They were well understood to convey the title which, according to the common law of European sovereigns respecting America, they might rightfully convey, and no more. *This was the exclusive right of purchasing such lands as the natives were willing to sell* [emphasis added]. The Crown could not be understood to grant what the Crown did not affect to claim; nor was it so understood.[98]

By the logic of the *M'Intosh* exclusion, Crown assertions of sovereignty (inherited by the US after independence) could not directly be adjudicated in US courts. In the passage above, however, Chief Justice Marshall has no hesitation in defining the legal content of the sovereignty asserted. *Worcester* takes a restrictive view of what the Crown originally claimed, namely an exclusive right, as against all other European powers, to purchase such lands as Indigenous peoples were willing to sell – in other words, an exclusive right among European powers to engage in treaty-making with Indigenous peoples in the territory claimed. This view does, in fact, seem broadly to conform to the Crown policy of treaty-making from the time of contact until Canadian confederation.[99] *Worcester* is blunt about the limits of the grants originally conveyed through royal charters: "these grants asserted a title against

Europeans only, and were considered blank paper so far as the rights of the natives were concerned."[100]

Nonetheless, at least in *M'Intosh*, Chief Justice Marshall allows for some element of expansion or evolution in the legal content of Crown and state sovereignty, such that the original claim of discovery might be "convert[ed] ... into conquest":

> However extravagant the pretension of converting the discovery of an inhabited country into conquest may appear; if the principle has been asserted in the first instance, and afterwards sustained; if a country has been acquired and held under it; if the property of the great mass of the community originates in it, *it becomes the law of the land and cannot be questioned* [emphasis added]. So, too, with respect to the concomitant principle that the Indian inhabitants are to be considered merely as occupants, to be protected, indeed, while in peace, in the possession of their lands, but to be deemed incapable of transferring the absolute title to others. *However this restriction may be opposed to natural right, and to the usages of civilized nations, yet if it be indispensable to that system under which the country has been settled, and be adapted to the actual condition of the two people, it may perhaps be supported by reason, and certainly cannot be rejected by courts of justice* [emphasis added].[101]

This is a fuller statement of the *M'Intosh* exclusion, accompanied by a strikingly weak apology for the "restriction" imposed on Indians through "conquest" at the hands of European settlers. This fuller statement is instructive. It shows that the *M'Intosh* exclusion both (1) forbids domestic courts from questioning the state assertions of sovereignty that underlie the domestic legal order and thus the authority of its courts, and (2) allows for the legal content of the sovereignty asserted to evolve and to expand[102] with the social and political imaginary of the "conquering" state (or of the "great mass of the community"), even if the resulting legal significance is "opposed to natural right, and to the usages of civilized nations."

The passage thus makes clear that Chief Justice Marshall is not *stipulating* that discovery may be converted into conquest on the basis of legal principles. It is rather *in spite of* basic legal principles (of "natural right" and "the usages of civilized nations") that domestic US courts must recognize that conquest has "becom[e] the law of the land and cannot be questioned." The forces driving this recognition are found in the social and political context and include the *assertion* that discovery has become conquest; subsequent adherence to that principle; the acquisition and holding of the country under it; and the origin of the property of the "great mass of the community" in that principle. These are the factors that Chief Justice Marshall points to as converting discovery into conquest, so far as the domestic "law of the land" is concerned.

Similarly with "the concomitant principle that the Indian inhabitants are to be considered merely as occupants," Chief Justice Marshall describes this "restriction" as opposed to basic legal principles but nonetheless as "indispensable" to the legal system "under which the country has been settled" and as "adapted to the actual condition" of its Indigenous and non-Indigenous inhabitants ("the two people"). However weakly this principle may "perhaps be supported by reason," it must be accepted by the country's courts of justice.

In the reasoning of Chief Justice Marshall, legal interpretation must account for social and political context. There may be elements of the social and political context that are indispensable to the domestic legal order (at least as perceived in the social and political imaginary in which the judicial interpretation is embedded). Courts of justice within that legal order must first accept these elements if they are to pronounce upon and reason about "the law of the land," for otherwise they would undermine the very legal order from which they derive their authority as domestic courts. This is one way of rendering the positivist dimension of the thought expressed so succinctly in the *M'Intosh* statement quoted earlier: "Conquest gives a title which the Courts of the conqueror cannot deny, whatever the private and speculative opinions of individuals may be, respecting the original justice of the claim which has been successfully asserted."[103]

This interpretation of *M'Intosh* clearly resonates with basic elements of legal positivism, including the core tenet of Hartian positivism that every functioning legal system has a "rule of recognition" consisting of the system's fundamental criteria of legal validity. The legal validity of all other rules, principles, and propositions within the legal system derives from these criteria.

However, the legal opinions of Chief Justice Marshall in *M'Intosh*, *Cherokee Nation*, and *Worcester* are also rich in a key dimension that is lacking in Hartian legal positivism: careful attention to the judicial task of *continuously translating* shifting aspects of social and political context into legal principles – in other words giving legal expression to the evolving social and political imaginaries in which courts are embedded. Dividing the *M'Intosh* exclusion into two elements, as suggested above, the first element (that domestic courts cannot question state assertions of sovereignty) resonates with positivism, while the second (that the courts must continuously adapt the legal content of such assertions within changing social and political context) is decidedly dissonant. This work of legal translation is the lifeblood of the common law.

This need for ongoing legal interpretation of social and political context – for continuous legal articulation of evolving social and political imaginaries – together with the positivist urge to suppress and deny this legal creativity, help explain the ambiguity that surrounds many legal terms left floating uncertainly between statements of fact and expressions of legal imagination. For instance, in *M'Intosh*, the term "conquest" naturally suggests military conquest, and thus points to established bodies of law dealing with factual situations of military conquest.[104] Yet Chief Justice Marshall is not using the term in quite that sense in *M'Intosh*. Instead, he is applying the term to the situation of a European power having "discovered" Indian territory and having acquired a degree of *de facto* control over it. This application of the term is a legal doctrinal development, holding that certain situations that we would not factually classify as "conquest," according to common use of that term, will be so classified as a matter of law. The factual reference of the term is stretched through legal convention. As noted above, Chief Justice Marshall acknowledges that it may well seem an "extravagant ... pretension" to use the term "conquest" in this way.[105]

Why then does he use the term? Undoubtedly because it allows the situation before his Court to be brought, by analogy, under legal principles drawn from established bodies of law dealing with conquest, modified as the chief justice thought necessary for the context of Indigenous–US relations.[106] In this way, the application of the term "conquest" in *M'Intosh* is a *legal* interpretation of the relevant social and political context; it amounts to a synthesis of the complex social, political, and legal terrain of Indigenous–state relations then prevailing in the New World under the banner of a body of law developed to govern situations of actual military conquest, moulded to the particular context of Indigenous–US relations.

Cherokee Nation introduced another striking legal synthesis of Indigenous–state relations by characterizing Indian nations as "domestic dependent nations."[107] Chief Justice Marshall's understanding of Indigenous–state relations seems to have undergone considerable creative evolution between *M'Intosh*, on one hand, and *Cherokee Nation* and *Worcester* on the other.[108] His judgment in the *Worcester* case, in particular, emphasizes the self-governing status of Indian nations – "independent of each other and of the rest of the world, having institutions of their own, and governing themselves by their own laws"[109] prior to the arrival of Europeans – and concludes that the self-governing status of the Cherokee Nation is protected by treaty and federal law.[110] Moreover, *Worcester* insists on the formally equal status of Indian nations: "The words 'treaty' and 'nation' are words of our own language, selected in our diplomatic and legislative proceedings by ourselves, having each a definite and well understood meaning. We have applied them to Indians, as we have applied them to the other nations of the earth. They are applied to all in the same sense."[111]

The power of Chief Justice Marshall's reasoning in these judgments lies in the legal creativity with which he draws together broad and complex social, political, and legal terrain under notions such as "conquest" and "domestic dependent nation." The point here is not to endorse either of these notions as successful syntheses of that complex terrain. The point is rather to underscore the experimental quality of Chief Justice Marshall's legal reasoning in the Marshall trilogy. He is trying out different formulations as his legal imagination attempts to get a handle on the complex social and political context of Indigenous–state relations that has been presented to his Court in the form of specific legal disputes requiring resolution. While he accepts successful Crown (and later US) assertions of sovereignty as a matter of fact that underpins the authority of US courts, he looks to the historical, social, and political relationships between Indigenous peoples and European powers and settlers (as those relationships are perceived in the social and political imaginary in which he lives and thinks) as the source of legal content for state sovereignty.

Conclusion

In other words, there are considerable affinities between the interpretive approach found in the Marshall trilogy and that of the dissent in *Caron*. This interpretive approach recognizes the institutional context of domestic courts and the essential importance of successfully asserted state sovereignty to the legal system they inhabit, but at the same time looks to the context of historical, social, and political relations in which sovereignty is asserted as a primary source of the meaning, the legal content, and the lawful authority of the sovereignty thus asserted.

As explained above, the Supreme Court of Canada has consistently cited the Marshall trilogy, particularly *M'Intosh*, for the proposition that the Crown acquired sovereignty and underlying title to lands in North America by "discovering" it (i.e., through simple assertion of sovereignty to the exclusion of other European powers). This application of the Marshall trilogy rests on a narrowly positivist reading that ignores the legal creativity with which Chief Justice Marshall tried to make sense of existing social and political contexts as, for instance, situations of "conquest" or "domestic dependent nations." This vital dimension of Chief Justice Marshall's legal reasoning reflects the common law style that draws from "a repository of inexhaustible legal reasons"[112] imbued with moral reasoning, with respect for existing customs and practices, with historical and judicial precedent, and with reasoning by analogy. Those are precisely the aspects of the Marshall trilogy's interpretive approach that hold the most promise for Canadian courts grappling with the task of reworking and rearticulating notions of sovereignty in a period of ideological transition.

Of course, the ideological transition we are currently living through – the repudiation of colonialism through official and unofficial channels, with the often stated (if still vague and contested) aim of reconciliation – is entirely different from the one Chief Justice Marshall was facing, which was in essence a consolidation and stabilization of state power in relations with Indigenous peoples whose populations and military strength were in steep decline. As the dissent stated in *Caron*, referring to the years following Canadian confederation, "the political climate at the time was imbued with improvisation."[113] The same was true of the period and context in which the Marshall trilogy was issued, which called for a corresponding degree of improvisation and creativity in the common law. The discussion above shows some of the ways in which the Marshall trilogy answered that call. The Marshall trilogy gave legal expression to rapidly evolving Indigenous–state social and political relations, in accordance, as Chief Justice Marshall explicitly acknowledged, with the governing ideology of European civilizational superiority. If we as a country today reject that ideology, then the very logic of the Marshall trilogy itself calls for revision of the legal conclusions reached in those cases, including the subordination of pre-existing Indigenous sovereignty to asserted Crown sovereignty under such categories as "conquest" and "domestic dependent nations."

Today, too, the political and legal climate of Indigenous–state relations in Canada is "imbued with improvisation." Indeed, improvisation has been a constant in the elaboration of state sovereignty, and in the related legal doctrines found in the case law.[114] This chapter has highlighted the tension and ambiguity running through Canadian case law addressing Crown assertions of sovereignty in relation to Indigenous peoples and pre-existing Indigenous legal orders. The chapter has indicated how this tension and ambiguity are structured in part by the dynamic tension between two competing legal interpretive approaches: the institutional positivist approach and the historically grounded pluralist approach. The chapter does not purport to resolve that interpretive tension, nor to vindicate either the positivist or pluralist interpretive orientation. I hope the discussion has shown, however, that the reception of the Marshall trilogy in Canadian law has been narrowly positivist, and that we may benefit from a greater appreciation of the pluralist orientation embodied both in the Marshall trilogy itself and in modern judgments such as the dissenting reasons in *Caron*. The *Caron* case warrants attentive reading precisely for the sharpness with which it brings the dynamic tension between institutional positivism and historically grounded pluralism into relief; that is, as contrasting practices of judicial interpretation that present alternative visions of Indigenous–state legal relations within domestic law.

NOTES

1 John Borrows, "Origin Stories and the Law: Treaty Metaphysics in Canada and New Zealand," in *Indigenous Peoples and the State: International Perspectives on the Treaty of Waitangi*, ed. Mark Hickford and Carwyn Jones (Abingdon, UK: Routledge, 2019), 38.
2 Benjamin Berger, "Children of Two Logics: A Way into Canadian Constitutional Culture," *International Journal of Constitutional Law* 11, no. 2 (2013): 328.
3 *Johnson v. M'Intosh*, 21 US 543 (1823) [hereafter *M'Intosh*], at 588.
4 Gerald Friesen, *The Canadian Prairies: A History* (Toronto: University of Toronto Press, 1987), 137.
5 *British North America Act, 1867*, 30–31 Vict, c 3 (UK) [hereafter *BNA Act, 1867*], since renamed the *Constitution Act, 1867*.
6 *Address to Her Majesty the Queen from the Senate and House of Commons of the Dominion of Canada*, 16 and 17 December 1867 [hereafter *1867 Address*], being Schedule A to the *Rupert's Land and the North-Western Territory Order* [hereafter *1870 Order*], 23 June 1870, in RSC 1985, Appendix II, No.
7 *Caron v. Alberta*, 2015 SCC 56 [hereafter *Caron*].
8 *Address to Her Majesty the Queen from the Senate and House of Commons of the Dominion of Canada*, 29 and 31 May 1869 [hereafter *1869 Address*], being Schedule B to the *1870 Order*.
9 *Caron*, at para 19.
10 The text of the English version of the Declaration is from the journal of Alexander Begg, as reproduced in Alexander Begg, *Alexander Begg's Red River Journal and Other Papers Relative to the Red River Resistance of 1869–70*, ed. W.L. Morton (Toronto: Chaplain Society, 1956), 218–20. See also Thomas Flanagan, "Political Theory of the Red River Resistance: The Declaration of December 8, 1869," *Canadian Journal of Political Science* 11, no. 1 (March 1978): 153–64, where the English text is reproduced at 153–5, and the

French at 155–7. The Declaration is signed by John Bruce as "President" and Louis Riel as "Secretary" of the "Provisional Government" that it proclaims.
11 Quoted in Flanagan, "Political Theory," 155.
12 Ibid., 154. Flanagan argues that the two authors cited by the Declaration in support of this principle – William Barclay (1541–1605) and Jean-Baptiste Du Voisin (1744–1813) – were in fact absolute monarchists who provide questionable authority, at best, for the principle asserted by the Declaration. Ibid., 162–4.
13 Quoted in Flanagan, "Political Theory," 154.
14 Ibid. The French text of the Declaration – at least in the version labelled as authentic by Father George Dugas, who may in fact have drafted the text at Riel's request – refers to "nos droits et nos intérêts" without qualification or mention of being British subjects: see Flanagan, "Political Theory," 156–8.
15 Quoted in Flanagan, "Political Theory," 155.
16 *Manitoba Act, 1870*, SC 1870, c 3, reprinted in RSC 1985, Appendix II, No 8.
17 See, for example, *Manitoba Metis Federation Inc. v. Canada (Attorney General)*, [2013] 1 SCR 623 [hereafter *MMF*].
18 See, for example, Friesen, *Canadian Prairies*, 130–241.
19 *British North America Act, 1871*, 34–35 Vict, c 28 (UK) [hereafter *BNA Act, 1871*], reprinted in RSC 1970, Appendix II.
20 *Alberta Act*, 1905, 4–5 Edward VII, c 3 (Canada), reprinted in RSC 1985, Appendix II, No 20; *Saskatchewan Act*, 1905, 4–5 Edward VII, c 42 (Canada), reprinted in RSC 1985, Appendix II, No 21.
21 *Constitution Act, 1982*, being Schedule B to the *Canada Act, 1982* (UK), 1982, c 11, s 35: (1) "The existing aboriginal and treaty rights of the aboriginal peoples of Canada are hereby recognized and affirmed. (2) In this Act, 'aboriginal peoples of Canada' includes the Indian, Inuit and Métis peoples of Canada."
22 See, for example, Robert M. Cover, "The Supreme Court, 1982 Term – Forward: *Nomos* and Narrative," *Harvard Law Review* 97, no. 1 (1983–4): 4–68.
23 The Marshall trilogy consists of *Johnson v. M'Intosh*, 21 US 543 (1823); *Cherokee Nation v. Georgia*, 30 US (5 Pet) 1 (1831); *Worcester v. the State of Georgia*, 31 US (6 Pet) 515 (1832). The Supreme Court of Canada has consistently cited these judgments, especially *M'Intosh and Worcester*, as foundational for Aboriginal law in Canada: see, for example, *Wewaykum Indian Band v. Canada*, 2002 SCC 79, at para 75; *R. v. Van der Peet*, [1996] 2 SCR 507, at paras 35–7; *R. v. Sioui*, [1990] 1 SCR 1025 at 1053–4; *R. v. Sparrow*, [1990] 1 SCR 1075 at 1103; *Guerin v. The Queen*, [1984] 2 SCR 335 at 377–80; *Calder v. Attorney-General of British Columbia*, [1973] SCR 313 at 320–1, 382–5.

24 On the virtues of parochialism, in the sense intended here, see David Dyzenhaus, "The Genealogy of Legal Positivism," *Oxford Journal of Legal Studies* 24, no. 1 (Spring 2006): 39–67, https://doi.org/10.1093/ojls/24.1.39, in particular these comments at 66: "But parochialism here is a virtue. It is only the fact that the legal theories of Dworkin and the neo-Benthamites are anchored not only in particular legal traditions, but in politically partisan accounts of those traditions, that permits them to provide insights both about the low ground of participant engagement with legal practice and about the high ground of abstract theory, as well as about the levels in between."

25 Using this word, too, in the non-pejorative sense found in the passage quoted in the previous note and further clarified in the following passage, also from Dyzenhaus, "Genealogy," 66: "Once we see that parochialism is a necessary component of productive engagement between rival legal theories, we can also see how that engagement is never quite on the theorist's terms, if only because engagement is with practices for which the theorist has to account, even if part of his account is that the practices embed institutional mistakes."

26 *Caron*, at para 8.
27 Borrows, "Origin Stories," 30.
28 *Caron*, at para 19.
29 Ibid., at para 20.
30 Ibid., at para 23.
31 Ibid., at para 23. Father Noël-Joseph Ritchot, the delegate of the Métis provisional government who took the lead in negotiations with Prime Minister Macdonald and Minister Cartier, in fact kept a detailed record of the Ottawa negotiations in his diary. This portion of Father Ritchot's diary was published in George F.G. Stanley, "Le journal de l'abbé N.-J. Ritchot – 1870," *Revue d'histoire de l'Amérique française* 17, no. 4 (1964): 537–64, https://doi.org/10.7202/302314ar.

There has been extensive academic and legal debate over the interpretation of this diary, particularly in the context of the Manitoba Métis Federation case that eventually reached the Supreme Court of Canada: see the Court's 2013 reasons in *MMF*. The Supreme Court did not mention the diary in *MMF*, though it had been the subject of extensive debate at trial. For academic commentary, see, for example, Darren O'Toole, "Section 31 of the *Manitoba Act, 1870*: A Land Claim Agreement," *Manitoba Law Journal* 38, no. 1 (2015): 73–118; Thomas R. Berger, "The Manitoba Métis Decision and the Uses of History," *Manitoba Law Journal* 38, no. 1 (2015): 1–27; Thomas Flanagan, "The Case Against Metis Aboriginal Rights," *Canadian Public Policy* 9, no. 3 (September 1983): 314–25, https://doi.org/10.2307/3550780. Flanagan was an expert witness for Canada at trial in *Manitoba Metis*

Federation Inc. v. Canada (Attorney General), 2007 MBQB 293, where the trial court discusses Father Ritchot's diary at length.
32 *Caron*, at para 190.
33 Ibid., at para 176.
34 Ibid.
35 See Stanley, "Le journal," 548–9.
36 See section 23 of the *Manitoba Act, 1870*: "Either the English or the French language may be used by any person in the debates of the Houses of the Legislature, and both those languages shall be used in the respective Records and Journals of those Houses; and either of those languages may be used by any person, or in any Pleading or Process, in or issuing from any Court of Canada established under the *British North America Act, 1867*, or in or from all or any of the Courts of the Province. The Acts of the Legislature shall be printed and published in both those languages."
37 The federal obligation of legislative bilingualism still holds in section 133 of the *BNA Act, 1867*, since renamed the *Constitution Act, 1867*: "Either the English or the French Language may be used by any Person in the Debates of the Houses of the Parliament of Canada and of the Houses of the Legislature of Quebec; and both those Languages shall be used in the respective Records and Journals of those Houses; and either of those Languages may be used by any Person or in any Pleading or Process in or issuing from any Court of Canada established under this Act, and in or from all or any of the Courts of Quebec. The Acts of the Parliament of Canada and of the Legislature of Quebec shall be printed and published in both those Languages."
38 In his diary, Father Ritchot notes the following with respect to the first clause in the instructions he received from the Métis provisional government (which stated that the Territory should enter the Union as a province): "Le projet de constituer une petite province … accompagné du projet de faire rentrer le reste des terres de Rupert et du Nord-Ouest dans la Confédération comme province ne me paraît pas contredire le contenu de la 1ère clause de nos instructions." Quoted in Stanley, "Le journal," 561. That is, Father Ritchot considered that it was consistent with the provisional government's demand that Canada should commit first to create the province of Manitoba over a small portion of the Territory, and subsequently to admit the rest of the Territory as a further province, or further provinces. As he reiterates later in the diary: "Je comprends que l'intention est de former plus tard des territoires restés en dehors du Manitoba, d'autres provinces." Ibid., 563.
39 *R. v. Mercure*, [1988] 1 SCR 234 [hereafter *Mercure*].
40 See *Haida Nation v. British Columbia (Minister of Forests)*, [2004] 3 SCR 511 [hereafter *Haida Nation*], at para 20: "Treaties serve to reconcile

pre-existing Aboriginal sovereignty with assumed Crown sovereignty, and to define Aboriginal rights guaranteed by s. 35 of the *Constitution Act, 1982*"; *Taku River Tlingit First Nation v. British Columbia (Project Assessment Director)*, [2004] 3 SCR 550 [hereafter *Taku River Tlingit*], at para 42: "The purpose of s. 35(1) of the *Constitution Act, 1982* is to facilitate the ultimate reconciliation of prior Aboriginal occupation with *de facto* Crown sovereignty"; *Delgamuukw v. British Columbia*, [1997] 3 SCR 1010 [hereafter *Delgamuukw*], at para 126: "[A]boriginal title arises from the prior occupation of Canada by aboriginal peoples. That prior occupation is relevant in two different ways: first, because of the physical fact of occupation, and second, because aboriginal title originates in part from pre-existing systems of aboriginal law"; *Guerin v. The Queen*, [1984] 2 SCR 335 [hereafter *Guerin*] at 379: "Their [Indians] interest in their lands is a pre-existing legal right not created by Royal Proclamation, by s. 18(1) of the *Indian Act*, or by any other executive order or legislative provision."
41 *MMF*, at para 66.
42 *Caron*, at para 1.
43 Ibid., at para 115.
44 Ibid.
45 Ibid., at para 4.
46 Ibid., at para 116.
47 Ibid.
48 Ibid., at para 6.
49 Ibid., at para 130.
50 Ibid., at para 46.
51 Ibid., at para 183.
52 Ibid., at para 235.
53 Ibid., at para 219.
54 Ibid., at para 236.
55 Ibid., at para 240.
56 On law as autopoietic, see, for example, Gunther Teubner, *Law as an Autopoietic System*, trans. Anne Bankowska and Ruth Adler, ed. Zenon Bankowski (Cambridge, MA: Blackwell Publishers 1993).
57 *Caron*, at para 103. See also para 46: "the express and mandatory language respecting legislative bilingualism used by the imperial Parliament in s. 133 of the *Constitution Act, 1867* and by the Parliament of Canada in the *Manitoba Act, 1870* stands in marked contrast to the complex web of instruments, vague phrases, political pronouncements and historical context on which the appellants' claims depend." This suggests that the majority's real point about the contrasting instruments involved is focused not so much on constitutional entrenchment as on the fact that the *Manitoba Act, 1870* explicitly mentions linguistic rights, while the

1870 Order does not. As noted in the text below, this point fails to grapple with the fact that the *1870 Order* placed the Territory outside the new province of Manitoba under the legislative authority of the Parliament of Canada, which unquestionably did have an express and constitutionally entrenched obligation of legislative bilingualism under section 133 of the *Constitution Act, 1867*.

58 *BNA Act, 1871*, preamble.
59 *Caron*, at para 214.
60 Ibid.
61 Ibid., at para 56.
62 Borrows, "Origin Stories," 34.
63 *1870 Order; Constitution Act, 1982*, Schedule, Item 3.
64 Prior to the adoption of the *Constitution Act, 1982*, the *1870 Order* could be amended by legislation of the British Parliament, though by the early twentieth century a convention was established that the British Parliament would only do so on request from the Canadian Parliament. See discussion in, for example, *Re: Resolution to amend the Constitution*, [1981] 1 SCR. 753 [hereafter *Patriation Reference*]. With the adoption of the *Constitution Act, 1982*, amendment of constitutional documents, such as the *1870 Order*, are governed by the cumbersome procedures laid out in sections 38 to 48 of that Act.
65 *Mikisew Cree First Nation v. Canada (Governor General in Council)*, [2018] 2 SCR 765 [hereafter *Mikisew Cree II*]; *Newfoundland and Labrador (Attorney General) v. Uashaunnuat (Innu of Uashat and of Mani-Utenam)*, 2020 SCC 4 [hereafter *Uashaunnuat*]; *Nevsun Resources Ltd. v. Araya*, 2020 SCC 5 [hereafter *Nevsun*]. On *Mikisew Cree II*, see Robert Hamilton and Joshua Nichols, "In Search of Honorable Crowns and Legitimate Constitutions: *Mikisew Cree First Nation v Canada* and the Colonial Constitution," *University of Toronto Law Journal* 70, no. 3 (2020): 341–75. On *Uashaunnuat* and *Nevsun*, see Ryan Beaton, "Performing Sovereignty in a Time of Ideological Instability: BC's Bill 41 and the Reception of *UNDRIP* into Canadian Law," *University of British Columbia Law Review* 53, no. 4 (2021): 1017–63.
66 There is a vast literature on legal positivism. In the Anglo-American legal world, the discussion has been organized largely around the "Hart–Dworkin debate." A helpful overview can be found in Scott J. Shapiro, "The 'Hart-Dworkin' Debate: A Short Guide for the Perplexed," in *Ronald Dworkin*, ed. Arthur Ripstein (Cambridge: Cambridge University Press, 2007), 22–55, https://doi.org/10.1017/CBO9781139167109.002 .
67 Plausible positivist descriptions of the Canadian legal system might characterize its rule of recognition as including rules found in written constitutional documents, in unwritten constitutional principles,

and in case law precedent. On unwritten constitutional principles in Canada, see, for example, *Re Manitoba Language Rights*, [1985] 1 SCR 721 at 752: "in the process of Constitutional adjudication, the Court may have regard to unwritten postulates which form the very foundation of the Constitution of Canada." The Court affirmed that statement in *Reference re Secession of Quebec*, [1998] 2 SCR 217, at para 54. See also *Reference re Remuneration of Judges of the Provincial Court (P.E.I.)*, [1997] 3 SCR 3, at paras 82–109 addressing "The Unwritten Basis of Judicial Independence" in the Canadian Constitution. The Court has also stressed, however, in *Babcock v. Canada (Attorney General)*, [2002] 3 SCR 3, at para 55, that "[t]he unwritten principles must be balanced against the principle of Parliamentary sovereignty." The precise role for unwritten principles in adjudication continues to divide the Court: see, for example, *Quebec (Attorney General) v. Canada (Attorney General)*, [2015] 1 SCR 693; *Trial Lawyers Association of British Columbia v. British Columbia (Attorney General)*, [2014] 3 SCR 31.

68 H.L.A. Hart, *The Concept of Law*, ed. Leslie Green, Joseph Raz, and Penelope A. Bulloch, 3rd ed. (Oxford: Oxford University Press, 2012), 250. Dennis Patterson, writing as a legal positivist, glosses this point by saying that the "constitution is law because everyone regards it as such. Validity is best explained as a psychosocial phenomenon." Dennis Patterson, "Theoretical Disagreement, Legal Positivism, and Interpretation," *Ratio Juris* 31, no. 3 (September 2018): 273, https://doi.org/10.1111/raju.12216.

69 Scott J. Shapiro writes that an account of legal interpretation is positivistic when "it roots interpretive methodology in social facts." Scott J. Shapiro, *Legality* (Cambridge, MA: Harvard University Press, 2011), 372. Patterson, "Theoretical Disagreement," 261n2, adopts Shapiro's characterization of positivistic legal interpretation. See also Dyzenhaus, "Genealogy," 45: "Positive law, properly so called, is not merely law whose existence is determinable by factual tests but law whose content is determinable by the same sort of tests." Shapiro and Patterson write as positivists, while Dyzenhaus writes as a critic of positivism.

70 Unless directed to do so by some legal rule or authority whose validity is established by factual tests; see the following note and accompanying text.

71 For instance, a constitutional provision enshrining equal rights is, on the positivist view, legally binding only because it is accepted as part of the constitution, not because of its moral content. Yet the fact that it is so binding may require judges to engage in moral reasoning about the meaning of "equality" in order to interpret the precise content of equality rights. Their judicial interpretations are legally valid because they remain authorized ultimately by factual tests (i.e., by proper "social pedigree"). Such "incorporation" of moral reasoning into assessments of legal validity is accepted by "soft" or "inclusive" positivists. Inclusive legal positivists

"hold that when moral considerations are incorporated into a legal order's criteria for legal validity, and when argument on the basis of such criteria yields a correct answer, there is no reason to deny that the answer is fully determined by law." Dyzenhaus, "Genealogy," 44. By contrast, "exclusive" legal positivists hold that any such arguments on the basis of moral considerations are about what the law ought to be, not about what it is.

72 Dyzenhaus, "Genealogy."
73 Ibid., 45.
74 Ibid., 46.
75 Ibid. See also James Tully's characterization of common law reasoning in Tully, *Strange Multiplicity: Constitutionalism in an Age of Diversity* (Cambridge: Cambridge University Press, 1995), 103–24. Tully draws notably on Sir Matthew Hale's defence of the common law against Thomas Hobbes's deductive rationalism.
76 In other words, the positivist focus on sovereign or legislative intent as the sole source of legal validity implies that judicial interpretation of, for example, the historical relations between Indigenous peoples and the state cannot *really* be *legal* interpretation, because such relations are not a source of law from the positivist perspective – except perhaps indirectly if some statute or constitutional provision authorizes the courts to draw legal conclusions from such relations. The majority in *Caron* exemplifies this indirect approach, interpreting the legal significance of the 1870 negotiations and agreement between Canada and the Métis provisional government through the lens of British and Canadian sovereign intent – i.e., the majority does its best to reconstruct the intent of the Dominion Parliament embodied in the *Manitoba Act, 1870* and of the British Crown embodied in the *1870 Order*, which was in turn authorized through the legislative intent of the British Parliament embodied in section 146 of the *BNA Act, 1867*. The dissent interprets these same instruments but derives the legal content and lawful authority of these instruments from the historic negotiations and agreement themselves, to a much greater extent than the majority.

Of course, the positivist perspective recognizes that sovereign intent cannot resolve every legal question that may arise. When this happens, judges may have to fill in the gaps (e.g., through moral reasoning, including at times moral reasoning about historical political relations). The positivists whom Dyzenhaus has been discussing in the lead-up to the passage quoted here – John Austin in particular – wanted to dispense with what they considered "the 'childish fiction' of the common law that judges do not make the law." Dyzenhaus, "Genealogy," 48; see also ibid., 53. But this desire to do away with the "childish fiction" is part of a prescriptive program, which Hart renounces in his own stated desire to stick with

"descriptive sociology." Hence Hart's need to move off this first horn of the dilemma.
77 Dyzenhaus, "Genealogy," 53.
78 Ibid., 62.
79 *Tsilhqot'in Nation v. British Columbia*, [2014] 2 SCR 257 [hereafter *Tsilhqot'in Nation*].
80 *R. v. Sparrow*, [1990] 1 SCR 1075 [hereafter *Sparrow*].
81 Dyzenhaus, "Genealogy," 46.
82 For a helpful discussion of the role of *de facto* sovereignty in the Marshall trilogy and in recent Canadian Aboriginal case law, see Kent McNeil, "Shared Indigenous and Crown Sovereignty: Modifying the State Model," *Articles & Book Chapters* (2020): 2815, https://digitalcommons.osgoode.yorku.ca/scholarly_works/2815. For a discussion, drawing on Carl Schmitt, of the never-ending contest (e.g., between Congress and the Supreme Court) in US constitutionalism to claim the voice of popular sovereignty and the power to (in Schmitt's language) decide on the exception, see Paul W. Kahn, *Political Theology: Four New Chapters on the Concept of Sovereignty* (New York: Columbia University Press, 2011). While Schmitt was a strident critic of legal positivism, particularly of Hans Kelsen's legal formalism, Schmitt's own political theology draws a similar line between law and politics, such that legitimacy and lawful authority within a legal system ultimately flow from the successful (*de facto*) assertion of sovereignty, an assertion that itself lies beyond the scope of adjudication as to legal validity; like the positivists' rule of recognition, the assertion of sovereignty is successful/accepted, or it is not. Common law reasoning is arguably opposed, in this respect, both to legal positivism and to Schmitt's political theology.
83 *M'Intosh*, at 588.
84 For a recent discussion of the act of state doctrine in Canadian law, see *Nevsun*. The majority in *Nevsun* states, at para 28: "The act of state doctrine is a known (and heavily criticized) doctrine in England and Australia. It has, by contrast, played no role in Canadian law."
85 *Coe v. Commonwealth of Australia*, [1979] HCA 68, at para 3 of the reasons of Justice Jacobs, dissenting in the outcome (the appeal before the Court dealing with an application to amend pleadings), though this substantive point was not in dispute between members of the Court. The principal reasons of the Court were written by Justice Gibbs, who similarly stated at para 12 of his reasons: "The annexation of the east coast of Australia by Captain Cook in 1770, and the subsequent acts by which the whole of the Australian continent became part of the dominions of the Crown, were acts of state whose validity cannot be challenged."
86 *Mabo v. Queensland (No. 2)*, [1992] HCA 23, at para 31 of the reasons of Justice Brennan.

87 *Sparrow*, at 1106, quoting Noel Lyon, "An Essay on Constitutional Interpretation," *Osgoode Hall Law Journal* 26, no. 1 (1988): 100.
88 *Sparrow*, at 1103. For a detailed look at this tension in the *Sparrow* reasons, see Mark Walters, "'Looking for a knot in the bulrush': Reflections on Law, Sovereignty, and Aboriginal Rights," in *From Recognition to Reconciliation: Essays on the Constitutional Entrenchment of Aboriginal and Treaty Rights*, ed. Patrick Macklem and Douglas Sanderson (Toronto: University of Toronto Press, 2016), 35–62.
89 See *Tsilhqot'in Nation*, at para 69, where the Court states that "[t]he doctrine of *terra nullius* (that no one owned the land prior to European assertion of sovereignty) never applied in Canada, as confirmed by the *Royal Proclamation* of 1763" and simultaneously affirms that "[a]t the time of assertion of European sovereignty, the Crown acquired radical or underlying title to all the land in the province [of British Columbia]."
90 *Haida Nation*, at para 20: "Treaties serve to reconcile pre-existing Aboriginal sovereignty with assumed Crown sovereignty, and to define Aboriginal rights guaranteed by s. 35 of the *Constitution Act, 1982*."
91 *Taku River Tlingit*, at para 42: "The purpose of s. 35(1) of the *Constitution Act, 1982* is to facilitate the ultimate reconciliation of prior Aboriginal occupation with *de facto* Crown sovereignty."
92 See *Delgamuukw*, at para 126: "[A]boriginal title arises from the prior occupation of Canada by aboriginal peoples. That prior occupation is relevant in two different ways: first, because of the physical fact of occupation, and second, because aboriginal title originates in part from pre-existing systems of aboriginal law"; *Guerin*, at 379: "Their [Indians] interest in their lands is a pre-existing legal right not created by Royal Proclamation, by s. 18(1) of the *Indian Act*, or by any other executive order or legislative provision."
93 See *Haida Nation*, at para 20: "Where treaties remain to be concluded, the honour of the Crown requires negotiations leading to a just settlement of Aboriginal claims." See also ibid., para 25: "Put simply, Canada's Aboriginal peoples were here when Europeans came, and were never conquered. Many bands reconciled their claims with the sovereignty of the Crown through negotiated treaties. Others, notably in British Columbia, have yet to do so. The potential rights embedded in these claims are protected by s. 35 of the *Constitution Act, 1982*. The honour of the Crown requires that these rights be determined, recognized and respected. This, in turn, *requires the Crown, acting honourably, to participate in processes of negotiation* [emphasis added]." In *Tsilhqot'in Nation*, at para 17, the Court confirmed that para 25 of *Haida Nation* was speaking of a *legal* duty: "The Court in *Haida* stated that the Crown had not only a moral duty, but *a legal duty to negotiate in good faith to resolve land claims*

[emphasis added]." Note, however, that the British Columbia Supreme Court, for one, explicitly declined to read *Haida Nation* and *Tsilhqot'in Nation* as affirming "a new principle of general application compelling negotiation in all aboriginal litigation." See *Songhees Nation v. British Columbia*, 2014 BCSC 1783, at para 19. Courts are generally reluctant to compel, as opposed to encourage, negotiations. It remains to be seen whether of circumstances may prompt more specific court orders compelling the Crown to negotiate. Some duty-to-consult judgments arguably impose more specific obligations to negotiate *if the Crown wishes to pursue its proposed course of action*. See, for example, *Tsleil-Waututh Nation v. Canada (Attorney General)*, 2018 FCA 153. This is different, however, from imposing on the Crown a stand-alone obligation to negotiate, independent of any specific action the Crown wishes to pursue.

94 *Calder v. Attorney-General of British Columbia*, [1973] SCR 313, at 380 (*per* Justice Hall). See also *Guerin*, at 380; *Sparrow*, at 1103; *Wewaykum Indian Band v. Canada*, 2002 SCC 79, at para 75.

95 *Cherokee Nation v. Georgia*, 30 US (5 Pet) 1 (1831) [hereafter *Cherokee Nation*]; *Worcester v. the State of Georgia*, 31 US (6 Pet) 515 (1832) [hereafter *Worcester*].

96 Antony Anghie, *Imperialism, Sovereignty and the Making of International Law* (Cambridge: Cambridge University Press, 2005).

97 *M'Intosh*, at 572–3.

98 *Worcester*, at 544–5.

99 See, for example, Darlene Johnston, *The Taking of Indian Lands in Canada: Consent or Coercion?* (Saskatoon: Native Law Centre, University of Saskatchewan, 1989), 67–73; John Borrows, "Wampum at Niagara: The Royal Proclamation, Canadian Legal History, and Self-Government," in *Aboriginal and Treaty Rights in Canada*, ed. Michael Asch (Vancouver: UBC Press, 1997), 155–72. See also the two sets of dissenting reasons by Justices Strong and Gwynne, respectively, in *St. Catharines Milling and Lumber Co. v. The Queen*, (1887) 13 SCR 577. Of course, Indigenous leaders often had to negotiate under the considerable pressure of European expansion and settlement.

100 *Worcester*, at 546.

101 *M'Intosh*, 591–2.

102 And *to contract*, as *Worcester* suggests. For instance, while Chief Justice Marshall emphasized the conquest of Indian Nations in *M'Intosh*, he took pains in *Worcester*, at 546, to explain that in the royal charters that planted colonies in the new world, "[t]he power of war is given only for defence, not for conquest." In *Worcester*, Chief Justice Marshall was consciously responding to the rapidly evolving social and political

context of Indigenous–state relations, including the intense public focus on Georgia's efforts, supported by President Andrew Jackson, to remove the Cherokee Nation from within its state boundaries: see, for example, Joseph Burke, "The Cherokee Cases: A Study in Law, Politics, and Morality," *Stanford Law Review* 21, no. 3 (February 1969): 500–31, https://doi.org/10.2307/1227621.
103 *M'Intosh*, at 588.
104 Chief Justice Marshall would surely have had *Campbell v. Hall*, (1774) 1 Cowp 204, 98 ER 1045, in mind. *Campbell* was a landmark case decided in 1774 by the Court of King's Bench in England; the case addressed fundamental aspects of legal regimes applicable to territories conquered by the British Crown. This is not to say that Chief Justice Marshall intended to import the reasoning from *Campbell* wholesale into US law governing relations between Indigenous peoples and the United States. *M'Intosh* does not, for instance, hold that upon conquest the laws of Indigenous peoples were incorporated into the laws of colonial Britain or, later, of the United States. However, Chief Justice Marshall's choice of the term "conquest" to frame Indigenous–US relations would have called *Campbell* to mind as a point of reference as *M'Intosh* attempted to craft a satisfactory legal regime to govern those relations.
105 *M'Intosh*, at 591.
106 See note 104 above.
107 *Cherokee Nation*, at 17.
108 See Burke, "Cherokee Cases."
109 *Worcester*, at 542–3.
110 Ibid., at 595.
111 Ibid., at 559–60.
112 Dyzenhaus, "Genealogy," 46.
113 *Caron*, at para 136.
114 On the fluidity of "sovereignty" in legal interpretation, see, for example, Walters, "Reflections on Law," 40: "As a construct of ordinary legal discourse, sovereignty is, like all ordinary legal constructs, something that must be constantly interpreted and reinterpreted over time to ensure that it contributes to the general understanding of law as an enterprise that integrates legality and legitimacy." See also Anghie, *Imperialism*.

9 "To Invite New Worlds": Indigenous Constitutionalism and the Search for a Jurisgenerative Federalism in Canada

ROBERT HAMILTON

We're in our ship, and all of our ways are in there. Our way of doing, our way of governing, our way of business, our language, our belief system. And you're in your ship, with your customs, and your way of governing, and your language, and your courts, and your laws, and your governance over yourselves, as we travel along on this river of life together. And we weren't supposed to poke holes in each other's vessel. The rule here is we don't steer the other one's boat.
– Kanenhariyo (Seth LaFort)[1]

Introduction

Resource development projects have frequently been a source of conflict between Indigenous peoples and the federal and provincial governments. Two pipeline projects – the Trans Mountain Expansion and Coastal Gaslink – are two recent, and prominent, flashpoints. As of this writing, a number of Indigenous nations in southern British Columbia have recently lost a duty to consult decision at the Federal Court of Appeal in which they alleged that federal approval of the Trans Mountain project should have been quashed on the basis that the Crown inadequately discharged its duty to consult and accommodate.[2] Further north, Wet'suwet'en peoples have been engaged in a battle with the government of British Columbia over the Coastal Gaslink pipeline. In each instance, Indigenous peoples have asserted Indigenous law as one basis for their actions.[3] Such conflicts are increasingly framed as contests between competing legal orders rather than disputes over rights; the disputes are about jurisdiction. This reflects the fact that the place of Indigenous peoples in the constitutional order in Canada has never been settled. While some Indigenous peoples do assert that they have never been a part of Canada and wish to remain fully apart from its legal and political frameworks, most do not assert secession as a goal. Nonetheless, they do question the authority of federal and provincial governments to make unilateral decisions in relation to their lands and resources. The conflicts, in this sense, can be seen as challenges to Canadian federalism.

This is all the more evident when we consider the shift to the language of self-determination. The recognition of Indigenous peoples as *peoples* in the United Nations Declaration on the Rights of Indigenous Peoples mandates that states recognize Indigenous self-determination.[4] The ability of Canada's constitutional order to adapt to the demands of Indigenous peoples may determine much about how the relationship between Indigenous peoples and the state develops in the coming years and decades. As Indigenous peoples continue to resist the unilateral imposition of colonial forms of governance, an inability to adapt institutions of Canadian federalism and doctrines of constitutional interpretation may make the development of productive shared governance mechanisms difficult. As James (Sa'ke'j) Youngblood Henderson writes, "The biggest problem that Canadians and Aboriginal peoples face in constitutional governance is the familiarity of the inherited system of constitutional and conventional federated governance."[5] The inherited system creates horizons that limit the legal and political possibilities imagined by federal and provincial governments and much of the Canadian public. To create the conditions for the rearrangements of constitutional authority required to meaningfully recognize Indigenous self-determination, inherited ideas about Canada's federal order have to be reassessed and challenged.

This chapter enters these debates by suggesting that the federal order can be reformed to meet Indigenous demands for self-determination only when that order becomes jurisgenerative; federalism, in its myriad dimensions, must facilitate the coexistence and growth of multiple legal and normative orders. The first part of the chapter defines terms: how laws can be said to be either jurisgenerative or, conversely, jurispathic, is crucial to imagining and assessing alternative structures. The second section explores the challenges and opportunities associated with a jurisgenerative federalism in terms of institutions and practices of federalism. The final part reflects on the role of the courts in facilitating the growth of a jurisgenerative federal association.

The Jurispathic Character of Aboriginal Law and Canadian Federalism

The terms *jurisgenerative* and *jurispathic* are drawn from Robert Cover's work. Jurisgenerative refers to the production of law and legal meaning.[6]

Communities continually produce legal norms as they "constantly create and maintain a world of right and wrong, of lawful and unlawful, of valid and void."[7] The creation of law in this context does not refer only to the production of positive law, such as statutes or regulations, but also to the continual generation of a normative world within communities – what Cover refers to as a *nomos*. Law is constituted by practices and interpretations that are shaped by this normative world. The production of legal meaning within communities "requires no state. ... [It] takes place always through an essentially cultural medium."[8] This emphasis on non-state conceptions of law decentres the state and prioritizes plural legal communities.

The creation of law is tied to the interpretive function of communities. Legal communities are "[a]utonomous interpretive communities" – communities that generate norms through the creation of shared meaning. This shared meaning, in turn, is crafted through narrative: "no set of legal institutions or prescriptions exist apart from the narratives that locate it and give it meaning."[9] The prescriptions and demands – the "oughts" – that constitute the normative universe of a given community and frame conceptions of legality and interpretations of law are bound up with layers of discourse and narrative.[10] Legal interpretation and the production of legal meaning cannot be separated from what Edward Said called the "structures of attitude and reference" of a given interpretive community.[11] The meaning of law, then, "is determined by our interpretive commitments."[12] These interpretive commitments, in turn, are shaped by the practices of communities. Together, the practices of communities and the shared production of meaning through collective narratives and multiple points of interpretation are jurisgenerative: they create law – what Judith Resnick refers to as the "lived, thick experience of law's meaning."[13] Quite apart from positive articulations or recognition from state authorities, autonomous interpretive communities create law and legal meaning on an ongoing basis. Cover's descriptive analysis aligns with the argument of Indigenous peoples that self-determination involves the recognition of their own internal legal orders. Indigenous claims for self-determination, as Robert Williams Jr. has argued, "most often assert a claim for the restoration of indigenous peoples' jurisgenerative power; that is, a claim for the power of indigenous communities to resume living by a law of their own choosing and creation."[14]

Jurisgenerative processes must be considered not only in respect of a community's internal laws but also of the shared and contested legal norms of multiple communities. The relationship between state law and discrete legal communities is of particular importance. To use one of Cover's examples, what "freedom of religion" means for state actors may not align with what it means for a particular religious group.[15] Cover's central intervention is to argue that both interpretations *are* law. Law cannot be divorced from the interpretive communities that give it meaning and adjudication, therefore, it is not a practice of determining what the law *is* but of choosing one legal interpretation over the other, of eliminating one legal meaning in favour of another. Put more simply, there is no single, universal "law" that exists apart from interpretation and application through specific practices. Law is always created through interpretation, which means it is always the site of contested interpretations and layers of meaning.

It is in this sense that adjudication is jurispathic: it destroys legal meaning. State law, therefore, in its insistence on a singular interpretive frame, "destroys the world that 'interpretation' calls up."[16] The *nomos*, the field of interpretation and narrative through which law is given meaning, cannot be "fused with the force of the state."[17] The state tends towards a jurispathic approach that destroys the legal realities of subnational groups – the legal meaning created by those groups – by establishing a rigid hierarchy of law. The state and state courts are a "solution" to the problem of pluralism – to a radical indeterminacy and relativism brought on by "too much law."[18] The executive and legislative branches in Canada have long histories of erasing Indigenous legal orders. Outlawing of the potlach, for example, undermined the processes through which coastal nations made and interpreted law.[19] The *Indian Act* sought to replace Indigenous forms of governance with state forms and purported to limit Indigenous law-making authority to a power to pass by-laws in relation to small number of issues.[20] Territorially, even that limited law-making authority was confined to reserves that comprise only a small portion of any nation's traditional territory. The residential school system systematically removed children from their parents and communities with the express aim of preventing the transmission of language and culture.[21] Many of the most harmful legacies of these policies continue to impact Indigenous peoples. Yet, the jurispathic character of state law is not displayed only through these evidently colonial laws.

Courts play a unique and important role. The need for courts is not historically articulated as law creating but as law confining; their task is to eliminate interpretations, synthesizing disparate views into a workable doctrine. The doctrine of *stare decisis*, however malleable in practice, is premised not on the generation of law but on stasis, hierarchy, and univocal statements of authority. Courts sit atop a hierarchy of state authority, and their interpretations, which "crush competing nomoi of autonomous communities," guide the use of force in the state.[22] In this way, "constitutional interpretation is ... inextricably bound up with the real threat or practice of violent deeds."[23] The connection between judicial interpretation and the use of state violence is clear, for example, in the many decisions the Canadian Supreme Court has held against Indigenous claims to constitutional rights, thereby calling on the force of the state, even if implicitly, to enforce their decisions.[24] In historical cases, the jurispathic role of the courts is clear. The 1928 *R. v. Syliboy* decision, for example, held that the Mi'kmaq could not enter into treaties because treaties "are unconstrained Acts of independent powers. But the Indians were never regarded as an independent power." Rather, a "civilized nation first discovering a country of uncivilized people or savages held such country as its own until such time as by treaty it was transferred to some other civilized nation. The savages' rights of sovereignty even of ownership were never recognized."[25] As recently as 1982, the central conclusions of the *Syliboy* decision were upheld by the Nova Scotia Court of Appeal.[26]

The contemporary courts may seem a more controversial example of jurispathic law. Especially since the inclusion of "Aboriginal and treaty rights" in the Constitution in 1982,[27] the courts have often seemed to be expanding the definition of Aboriginal rights and protecting a sphere of Indigenous autonomy from intransigent government actors.[28] Indeed, elements of the doctrine of Aboriginal rights create space for Indigenous laws in important respects. In *Tsilhqot'in Nation*, for example, the Supreme Court of Canada held that the interest that Aboriginal title protects includes jurisdiction over title lands. There is a public law dimension to Aboriginal title that supports the exercise of self-government.[29] Further, in demonstrating the historical occupation of territory required to ground a title claim, a nation can bring forward evidence that their laws governed the use of that territory.[30] The doctrine of Aboriginal title has evolved in a way that may support jurisgenisis insofar as it recognizes the rights of the title-holding group to manage their title lands collectively, and to rely on their internal legal traditions to ground claims for title.

The development of the duty to consult has compelled federal and provincial governments to dialogue with Indigenous peoples where it considers actions that may affect their rights. Viewed optimistically, this doctrine created what Brian Slattery has referred to as a "generative constitution" and Henderson has called "dialogical governance."[31] Further, while the Supreme Court has not recognized a right of self-government, it has made important statements recognizing "Aboriginal sovereignty" and the need to recognize "shared sovereignties."[32] Lower courts have made similarly encouraging remarks: the British Columbia

Supreme Court held in *Campbell v. British Columbia (Attorney General)* that the inherent right of self-government was not extinguished by the assertion of British sovereignty and the passage of the *British North America Act, 1867*, and in *Restoule v. Canada*[33] the Ontario Superior Court relied on "Anishinaabe principles of respect, responsibility, reciprocity and renewal to understand the intention of the signatories at the time of signing"[34] in the process of treaty interpretation.

Yet, a jurispathic tendency has continued to undergird the architecture of Aboriginal rights, a tendency seen clearly in the *R. v. Sparrow*[35] and *R. v. Van der Peet*[36] decisions. In *Sparrow*, Ronald Sparrow was charged with violating *Fisheries Act, 1985* regulations for fishing with a net exceeding the allowable length. Sparrow argued that "the regulation of fishing was an inherent aspect of the aboriginal right to fish" and "that the right to regulate is part of the right to use the resource"[37] – that is, it included a jurisdictional element through which Indigenous law would regulate the subject matter of the right. The Court disagreed, holding that overriding legislative power and regulatory authority was "always" held by the Crown.[38] Adopting Cover's analysis would lead to the conclusion that Ronald Sparrow's understanding of the law, grounded as it was in the lived practices and normative universe of the Musqueam people and their understanding of the nature of the Canadian Constitution and their place in it, is as much "the law" as that articulated by the Supreme Court.[39] The Court decided not merely whether the Department of Fisheries and Oceans had violated Mr. Sparrow's Aboriginal rights; they chose between legal orders and, in so doing, prioritized one at the expense of the other. In *Van der Peet*, the Court designed a restrictive culture-based test for establishing Aboriginal rights that considerably narrowed the scope of constitutional protection for those rights by requiring that an activity be "integral to the distinctive culture" in question at the date of contact in order to be recognized as a right.[40] While the Court recognized that Indigenous legal perspectives ought to shape the nature of the right in question, it designed a legal test that narrowly circumscribed those rights and relied on problematically essentialized conceptions of Indigenous identity and culture.[41] While motioning towards a generative conception of Aboriginal rights, the Court tailored those rights to the demands of the nation state.

The combined effect of these two cases was to limit Aboriginal rights to a narrow range of "cultural" practices that are subject to government regulation and unilateral infringement, with cultural practices subject to judicial oversight through a proportionality analysis. Regardless of what one believes about the sagacity of these decisions, the regime they structure is jurispathic in the two senses outlined here: in shaping the doctrine, the Court eliminated competing interpretations of the constitutional norms at issue, while the doctrine itself makes a constitutional basis for the exercise of Indigenous law and jurisdiction difficult to find. Thus, section 35 has given rise to a judicially structured rights regime that accepts the Crown's unilateral claims. These concessions to the pretences of the Crown can be understood as emanating from the *nomos* that inform judges' decision-making. Their normative vision of the place of Indigenous peoples in Canada's constitutional order shapes the narratives that their interpretive community internalizes and then deploys. This interpretive community has not to date been able to consider serious challenges to the Crown's unilateral sovereign authority or inherited notions of state territoriality or federal constitutionalism.[42] As a result, the model of Aboriginal rights they constructed fixed Indigenous peoples as cultural minorities without a meaningful place in the scheme of the federal association. Section 35, as interpreted by the judiciary, has proven jurispathic, despite the fact that the jurispathic tendencies sit in tension with many of the more expansive ideas the Court has at times put forward.[43]

A recent example illustrates the tensions that pull at the structure built atop this foundation. In *Mikisew Cree First Nation v. Canada*,[44] the Mikisew Cree First Nation argued that the Crown duty to consult and accommodate applies to the preparation of legislation. The majority of the Court disagreed, holding that such a duty would unduly impinge on parliamentary sovereignty and the separation of powers.[45] Two very different constitutional interpretations were being put forward. The factums of two interveners, the Federation of Sovereign Indigenous Nations (FSIN) and the Grand Council of the Crees (GCC), show how the normative vision of the interpretive community shapes the legal interpretation of the parties. The FSIN wrote: "the approach endorsed by the Federal Court of Appeal in *Mikisew* [which held against the recognition of the duty to consult in these circumstances] is a condescension to the unique political status afforded to Indigenous nations which have entered into Treaty."[46] The GCC argued:

> This formalistic approach freezes the doctrines of separation of powers and Parliamentary sovereignty at a time before the emergence of the constitutional duty to consult Indigenous peoples. It takes no account of the modern reality of governance in Canada. Rather than seeking to reconcile the doctrines with the duty, it draws an irreconcilable opposition between them so as to exclude any application of the duty to consult at any stage in the process leading to the development of legislation.

The approach proposed by the Mikisew Cree, the GCC argued, takes the path of reconciliation and recognizes the Constitution as representing and encompassing evolving social norms. By taking account of modern governance realities, this approach seeks to reconcile constitutional doctrines with constitutional duty rather than discarding one in favour of the other:

> This approach balances the need for effective legislative action with the constitutional duty to consult Indigenous peoples and protect their Aboriginal and treaty rights in the framework of section 35 of the *Constitution Act, 1982*. This path is preventive, not curative. It fosters negotiation over litigation so as to comply with the honour of the Crown and the overarching objective of reconciliation between Indigenous peoples and Government.[47]

The narratives that shape the legal meaning the Grand Council of the Crees assign to section 35 and their understanding of the obligations it creates are shaped by their normative understanding of the development of the constitutional order. The attorney general for Canada presented a competing view of the Constitution:

> The principle of parliamentary sovereignty and the duty to consult do not overlap because the courts cannot supervise the law-making process in Parliament and the Crown (the Executive) does not control that process. In this appeal it is important to note that not all actions of Ministers and their government departments are executive acts. Ministers, as members of the legislature, are also involved in acts, such as the development of legislation, that are part of the law-making process of Parliament. Parliamentary sovereignty and the duty to consult only purport to overlap in this case because the appellants have taken the position that the decision of Cabinet to propose legislation to Parliament is not part of the law-making process of Parliament and is therefore subject to the duty to consult. That position is inconsistent with the constitutional principles underlying our parliamentary system.[48]

Similarly, the attorney general of Alberta argued:

> The separation of powers is a constitutional principle fundamental to our democratic government. The legislative branch makes policy choices and enacts laws, the executive implements those policies and laws and the judiciary interprets and enforces the laws. Each branch of government plays an essential role, but must be sensitive not to intrude into the spheres reserved to others.[49]

The federal and provincial governments emphasized a constitutional narrative that imagines the constitutional past as fixed and subject to clear and identifiable rules and procedures from which one cannot deviate. To understand constitutional obligations, one need only employ a formalistic reading of the rules. The forward-looking vision that shapes the narratives offered by the federal and provincial Crowns sees Indigenous peoples as enjoying discrete *Charter*-analogous rights that in no way challenge the conventional constitutional order as understood from the Crown perspective. The majority of the Court agreed with the Crown vision of the Constitution and their interpretation of constitutional text and convention.

Whatever one may think of whether this decision accords with previous case law, it is clear that it does not accord with the constitutional interpretation of the Indigenous peoples concerned. Here, Cover's insight that law is "a bridge linking a concept of reality to an imagined alternative"[50] is apposite: what is at issue is not a rote application of "rule" to "fact," but a determination of Indigenous peoples' place in the constitutional order in the future and whose vision ought to be determinative in that regard. The jurispathic character of the Court's decisions – the extent to which adjudication suppresses law – is evident: the interpretations that have been given priority interpret section 35 in a way that fails to allow for the flourishing of Indigenous legal norms within a federal association. State "aboriginal law" is, therefore, "world maintaining." That is, it supports and maintains a given normative universe and "destroys legal meaning in the interest of social control."[51]

A final example illustrates the "world-maintaining" nature of this body of law. In *Coastal GasLink Pipeline Ltd. v. Hudson*,[52] the Supreme Court of British Columbia was asked to issue an injunction against pipeline protestors. The protestors relied on Indigenous law as a defence, claiming that they were preventing the company from entering their territory on the basis of Wet'suwet'en law.[53] The Court responded as follows:

> As a general rule, indigenous customary laws do not become an effectual part of Canadian common law or Canadian domestic law until there is some means or process by which the indigenous customary law is recognized as being part of Canadian domestic law, either through incorporation into treaties, court declarations, such as aboriginal title or rights jurisprudence or statutory provisions. ... While Wet'suwet'en customary laws clearly exist on their own independent footing, they are not recognized as being an effectual part of Canadian law.[54]

While recognizing the *existence* of Wet'suwet'en law, the Court held that it was unable to give it meaning – to interpret and apply it – until such time as it was given positive recognition in an approved form. Nowhere can be found a more explicit example of the Court choosing between, and eliminating, forms of law. The invocation of jurisdiction – the Court simply does not have the jurisdiction to recognize Indigenous law – illustrates how legal technicality is relied on to mask the Court's role in mediating normative claims.[55]

The interpretive commitments that are brought to bear on the interpretation of a given constitutional clause are shaped by an interpretive community's understanding of the present and desires for the future; as Cover explains, "a *nomos* is a present world constituted by a tension between reality and vision."[56] Interpretation of law accords with this vision. In the case of Aboriginal rights, the interpretations given to the Constitution are shaped by the distinct views about the place of Indigenous peoples in Canada's constitutional order. As Henderson has argued, "[t]he underlying cultural and constitutional realities of Aboriginal peoples have not been recognized and incorporated into constitutional governance and democracy."[57] This has a tangible impact because, as Cover notes, "while one dimension of the agonistic element [of constitutional interpretation] may be argument; another more important dimension is violence."[58] That is, unlike literary interpretation, the interpretation of legal texts – written or unwritten – guides the state's use of force. The stakes of constitutional interpretation are high.

In assessing the usefulness of this analysis to the Canadian context, especially with a prescriptive eye turned towards the articulation of productive alternative visions for law and policy, it is important to keep in mind the capacious sense in which Cover uses the term "interpretation." Constitutional interpretation is not the exclusive purview of the courts; it "may be the act of judges or citizens, legislators or presidents, draft resistors or right-to-life protestors."[59] The process of constitutional interpretation is diffused throughout society, with autonomous communities of meaning interpreting constitutional provisions in light of their distinctive normative underpinnings. Considering how jurisgenesis can be fostered in a federal state, then, requires analysis of the myriad actors who give constitutions meaning through interpretation and practice.

Jurisgenesis in the Federal State

While the vocabulary of "jurispathic law" may provide a helpful way to analyse and describe Canadian Aboriginal law, it hardly provides new information: that colonialism sought to eliminate Indigenous forms of law and jurisdiction is clear. The more interesting question is how state law can be challenged and reformed to create space for a jurisgenerative constitutional order to develop. An initial question, then, is the extent to which the jurispathic tendencies of the state can be mitigated in the facilitation of jurisgenerative possibilities. Can the totalizing impulses of the nation state be prevented from reducing normative and legal pluralism, and can state law be reformed so that it actually encourages the growth and flourishing of such pluralism?[60]

Robert Post argues that Cover is intensely pessimistic about the possibility of fostering jurisgenesis in the state. The state can only go so far as to adopt an "imperial" or "world-maintaining" position towards competing *nomoi*.[61] The state can strive for coexistence of multiple normative orders, but, to quote Cover, it can do so only under "an organizing principle itself incapable of producing the normative meaning that is life and growth."[62] Post reads Cover as voicing a familiar critique of a liberal constitutional order: that it might recognize plurality to an extent but can never help but to impose its own hegemony and bring competing value systems within its bounds. A state-based approach would "use violence to crush and displace the autonomous communities where nomos is actually forged."[63] Thus, while Cover recognizes that some principles of constitutionalism – in particular freedom of association – may provide space for competing *nomoi*, ultimately Post argues that Cover sees nothing more than a "passive and ultimately libertarian role for the state."[64] The state is "unrelentingly evacuated of meaning … exhausted by its bureaucratic and administrative structures," supported by judges whose role is "to kill the diverse legal traditions that compete with the state."[65] In Post's view, Cover thus removes from the state any reformative possibilities; his state is one "evacuated of political deliberation" that can only ever be jurispathic.[66] If correct, the state could not be the site of the jurisgenerative negotiation of shared legal orders between distinct communities, nor the site of flourishing normative and legal pluralism.

While recognizing many of these features of Cover's understanding of the state, Judith Resnick reads Cover as less unequivocally pessimistic about the possibility that the state might facilitate jurisgenesis.[67] Cover's concern, on her reading, is to explain and lay bare why the state fears the *jurispotence* of normative communities.[68] That is, "he wanted the state's actors … to be uncomfortable in their knowledge of their own power, respectful of the legitimacy of competing legal systems, and aware of the possibility that multiple meanings and divergent practices ought sometimes to be tolerated, even if painfully so."[69] This, in turn, can cause state decision-makers to recognize that their ability to impose a single conception of legality "stems from power itself rather than adopt a more comfortable (but false) proposition that a legal regime triumphs because it is superior."[70] Resnick rejects Post's argument, positing instead that Cover was in fact fundamentally concerned with the interactions between state and non-state legal orders.[71] The fact that state law is jurispathic does not render it irredeemable; it is when state law and adjudication mask their role through formalistic and technical reasoning that obscures the normative basis of decisions and the nature of the power relations at play that problems of legitimacy arise. Where the nature of disputes is clear, "competition and complementation among legal systems could itself be generative."[72]

This more nuanced view sees Cover as rejecting an "all-or-nothing" approach to the role of the state in generative legal interactions. Rather, the state is one actor – or one collection of actors – among many engaged in processes of contestation and negotiation through which law is worked out. While courts may play a jurispathic role insofar as they choose one law at the expense of another, a recognition of that role can cause them to adopt positions that are attentive to how and where they impose rigid singularity. The state, in other words, can be prodded into recognizing the legitimacy of competing legal orders and leaving open spaces for the generative development of shared norms between communities. This view has the benefit of recognizing the iterative processes through which norms are negotiated through shifting practices and resists the urge to homogenize either state actors or paideic communities. It adds complexity and nuance to the picture, even if the result is discomfort.

What can this tell us about jurisgenerative federalism? First, in order for the jurisgenerative nature of communities to flourish, the laws of one community must allow space for the existence of competing orders. While the competition between legal orders always has jurispathic results, law can be intentionally shaped in ways that minimize this tendency. Second, a process of jurisgenisis will occur *between* communities: the interaction of legal orders is in itself generative. So, what features of a political and legal order may allow for this? This question can be answered by examining actual practices and features of federal constitutional orders that are jurisgenerative – that is, that provide space for the construction of legal meaning by plural communities, both independently and through their interactions.

The starting point has to be the recognition of the existing legal orders of Indigenous peoples. The jurispotence of Indigenous peoples is evident, and how the Canadian constitutional order responds will shape

Crown–Indigenous relations in the years to come. While it has long been recognized that Indigenous peoples possess binding internal community norms, these have frequently been branded as customary law. Identified as such, they were considered as *outside*, and frequently *lesser than* state legal orders.[73] Much recent work, however, has argued persuasively in favour of seeing Indigenous law *qua* law, rejecting colonial hierarchies that minimize Indigenous jurisdiction.[74] There are countless examples of this growing jurispotence *within* Indigenous communities, including the development of tribal parks, the construction of big houses, and the revitalization of legal orders and grounded political authority. This has been accompanied by heterogeneous Indigenous theorizing about the nature of these movements and their development.[75]

There are also potential examples of jurisgenerative interaction of state and Indigenous legal orders at the institutional level. A first type of example are existing structures of shared decision-making and co-management – what I have elsewhere referred to as "interstitial federal institutions."[76] These include, for example, modern treaty bodies, reconciliation agreements, and co-management boards. Each of these examples have detractors and supporters with important arguments. Yet, what they all include to various extents are a recognition of Indigenous jurisdiction and the development of shared decision-making bodies through which inter-societal law can be generated.

The pipeline disputes outlined in the introduction provide two more salient examples. First, the role of Indigenous project assessments in the Trans Mountain Pipeline Expansion decision is worth considering. Both the Tsleil-Waututh and Sto:lo developed assessments of the proposed project. These assessments, which incorporate both contemporary scientific analysis and traditional knowledge, determined that the risk of the project was too great to justify its approval. These are expressions of Indigenous law.[77] How the courts deal with these types of assessments is important, as they provide courts an opportunity to recognize Indigenous jurisdiction. In *Tsleil-Waututh Nation v. Canada*, the Federal Court of Appeal noted these project assessments and suggested that they could have been considered in the consultation and accommodation process.[78] The court was prepared to note their importance, but by situating them in the duty to consult doctrine, the court also indicated that such assessments would not represent a final decision about projects, or even be equivalent to Crown decision-making processes. In *Coldwater v. Canada*, the follow-up decision held that the duty to consult and accommodate had been adequately discharged; there was no discussion of these Indigenous assessments. If given a meaningful role in project approvals, these assessments could represent an important intersection of state and Indigenous law. As Sarah Morales argues, "Although Indigenous-led assessment processes will not resolve every conflict between Indigenous peoples, government and industry proponents, they do offer a way forward that respects Indigenous laws and legal processes, international law and Canadian common law. They put Indigenous laws and norms at the centre of the process and uphold the right to self-determination of First Nations."[79]

A second example is the direct action of some Wet'suwet'en peoples against the Coastal Gaslink pipeline and, subsequently, solidarity movements across the country. In light of the proposed development of the Coastal Gaslink pipeline, Wet'suwet'en hereditary chiefs established blockades in their traditional territory and issued an eviction notice to the pipeline company. The company sought and received an injunction to remove the protestors.[80] Upon Royal Canadian Mounted Police enforcement of the injunction, solidarity movements developed across the country, including rail blockades and numerous demonstrations.[81] Such resistance can be jurisgenerative – an example of what Cover calls "redemptive constitutionalism."[82] What is crucial here is to understand that dissenters are "doing constitutional law, not just talking about it."[83] Just as the constitutional interpretation of judges is transformed into deeds through "the ecology of roles and the social cooperation in domination," so the deeds of resistance transform the "interpretation of the dissenting community into a species of true constitutionalism."[84] Put another way, there are a number of roles in the state – police being the most prominent example – through which the constitutional interpretation of the courts is given effect through force. Resistance works against this, bringing competing constitutional visions into being through practice. Crucially, "[t]he citizen or dissenter's constitutional interpretation cannot be *less* the deed than that of the state's officials."[85]

Because the constitutional interpretation of the state is given effect through force and violence, the interpretation of dissenting communities also must be given effect through action: "the extension of constitutional politics from argument to action – from briefs to pickets or sit-ins or even bombings – is in part compelled by the logic of constitutional interpretation."[86] Resistance shapes the interpretation of constitutional norms in foundational ways. As Cover writes, "Legal precepts and principles are not only demands made upon us by society, the people, the sovereign, or God. They are also signs by which each of us communicates with others." Law, then, is "a resource in signification," and "an act signifies something new and powerful when we understand that the act is in reference to a norm."[87] Cover does not advocate violence; rather, he points out that the logic of constitutional interpretation backed by state force compels competing interpretations to be put forward through practice and resistance to that force. Such actions bring competing interpretations of law to the fore and imbue those practices with legal meaning.[88]

Accepting the diverse production of legal meaning, and the correlative plurality of law, the question then becomes one of implications. What are the implications for structuring constitutional and federal arrangements that flow from this conclusion? A first step is to distinguish between normative and practical approaches to exploring this issue. A normative approach would say that this pluralism is a good in itself, and that political and legal structures should be designed to facilitate its flourishing. This is not a line of argument I wish to pursue here. The alternative is a practical approach. It begins by asking, in light of the *fact* of pluralism, what types of legal and political structures are apt to lead to the most peaceful and productive relationships possible by minimizing relations and practices of domination and enhancing freedom and dignity.[89] Here pluralism is valued in an instrumental sense: systems that seek to undermine pluralism are unstable. Whether they are unjust in an abstract or absolute sense is immaterial; their perceived injustice by individuals or communities subject to domination will give rise to practical political problems as individuals and groups seek legitimate forms of political authority. Thus, while it may well be morally unjustifiable in most cases for a majority to impose its values upon minority communities – or for more powerful communities to impose themselves on those less powerful through force (of which law is a central part) – consensus on this point is not necessary in order for us to agree that antagonistic strife is less likely where pluralism is respected. In this sense, a jurisgenerative federalism provides a workable path to legitimate constitutional authority.

In considering the diverse range of practices through which communities generate law internally and between themselves, several key features emerge. Jurisgenerative models of federal association must be agonistic rather than antagonistic in nature; that is, recognizing that conflict over norms is unavoidable in political communities, a generative federalism must be designed not to eliminate competing views in an attempt to solidify a singular vision, but to accept and mediate such strife. In so doing, it should seek to provide systems and practices whereby these conflicts can be negotiated rather than developing into open antagonism.[90] A central feature of this is space for dialogue, not only in relation to the adjudication of competing claims, but in respect of the rules that govern such adjudication.

It is frequently said that "a federal system is a dialogical system."[91] The term "dialogical" so used primarily denotes communication between branches of government or between government and the courts and is frequently used in a descriptive, rather than normative, sense.[92] Peter Hogg, for example, employs the term in this sense in conceptualizing the relationship between courts and legislatures in the Canadian system.[93] This form of dialogical governance – one in which structures of governance are designed to facilitate the development, articulation, and interpretation of norms through dialogue between discrete branches or actors in the system – is frequently understood as an important feature of a functioning federal system. How accommodating it is to legal pluralism, however – how jurisgenerative its potential – varies with the circumstances. Who, for example, is the dialogue between? A dialogue between the courts and legislature may well work to ensure that dominant interpretations of law align with the views of a majority of the citizenry. This, however, does little to accommodate a plurality of perspectives and the legal orders of "autonomous communities" unless more actors are included in the dialogue. The voices of non-governmental organizations, religious associations, political groups, government commissions, Indigenous governments, and so on can also be considered as in dialogue with state institutions. The extent to which these types of actors can influence the shape of the shared legal norms that affect them will determine in part how effective dialogue can be at facilitating democratic engagement that respects the "norm generating autonomy" of constituent members.

It follows that the effect of the dialogical character of federalism can be overstated if one assumes inherited constitutional visions and prioritizes certain actors and languages of engagement.[94] Dialogical federalism refers to institutions and actors within a given governance terrain engaging in ongoing dialogues through which norms are adjudicated, laws are articulated and interpreted, and policies are worked out. In the abstract, we can imagine this taking place in a homogenous political community in which dialogue happens in relation to, or against the backdrop of, a single *nomos* shared by all those involved. Political communities, however, are not homogenous, and the dialogues occurring often mediate not only distinct interests within a normative community but also contrasting constitutional visions of distinct communities themselves. Distinct communities are in constant dialogue both within themselves and with the state in respect of the negotiation of internal and shared norms.

A constitution, written or unwritten, is given meaning by a plurality of voices engaged in discrete interpretative exercises. Dialogical interpretation avoids what Mikael Bhaktin refers to as a "monological closing," which occurs when the dominant classes impose a single narrative or interpretive frame: a unilateral meaning-making.[95] The importance of this insight can be seen when combined with Cover's insistence that "*legal* interpretation, unlike its purely literary cousins, must be in bed with force and violence."[96] Thus, a closed or monological form of legal interpretation, which is backed by the violence of the state, deploys that violence in the service of a singular constitutional vision. That unilateralism can be challenged through an emphasis on the dialogical nature of the creation of meaning in the social sphere.[97] As James Tully points out, even more than dialogical, this should be construed as multilogical.[98] The monological is antonymous to the multilogical. In a monological frame, power is centralized and hierarchical. The tensions, negotiation, contestation, and accommodation that characterize political communities are subsumed within a single overarching narrative and vision. The result is a top-down form of unilateral and univocal meaning-making. The shared creation of legal meaning within communities is lost when the social reality is shaped in ways that promote monological rather than multilogical engagement between citizens, governments, and groups (cultural, linguistic, religious, etc.).[99] This form of monological reasoning characterizes the contemporary modern constitution in its relation to Indigenous peoples.[100] It stands in contrast to multilogical processes of reciprocal elucidation through which new forms of association and engagement are negotiated and take shape.[101]

This concept of dialogical or multilogical reciprocal elucidation comes into play in at least two ways in relation to federalism. First, it provides a lens through which the actors can be understood: they are always acting dialogically – that is, through dialogue with other actors in the system. As mentioned, the Canadian courts have been characterized as being in a dialogical relationship with the legislative branch, particularly after the introduction of the *Charter of Rights and Freedoms*.[102] This can be expanded to include a number of different actors. The Truth and Reconciliation Commission, for instance, has shaped discourses in many public and private institutions in Canada. Law schools, to take one example, have been engaging in internal dialogues about how to best respond to the Truth and Reconciliation Commission's Calls to Action. Norms are under constant negotiation through which rights, obligations, jurisdictions, and subject positions are worked out. Second, a dialogical or multilogical framework provides a mode of analysis for understanding the texts and representations of the constitutional order. When we ask, for example, what the law "is" or what the Constitution or a piece of legislation "says" about a subject, a dialogical interpretive frame acknowledges the several interpretive communities that give these laws meaning. There is a recognition that the meaning of a certain law, or indeed the meaning of the concept of law itself, is not fixed; rather, it is worked out through contestation and negotiation. Legal meaning must be open in this way to avoid what Tully refers to as "hegemonic ventriloquism," a process in which "the more powerful partners consult with and listen to the less-powerful others and then translate what they hear into the presumptively universal or higher language of their hegemonic discourses."[103]

Many Indigenous traditions tend to be highly dialogical in nature in both of these senses. As John Borrows writes, "an especially broad source of Indigenous legal tradition is formed through processes of persuasion, deliberation, council, and discussion. ... the proximate source of most Indigenous law is developed through people talking with one another."[104] Henderson echoes this: "First Nations' consciousness is attached to dialogue and performative legal traditions," and "Aboriginal legal traditions exhibit a deep respect for diversity in relationships, and a rejection of singularity."[105] That is, law is worked out through dialogue and in a way that incorporates a plurality of perspectives. These forms of dialogical engagement inform the interpretative lenses Indigenous peoples bring to the legal questions they face, both within their distinct legal orders and in the development of shared constitutional principles, including their visions of an evolving, decolonized, constitutional order.

Through dialogical engagement, new languages of constitutionalism can be developed, leading to "a constitutionalization of an openness to dialogue and innovative collaboration that serves as a freedom from old dogmas of institutional design of democratic society and the structure of constitutional law."[106] As Tully writes, "intercultural dialogues are the best and most effective way, for they enable Westerners to see their conventional horizon as a limit and the dialogues are themselves the intimations of and indispensable groundwork for a future non-colonial relationship between genuinely free and equal peoples."[107] That is, legal meaning is diffuse within a constitutional order characterized by the dialogical engagement of a plurality of distinct voices. These forms of dialogic engagement create obligations on the parties for constructive engagement, obligations that require "mutuality, honesty, and creativity in complex consultation, discussions, and negotiations."[108] Embracing the dialogical possibilities of a jurisgenerative federalism would allow for the development of modes of governance based not on inherited imperial terms relating to "organization or institutions of power," but instead "in terms of relationships."[109] Institutions and practices of governance, therefore, must be mutually created that can allow for the parties to carry out their obligations in these dialogical arenas.[110]

This form of engagement can then allow foundational concepts that support jurispathic hegemonies to be questioned. Sovereignty, for example, is a concept that has done considerable work in limiting the reach of Indigenous legal orders and providing courts with a basis on which to grant prominence to state norms. While sovereignty has always been a contested concept in the Western tradition, absolute or exclusive authority is a central feature. As with the other concepts discussed in this chapter, though, contemporary conceptions are often projected into the past in a way that not only misconstrues the past but also limits possibilities that can be imagined for the future.[111] Especially in colonial spheres, the putative attributes of sovereignty never aligned with legal and political realities. Colonial spaces were legally pluralistic, and imperial authority extended unevenly.[112] Territorial jurisdictions were formed in halting and partial ways through a range of discrete practices. While sovereign authority, conceived of as authority through fixed territorial bounds, became more entrenched with the development of the nation state, it was not until the twentieth century that modern forms of state and sovereignty emerged in their currently cognizable form.[113] Thus, the current notion of sovereignty relied on by the courts serves more to justify a constitutional framework that minimizes Indigenous jurisdiction than to apply an uncontested legal precept. Without questioning the validity of the Crown's sovereignty – something a domestic court undoubtedly feels constrained from doing – the attributes of sovereignty can nonetheless be subject to change over time.[114]

Negotiated forms of sovereignty can lead to rethinking the state itself. New forms of federation and constitutional governance must not blindly accept inherited conceptual givens. Received concepts of state and sovereignty are not fixed or immutable; they have always been subject to revision and have to be considered as open to processes of negotiation and contestation.[115] The idea of the state as having absolute authority through fixed bounds is deeply entrenched: "The most general feature of the state as a political form ... is its grounding in the territorialisation of political power."[116] Yet, as François Rocher and Marie-Christine Gilbert argue, "It is important to recall that pluralistic federalism suggests a model of governance that is open to asymmetries and plural identities, while also promoting conciliation between competing national initiatives. It allows us to think of the modern nation-state in terms that extend beyond monistic and unitary sovereignty, to re-conceptualize the state in multinational terms that accord with the principle of autonomy."[117] A fixed conception of the nation state leads to only two options: either the state has absolute authority throughout its territorial bounds, including those occupied by Indigenous peoples, or Indigenous peoples secede and create their own states. As Tully points out, however, this is a false dichotomy: "jurisdiction can be shared as well as exclusive."[118] The practices of diverse federalism outlined above suggest reconceptualizing these foundational principles in ways that avoid the imposition of singularity and support the diffusion of normative and legal meaning.

A jurisgenerative federalism, then, is one in which constitutional norms and federal relationships are open to ongoing negotiation to reflect the diverse legal meanings of constituent communities. As the examples above suggest, this can be achieved in part through the development of institutions of government that incorporate a plurality of voices and rework conventional jurisdictional lines. This shift can be supported by the development of constitutional narratives that challenged inherited notions of federalism, jurisdiction, sovereignty, and state territoriality. These discourses can be generative responses to practices of Indigenous peoples, both framed as explicit resistance and as exercises of inherent jurisdiction. The reality of legal pluralism and the diverse production of legal meaning can thereby be given effect in a shared constitutional order. Given Cover's emphasis on the role of the courts and the reality that parties will continue to rely on litigation, even if only engaged in it strategically, the role of the courts in a generative order must also be considered.

Returning to the Courts

Because law is grounded in practice, judges have only so much power in these processes. Their power is limited by two key features: first, their decisions are meaningless without an apparatus to carry them out; second, legal meaning – including the meaning of the pronouncements of the courts – will always be contested by competing normative communities. Further, given what has been discussed above, we can see that from "a position that starts as neutral – that is, nonstatist – in its understanding of the law, the interpretations offered by judges are not necessarily superior."[119] What role, then, can courts play in fostering a jurisgenerative federalism? And, given what has been discussed above about the nature of Canadian courts' treatment of Indigenous issues, how can the courts adapt their doctrine to facilitate a more generative order?

In his early work on American slavery litigation, Cover provides an analysis that may be helpful. Cover identifies what he refers to as the "judicial can't,"[120] an evocative phrase he coined in response to a phenomenon he observed in slavery cases: anti-slavery judges who upheld the legality of slavery on the basis that they "could not" do otherwise. This underlying conflict was revealed both through the personal correspondence of judges and, perhaps most interestingly, in the written decisions themselves. In *Miller v. McQuerry*, for example, Justice John McLean drew a distinction between matters of conscience (i.e., morality) and matters of law. He wrote that the "abstract principles of slavery" involve "the laws of nature, and immutable principles of right."[121] These issues, McLean held, are matters to be dealt with by "the people ... and their representatives." As to the role of judges: "this is a field which judges cannot explore ... they look to the law and the law only."[122] In the formalism characteristic of much nineteenth-century common law adjudication, McLean sharply divides the roles of the legislative and judicial branches: the former may take into consideration issues of conscience when drafting laws; the latter may only apply the iterations of law so drafted. To disrupt this arrangement, McLean argued, "would undermine and overturn the social compact."[123] We see the emergence of the "judicial can't" here, as McLean signals his recognition that slavery may violate "the laws of nature, and immutable principles of right" while holding himself powerless to find that they violate "the law."

In the contemporary Canadian context, the "judicial can't" circumscribes the actions courts consider available to them in two ways: with respect to (1) the limit of state sovereignty and the underlying title of the Crown, and (2) the challenge of recognizing and giving meaningful effect to Indigenous law. I address each in turn.

While there is, of course, a long history of courts being deferential on political questions[124] and attuned to both their role in the constitutional order, where the question of sovereignty and underlying title is concerned Canadian courts inherited a specific "can't" directly from an American justice writing two decades before McLean penned his decision in *Miller*. In *Johnson v. McIntosh*, Chief Justice Marshall wrote that "[c]onquest gives a title which the Courts of the conqueror cannot deny."[125] This specific idea – that by way of "discovery" European nations acquired absolute sovereignty and underlying title to lands in North America, thereby reducing the political character of the nations occupying those lands – was taken up explicitly by Canadian courts and forms the foundation of section 35 case law.[126] As in the US cases, this is seen as an essentially uncontestable "judicial can't."

What must be considered, then, is whether the scope of this limitation can be minimized without violating this prohibition. The Canadian Supreme Court has indeed shown some appetite for this. In *Haida*

Nation, for example, the Court referred to Crown sovereignty as *de facto*, seeming to imply that it lacked a legal foundation.[127] In the Court's view, the Crown's sovereignty would be perfected, in some sense, by ensuring that the procedural process outlined in the duty to consult and accommodate is followed. The Court seems to envision what Ryan Beaton has called a "judicially mediated" form of sovereignty wherein the acquisition of Crown sovereignty can be legitimized through judicial supervision of its exercises.[128] In *Mitchell v. M.N.R.*, the Court acknowledged the existence of both Crown and Indigenous "sovereignties," seeming to recognize a less-than-absolute form of Crown sovereignty that could admit of the existence of parallel forms.[129] Yet, for the reasons already outlined, these concessions have not led to a doctrine that excises Crown unilateralism or meaningfully accommodates Indigenous self-determination. Contests over jurisdiction are reframed as contests over rights, and foundational questions of political authority remain obscured.

Fair enough. As Chief Justice Marshall wrote, such engagement "savours too much of the exercise of political power to be within the proper province of the Judicial Department."[130] It is understandable, and advisable, for courts to withdraw from issues they consider explicitly political or beyond their constitutional mandate. Where Indigenous peoples are concerned, however, what the courts have neglected to realize is the how much their interpretation of the scope of their "can't" frames the constitutional relationships of the parties and engages the courts in deeply political affairs. By reading that which they cannot question – the sovereignty of the Crown and its underlying title and legislative power – as necessarily placing Indigenous peoples in a constitutional arrangement in which they have no jurisdiction or authority, the courts have done the political work of determining the constitutional order.

How might courts do otherwise, respecting their constitutional role but, to paraphrase Justice McLean, without "undermining and overturning the social compact"? This can be done by first limiting and defining the attributes of Crown sovereignty, moving to a reliance on what Joshua Nichols and I have elsewhere called a *thin* version of Crown sovereignty.[131] This is not the same thing as supervising Crown conduct to ensure it is constitutionally valid. Judicial review is hardly contentious in Canada, especially after section 52 of the *Constitution Act, 1982* was introduced into the constitutional order. This has also been a central feature of the courts' Aboriginal rights jurisprudence. The argument here is that the judicial supervision of Crown action has deployed tools inappropriate to the task of mediating between competing legal orders, and it has done so because it has assumed a greater "judicial can't" than necessary. The doctrine has thus been jurispathic in that it has sidelined Indigenous legal orders, and it has been excessively political in that it has resolved questions of constitutional authority that ought to be subject to political negotiation. Courts can create spaces for the negotiation of contested constitutional principles, norms, and authority by signalling that they are open to reviewing the assumption of Crown sovereignty. In doing so, they must be attentive to how they distribute negotiating power between the parties. Negotiating power must be distributed equally to allow for the development of jurisgenerative institutions and principles. This can be accomplished by compelling, rather than merely voicing a preference for, negotiated solutions.

The second "judicial can't" that limits the courts' ability to develop generative doctrine concerns the interpretation and application of Indigenous law. The clearest example of this is the *Coastal Gaslink* decision dealt with above, where the Supreme Court of British Columbia held that it could not recognize Indigenous law until such time as that law was given positive recognition through treaty or other instrument. While recognizing that Wet'suwet'en law *exists*, the Court held it simply could not do anything with it. One response to this is to highlight the body of case law this decision ignored. The Supreme Court has recognized on several occasions that the doctrine of continuity applies in respect of Indigenous law. That doctrine holds that where Britain, acting as a colonial power, acquired new territory, the laws of the peoples existing in that place continued to exist until such time as they were explicitly modified or extinguished.[132] The most often cited historical example of this in the Canadian context is likely the 1867 *Connolly v. Woolrich* decision, in which the Quebec court held that a marriage recognized under Cree law was valid and could be upheld as legally binding in Quebec. The *Campbell* decision is perhaps the most notable contemporary example, where the Supreme Court of British Columbia held explicitly that Indigenous rights of self-government survived the assertion of Crown sovereignty and were not extinguished. While these cases diverge from the *Coastal Gaslink* analysis, the Court in *Coastal Gaslink* nevertheless brought forward an important question: How can Canadian courts apply Indigenous law? It is beyond the scope of this chapter to address this issue in detail. Indeed, the issue is a fraught one, as it is by no means clear that Indigenous legal orders are amenable to application in state courts, or that Indigenous peoples wish for colonial courts to "apply" their law in a conventional sense. A more fruitful avenue appears to be for the courts to modify the tools they use to adjudicate Indigenous–state disputes. Tools of jurisdiction allow the courts to create space for the application of Indigenous law without requiring them to either engage with it substantively or continue the current practice of relying on it merely as evidence that a common law test (e.g., occupation) is met.

Conclusion

Indigenous peoples have frequently been victims of what Roger Merino calls the "inclusion/exclusion paradox."[133] In one sense, they have been subsumed within a constitutional order and assigned a place in that order to which they did not consent. Within this structure, they are considered subjects of the Crown rather than distinct peoples or political entities. Their jurisdiction is delegated and dependent on the state for recognition. In another sense, they are excluded from the constitutional order. Without recognition of their jurisdiction, they sit outside the division of powers, unable to make constitutional claims to jurisdiction and decision-making authority. While the doctrine of Aboriginal rights has sought in various ways to resolve this paradox, it has to date been unable to do so. Similarly, while institutions and practices of governance have begun to incorporate Indigenous decision-making, the development of consent-based decision-making structures that give meaningful effect to Indigenous self-determination are only in the nascent stages of development. Robert Cover's analysis, which clarifies the mechanisms through which dominant systems of law reduce competing visions, provides a lens through which these processes in Canada can be understood and prescriptive alternatives can be imagined. It provides one avenue for seeing how constitutional doctrine and practices of governance can be opened up to "invite new worlds" through shared constitutional practices and norms.

NOTES

1 This explanation of the nature of *Tyohate*, the Two Row Wampum, was provided by Kanenhariyo (Seth LaFort) in a 15 February 2020 meeting between Mohawk leaders and Minister of Indigenous Services Marc Miller. See "Complete Transcripts of Meeting between Marc Miller and Kanyen'kehaka (Mohawk)," Real People's Media, accessed 6 June 2023, https://realpeoples.media/complete-transcripts-of-meeting-between-marc-miller-and-kanyenkehaka-mohawk.
2 *Coldwater v. Canada (Attorney General)*, 2020 FCA 34.
3 Ibid.

4 See Mauro Barelli, *Seeking Justice in International Law: The Significance and Implications of the UN Declaration on the Rights of Indigenous Peoples* (London: Routledge, 2016); Jackie Hartley, Paul Joffe, and Jennifer Preston, eds., *Realizing the UN Declaration on the Rights of Indigenous Peoples: Triumph, Hope, and Action* (Saskatoon: Purich Publishing, 2010). For academic literature considering domestic implementation in relation to section 35 Aboriginal rights, see many of the chapters in John Borrows, Larry Chartrand, Oonagh E. Fitzgerald, and Risa Schwartz, eds, *Braiding Legal Orders: Implementing the United Nations Declaration on the Rights of Indigenous Peoples* (Waterloo, ON: CIGI Press, 2019).
5 James (Sa'ke'j) Youngblood Henderson, "Dialogical Governance: A Mechanism of Constitutional Governance," *Saskatchewan Law Review* 72, no. 1 (2009): 34.
6 Robert M. Cover, "The Supreme Court, 1982 Term – Forward: *Nomos* and Narrative," *Harvard Law Review* 97, no. 1 (1983–4): 7.
7 Ibid., 4.
8 Ibid., 11.
9 Ibid., 4.
10 Ibid., 5.
11 Edward Said, *Culture and Imperialism* (New York: Vintage, 1993).
12 Cover, "*Nomos* and Narrative," 7.
13 Judith Resnick, "Living Their Legal Commitments: Paideic Communities, Courts, and Robert Cover," *Yale Journal of Law and the Humanities* 17, no. 1 (2005): 42. Flowing from this logic, Robert Cover posits a hypothetical that has particular salience in the context of Indigenous–state relations: "If there existed two legal orders with identical legal precepts and identical, predictable patterns of public force, they would nonetheless differ essentially in meaning if, in one of the orders, the precepts were universally venerated while in the other they were regarded by many as fundamentally unjust." Cover, "*Nomos* and Narrative," 7.
14 Robert A. Williams Jr., "Sovereignty, Racism, Human Rights: Indian Self-Determination and the Postmodern World Legal System," *Review of Constitutional Studies* 2, no. 2 (1995): 149.
15 Cover, "*Nomos* and Narrative."
16 Robert M. Cover, "Violence and the Word," *Yale Law Journal* 95 (1986): 1601–12. See also Robert C. Post, "Who's Afraid of Jurispathic Courts? Violence and Public Reason in *Nomos and Narrative*," *Yale Journal of Law and the Humanities* 17, no. 1 (2005): 10.
17 Post, "Violence and Public Reason," 10.
18 Jonathan Havercroft makes a similar point about absolute conceptions of sovereignty. As he points out, Hobbes and Spinoza were both drawn to notions of absolute sovereign authority as a way to fend off the dangers

of epistemological indeterminacy. See Jonathan Havercroft, *Captives of Sovereignty* (Cambridge: Cambridge University Press, 2011), 1–10.
19 See, for example, Tina Loo, "Dan Cranmer's Potlach: Law as Coercion, Symbol, and Rhetoric in British Columbia, 1884–1951," *Canadian Historical Review* 73, no. 2 (1992): 125–65, https://doi.org/10.3138/CHR-073-02-01.
20 See Wayne Daugherty and Dennis Madill, *Indian Government under Indian Act Legislation, 1868–1952* (Ottawa: Research Branch Department of Indian and Northern Affairs, 1980). See *Logan v. Styres*, (1959) 20 DLR (2d) 416.
21 See Truth and Reconciliation Commission of Canada, *Final Report of the Truth and Reconciliation Commission of Canada*, 6 vols. (Montreal: McGill-Queen's University Press, 2015).
22 Post, "Violence and Public Reason," 12.
23 Robert M. Cover, "The Bonds of Constitutional Interpretation: Of the World, the Deed, and the Role," *Georgia Law Review* 20, no. 4 (Summer 1986): 816.
24 In *R. v. Marshall*, for example, the court held that while it had recognized a treaty right to fish commercially, that right did not prohibit the Department of Fisheries and Oceans (DFO) from regulating the exercise of the right as the Mi'kmaq claimed. The unstated conclusion of this was that the DFO had authority to forcibly restrain the Mi'kmaq from fishing, as they indeed did in scenes of considerable violence: *R. v. Marshall*, [1999] 3 SCR 456, at paras 57–9; *R. v. Marshall*, [1999] 3 SCR 533, at paras 24, 38.
25 *R. v. Syliboy*, [1929] 1 DLR 307.
26 *R. v. Simon*, 1982 CanLII 3703 (NS CA); 49 NSR (2d) 566.
27 See *Constitution Act, 1982*, being Schedule B to the *Canada Act, 1982*, s 35.
28 Indeed, some have argued that the courts have radically expanded Aboriginal rights beyond a defensible interpretation. See Alex Cameron, *Power without Law: The Supreme Court of Canada, the Marshall Decisions, and the Failure of Judicial Activism* (Montreal: McGill-Queen's University Press, 2009).
29 Brian Slattery, "The Constitutional Dimensions of Aboriginal Title," *Supreme Court Law Review* 71, no. 3 (2015): 45–66.
30 See *Tsilhqot'in Nation v. British Columbia*, 2014 SCC 44.
31 See Brian Slattery, "The Generative Structure of Aboriginal Rights," *Supreme Court Law Review* 38, no. 2 (2007): 595–628; Henderson "Dialogical Governance." For a critique of the duty to consult and suggestions for modifications to the doctrine that may help it realize its generative goals, see Robert Hamilton and Joshua Nichols, "The Tin Ear of the Court: *Ktunaxa Nation* and the Foundations of the Duty to Consult," *Alberta Law Review* 56, no. 3 (2019): 729–60.
32 *Haida Nation v. British Columbia (Minister of Forests)*, 2004 SCC 73 [hereafter *Haida Nation*]; *Mitchell v. M.N.R.*, [2001] 1 SCR 911 [hereafter *Mitchell v. M.N.R.*].

33 *Restoule v. Canada (Attorney General)*, 2018 ONSC 7701.
34 Darcy Lindberg, "Historical Lawsuit Affirms Indigenous Laws on Par with Canada's," *The Conversation*, 15 January 2019, https://theconversation.com/historical-lawsuit-affirms-indigenous-laws-on-par-with-canadas-109711.
35 *R. v. Sparrow*, [1990] 1 SCR 1075 [hereafter *Sparrow*].
36 *R. v. Van der Peet*, [1996] 2 SCR 507 [hereafter *Van der Peet*].
37 *Sparrow*, at 1043.
38 On the problematically ahistorical nature of this claim, see Hamar Foster, "Forgotten Arguments: Aboriginal Title and Sovereignty in Canada Jurisdiction Act Cases," *Manitoba Law Journal* 21, no. 3 (1992): 343–89.
39 As Cover writes, "within the domain of constitutional meaning, the understanding of the Mennonites assumes a status equal (or superior) to that accorded to the understanding of the Justices of the Supreme Court. In this realm of meaning – if not in the domain of social control – the Mennonite community creates law as fully as does the judge." Cover, "*Nomos* and Narrative," 28.
40 *Van der Peet*, at paras 45–63.
41 For classic commentary, see Russel Lawrence Barsh and James (Sa'ke'j) Youngblood Henderson, "The Supreme Court's *Van der Peet* Trilogy: Naive Imperialism and Ropes of Sand," *McGill Law Journal* 24 (1997): 993–1009.
42 Their conceptions of history and their legal citations make this clear.
43 It is important to note that, for Cover, all adjudication is jurispathic by its very nature. That it is jurispathic is not the problem per se; the problem arises when courts elide their jurispathic nature.
44 *Mikisew Cree First Nation v. Canada (Governor General in Council)*, [2018] 2 SCR 765 [hereafter *Mikisew Cree II*].
45 For overview and analysis, see Joshua Nichols anda Robert Hamilton, "In Search of Honourable Crowns and Legitimate Constitutions: *Mikisew Cree* and the Colonial Constitution," *University of Toronto Law Journal* 70, no. 3 (Summer 2020): 341–75, https://doi.org/10.3138/utlj.2019-0115.
46 Factum of the Intervener, Federation of Sovereign Indigenous Nations, in *Mikisew Cree II*, at para 15.
47 Factum of the Intervener, Grand Council of the Crees, in *Mikisew Cree II*.
48 Factum of the Respondent, Governor General in Council, in *Mikisew Cree II*, at para 4.
49 Factum of the Intervener, Attorney-General of Alberta, in *Mikisew Cree II*, at paras 5–6.
50 Cover, "*Nomos* and Narrative," 9.
51 Ibid., 11.
52 *Coastal GasLink Pipeline Ltd. v. Huson*, 2019 BCSC 2264 [hereafter *Coastal GasLink*].
53 Ibid., at paras 1, 51–2.

54 Ibid., at paras 127–9.
55 See Resnick, "Living Their Legal Commitments," 25.
56 Cover, *"Nomos* and Narrative," 9.
57 Henderson, "Dialogical Governance," 36.
58 Robert M. Cover, "Bonds of Constitutional Interpretation," 817.
59 Ibid., 821.
60 For an overview of various approaches to pluralism in liberal theorizing, see Duncan Ivison, *Can Liberal States Accommodate Indigenous Peoples?* (Cambridge: Polity, 2020).
61 Post, "Violence and Public Reason," 11.
62 Cover, *"Nomos* and Narrative," 16.
63 Post, "Violence and Public Reason," 12.
64 Ibid., 11.
65 Cover, "Bonds of Constitutional Interpretation," 819.
66 Post, "Violence and Public Reason," 15.
67 Resnick, "Living Their Legal Commitments," 24. Resnick is not sanguine about Cover's view of the state: "rather than posit the legal commitments of normative communities as impermissibly disruptive of the congenial order of the nation-state, Cover identified the state as the aggressive force, *jurispathic* in its ability to quash such communities' own commitments when they are odds with national norms."
68 Ibid., 25.
69 Ibid.
70 Ibid., 25–6.
71 Ibid., 26.
72 Ibid., 30.
73 Louis Althusser aptly captures this characterization: "This activity of systematization is accordingly to be understood not only as elimination of the *contradictions* that can arise among the rules of existing law, but also, and above all, as elimination of the eventual contradictions that may arise between the rules already defined in the internal system of law and the paralegal limit-practices of case law, the essential role of which is to identify 'cases' that the law has not yet really integrated and systematized. In this regard, case law must obviously be brought into relation with *law's outside*, the existence of which the history of law recognizes in the form of what is known as *'customary'* as opposed to *written* legislation." Louis Althusser, *On the Reproduction of Capitalism: Ideology and Ideological State Apparatuses* (London: Verso, 2014), 58.
74 John Borrows, *Canada's Indigenous Constitution* (Toronto: University of Toronto Press, 2010).
75 Ibid. See also Glen Sean Coulthard, *Red Skin, White Masks: Rejecting the Colonial Politics of Recognition* (Minneapolis: University of Minnesota Press, 2014); Gordon Christie, *Canadian Law and Indigenous Self-Determination: A Naturalist Analysis* (Toronto: University of Toronto Press, 2019); Aaron Mills, "The Lifeworlds Of Law: On Revitalizing Indigenous Legal Orders

Today," *McGill Law Journal* 61, no. 4 (June 2016): 847–87, https://doi.org/10.7202/1038490ar; Audra Simpson, *Mohawk Interruptus: Political Life across the Borders of Settler States* (Durham, NC: Duke University Press, 2014); Dale Turner, *This Is Not a Peace Pipe: Towards a Critical Indigenous Philosophy* (Toronto: University of Toronto Press, 2006); Robert A. Williams Jr., *Linking Arms Together: American Indian Treaty Visions of Law and Peace, 1600–1800* (Routledge: New York, 1999); Leanne Betasamosake Simpson, *As We Have Always Done: Indigenous Freedom through Radical Resistance* (Minneapolis: University of Minnesota Press, 2017).

76 See Robert Hamilton, "Indigenous Peoples and Interstitial Federalism in Canada," *Review of Constitutional Studies* 24, no. 1 (2019): 43–84.
77 Sarah Morales, "Indigenous-led Assessment Processes as a Way Forward," Centre for International Governance Innovation, 4 July 2019, https://www.cigionline.org/articles/indigenous-led-assessment-processes-way-forward.
78 *Tsleil-Waututh Nation v. Canada (Attorney General)*, 2018 FCA 153, at paras 649–53, 681–2.
79 Morales, "Indigenous-led Assessment."
80 *Coastal GasLink*.
81 See Jillian Kestler-D'Amours, "Understanding the Wet'suwet'en Struggle in Canada," *Al Jazeera*, 1 March 2020, https://www.aljazeera.com/news/2020/03/understanding-wet-struggle-canada-200301200921070.html.
82 Cover, "Bonds of Constitutional Interpretation," 832. The redemptive aspect is important for Cover. By deliberately choosing a term weighted with religious significance, Cover wanted to illustrate how resistance and dissent can be illustrative of a redemptive constitutional vision – a constitutional vision that seeks to redeem an existing constitutional order to bring it in line with a different vision of the future.
83 Ibid.
84 Ibid.
85 Ibid.
86 Ibid., 832–3.
87 Cover, "*Nomos* and Narrative," 8.
88 Indeed, this seems to be recognized about the Idle No More movement. While that movement garnered largely positive attention, it is important to note that many acts of Indigenous resistance that were extensively criticized at the time were required to gain greater recognition of Indigenous claims. Virtually all of the major victories at the Supreme Court, for example, either began with or were closely associated with acts of civil disobedience and resistance. See, for example, Ward Churchill, *Struggle for the Land: Native North American Resistance to Genocide, Ecocide, and Colonization* (Winnipeg: Arbeiter Ring, 1999); Coulthard, *Red Skin,*

White Masks; J.R. Miller, "Aboriginal Rights, Land Claims, and the Struggle to Survive," in *Sweet Promises: A Reader on Indian–White Relations in Canada*, ed. J.R. Miller (Toronto: University of Toronto Press, 1991), 405–20.
89 Of course, the normative enters the debate again here. Why ought we to avoid relationships of domination? We can again resort to a practical argument – those will lead to resistance – or accept a basic minimum in terms of the normative argument: while we might well disagree on a number of moral issues, we can presume that "might is right" is not tenable.
90 On the distinction between agonistic and antagonistic, see Chantal Mouffe, *Agonistics: Thinking the World Politically* (London: Verso, 2013), 7.
91 Patrick E. Higginbotham, "The Continuing Dialogue of Federalism," *Kansas Law Review* 45 (1997): 985.
92 Peter W. Hogg and Ravi Amarnath, "Understanding Dialogue Theory," in *The Oxford Handbook of the Canadian Constitution*, ed. Peter Oliver, Patrick Macklem, and Nathalie Des Rosiers (Oxford: Oxford University Press, 2017), 1057.
93 Peter Hogg, "The Law-Making Role of the Supreme Court of Canada: Rapporteur's Synthesis," *Canadian Bar Review* 80, no. 1/2 (2001): 180; Henderson, "Dialogical Governance," 46. See also Peter W. Hogg and Allison A. Bushell, "The *Charter* Dialogue between Courts and Legislatures (Or Perhaps the *Charter of Rights* Isn't Such a Bad Thing after All)," *Osgoode Hall Law Journal* 35, no. 1 (Spring 1997): 75–124; Hogg and Amarnath, "Understanding Dialogue Theory," 1053.
94 As James Tully notes, "It is necessary to call into question and amend a number of unexamined conventions, inherited from the imperial age, that continue to inform the language of constitutionalism in which the demands are taken up and adjudicated." James Tully, *Strange Multiplicity: Constitutionalism in an Age of Diversity* (Cambridge: Cambridge University Press, 1995), 34.
95 Ken Hirschkop, "Bakhtin, Discourse, and Democracy," *New Left Review* 160 (1986): 92–111; Zali Gurevitch, "Plurality in Dialogue: A Comment on Bakhtin," *Sociology* 34, no. 2 (May 2000): 243–63, https://doi.org/10.1177/S003803850000016X. Charles Taylor emphasizes the important of Bakhtin's "inner dialogicality" in processes of political recognition: Charles Taylor, "The Politics of Recognition," in *Multiculturalism: Examining the Politics of Recognition*, ed. Amy Gutmann (Princeton: Princeton University Press, 1994), 33.
96 Sarah Krakoff, "Law, Violence, and the Neurotic Structure of American Indian Law," *Wake Forest Law Review* 49, no. 3 (2014): 743–56.
97 Craig Brandist, "The Bhaktin Circle," *Internet Encyclopedia of Philosophy*, accessed 6 June 2023, https://iep.utm.edu/bakhtin-circle.

98 James Tully, *Public Philosophy in a New Key*, vol. 1, *Democracy and Civic Freedom* (Cambridge: Cambridge University Press, 2008).
99 Mark Kingwell, *A Civil Tongue: Justice, Dialogue, and the Politics of Pluralism* (University Park: Pennsylvania State University Press, 1995), 64: "Citizens are never engaged in the discernment and cultivation of common goods; instead they pursue their goals in isolation from one another, blind to the ambitions and desires of the persons with whom they happen to share a society."
100 Tully, *Strange Multiplicity*, 115–16.
101 James Tully, "Deparochializing Political Theory and Beyond: A Dialogue Approach to Comparative Political Thought," *Journal of World Philosophies* 1, no. 1 (2016): 64.
102 Hogg and Bushell, "*Charter* Dialogue."
103 Tully, "Deparochializing Political Theory," 64.
104 Borrows, *Canada's Indigenous Constitution*, 35.
105 Henderson, "Dialogical Governance," 71.
106 Ibid., 33. The evolving languages of federalism and constitutionalism can be seen in Carwyn Jones's discussion of the New Zealand constitution in chapter 6 of this volume, in particular, the way in which the unwritten constitution and the Treaty of Waitangi sit in tension with the unitary state.
107 Tully, *Public Philosophy*, 276–7.
108 Henderson, "Dialogical Governance," 59. Here we see the importance of what Michael Asch discusses in chapter 2 of this volume as "mutual consent, freely given."
109 Henderson, "Dialogical Governance," 34.
110 Douglas White III, for example, emphasizes the need to develop consent-based decision-making structures. See Douglas White III Kwulasultun, *Consent* (Vancouver: Union of British Columbia Indian Chiefs, 2019).
111 Jeremy Webber identifies five "types" of sovereignty: the final power of decision; status as a state in international law; the originating source of law; unified and rationalized order of law; and unified representation of political community. Webber argues that the notion or type of sovereignty that is put to work has a considerable impact on shaping the legal and constitutional relationships between parties. Understanding how parties are using the concept differently can open up ground for negotiated solutions. See Jeremy Webber, "Contending Sovereignties," in *The Oxford Handbook of the Canadian Constitution*, ed. Peter Oliver, Patrick Macklem, and Nathalie Des Rosiers (Oxford: Oxford University Press, 2017), 291–9. The need to restructure federal relations around less absolute conceptions of sovereignty has been noted elsewhere: see François Rocher and Marie-Christine Gilbert, "Re-federalizing Canada: Refocusing the Debate on Decentralization," in

The Case for Decentralized Federalism, ed. Ruth Hubbard and Gilles Paquet (Ottawa: University of Ottawa Press, 2010), 121.

112 Lauren Benton, *A Search for Sovereignty: Law and Geography in European Empires, 1400–1900* (Cambridge: Cambridge University Press, 2010); Lauren Benton and Richard J. Ross, eds., *Legal Pluralism and Empires, 1500–1850* (New York: New York University Press, 2013).

113 See generally Eric Hobsbawn and Terence Ranger, eds., *The Invention of Tradition* (Cambridge: Cambridge University Press, 1983).

114 The courts have long held, for example, that Crown prerogatives, which are expressions of the attributes of sovereign authority, are justiciable. See Paul Daly, "Royal Treatment: The Crown's Special Status in Administrative Law," *Review of Constitutional Studies* 22, no. 1 (2017): 81–102; Christopher Vincenzi, *Crown Powers, Subjects and Citizens* (London: Pinter, 1998).

115 Quentin Skinner, "A Genealogy of the Modern State," *Proceedings of the British Academy* 162 (2009): 360; Bob Jessop, *The State: Past, Present, Future* (Cambridge: Polity, 2016), 53–6.

116 Martin Jones and Bob Jessop, "Thinking State/Space Incompossibly," *Antipode* 42, no. 5 (2010): 1120, https://doi.org/10.1111/j.1467-8330.2010.00796.x.

117 Rocher and Gilbert, "Re-federalizing Canada," 121.

118 Tully, *Public Philosophy*, 276–7.

119 Cover, "*Nomos* and Narrative," 29.

120 Robert M. Cover, *Justice Accused: Antislavery and the Judicial Process* (New Haven, CT: Yale University Press, 1975), 119.

121 Quoted in ibid., 119–20.

122 Ibid.

123 Quoted in ibid., 120.

124 Unlike the United States, Canada does not have an explicit "political questions doctrine." Canadian courts may decline jurisdiction for a number of reasons, though the political nature of the question is not relied on explicitly in doing so. See D. Geoffrey Cowper and Lorne Sossin, "Does Canada Need a Political Question Doctrine?," *Supreme Court Law Review* 16 (2002): 343–70; Geoffrey Sawer, "Political Questions," *University of Toronto Law Journal* 15, no. 1 (1963): 49–61, https://doi.org/10.2307/824907. Two examples where the court seems to have come close to applying a political questions doctrine are *Reference re Secession of Quebec*, [1998] 2 SCR 217 and *Canada (Prime Minister) v. Khadr*, [2010] 1 SCR 44.

125 *Johnson & Graham's Lessee v. McIntosh*, 21 US 543 (1823), at 588.

126 See, for example, *Guerin v. The Queen*, [1984] 2 SCR 335; *Sparrow*.

127 *Haida Nation*.

128 Ryan Beaton, "*De Facto* and *de Jure* Crown Sovereignty: Reconciliation and Legitimation at the Supreme Court of Canada," *Constitutional Forum* 27, no. 1 (2018): 25–3; Richard Stacey, "Honour in Sovereignty: Can Crown Consultation with Indigenous Peoples Erase Canada's Sovereignty Deficit?," *University of Toronto Law Journal* 68, no. 3 (Summer 2018): 405–39, https://doi.org/10.3138/utlj.2017-0110.
129 *Mitchell v. M.N.R.*
130 *Cherokee Nation v. Georgia*, 30 US (5 Pet) 1 (1831), at 20.
131 Hamilton and Nichols, "Tin Ear."
132 Mark D. Walters, "The Golden Thread of Continuity: Aboriginal Customs at Common Law and under the *Constitution Act, 1982*," *McGill Law Journal* 44, no. 3 (1999): 711–52.
133 See chapter 5 by Roger Merino in this volume.

Conclusion:
The Futures of Federalism

JOSHUA NICHOLS

Where do Indigenous peoples fit within the constitutional order? This question seems simple and direct, like we could just refer to the provisions of the Constitution and discover the answer. But as soon as we take this step we find that we have departed from the black-and-white confines of explicit rules and passed into the more open-textured, grey expanse that surrounds the concepts of sovereignty and the rule of law. At this more foundational level of the constitutional order, the apparently hard-and-fast rules that we rely upon in the present moment lose their distinct edges. If we are to make our way down here, we need to understand the concept of law "as a process, an enterprise, in which rules have meaning only in the context of institutions and procedures, values, and ways of thought."[1] This is a helpful guide when thinking about the diverse practices of treaty-making. If we approach these practices with a concept of law that is confined to a consideration of the relationship between a unitary sovereignty and statutes, we will understand treaties as legal documents within the domestic legal system and look for their meaning by considering the relevant legislation and case law. By adopting this understanding of the concept of law we position treaties as a legal puzzle whose place can be found within the confines of the existing legal system. This is certainly one way to proceed, but it omits the deeper problems that we encounter when we understand treaty-making as an ongoing relationship between Indigenous peoples, governmental authority, and the principles of diverse constitutionalisms (e.g., treaty practices involve the legal traditions of each member involved, and their meaning inheres in the fraught and open-textured ground of shared understanding).

If we begin from the perspective that treaty-making concerns an ongoing relationship across diverse legalities, it becomes clear that the meaning of the treaties cannot be found within the confines of a single legal system. Rather, once we take treaty practices seriously as jurisgenerative practices that exist across or between different legalities, we see that treaties are not simply contracts but legal problems, because when we attempt to determine their meaning, we do not have clear and singular interpretations available.[2] Understood in this way, treaties[3] are not a new line of code waiting to be integrated into a legal system. Rather, treaty practices cast light onto the processes, institutions and procedures, values, and ways of thought that connect European colonialism and constitutionalism with the diverse legalities of their Indigenous treaty partners. By approaching the practices of treaty-making as a legal problem we are not simply casting light on the past (e.g., the historical vagaries of negotiation, interpretation, and political conflict). Rather, adopting this view of treaties shows us the one-sided and ultimately arbitrary processes and rules that have accumulated within the Canadian legal system over time that serve to continue the troubling legacy of imperial tyranny by providing it with a veneer of constitutional legality.

All too often the work of legal interpretation is limited to the textual provisions of treaties understood in a narrow and formalistic way. This style of legal interpretation can transform them into surrender agreements, but this only works by omissions and elisions that serve to testify against the legitimacy of their legal character. For example, in 2007, the UN General Assembly adopted the United Nations Declaration on the Rights of Indigenous Peoples (UNDRIP), and at that time only four countries opposed it: Australia, New Zealand, the United States, and Canada.[4] Each of these states had developed legal mechanisms within their domestic constitutional orders based on the premise of a unilateral sovereignty bundled together with legislative power and underlying title.[5] Indigenous peoples within these legal orders hold a *sui generis* set of rights and various delegated powers. Thus, the UNDRIP casts light on the models of constitutional containment these states had developed and the legal problems that these models posed. The light at the international level helped to show that despite local variation, Indigenous peoples do not have a form of jurisdiction that can provide the kind of legal legitimacy self-determination requires. This approach of constitutional containment has effectively positioned Indigenous peoples in what Roger Merino calls an "inclusion/exclusion paradox."[6] Indigenous peoples are constitutionally incorporated as cultural minorities with some *sui generis* rights, but their claims to sovereignty must be renounced. This is a coercive approach that is not underpinned by voluntary consent. Yet, the courts begin from the presumption that the state has sovereignty and Indigenous peoples are proportionately diminished.

The paradox of inclusion/exclusion is a two-way street. If the legal standing of Indigenous peoples is diminished, the governments of settler states have proportionately greater powers. Thus, when Indigenous peoples are confined to a legal standing to which they do not consent, the state acquires a form of sovereignty that cannot fit within the confines of the constitutional order. As long as the relationship remains unbalanced, the foundations of these states cannot account for themselves. The courts are put in an impossible position. They cannot simply allow the foundations of the state to float. They must ground the machinery of the constitutional order, which requires ensuring that the prerogative powers of the executive are contained within the constitution – i.e., the rule of law. In this way, courts within states whose governments have established systems of internal colonization are tasked with a problem that cannot be resolved from a structural perspective.

However, the practices of treaty federalism remind us that the concept of sovereignty is composed of a combination of necessary and negotiable legal qualities and can be understood in "thick" and "thin" versions. This awareness makes it possible to see that courts within settler states have been using a thick version of sovereignty, which has had real constitutional costs. The thick version of state sovereignty entails diminishing Indigenous peoples to either cultural minorities or tribal governments subject to plenary congressional power. To give this diminishment the appearance of legal validity, courts must marshal their interpretive resources to convert treaties into surrender documents that annihilate the political existence of Indigenous peoples.[7] The resulting legal incoherence becomes precedent and is woven into the fabric of the constitutional order.

In contrast, the concept of Indigenous self-determination as it is expressed in the practices of treaty federalism allows us to see how a thin version of sovereignty can open jurisdictional space within the constitutional order that parties can fill through negotiations. This approach allows the courts to maintain their judicial neutrality while using a thin version of sovereignty to open up a path towards meaningful Indigenous self-determination that does not compromise either the territorial integrity or political unity of existing states. The chapters in this book use treaty federalism and assume a thin conception of sovereignty to explore the various possibilities it holds for the future of Canada and other states with legacies of internal colonial practices.

To date, courts have largely acted as if that thick sovereignty can be coherently and constitutionally contained. Yet, this has been accomplished by diminishing, but never fully eliminating, Indigenous jurisdiction. Even in the nineteenth century, the courts maintained that Indigenous peoples had legal rights. While these rights were characterized as a "mere burden" on the Crown (as Lord Watson states in *St. Catharines Milling and Lumber Co. v. The Queen*), the court admitted that "[i]t has never been contended that the Indian title amounted to nothing."[8] The refusal to simply declare Indigenous rights non-justiciable cannot be attributed to a moral sense among members of the judiciary. Rather, it reflects the "compulsion to legality" characteristic of state action, which David Dyzenhaus defines as a "compulsion to justify all acts of state as having a legal warrant, the authority of law."[9] This compulsion has drawn the courts into the task of providing a legal foundation for sovereignty over Indigenous peoples.[10] It is an impossible task.

Thus, the courts have looked to various precedents to piece together workable solutions on a case-by-case basis. But the solutions they find in the case law are based on pseudo-legal fictions that attempt to explain the diminishment of Indigenous peoples by claiming they are different in kind from Europeans (i.e., the so-called standard of civilization). Courts can no longer simply say "savages" or "nomads" and expect the question before them to be resolved. The legal magic of these fictions has long expired. The courts now attempt to conceal their continued reliance on these incantations by generating new versions of them.[11] This attempt to hold the Constitution together is failing because the racist practices of European colonial empires cannot be reconciled with the demands of modern constitutionalism. The solution that this book puts forward is a negotiated merger of sovereignty with the role of the judiciary being to constitutionally restrain the legal authority of government (to thin or deflate it) in a way that allows for legitimate negotiations, or voluntary consent as Michael Asch describes it.[12] We argue it is also the same approach to the problem that the practices of treaty federalism help to facilitate.

What the courts have largely overlooked is that if the relationship begins on equal footing, it is possible to justify the legal character of the relationship because it is grounded on mutual consent. As James (Sa'ke'j) Youngblood Henderson describes, once we reconsider the foundations of Aboriginal rights jurisprudence, we see that the practices of treaty federalism are not foreign to the domestic constitutional machinery of settler states. Rather, these are already deeply pluralistic legal practices that work with the common and civil legal traditions in grappling with the legality of the sovereign authority of settler states. When we understand the work of legal interpretation and the diverse practices of treaty federalism in this light, it is clear that Indigenous legalities should not be viewed as an optional reference point for constitutional interpretation but as a part of the engine of federalism that is misfiring and, if left unattended, may well completely break down. The practices of treaty federalism are flexible, so they could be placed in a variety of related constitutional machinery to balance the inherent right of self-determination with the territorial integrity and political unity of existing states.

The principles of treaty federalism offer tools to assist courts and legislators in making this solution to the problem of constitutional legitimacy within settler states explicit. These principles serve to remind courts that the Canadian state does not hold sovereignty over Indigenous peoples, who are thus not merely the objects of plenary legislative authority under section 91(24) of the *Constitution Act* (i.e., the notion that the term "Indians" in section 91[24] refers to race is merely expired legal magic – a race cannot sign a treaty, only nations or peoples can). Rather, Canadian sovereignty can only be legally understood as being shared among treaty partners, and section 91(24) is, as Larry Chartrand maintained, "a 'treaty power' to negotiate with nations and peoples who occupy and possess territory that Canadian authority wished to acquire."[13] This reminder is much needed as the courts have an obligation to determine the constitutional limits of governmental authority, and this means interpreting section 91(24) as "[a] power that is broad in its application to various Indigenous peoples (so none are excluded), but non-existent as to its capacity to allow unilateral action."[14]

The chapters in this book take the unitary nation state as simply a model while recognizing that the distribution of jurisdiction within actual states is highly variable and that federalism (of one form or another) is in fact the norm. This opens up the possibility that Indigenous peoples could have their inherent right of self-determination realized within existing states as partners in a federal system.[15]

NOTES

1 Harold J. Berman, *Law and Revolution: The Formation of the Western Legal Tradition* (Cambridge, MA: Harvard University Press, 1983), 11
2 For the distinction between puzzles and problems, see James F. Conant's excellent lecture, "Thomas Kuhn on the Difference between Puzzles and Problems," Wissenschaftskolleg zu Berlin – Institute for Advanced Study, YouTube video, 1:12:59, 11 May 2017, https://www.youtube.com/watch?v=gfC68drP_Dc. For the meaning of the concept of jurisgenerative, see Robert M. Cover, "Foreword: *Nomos* and Narrative," *Harvard Law*

Review 97, no. 1 (1983–4): 4–68. Finally, for the concept of legalities, see Aaron Mills's pathbreaking work; in particular, "The Lifeworlds of Law: On Revitalizing Indigenous Legal Orders Today," *McGill Law Journal* 61, no. 4 (2016): 847–84.

3 I am using the concept of treaties in the broadest sense so as to include historical, modern, and international instruments such as the Royal Proclamation of 1763 and the United Nations Declaration on the Rights of Indigenous Peoples, which articulate legal and normative treaty frameworks. For an excellent example of this more holistic approach, see Michael Asch's compelling and powerful study of treaty-making practices in his *On Being Here to Stay: Treaties and Aboriginal Rights in Canada* (Toronto: University of Toronto Press, 2014).

4 UN General Assembly, United Nations Declaration on the Rights of Indigenous Peoples (UNDRIP), 2 October 2007, A/RES/61/295.

5 Examples of this can easily be seen in *R. v. Sparrow*, [1990] 1 SCR 1075 [hereafter *Sparrow*], at 1109, and in *United States v. Kagama*, 118 US 375 (1886) [hereafter *Kagama*], at 383–5. In both of these instances, state sovereignty is predicated on unilateral assertions that claim to be based in a confusing amalgam of fact and law known as the doctrine of discovery. The court does not need to argue for the legal asymmetry between the parties; it simply utilizes the resources of judicial notice to state that "Indian tribes are wards of the nation" (*Kagama*, at 383), or that "there was from the outset never any doubt that sovereignty and legislative power, and indeed the underlying title, to such lands vested in the Crown" (*Sparrow*, at 1109). The courts have bolstered this position by leaning on the principle of sovereign incompatibility, but the live question is what necessarily comes with sovereignty. It seems patently obvious that underlying title and legislative power are not things that are automatically distributed within a state. Rather, the distribution of jurisdiction is subject to explicit negotiations and customary change over time.

6 See chapter 5 by Robert Merino in this volume.

7 In *Worcester v. the State of Georgia*, 31 US (6 Pet) 515 (1832) [hereafter *Worcester*], at 518–19, Chief Justice Marshall argues that were the court to interpret the Treaty of Hopewell as constituting a surrender of self-government on the basis of the phrase "managing all their affairs," the court "would convert a treaty of peace covertly into an act annihilating the political existence of one of the parties."

8 *St. Catharines Milling and Lumber Co. v. The Queen*, [1888] UKPC 70; *Johnson v. M'Intosh*, 21 US 543 (1823), at 603.

9 David Dyzenhaus, "The Puzzle of Martial Law," *University of Toronto Law Journal* 59, no. 1 (Winter 2009): 42, https://doi.org/10.3138/utlj.59.1.1.

10 *Reference re Secession of Quebec*, [1998] 2 SCR 217, at para 150. See also Robert Hamilton and Joshua Nichols, "Reconciliation and the Straitjacket: A Comparative Analysis of the *Secession Reference* and *R v Sparrow*," *Ottawa Law Review* 52, no. 2 (2021): 403–53.
11 *MP v. Secretary of State for the Home Department*, [2006] EWHC 1000 (Admin), at para 103. David Dyzenhaus cites this phrase in Dyzenhaus, "Puzzle of Martial Law," 61.
12 See chapter 2 by Michael Asch in this volume.
13 Larry Chartrand, "The Failure of the Daniels Case: Blindly Entrenching a Colonial Legacy," *Alberta Law Review* 51, no. 1 (2013): 185, https://doi.org/10.29173/alr63.
14 Ibid., 188.
15 Chief Justice Marshall attempted to do this by developing the concept of "domestic dependent nations" in *Cherokee Nation v. Georgia*, 30 US (5 Pet) 1 (1831). This concept was designed to reflect the legal position that the Cherokee had developed through negotiation with the United States, not their original status, and it served to limit the sovereignty of both parties by merging them. Marshall added emphasis to this point in *Worcester* when he explicitly rejected both the doctrine of discovery and the civilization thesis. In other words, the position that Marshall developed through the trilogy maintains that Aboriginal peoples enter negotiations as sovereigns, not as wards. This understanding of domestic dependent nations placed the emphasis on the fact that any rights that are not explicitly extinguished or limited by treaty are held in reserve by the tribe; it remained the dominant approach in the US through to *Ex Parte Crow Dog*, 109 US 556 (1883), until it was effectively transformed by *United States v. Kagama*, 118 US 375 (1886), which reinterprets Marshall's notion of domestic dependent nations by placing the emphasis squarely on "dependent." For a detailed historical account of this transition, see Sidney L. Harring, *Crow Dog's Case: American Indian Sovereignty, Tribal Law, and the United States Law in the Nineteenth Century* (Cambridge: Cambridge University Press, 1994), and for a legal analysis of the plenary power of Congress, see Robert N. Clinton, "There Is No Federal Supremacy Clause for Indian Tribes," *Arizona State Law Journal* 34 (2002): 113–260; and Philp Frickey, "(Native) American Exceptionalism in Federal Public Law," *Harvard Law Review* 119, no. 2 (2005): 433.

Printed in the USA
CPSIA information can be obtained
at www.ICGtesting.com
CBHW020931221124
17326CB00004B/4